W9-BYK-026

A People's History of the U.S. Military

## Also by Michael A. Bellesiles

*1877: America's Year of Living Violently*

*Arming America: The Origins of a National Gun Culture*

*Documenting American Violence: A Sourcebook*
(co-edited with Christopher Waldrep)

*Ethan Allen and His Kin: Correspondence, 1772–1819*
(co-edited with John Duffy)

*Lethal Imagination: Violence and Brutality in American History* (editor)

*Revolutionary Outlaws: Ethan Allen and the
Struggle for Independence on the Early American Frontier*

*A Survival Guide for Teaching*

*Weighed in an Even Balance*

# A People's History of
# the U.S. Military

Ordinary Soldiers Reflect on Their Experience of
War, from the American Revolution to Afghanistan

MICHAEL A. BELLESILES

Requests for permission to reproduce selections from this book should be mailed to:
Permissions Department, The New Press, 38 Greene Street, New York, NY 10013.

Published in the United States by The New Press, New York, 2012
Distributed by Perseus Distribution

LIBRARY OF CONGRESS CATALOGING-IN-PUBLICATION DATA
Bellesiles, Michael A.
A people's history of the U.S. military : ordinary soldiers reflect on their experience
of war, from the American Revolution to Afghanistan / Michael A. Bellesiles.
p. cm.
Includes bibliographical references and index.
ISBN 978-1-59558-628-5 (hc. : alk. paper)
1. United States—History, Military.  2. Soldiers—United States—Diaries.  3. Soldiers—United
States—Anecdotes.  4. Soldiers' writings, American.  5. United States—Armed Forces—
Diaries.  6. United States—Armed Forces—Biography—Anecdotes.  I. Title. II. Title: Ordinary
soldiers reflect on their experience of war, from the American Revolution to Afghanistan.
E181.B535 2012
355.00973—dc23

2012012226

Now in its twentieth year, The New Press publishes books that promote and enrich public
discussion and understanding of the issues vital to our democracy and to a more equitable
world. These books are made possible by the enthusiasm of our readers; the support of a
committed group of donors, large and small; the collaboration of our many partners in
the independent media and the not-for-profit sector; booksellers, who often hand-sell
New Press books; librarians; and above all by our authors.

www.thenewpress.com

*Composition by Westchester Book Composition*
*This book was set in Adobe Garamond*

Printed in the United States of America

2   4   6   8   10   9   7   5   3   1

*For Matt and Mark,*
*brothers in word and deed*

# Contents

# Introduction

A great deal of America's history gets thrown in the trash. It is just so much clutter that gets in our way and has no apparent meaning. Old buildings get torn down, historical sites are paved over for parking lots, and personal documents from an earlier age are discarded. Ours is a society oriented toward the present, with little patience for the past.

As a teenager I haunted junk shops in Los Angeles, mostly looking for cheap used books, since that was about all I could afford. Back in the 1960s these shops were full of souvenirs brought back from World War II and the Korean War, with display cases filled with knives, uniform patches, and medals. In my childish veneration of heroism, I could not understand getting rid of medals. But one day the nature of my society became clearer to me. I was in one of my favorite junk shops and noticed a beautiful leather-bound photo album. Cautiously, I began to leaf through the yellowing pages. Early in the album, a young soldier stands to clumsy attention in his doughboy uniform. Later on, the same young man leans proudly against a car, then is part of a couple holding a baby; there follows the usual snapshots of people laughing on a picnic, formal portraits, birthday celebrations, a few soldiers in World War II uniforms, and then an abrupt end, followed by blank pages.

The shop's owner, a friendly woman who was used to my interest in old things, told me that someone would probably buy the album for their own use. "What will they do with the photos?" I asked.

"Oh, they'll get thrown away."

Americans are notoriously uninterested in their nation's history, with surveys consistently discovering a vast void of historical knowledge even among college graduates. This avoidance of the past generally extends beyond our national story to include personal history and even memory. I am often astounded to find that people my age have somehow completely forgotten key events that occurred during their lifetimes, including entire wars. But then, growing up, I was surrounded by war. There were U.S. Navy vessels in the harbor, a visible military-industrial complex that employed the parents of many classmates, and veterans everywhere. My father served in World War II, my uncle Charles took part in the Normandy invasion and received a Silver Star for gallantry, my uncle Frank piloted a bomber over Germany, and our neighbor Dale Lundbergh flew fighters in the Pacific. Yet nobody wanted to talk about the war. My mother kept an album of clippings during World War II, but she didn't want it in the house and gave it to her brother; I never learned why.

History opened up for me one day at school when I returned to my math class because I had left behind a book I was reading. In this large urban high school of four thousand, I was just another dumb kid quietly doing my work, until that afternoon. When I saw that my book was not where I had left it, but sitting on the teacher's desk, I immediately assumed I was going to get in trouble again for reading in class. Instead my math teacher picked up the book and asked why I was reading a memoir, written by a German soldier, about the first months of World War I. That began several years of conversations with Harvey Green, one of the men who had planned the escape from Stalag 17, and started me on my circuitous path to a PhD in history.

I soon learned that the Los Angeles school system was full of veterans, many of them wanting to tell their stories but doubting that anyone wanted to hear them. I listened as they talked about the segregated military, the liberation of concentration camps, the loss of good friends in battle, struggling to survive in a prison camp, first hearing of the atomic bomb, coming home—these latter stories usually ending with a quick intake of breath and a change of subject. I may have been the only student to know that my history teacher had been wounded in Italy, or that my physics teacher had splashed ashore at Okinawa, and I am certain that none of my classmates could imagine our diminutive female English teacher working in an airplane factory during the war. Paul Liley, my photography teacher who became a lifelong friend, had what sounded like a fairly safe job, photographing sites for bombing runs against Japanese targets, until he flew over a city they had just hit and realized that those were the remains of houses down there. He started drinking heavily after that run. Thanks to Green, I heard all their stories, listening closely, and saddened when they said that I showed more interest than their own children. And then friends of mine started going to Vietnam; a few did not return.

It makes a sort of sense that people did not want to hear these veterans talk of their experiences: they did not want to acknowledge our military heritage or their shared responsibility for these wars. One of my teachers had served in Korea, a war largely unknown to me. He told me that the strangest thing was coming home to a country that seemed to have no conception that there was a war on. Years later other Korean veterans would tell me much the same story, of returning to their homes in Ohio or New York and encountering a willful ignorance of America's involvement in an Asian war. The distance between returning soldiers and the civilian population is often enormous, reinforcing the sense of alienation many veterans feel from their own country. In my years of volunteer work with vets, the expression I believe I have most often heard is "no one cares."

War has always played a complex role in American history, largely as we like to believe that democracies do not turn to war willingly. There are politicians who like to say that ours is a country devoted to peace, which indicates that they know nothing of American history. Ours, as Geoffrey Perret has written, is a country made by war.[1] George Washington notoriously wrote, "I heard the bullets whistle, and, believe me, there is something charming in the sound," while William Tecumseh Sherman famously declared that "war is hell."[2] A recent president proclaimed the United States "a peace-loving nation" while himself launching two wars.

Amid the diversity of commentary on the American relation with warfare, a voice seldom heard is that of the common soldier. Americans routinely praise the average soldier and give him many names: Cousin Jonathan, Yank, Johnny Reb, Doughboy, G.I., Grunt. But while the generalizations abound, that voice is muted, if not deliberately silenced. In historical accounts, the soldier is the expendable extra, necessary as part of the glorious scene, but seldom the subject of the viewer's gaze. Prior to World War II there are generic heroes, such as Daniel Chester French's famous minuteman statue or, more commonly, one of the figures in a long line of soldiers in some historic painting. Yet the soldier as an individual remains obscure, rarely the subject of attention or narrative. Photography should have changed that anonymity. Anyone who has looked at the somber faces frozen in Mathew Brady's Civil War photographs recognizes the humanity beneath the uniform; but they are still silent voices from the past, accompanied by a Ken Burns soundtrack of melancholic violin music. This book aims to bring the military experience of common soldiers to the forefront, to fulfill Walt Whitman's longing to record their song of democratic service.

The average soldier is not ignored due to a lack of material. A surprisingly large number of veterans from the Revolution through our current wars have recorded their combat experiences in letters, diaries, memoirs, and, more recently, on tape, film, and blogs. While this book strives to avoid generalization, it is evident from these records that the common soldiers thought more of food than fame, longed more for home than heroism. They saw marching where others perceived strategy, the chaos of destruction where scholars describe tactics. Above all else, their voices are worth hearing, for theirs are the voices of everyday heroes, the great diversity of Americans willing to risk everything in service to their country.

The impetus for this book came out of the local garbage dump. One day my neighbor Billy Angier, a veteran who works at the dump, brought over a box he thought might interest me. In the box was a diary from World War I, as well as some sketch pads with rather good pencil studies of French scenes in 1918 and 1919. I was floored that anyone could just chuck these books into the trash, but then it is easy to understand that someone living in the twenty-first century would find little of interest in a small book filled with cryptic handwriting. As I talked with Billy, it suddenly hit me that I needed to do something—no matter how minor—to save these stories from the trash heap of history.

As a bartender, I have met an inordinate number of veterans, far too many of whom seem to need a drink. Years ago I had a regular who wore a jacket that said on the back, "I know I'm going to heaven, because I've served my time in hell." When I asked about it, he just said that he got it in Saigon in 1969. He thought that was sufficient explanation, and indeed it was. I quickly learned not to pry unless invited and, over time, attempted to evoke these invitations by volunteering my time to help veterans in as many ways as possible. I found that I could best assist veterans by encouraging them to apply to college, helping them to fill out the applications, offering to proofread essays, encouraging them to hang in there. Along the way, I got their stories and made friendships. I am just sorry that I cannot include all their tales in these pages.

This book seeks to avoid abstractions, to give the human experience of war from the perspective of the common soldier—by which I mean a soldier low in rank, not valor. Back when I taught a course on the Vietnam War, I came across Stuart A. Herrington's memoir, *Silence Was a Weapon*. He begins modestly doubting the value of his book: "I was also inhibited by the fact that I was a low-level actor in the overall sweep of events that unfolded around me in Vietnam. Captains don't write the histories of wars—generals inherit that task. The whole world awaited General Westmoreland's memoirs, but who would be interested in the thoughts of one of the thousands of junior officers who served in Vietnam?"[3] Yet it is not clear to me why anyone would be interested in General Westmoreland's prevarications and convoluted justifications.[4] If the Vietnam War demonstrates anything, it is that those who make and guide policy often have no clue what is going on and a lot less knowledge of reality than the average soldier in the field. The memoirs of senior officers in the past half century have a curious sameness about them, as though they were all the product of the school of special pleading and excuse making. In contrast, there is nothing approaching uniformity in the memoirs and letters of, or interviews with, common soldiers. Each is the creation of an individual experiencing war in his or her own way. These are the stories I wish to tell here; these are the tales of American democracy under stress.

One of the primary strengths of soldiers as observers is that they view one another without contempt or sentiment. It is this realism that preserves their sense of camaraderie beyond the end of their service to their country and makes their narratives compelling. They have seen one another in the worst conditions known to humanity, shared the limits of endurance, and understood that there is far less to war than the valiant charges of imagination and far more than fields of dead bodies. They come to truly know one another as people, and often extend the support and forgiveness that they long for themselves. Their shared suffering, often in the face of public indifference, convinces them that they are in it together, generally without any hint of entitlement.

The American military experience is unique in world history. Starting with their Revolution, Americans have persistently grappled with the role of the citizen as soldier. What are the consequences of giving up one's freedom in order to fight for liberty? Is it possible to have a democratic army? Does the Republic owe anything to those who serve the common cause? Do soldiers and veterans pose a threat to republican principles? The answers to these questions have varied wildly, alternately undermining American military efforts and giving strength to the nation's endeavors. Baron Friedrich von Steuben's dream of a "community of the line" was often realized, granting solidarity to soldiers from widely dispersed regions and backgrounds; it was just as often violated in acrimonious and counterproductive efforts to maintain a traditional military hierarchy and discipline, or crushed under the weight of bigotry. On leaving service, veterans usually found the country for which they fought far from grateful and appallingly parsimonious. It is nearly as common for veterans to miss their years of military camaraderie as for them to suffer long-term trauma from their tour of duty. Military service can shatter and give meaning to lives; it is rarely a neutral encounter. The horror of war embraces everyone, victors and losers. Even Hugh Thompson, who heroically put himself between Lieutenant William Calley and several Vietnamese civilians at My Lai, remained haunted by his own limitations: "I wish I could have saved more."[5]

I have sought in this book to avoid empty rhetoric and rote descriptions of glorious battles in favor of authentic voices describing the reality of the military experience and its aftermath. A few officers are included, primarily from the junior ranks, in order to provide a sense of the attitudes they shared with enlisted men or to relate perspectives not covered elsewhere. The documents reveal altered ways of thinking reflective of larger social change, such as the acceptance of blacks and women as comrades-in-arms. Similarly, attitudes toward war itself, though never uniform in any given period, indicate changing social mores and particular circumstances. While veterans of the Revolution evaluated their military experiences in a number of ways, most agreed in finding enormous value in their service. In contrast, those who fought in the War of 1812 generally had no idea why a war had been necessary, while many soldiers in the Indian wars of the nineteenth century doubted the morality of these conflicts. Veterans of World War II rarely question the legitimacy of the "Good War," especially after the liberation of the concentration camps, while the memories of Korean and Vietnam veterans are marked by confusion and anger.

I have brought the Korean and Vietnam Wars together into a single chapter for two reasons. As we move further away from the years in which Vietnam dominated the politics and culture of the United States, it becomes increasingly evident that the earlier war in Korea has been unfairly overlooked as part of America's Cold War conflict with a perceived international communist threat. Additionally, my conversations with veterans of both wars persuade me that they shared a number of essential experiences. Though opposition to the Vietnam War differed from the general lack of attention given to the Korean War, military personnel serving in both wars returned home to sweeping indifference, and remember keenly their alienation from a public unaware of or disinterested in the sacrifices they had made for their country.

Often a veteran will tell me, as one Vietnam vet who is now a lawyer recently said, "There is really nothing to say." He then started talking about a Vietcong surprise attack on his base, during which he had run to his tank as mortars fell within the wire, climbed the side, pivoted the turret toward the suspected origin of the mortar attack, and fired. The shell took off the top of the latrine on its trajectory into the jungle. As he watched, the latrine walls collapsed, and there stood one of his buddies with his pants around his ankles, a roll of toilet paper in his hand, looking completely gobsmacked. "I couldn't help but laugh," he said. "I shouldn't have, but I did." Nope, no stories here.[6]

This modest belief that they have no stories worth hearing speaks to a larger problem faced by anyone who works with veterans: their culture of macho stoicism. They are supposed to suck up any pain and keep moving—an attitude very useful in wartime, but less so after one's military service ends. Far too many veterans have hesitated to seek medical and psychological aid because they do not want to sound like whiners or appear weak. They keep silent about their experience, grit their teeth, and press on as best they can, often in the face of debilitating difficulties. As Nancy Sherman has written, "The Stoic doctrine is essentially about reducing vulnerability." The soldier and veteran avoid "ordinary emotions, like fear and grief." Many feel shame that they made it home safely when so many friends and comrades-in-arms did not. "And then once home, they worry that their real family is back on the battlefield, and they feel guilt for what feels like a misplaced intimacy." Many internalize these conflicting emotions, intensifying psychological trauma. Tragically, an inordinate percentage of veterans blame themselves and end up taking their lives. Sometimes, though, the Stoic armor slips away to reveal that the veteran's emotions and doubts are testaments to their morality and humanity. Those who work with veterans often find that encouraging them to tell their stories is a powerful first step on that path to acceptance and a renewed sense of personal honor.[7] Put another way, far too many veterans drink to forget, whereas the first thing they should do is remember—the forgetting will come with time.

In hopes of giving voice to these common soldiers and maybe even fostering a dialogue over the treatment of veterans, this book goes further than the final battle to examine the impact of homecoming and the long-term treatment of veterans. Communities may have turned out for victory parades, but the degree to which they aided returning soldiers in dealing with the effects of military service is a little-explored topic in American history.

What comes across most compellingly in these recollections, however, is the unique diversity of voices. These documents express tragedy and humor, anger and wit, as they describe battles and the daily life of soldiers, brotherhood and patriotism, emotional homecomings and the lingering costs of war.

This book is organized chronologically, its ten chapters following America's military heritage from the Revolution through our current wars. While I have tried to address a breadth of themes of military service, there are still many that must be bypassed. Any given chapter in this book could easily be expanded into a book; in fact, three books in the People's History series already address the American Revolution, the Civil War, and the Vietnam War.[8] This book focuses on those who served the United States, therefore excluding other American soldiers, including Loyalists during the American Revolution, Confederates in the Civil War, and Native Americans in numerous conflicts. Given the limitations of space, and to avoid repetition, I have attempted to raise issues of primary importance in the specific war under discussion; each chapter thus explores a different theme of America's military experience. For instance, a discussion of the complex nature of democratic warfare dominates the first chapter on the American Revolution, while My Lai made atrocities and civilian casualties troubling issues during the Vietnam War. There is very little in this book about peacetime service—but then the American military has experienced little peacetime service.

Studs Terkel and Alfred Young serve as inspirations for this work. Terkel devoted his career to bringing the American experience to life in the voices of common people.[9] Following his example, I have interfered little with the stories in this book. The military personnel included here speak in their own words, though I have followed Terkel's example in removing verbal tics and stumbles, and correcting minor spelling errors—most particularly in the early chapters where it is sometimes difficult to determine what word is intended by the rather eccentric spelling of a bygone age. Al Young is one of this country's great democratic historians, reconstructing our heritage from the bottom up, bringing unusual biographies to life, and teasing out larger historical meanings from the lives of common people. Young seeks to answer the question: "How does an ordinary person win a place in history?"[10] The privates, sergeants, and seamen in this book have all played important roles in our national saga, though that credit has far too often been denied them. What follows is their story, told in their own words, with great respect for the sacrifices they have made and the simple courage they displayed by just showing up to serve their country.

It must be noted, when dealing with personal narratives by figures generally ignored by history, that the validity of their statements often have to be taken at face value. There has been an unfortunate tendency for some people to lie about military service, even among those running for public office.[11] I have sadly encountered such prevarication in my own work over the years. As a consequence, I have made every effort to verify as much of the enclosed material as possible. I greatly appreciate the good humor with which most veterans willingly produce documentation of their service. While truly regrettable that it is necessary to ask, it is important that the reader have confidence in the historical record. Ultimately, though, it must be admitted that the specific details of most historical narratives cannot be verified as they are extremely private and the other participants are often no longer alive. To that degree, I once more follow Studs Terkel's example and remind the reader to be skeptical yet respectful. These are the truths as the speakers know them, and I am confident that any errors are not intended.

For many of the veterans with whom I have spoken over the years, there are two forms of storytelling: that for civilians, and the truth. Repeatedly I heard a variation on the sentence, "No one wants to know the truth of Vietnam," or Korea, or Iraq, or Afghanistan. In wartime, the unusual and unpleasant become normal and accepted. My father, who for a time fished dead bodies out of the North Atlantic, told me that, in war, "the strange becomes standard with routine." Veterans get the sense that there is no quicker way to alienate family and friends than to describe war in its grotesque reality. Tim O'Brien spoke powerfully of this distance between veterans and civilians in *The Things They Carried*. The truth in war requires an "absolute and uncompromising allegiance to obscenity and evil." War teaches young men that life is obscene, and they speak that harsh reality. Listening to a true war story leaves one embarrassed, so if you don't like filthy language "you don't care for the truth; if you don't care for the truth watch how you vote. Send guys to war, they come home talking dirty." In war, the truth is elusive and disgusting; war stories are therefore "beyond telling."[12] In thinking about writing of his service in Iraq, Tyler Boudreau weighed the alternatives. When he told people he had been in Iraq, the response was not animosity, but a "glassy-eyed smile" and meaningless avoidances like "Wow, man." The message was clear to Boudreau: "I got the picture real fast. If my story wasn't tragic, if it didn't make 'em cry, or if it didn't yank 'em to the edge of their seats, or get a big laugh, nobody wanted to hear it. They didn't want to hear the dry particulars. They wanted high-speed adventure and witty heroes who escaped death by the skins of their teeth and saved the day in the end."[13] In other words, they did not want the truth.

It is striking how rarely soldiers attempt to glorify combat. Jack Veness, one of Canada's great heroes from World War II, who testified at the Nuremberg Trials on witnessing the slaughter of Allied prisoners of war, had one of the more exciting military adventures of the war, escaping from the Germans and fighting with the French Resistance. Yet he did not hesitate to say that "anyone who romanticizes war hasn't been in one."[14] However, there is no mistaking that something of war attracts many people. In searching for a moral equivalent of war, William James noted: "Modern man inherits all the innate pugnacity and all the love of glory of his ancestors. Showing war's irrationality and horror is of no effect on him. The horrors make the fascination."[15] But often the encounter quickly loses its appeal, for the romance of war has little to do with its reality. One of the great reporters of World War II, Ernie Pyle, describes looking through some magazines at an airbase in Tunisia and being struck by how "war seemed romantic and exciting, full of heroics and vitality." But he couldn't feel that thrill. "I don't know what the hell's the matter with me," he said to the pilots. "Here we are right at the front, and yet the war isn't dramatic to me at all." Major Quint Quick of Bellingham, Washington, responded, "It isn't to me either. I know it should be, but it isn't. It's just hard work, and all I want is to finish and get back home."

Pyle found that the experience of war was not always the stuff of great drama, of inspiring speeches by commanders and heroic assaults by fearless troops. "Certainly there were great tragedies, unbelievable heroism, even a constant undertone of comedy. But when I sat down to write, I saw instead: men at the front suffering and wishing they were somewhere else, men in routine jobs just behind the lines bellyaching because they couldn't get to the front, all of them desperately hungry for somebody to talk to beside themselves, no women to be heroes in front of, damned little wine to drink, . . . just toiling from day to day in a world full of insecurity, discomfort, homesickness, and a dulled sense of danger." And it all came down to that "one really profound goal that obsesses every one of the Americans" he knew, home. That is the true romance of war: returning home alive.[16]

Over the years I have been honored to know many veterans, and many of their words appear in these pages. I hope that they all know how much I have appreciated our association and trust that this book is some small recompense for the confidences they have shared and the friendships they have extended. I have also been impressed by the many dedicated people who have done their best to aid veterans and to keep their stories alive. Eileen Hurst at Central Connecticut State University's Veterans History Project seems to never sleep as she works to record the widest possible diversity of military memories. I highly commend her efforts and those of the fine people at the Library of Congress and the Legacy Project.[17]

Veterans share a perception that their time in uniform was one of great camaraderie, of serving together and fighting for one another more than for any identifiable cause. Audie Murphy, the most decorated American soldier of World War II, explained his heroism in the simplest terms: "They were killing my friends."[18] Yet, far too often, when they come home they discover that the bond they prized is broken. There are too many examples of public hypocrisy, such as that displayed by Representative Dennis Rehberg of Montana, an adamant supporter of the Iraq War who turned around and voted against a bill to give troops mandatory rest periods between deployments.[19] For such a person, "supporting our troops" is limited to sending them into harm's way. "In the service, we were in it together," Paul Liley said about World War II. "I came home to the Red Scare, to commies under the bed, to suspicions of everyone's loyalty."[20] "In Iraq, we were in it together, it was a great feeling," recalls Joe O'Keefe. "I trusted those guys, we were on the same side."[21] The men and women who have served in the armed forces of the United States present a model for true patriotism, recognizing that we must rely on our fellow Americans. It is rare to encounter a soldier who ultimately saw the military as a chance to accumulate wealth; patriotism lies in service, not selfishness, and many of them wonder why these values do not translate to civilian life.

At the end of the First World War, Rudyard Kipling, who lost his son in the war, was called upon to write an inscription for the memorial to the nine hundred thousand British servicemen who died in that horrendous conflict. Kipling turned to Ecclesiasticus, offering the simple phrase: "Their name liveth for evermore."[22] But that turns out not to be true; far too often they end up in the trash. We owe the veterans this much, to see that their service to our nation is not forgotten.

# 1

# The American Revolution

The American Revolution sorely tested American character and beliefs. Many expected that all a virtuous people need do was to rise up in righteous anger and claim their victory. These patriots held that professional soldiers were either mercenaries or automatons, kept in line by money or fear, and incapable of resisting the courage of a free people. Naturally, they had no intention of paying the cost of fielding a well-trained army. In 1775 few Americans wanted to rely upon or to be professional soldiers; by 1776 it was clear that they had little choice but to create an army capable of standing up to the British.

In *Common Sense*, Tom Paine warned, "Now is the seed-time of continental union, faith, and honor. The least fracture now will be like a name engraved with the point of a pin on the tender rind of a young oak: the wound will enlarge with the tree, and posterity read it in full grown characters." Indeed, so many of the strengths and fractures inscribed on the Continental Army would inform the nation's further development.[1]

## The Sudden Advent of War

In the early months of 1775 towns around Boston began preparing for war, stockpiling arms and ammunition, and calling the militia out for training. For the previous few years New England's radical leaders had been warning that the British government was capable of any outrage, including military action. Yet when it finally came on April 19, 1775, the march of the British army out of Boston caught Americans by surprise. The reality of war hit the people of New England hard; the Lexington militia barely fired any of their muskets before being chased from town. Even though the slaughter of the British on their retreat from Concord back to Boston could be taken as an American victory, the sight of so many casualties and so much blood shattered any doubts of a peaceful solution to the colonies' disagreement with the Crown.

In 1825 Amos Barrett sat down to write his memories of that day, fifty years earlier, when he and the other minutemen faced the British attack. Like so many veterans, Barrett found he could remember the events of his military service "better than I can remember things 5 years ago." Barrett was a young man living in Concord when the British marched there from Lexington. He went on to serve at the Battle of Bunker Hill and rise to the rank of captain at Saratoga:

The 19th of April, 1775, the British landed about 1,000 of their best troops from Boston in boats abreast of Charleston river, above Charleston bridge in the night very privately, and I believe they did not take the road till they all met at old Cambridge. They kept the old road and every man they saw they took and kept so that they should not alarm the people, but some how they got word at Lexington that they were coming. There were a number of men collected on the common when the British got there, and the British ordered them to disperse, but they did not so quickly as they wished to have them, and the British fired on them and killed 7 or 8 and wounded a number more. Our men did not fire on them, though I heard after they had got by, 2 or three of our men fired and wounded some of them.

We at Concord heard that they were coming. The bell rung at 3 o'clock for alarm. As I was a minute man, I was soon in town and found my captain and the rest of my company at the post. . . . Before sunrise there were, I believe, 150 of us. . . . We thought we would go and meet the British. We marched down towards Lexington about a mile . . . and we saw them coming. We halted and staid till they got within about 100 rods, then we were ordered to the about face and marched before them with our drums and fifes going, and also the British (drums and fifes). We had grand music.

We marched into town and over the north bridge a little more than half a mile and then on a hill not far from the bridge, where we could see and hear what was going on. What the British came out after was to destroy our stores that we had got laid up for our army. There was in the town a number of entrenching tools which they carried out and burnt. At last they said it was best to burn them in the house and set fire to them in the house. But our people begged them not to burn the house and put it out. It wasn't long before it was set on fire again, but finally it was not burnt. There were about 100 barrels of flour in Mr. Hubbard's malt house. They rolled that out and knocked them to pieces and rolled some into the mill pond, which was saved after they were gone.

While we were on the hill by the bridge, there were 80 or 90 British came to the bridge and there made a halt. After a while they began to tear the plank off the bridge. Major Buttrick said if we were all [of] his mind, he would drive them away from the bridge—they should not tear that up.

We all said we would go. We, then, were not loaded. We were all ordered to load, and had strict orders not to fire till they fired first, then to fire as fast as we could. We then marched on.

Capt. Davis' minute company marched first, then Capt. Allen's minute company, the one that I was in next. We marched 2 deep. It was a long causeway, being round by the river. Capt. Davis had got, I believe, within 15 rods of the British, when they fired 3 guns, one after another. As soon as they fired them, they fired on us. The balls whistled well. We then were all ordered to fire that could fire and not kill our own men. It is strange there were no more killed, but they fired too high. Capt. Davis was killed and Mr. [Hosmer] and a number wounded. We soon drove them from the bridge, when I got over there were 2 lay dead and another almost dead. We did not follow them. There were 8 or 10 that were wounded and a running and a hobbling about, looking back to see if we were after them. We then saw the whole body coming out of town. . . . After a while we found them marching back towards Boston. We were soon after them. When they got about a mile and a half to a road that comes from Bedford and [Bilrica], they were waylaid and a great many killed. When I got there, a great many lay dead, and the road was bloody.[2]

In the days after the British retreat from Concord, thousands of militia members and individuals rushed to the Boston area, where the British army found itself besieged. Simon Fobes of Bridgewater, Massachusetts, who had just turned nineteen when the British marched on Concord, was one of these men. His father, "a firm friend to his country, but too old and feeble to take any active part himself," encouraged Simon to enlist. Fobes became a private in Captain Eliakim Smith's militia, "and to some extent learned military exercise" as part of General Israel Putnam's brigade. Initially, the volunteers acted to set their own rules:

While we lay at Dorchester, the non-commissioned officers and privates of our company agreed upon some by-laws, to be in force among ourselves, particularly with regard to pilfering and uncleanliness about the camp. If any one, on being accused and tried by a court-martial consisting of the sergeants of the company, was found guilty, he was fined or whipped at the discretion of the court. These by-laws were strictly enforced. A soldier was brought before the court for some misdemeanor, tried, found guilty, and sentenced to be whipped. He was immediately taken into an orchard, tied to an apple-tree, and smartly whipped with rods. Another was caught on a pear-tree stealing fruit, and he was tried and severely punished.[3]

Just days before his twenty-first birthday, Amos Farnsworth joined his Groton, Massachusetts, militia unit as they rushed toward Boston in the immediate aftermath of Lexington and Concord. His diary describes the army of volunteers collecting around Boston as they besieged the British, culminating in the ferocious Battle of Bunker Hill. Farnsworth, who continued to serve in the militia through the war, was a deeply religious man, as his diary records:

Wednesday morning, April 19, 1775. Was Alarmed with the news of the Regulars Firing At Our men At Concord. Marched and Came there where Some had Been killed. Pulled on and Came to Lexington where much hurt was Done to the houses there by braking glass And Burning Many Houses: but they [the British] was forced to retreat though they was more numerous then we And I saw many Dead Regulars by the way. Went into a house where Blood was half over Shoes.

Friday June. 16. . . . in the afternoon we had orders to be ready to march. . . . About Dusk Marched for Bunkers hill; under Command of our own Col. [William] Prescott. . . . Our Men marched to Bunker-Hill And begun their entrenchment And Carried it on with the utmost Vigor all Night. . . .

Saturday June ye 17. The Enemy appeared to be much Alarmed on Saturday Morning when they discovered Our operations and immediately began a heavy Cannonading from a battery on Corps-Hill [Copp's Hill] Boston and from the Ships in ye Harbour. We with little loss Continued to Carry on our works till 1 o'Clock when we Discovered a large Body of the Enemy Crossing Charles-River from Boston. They landed on a Point of land about a Mile Eastward of our Entrenchment And immediately disposed their army for an attack previous to which they Set fire to the town of Charlestown. It is supposed that the Enemy intended to attack us under the Cover of the Smoke from the burning Houses, the Wind favouring them in Such a Design; While on the other side their Army was extending Northward towards Mistick-River with an apparent Design of surrounding our Men in the Works, And of cutting off any Assistance intended for our Relief. They were however in some Measure, counteracted in this Design, and Drew their Army into closer Order.

As the Enemy approached, Our men was not only Exposed to the Attack of a very numerous Musketry but to the heavy Fire of the Battery on Corps-Hill, 4 or 5 Men of War, Several Armed Boats or Floating Batteries in Mistick-River, and a number of Field pieces. Notwithstanding we within the entrenchment, and at a Breast Work without, sustained the Enemy's Attacks with great Bravery and Resolution, killed and wounded great Numbers, and repulsed them several times; and after bearing, for about

2 Hours, as severe and heavy a Fire as perhaps ever was known, and many having fired away all their Ammunition, and having no Reinforcement: although there was a great Body of Men near By: we ware over-powered by Numbers and obliged to leave the Entrenchment retreating about Sunset, to a small Distance over Charlestown Neck.

...I Did not leave the Entrenchment until the Enemy got in. I then Retreated ten or Fifteen rods, then I received a wound in my right arm the ball going through a little below my Elbow.... Another ball struck my Back taking off a piece of Skin about as big as a Penny. But I got to Cambridge that night. The Town of Charlestown supposed to contain about 300 Dwelling-Houses, a great Number of which ware large and elegant, besides 150 or 200 other Buildings, are almost all laid in ashes by the Barbarity and wanton Cruelty of that infernal Villain Thomas Gage.[4]

After Bunker Hill, Congress took charge of the troops around Boston, appointing the Virginian George Washington commander of their new, hastily assembled, and untrained army. Washington, who had played a pivotal role in starting the war with France in 1754, had commanded Virginia's militia during the ensuing French and Indian or Seven Years' War. Demonstrating both competence and ambition, Washington had longed for a regular commission in the British army, but had been repeatedly rebuked. Now in 1775 his goal was to mold the new Continental Army into a respectable fighting force. At the beginning of the war, Washington loathed his soldiers and feared their predilection toward equality. He wrote his cousin Lund Washington from Boston that the New England militia "are by no means such Troops, in any respect, as you are led to believe of them from the Accounts which are published, but I need not make myself Enemies among them, by this declaration, although it is consistent with the truth. I daresay the Men would fight very well (if properly Officered) although they are exceedingly dirty & nasty people."[5] Shortly thereafter he wrote Richard Henry Lee that there is "an unaccountable kind of stupidity in the lower classes of these people which believe me prevails but too generally among the Officers of the Massachusetts part of the Army, who are nearly of the same Kidney with the Privates."[6] As late as September 24, 1776, Washington complained to John Hancock of his soldiers, "while those men consider, and treat him [an officer] as an equal, & (in the Character of an Officer) regard him no more than a broomstick, being mixed together as one common herd, no order, nor no discipline can prevail—nor will the Officer ever meet with that respect which is essentially necessary to due subordination."[7]

Washington's ill-kept army entered Boston on March 20, 1776, convincing many Americans that the war's end could not be far distant. But the British government felt very differently, giving the Howe brothers, Admiral Richard and General William, command of the largest military force to ever operate in the Americas. Washington moved his army to New York City to meet this new threat to what was now the independent nation of the United States. But the British command of the seas allowed the Howes to pick when and where they did battle with the rebels. In August, General Howe adroitly outflanked the Americans on Long Island, many units fleeing without firing a shot. After a crafty overnight evacuation of his army from Brooklyn to Manhattan, Washington's Continental Army was yet again defeated several times, most humiliatingly at Kip's Bay on September 15, where the militia threw aside their guns and ran at the approach of the British troops. Private Joseph Plumb Martin described the encounter:

I believe the enemy's party was small; but our people were all militia, and the demons of fear and disorder seemed to take full possession of all and everything on that day. When I came to the spot where the militia were fired upon the ground was literally covered with arms, knapsacks, staves, coats, hats and old oil flasks. . . . We soon came in sight of a large party of Americans ahead of us who appeared to have come into this road by some other route. We were within sight of them when they were fired upon by another party of the enemy. They returned but a very few shots and then scampered off as fast as their legs would carry them. When we came to the ground they had occupied, the same display of lumber [abandoned guns and material] presented itself as at the other place.[8]

The Continental Army suffered further defeats at Harlem Heights and White Plains, followed by the disastrous capture of Fort Washington, where the British took nearly three thousand prisoners and large stores of irreplaceable American military ordnance. As Washington's army retreated across New Jersey pursued by the British, many patriots wondered whether their rebellion would survive the year. That it did so was largely the result of the perseverance and resilience of Washington and his troops. On Christmas Eve 1776, Washington led his troops in a dangerous night crossing of the Delaware River. Violating all the rules of war, Washington divided his small army and attacked the British troops, mostly Hessians, at Trenton from both directions. Catching them completely by surprise, the Continentals finally managed a victory, which Washington followed up with a daring night march on Lord Charles Cornwallis's British regulars camped at Princeton, forcing them to retreat toward New York. In two weeks Washington reversed the trajectory of the war, demonstrating that in a revolution, the rebel simply had to stay alive to stay in the fight.

In the ensuing five years, the Americans experienced humiliations and stunning victories. In 1777 General Howe slowly but methodically drove the Continental forces before him in Pennsylvania, spending the winter in the new nation's capital of Philadelphia, while the Continental forces suffered through the long hard winter at Valley Forge. But at the same time, General John Burgoyne walked into a trap of his own making, suffering significant defeats at the battles of Bennington and Freeman's Farm before surrendering his army in October 1777, bringing France into the war on the American side. The British then shifted to a southern strategy, intending to reclaim their North American empire one state at a time. This approach started well, as Savannah and then Charleston fell to the British. The collapse of the militia at the Battle of Camden in August 1780 confirmed British military superiority and appeared to presage the loss of the Carolinas to the empire. At this point Washington made an inspired choice, sending his quartermaster general, Nathanael Greene, to take command of the shattered Continental forces in the South. Aided by one of the finest field commanders of the war, Daniel Morgan, Greene rebuilt his army and conducted one of the most brilliant campaigns of the war, leading the British on a merry chase across the South while picking off isolated enemy posts. Stunning victories at King's Mountain and Cowpens, and the brutal holding action at Guilford Courthouse, slowly wore down the British and drove General Cornwallis to seek escape from the southern morass in Virginia. Moving with commendable speed, Washington and his French allies, aided by a significant French naval victory off the mouth of the Chesapeake, surrounded Cornwallis's forces at Yorktown, resulting in the surrender of the British army in October 1781. Washington and most of his troops realized that their long war for independence was almost at an end, though it would take the British government another year to come to terms with that fact.

## Why They Fought

More than any other institution, the Continental Army helped mold a national identity. Those who served in the army, some 140,000 American men, came to feel an identification beyond their home community, finding in military service a commonality of interest in hardship and sacrifice. In the midst of war, the political identity of most soldiers came to differ significantly from that of other Americans in its nationalism. They had fought for the nation, not for their individual home states, and they now saw the nation as the point and the goal of the war. What makes these developments most significant to the future of the United States and its military is that these soldiers were overwhelmingly young, propertyless men from the lower strata of society, men who may have been lured into service by promises of regular food and pay, but who stayed from a sense of commitment to their fellow soldiers and to "the glorious cause."

At the war's start, the Continental Congress hoped to attract volunteers with an array of benefits. Since enlistees would lose income opportunities while serving, Congress prohibited creditors from suing soldiers. In addition to praising enlistees for their patriotism, Congress also promised them food, clothing, and one hundred acres of land. These assurances carried little substance and were quickly forgotten as those serving in the Continental Army were constantly ill fed and poorly clothed, and the promised land evaporated with the war's end. Nor did the United States deliver even on the mediocre pay that was the soldier's due. One soldiers' song complained of this lack of pay:

> What think you of a soldier that fights for liberty;
> Do you think he fights for money,
> or to set his country free? . . .
> Here's health to General Washington
> and every soldier's friend.
> And he that cheats a soldier out of his little pay
> May the devil take him on his back,
> To hell with him straightway.[9]

While young men enlisted in the Continental Army for many different reasons, most soldiers—coming from the poorest reaches of society—appear to have been attracted by bounties and promises of regular pay and food. This economic motivation in no way undermines the sincerity of the patriotism of common soldiers; as they repeatedly demonstrated during the war, these poor soldiers persevered when the more prosperous members of the militia turned and fled. Private George Morison, part of Arnold's daring trek through the Maine wilderness, asked the right question back in 1775, when his company received dangerously defective boats:

Sept. 28. Poled up the river all day. The water in many places being so shallow, that we were often obliged to haul the boats after us through rock and shoals, frequently up to our middle and over our heads in the water; and some of us with difficulty escaped being drowned.

This, however, was not the worst of our distresses, for many of the bateaux were so badly constructed, that whether in or out of them we were wet. Could we have then come within reach of the villains who constructed these crazy things, they would fully have experienced the effects of our vengeance. Many of them were little better than common rafts, and in several of them our provision and camp equipage were much injured. Avarice, or a desire to destroy us, perhaps both, must have been their motives—they could have had none else. Did they not know that their doings were crimes—that they were cheating their country, and exposing its defenders to additional sufferings and to death? Much of our provisions were destroyed, in consequence of the bad condition of several of these boats, which ought to have sustained those who died for want thereof. It is no bold assertion to say that they were accessory to the death of our brethren, who expired in the wilderness. These men could enjoy the sweets of domestic ease, talk about liberty and the rights of mankind, possibly without even a recollection of their parricidal guilt, which in minds subject to any reflection, would excite the most poignant remorse. May Heaven reward them according to their deeds.[10]

Class animosity is occasionally evident in the anger common soldiers felt for their negligent treatment. At the end of 1776 Eliphalet Wright wrote, "As affairs are now going on, the common soldiers have nothing to expect, but that if America maintain her independency, they must become slaves to the rich."[11] In 1779 and 1780, the privation forced upon the Continental soldiers drove some of them to mutiny. But even in violating military regulations, the mutineers insisted on their loyalty to the cause and to one another. These were not so much mutinies against the army or its officers, but against civilians—who did not care—and were easily suppressed. Ann Glover's petition to the North Carolina General Assembly attempted to explain the actions of her husband, Sergeant Samuel Glover, who was executed for his role in the mutiny of the North Carolina line in 1779:

THE PETITION OF ANN GLOVER.

State of North Carolina. To the Honorable the General Assembly of the said State now sitting. The Humble Memorial of Ann Glover, widow of Samuel Glover, late a soldier in this State, who enlisted himself some time in the year 1775, in the Continental Service in the Second Regiment raised here, Humbly Sheweth,

That your Petitioner's late Husband well and faithfully discharged his Duty as a Soldier and Friend to the Cause of American freedom and Independence, & marched to the Northward under the Command of Col. Robert Howe, who, if he was here, would bear honest and honorable Testimony that your Memorialist's deceased Husband was deemed by him and every other officer in that Battalion a good soldier, and never was accused of being intentionally Guilty of a breach of the Laws, Martial or Civil. Your Petitioner begs leave to inform your Honors that her late husband continued in the service of the United States of America upwards of three years, and then returned, by orders of his Commanding officers, to the Southward, at which time he had above twelve months' pay due for his services as a soldier, and which he ought to have received, and would have applyed for the sole support of himself, his wife, your Petitioner, and two helpless orphan Children. That many of the poor soldiers then on their March under Command of Gen. Hogun, possessed of the same attachment & affection to their Families as those in Command, but willing to endure all the dangers and Hardships of war, began their March for the Defence of the State of South Carolina, could they have obtained their promised but small allowance dearly earned for the support of their distressed families in their absence; but as they were sure of suffering for want of that subsistence which at that time & unjustly was cruelly withheld from them, a General Clamor arose among the common soldiery, and they called for their stipend allowed by Congress, but it was not given them, altho' their just due.

Give your poor Petitioner leave to apologize for her unhappy Husband's conduct, & in behalf of her helpless self, as well as in Favour of his poor Children on this occasion, and ask you what must the Feeling of the Man be who fought at Brandywine, at Germantown, & at Stony Point & did his duty, and when on another March in defence of his Country, with Poverty staring him full in the face, he was denied his Pay? His Brother soldiers, incensed by the same Injuries and had gone through the same services, & would have again bled with him for his Country whenever called forth in the service, looked up to him as an older Soldier, who then was a Sergeant, raised by his merit from the common rank, and stood forth in his own and their behalf, & unhappily for him demanded their pay, and refused to obey the Command of his superior Officer, and would not march till they had justice done them. The honest Labourer is worthy of his hire. Allegiance to our Country and obedience to those in authority, but the spirit of a man will shrink from his Duty when his Services are not paid and Injustice oppresses him and his Family. For this he fell an unhappy victim to the hard but perhaps necessary Law of his Country. The Letter penned by himself the day before he was shot doth not breathe forth a word of complaint against his cruel Sentence, Altho' he had not received any pay for upwards of fifteen months. He writes to your Humble Petitioner with the spirit of a Christian. This Letter is the last adieu he bid to his now suffering widow, & she wishes it may be read in public Assembly, and then returned her by some of the Members, who will take it with them when they return to Newbern, and leave it in the care of Major Pasteur. Your humble Petitioner, distressed with the recollection of the fatal catastrophe, will not trouble your Honours any longer upon the subject, but humbly request that you will extend your usual Benevolence & Charity to her & her two children, and make her some yearly allowance for their support.

I am, &c,

ANN GLOVER. New Bern, 10th Jan. 1780[12]

Despite the support of several officers and respectable citizens, and her pointed reminder of the biblical injunction from the Book of Luke that "the laborer is worthy of his hire," there is no indication that the assembly looked favorably upon Glover's petition.

Based on his narrative, it appears that John Hempstead of Connecticut was kept to his duty by his wife's last words to him as he left for war: "After I got Under Way my wife Called to me prety loud. I Stopt my hors and ask'd her What She wanted. Her answer was Not to let me hear that you are Shot in the Back."[13] A few soldiers admitted that they enlisted with friends out of a sense of shared enthusiasm, or out of dire necessity brought on by poverty. Some—especially when writing many years later—proclaimed patriotism as their motive force, while a great many simply referred to a sense of duty and commitment to their fellows. But it appears that the average soldier came, with time, to feel an affinity with his comrades-in-arms, and felt pride in serving with others who remained dedicated to their nation. As Steuben wrote at the war's end: "A desire of fame was my ruling motive for visiting America, but when I saw so many brave, so many good men encountering every species of distress for the cause of their country, the course of my ambition was changed, and my only wish was to be linked in the chain of friendship with those supporters of their country, and to render that country which had given birth to so many patriots, every service in my power."[14]

The winter encampment at Valley Forge typified the experiences that molded the outlook of the common Revolutionary soldier. Though 1777 had been a bumper year for agricultural production in the United States, Congress was unable to get any of that surplus to the army, while the public felt their need for profits far outweighed the nation's need for taxes to support the military. Yet the army held together. Valley Forge demonstrated to common soldiers the need to rely on one another. Reduced to eating mostly "Fire Cake," flour and water baked in the coals, soldiers at Valley Forge who had long known America's agricultural plenty found in their bare subsistence diet a constant reminder of their separation from civilian life. Occasionally they received "rusty Pork," meat that had gone bad and was inedible; they rendered off the fat and threw away the meat, then mixed it with water and "the Meal, I cannot call it flour, for it was hardly ground, . . . which served both for Meat and Bread," as Pennsylvania's Captain John Lacey recalled.[15]

As the soldiers recognized the new form of friendship created by their shared service and hardship, they sought to make sense of it. Albigence Waldo, an observant twenty-seven-year-old doctor who kept a diary at Valley Forge, shared the hardships of the troops as he chronicled the development of the "firmest Friendship" that held the army together. From Pomfret, Connecticut, Waldo served from the war's beginning until ill health forced him to resign in October 1779:

*December 14* [1777].— . . . The Army which has been surprisingly healthy hitherto, now begins to grow sickly from the continued fatigues they have suffered this Campaign. Yet they still show a spirit of Alacrity & Contentment not to be expected from so young Troops.

I am Sick—discontented—and out of humour. Poor food—hard lodging—Cold Weather—fatigue—Nasty Clothes—nasty Cookery—Vomit half my time—smoked out of my senses—the Devil's in't—I can't Endure it—Why are we sent here to starve and Freeze—What sweet Felicities have I left at home; A charming Wife—pretty Children—Good Beds—good food—good Cookery—all agreeable—all harmonious. Here all Confusion—smoke & Cold—hunger & filthyness—A pox on my bad luck. . . .

People who live at home in Luxury and Ease, quietly possessing their habitations, Enjoying their Wives & families in peace, have but a very faint Idea of the unpleasing sensations, and continual Anxiety the Man endures who is in a Camp. . . . These same People are willing we should suffer every thing for their Benefit & advantage, and yet are the first to Condemn us for not doing more!!

*December 21.* [Valley Forge] Preparations made for huts. Provisions Scarce. . . . Heartily wish myself at home, my Skin & eyes are almost spoiled with continual smoke. A general cry thro' the Camp this Evening among the Soldiers, "No Meat! No Meat!"—the Distant vales Echoed back the melancholy sound—"No Meat! No Meat!" Imitating the noise of Crows & Owls, also, made a part of the confused Musick.

What have you for your Dinners Boys? "Nothing but Fire Cake & Water, Sir." At night, "Gentlemen the Supper is ready." What is your Supper Lads? "Fire Cake & Water, Sir." . . .

*December 22.*— . . . I am ashamed to say it, but I am tempted to steal Fowls if I could find them, or even a whole Hog, for I feel as if I could eat one. . . . At 12 of the Clock at Night, Providence sent us a little Mutton, with which we immediately had some Broth made, & a fine Stomach for same. Ye who Eat Pumkin Pie and Roast Turkies, and yet Curse fortune for using you ill, Curse her no more, least she reduce your Allowance of her favours to a bit of Fire Cake, & a draught of Cold Water, & in Cold Weather too. . . .

*December 25, Christmas.*—We are still in Tents—when we ought to be in huts—the poor Sick, suffer much in Tents this cold Weather. . . . But very few of the sick Men Die. [Nearly three thousand of Washington's army of roughly eight thousand men were unfit for duty.]

*December 26.*—[Washington] has always acted wisely hitherto. His conduct when closely scrutinised is uncensurable. . . . Many Country Gentlemen in the interior parts of the States who get wrong information of the Affairs & state of our Camp, are very much Surprised at General Washington's delay to drive off the Enemy, being falsely informed that his Army consists of double the Number of the Enemy's—such wrong information . . . brings blame on his Excellency, who is deserving of the greatest encomiums; it brings disgrace on the Continental Troops, who have never evidenced the least backwardness in doing their duty, but on the contrary, have cheerfully endured a long and very fatiguing Campaign. . . .

*December 28.*—Yesterday upwards of fifty Officers in General Greene's Division resigned their Commissions—Six or Seven of our Regiment are doing the like to-day. All this is occasioned by Officers Families being so much neglected at home on account of Provisions. . . .

*December 29.*— . . . So much talk about discharges among the Officers—& so many are discharged—his Excellency lately expressed his fears of being left Alone with the Soldiers only. Strange that our Country will not exert themselves for his support, and save . . . a Cause of such unparalleled importance!!

*December 31.*—[Waldo considered going home, but was asked to stay on.] I concluded to stay—& immediately set about fixing accommodations for the Sick &c. &c.

*Sunday, January 4.*— . . . I was called to relieve a Soldier thought to be dying—he expired before I reached the Hut. He was an Indian—an excellent Soldier—and an obedient good natured fellow. He engaged for money doubtless as others do;—but he has served his country faithfully—he has fought for those very people who disinherited his forefathers—having finished his pilgrimage, he was discharged from the War of Life & Death. His memory ought to be respected, more than those rich ones who supply the world with nothing better than Money and Vice. . . . What a frail— dying creature is Man. We are Certainly not made for this world—daily evidences demonstrate the contrary.[16]

Through his long life, one private never let go of his pride in having served at Valley Forge. Joseph Plumb Martin's memoir is unique for its graphic re-creation of the daily life of the common Continental soldier. From the games they played to the exhaustion of long marches to the aftermath of battles, Martin describes the realities of military life during the American Revolution. Serving for most of the war, Martin witnessed the panic at Kip's Bay, the trials of Valley Forge, and the ultimate victory of Yorktown. Along the way he voices the spirit of camaraderie, the pride of service in a just cause, and the joy of a warm meal. Born in Becket in western Massachusetts in November 1760, Martin was the son of a minister who tended to lose his positions for "unministerial conduct." Receiving no formal education, Joseph Martin spent most of his youth on his grandparents' farm in Milford, Connecticut. Martin initially resisted the war fervor of 1775, known as the *rage militaire*. "The smell of war began to be pretty strong," he wrote, "but I was determined to have no hand in it." He was blunt about his reasons for avoiding service: "I felt myself to be a real coward. What— venture my carcass where bullets fly! That will never do for me." However, when a group of soldiers stayed at his family's farm in 1776, the fifteen-year-old Martin was inspired to enlist, joining the Connecticut state forces. After taking part in the battles around New York City later that summer, Martin enlisted in the Continental Army for the duration of the war, serving in the Eighth Connecticut Continental Regiment—Dr. Waldo's unit—under Captain David Bushnell, inventor of floating mines and of the first submarine, the *Turtle*. After the war, Martin moved to a farm in Maine, where he served as a selectman, town clerk, and justice of the peace. But he never prospered and lost his land, becoming a common laborer while remaining a voracious reader. Martin wrote this narrative in 1830 when he was seventy, and died in 1850, just short of his ninetieth birthday:

[1777] Starvation seemed to be entailed upon the army and every animal connected with it. The oxen . . . all died, and the southern horses fared no better. . . .

While we lay here there was a Continental Thanksgiving ordered by Congress; and as the army had all the cause in the world to be particularly thankful, if not for being well off, at least that it was no worse, we were ordered to participate in it. We had nothing to eat for two or three days previous, except what the trees of the fields and forests afforded us. But we must now have what Congress said—a sumptuous Thanksgiving. . . . Well—to add something extraordinary to our present stock of provisions—our country, ever mindful of its suffering army, opened her sympathizing heart so wide, upon this occasion, as to give us something to make the world stare. And what do you think it was, reader?—Guess.—You cannot guess, be you as much of a Yankee as you will. I will tell you: it gave each and every man *half a gill* of rice and a *table spoon full* of vinegar!!

After we had made sure of this extraordinary superabundant donation, we were ordered out to attend a meeting and hear a sermon delivered upon the happy occasion. . . . I remember the text, like an attentive lad at church . . . "And the soldiers said unto him, And what shall we do? And he said unto them, Do violence to no man, nor accuse anyone falsely." The preacher ought to have added the remainder of the sentence to have made it complete, "And be content with your wages." But that would not do, it would be too apropos; however, he heard it as soon as the service was over; it was shouted from a hundred tongues. . . . I had nothing else to do but to go home and make out my supper as usual, upon a leg of nothing and no turnips.

The army was now not only starved but naked; the greatest part were not only shirtless and barefoot, but destitute of all clothing, especially blankets. I procured a small piece of raw cowhide and made myself a pair of moccasins, which kept my feet (while they lasted) from the frozen ground, although, as I well remember, the hard edges so galled my ankles, while on a march, that it was with much difficulty and pain that I could wear them afterwards; but the only alternative I had was to endure this inconvenience or to go barefoot, as hundreds of my companions had to, till they might be tracked by their blood upon the rough frozen ground. But hunger, nakedness and sore shins were not the only difficulties we had at that time to encounter; we had hard duty to perform and little or no strength to perform it with. . . .

We were now in a truly forlorn condition,—no clothing, no provisions and as disheartened as need be. . . . However, there was no remedy, no alternative but this or dispersion. But dispersion, I believe, was not thought of, at least, I did not think of it. We had engaged in the defense of our injured country and were willing, nay, we were determined to persevere as long as such hardships were not altogether intolerable. . . . But we were now absolutely in danger of perishing, and that too, in the midst of a plentiful country. We then had but little and often nothing to eat for days together. . . . I am not writing fiction; all are sober realities.

. . . We were ordered . . . to go into the country on a foraging expedition, which was nothing more nor less than to procure provisions from the inhabitants for the men in the army and forage for the poor perishing cattle belonging to it, at the point of the bayonet. . . .

Our party consisted of a lieutenant, a sergeant, a corporal and eighteen privates. We marched till night when we halted and took up our quarters at a large farmhouse. . . . We were put into the kitchen. We had a snug room and a comfortable fire, and we began to think about cooking some of our fat beef. One of the men proposed to the landlady to sell her a shirt for some sauce [gravy]. She very readily took the shirt, which was worth a dollar at least. She might have given us a mess of sauce, for I think she would not have suffered poverty by so doing, as she seemed to have plenty of all things. . . . [We] took it into our heads that a little good cider would not make our supper relish any worse; so some of the men took the water pail and drew it full of excellent cider, which did not fail to raise our spirits considerably. Before we lay down the man who sold the shirt, having observed that the landlady had flung it into a closet, took a notion to re-possess it again. We marched off early in the morning before the people of the house were stirring, consequently did not know or see the woman's chagrin at having been overreached by the soldiers.[17]

Serving together, the members of the Continental Army became more than friends: they became brothers sharing experiences unknown to the general public. Within a few years, they came to take pride in their endurance and skill. In 1779, Ensign Daniel Gookin of New York wrote with admiration of the performance of his fellows: "To see with what patience the soldiers endured the fatigues of this march wading rivers, climbing mountains and a number of other things too tedious to mention, afford a pleasing prospect that in time we shall have soldiers equal to any in the world."[18]

## The Face of Battle

The Revolutionary battlefield was an intimate place. Personal and often face-to-face, eighteenth-century combat demanded a high degree of fortitude to advance across open ground toward a silent, well-armed enemy one could see or to stand one's ground as the bayonets drew closer. The muskets of the age could claim little accuracy—the command came, "ready, level, fire," aiming being no part of its use—and had an effective range of sixty to eighty yards. When Colonel William Prescott supposedly told his troops not to fire "until you see the whites of their eyes," he provided practical directions. The bayonet charge could be terrifying for all involved. Bayonets were usually more than two feet long, thrust into an enemy's body from the end of a leveled musket. It was perfectly understandable that many untrained troops fled at the sight of these sharpened blades.

Revolutionary battles could be horrible beyond the comprehension of the average soldier. The Battle of White Plains in October 1776—at which General Howe once more pummeled Washington's retreating army—seared the memory of infantryman Elisha Bostwick through the rest of his life. He observed a cannonball cut its way through men he knew and with whom he had served.

"The ball first took off the head of Smith, a Stout heavy man and dashed it open, then took Taylor across the Bowels, it then Struck Sergeant Garret of our Company on the hip [and] took off the point of the hip bone." Smith and Taylor died there on the field, while Garret was carried from the field only to die later that day. "To think, oh! what a sight that was to see within a distance of six rods those men with their legs and arms and guns and packs all in a heap." Though the cannonball had been fired from a distance, Bostwick could observe the enemy throughout the battle and saw the cannon that fired that lethal shot.[19]

Yet if the enemy was clearly visible in combat, so were one's comrades. Contrary to the popular mythology, Continental troops rarely fired on the British from behind cover. Washington sought the respect of his allies and opponents, following contemporary European military standards in keeping his units as well ordered as possible in compact formations. The men thus maneuvered and fired, advanced and received fire, fell back and reformed as a group. The best-trained units would stand shoulder to shoulder on the battlefield, the direct physical contact lending reassurance. Many soldiers stood fast for fear of looking a coward before their friends. By 1778 Continental officers could rely on their men to stand together. When General Anthony Wayne realized that he had been outfoxed by Cornwallis at Greenspring in July 1781, he boldly ordered his men to attack against superior odds, confident that they would hold together. As one of those present recorded in his diary: "our troops behaved well, fighting with great spirit & bravery. The infantry were oft broke; but as oft rallied & formed at a word."[20] What the officers came to admire was their men's resilience and endurance. Despite the horrors of this intimate war, the majority of the troops honored their commitment to their comrades and to their nation.

Combat could unhinge even well-trained soldiers. Some called it "cannon fever," some cowardice, but most found it difficult to explain the way in which competent and even courageous soldiers could suddenly collapse into incoherent conduct. For instance, Patrick Henry's son, John Henry, served with distinction at Saratoga. But as he walked amid the dead bodies after the battle, he broke his sword and threw it to the ground, shouting in anger and then suffering a mental collapse. After nine months, his mental health unimproved, he resigned his commission. Soldiers understood, if they could not explain, Henry's breakdown; to himself and his neighbors, Henry appeared less of a man.[21] After a battle in Virginia, Private Josiah Atkins plaintively wrote his mother: "How lamentable my circumstances. Once I lived in peace at home, rejoicing in the divine favor and smiles, but now I am in the field of war, surrounded with circumstances of affliction and heart-felt disappointment." Referencing the lament from Exodus, Atkins ended, "Once I enjoyed the pleasant company of many friends, but now I am among strangers in a strange land." Atkins never made it home.[22]

Those who had not experienced combat lived on images; those who had survived under fire knew that it defied simple categories. Most members of the army found refuge in their professionalism, bearing up under the trials of service with cool competence. The ability of the Continental Army was well displayed in Greene's southern campaign, which outmaneuvered the British at every turn and saw the Delaware Regiment march five thousand miles between April 1780 and April 1782.[23] By Yorktown the Continental Army had become a symbol of national pride, with crowds turning out wherever they marched, though the public would still not pay them.

Oliver Boardman, a private in the Connecticut Line, served at the battles of Saratoga under the command of Benedict Arnold. In his journal he recorded the ebb and flow of combat, the army's use of Indian scouts, friendly fire, the treatment of loyalists, the decay of Burgoyne's army, and the feelings of elation that came with victory:

Third [September] 18th [1777] This Morning at three O'Clock Struck our Tents, & took our Packs, & the whole of General Arnold's Division Marched on towards the Enemy by Columns, through the woods till our Right was in full view of their Camp, our advanced Party upon the Left, fired upon a Number, that was a digging potatoes. Wounded some, & took four or five Prisoners. Then we retreated to the Brow of a great Hill & Lay in the Bushes for them. Our Generals saw them Paraded & March forward, we tarried awhile & then marched to Camp. (9 Miles)

Friday 19th The Enemy came to Pay us a Visit, when they arrived within a Mile & a half, Our Men attacked them. A heavy fire began & lasted about four Hours & a half, we hear the Enemy have lost a great Number Besides Wounded 46 were taken Prisoners.

Saturday 20th [British] Deserters come In who say the Enemy are in as great Confusion as ever Militia was without Commanders. The Return of Colonel [Thaddeus] Cook's Regiment after the Battles. The first Battle: 11 Killed, 36 Wounded, 3 Missing; The Return of the Battle on Tuesday the Seventh of October: 2 Killed & 5 Wounded.

Sunday 21st This Morning Struck Tents & Paraded, General Arnold come to the Head of the Regiment & gave News that our Men had taken some out works at Ticonderoga with three Hundred Prisoners, at Least a Hundred of our own, & 3 Hundred Battoes Loaded with Baggage. Then we gave three Cheers, after it had all gone through the Camp Thirteen Cannon were fired for the thirteen united States then three Cheers were given through the Camp. This Afternoon a scout of our Indians took a

Tory, the General gave him to them for a while. They took him & Buried him up to his Neck & had their Pow wow around him, after that, they had him up and Laid him a side of a great fire & turned his head & feet a while to the fire, hooting & hollowing round him then he was hand Cuffed & sent to Albany Gaol.

Monday 22nd A sad Accident happened Yesterday of one Sentry who shot another being out of his Post, Belonging to the same Picquet.

Tuesday 23rd A Scout of our Indians took two Regulars Sentries Yesterday. After taking their hats from them they Painted their Faces & Brought them In. Besides, Our Indians Brought eight other Prisoners in—that were a going an Express to Montreal, one of them was a Deserter from our Train of Artillery at Quebec.

Wednesday 24th Our Indians went out & Brought in three Prisoners with a Rope round the Neck of each of them. . . . Besides another sad & Melancholy Accident happened of one Sentry's Shooting another Belonging to the same Picquet.

Thursday 25th A Party of our Men went out to take the Regulars' advanced Picquet. Our Men in surprise upon them demanded of them to lay down their Arms which they were about, till an Officer stepped up & Damned them off hearty. They directly took their arms made one fire & took to their heals. Our Men killed Six & took one Hessian Officer. . . .

Monday 29th Last Night a Colonel's Guard went out to take the Enemy's advanced Picquet. They being apprised of it Doubled their guard & put themselves in readiness for Defence. Our Men came up & Exchanged a few Shot[s,] one of our men was killed & three or four wounded. . . .

Sunday [October] 5th One Hessian deserted this Morning, He informs that several of his fellows were waiting the first opportunity to come off, also that they are very scant for Provision. This Afternoon two of the British Soldiers Deserted, they bring the same News about Provision. Taken and Deserted Seventeen to Day.

Tuesday 7th . . . This Afternoon about three O'Clock Burgoyne's flying Camp, commanded by Frasier [Brigadier General Simon Fraser], Advanced within about half a Mile of our advanced Picquet to Drive them from a Hill where Capt [Joseph] Blague and fifty men & myself one of the Number were Posted, at which they kept a Smart Cannonade for a Quarter of an Hour, while our Men mustered along & sent a party to come upon their Backs, where they soon fell at it on all sides, & Drove the Enemy from their Artillery. [Fraser fell back upon] the Hessian Camp where our General [Arnold], Little thought of Danger, forced his way through & Spared none till a Ball Break his Leg & killed his Horse. But his Brave Men not Discouraged with their Misfortune Drove them from their Camp & took it, with their Tents Standing & Pots Boiling, Besides three Pieces of Brass Cannon, Eight Brass Cannon in the whole, Two Twelves, the others Sixes & Nine Pounders, taken to Day. Fraser was killed.

Wednesday 8th Our Men kept a Constant Cannonade all Day into their other Encampment. . . .

Thursday 9th About Thirty Deserters came in last Night. They Inform that Burgoyne began his retreat last Night as soon as our Men Ceased firing & Left three Hundred Sick & Wounded. . . .

Friday 10th This Morning we paraded & marched after the Enemy up at Saratoga, & paraded over Night, upon a great Hill about South East from the Enemy. General [Philip] Schuyler's House with the rest of ye Buildings, Mills, Barracks &c at Saratoga were Burnt to Day [by the British].

Saturday 11th General [John] Fellows took a hundred Battoes [boats] Last Night, with Five Hundred Barrels of Pork, a quantity of Porter, & other Rich Stores With a Guard of a Sergeant & fifteen Men. About Noon we moved to the North-West of the Enemy in the Woods & built fires, & turned in upon the Ground. Upwards of Fifty taken & Deserted to Day.

Sunday 12th General [Horatio] Gates sent in a Flag of Truce. General Burgoyne sent one to answer it. General Gates sent the Second. . . .

Monday 13th A Scout of Rifle Men saw a scout of the Hessians & Canadians, one of our Men called to one of the Hessians in his Language to come to him, he Directly threw down his Gun & run to him. He informs us that they Drew all their Provision, which is to Last Seven Days. General Gates himself says, that the account from every Deserter & Prisoner agree so well that he has reason to Believe it, & contradicted by none. . . .

Wednesday 15th A Cessation of Arms to Day. Some of the British Soldiers come to our Sentries to get them some water. We are informed by our Officers that the Articles are agreed upon Between General Gates & General Burgoyne.

Thursday 16th A Parlay was beat at Midnight last Night, our Men answered it. By what we can learn his honour [Burgoyne] was about to Fall from his agreement with General Gates. We also Learn that he Dealt out Sixty Rounds of Cartridges to the British Soldiers, In order to try to do his Best & worst once more & ordered as many for the Hessians But they refused to take them. Our Generals are together taking the Matter into Consideration. Orders to Strike Tents immediately & every thing put up.

Our Generals sent in at Eleven O'Clock that they would give his Honour one Hour to Consider the Matter of his Agreement Yesterday And gave Orders for every man to be ready at the Minute after Twelve O'Clock when three Cannon will be fired, if he will not sign the Articles of Capitulation. Colonel [Daniel] Morgan received Orders for his Rifle Men to march immediately & Scale their works & Spare no Man they could find & The Army to follow & carry it through.

Our Scout took a Tory that Deserted from us at Ti [Fort Ticonderoga] & . . . without any trial they put a Rope round his Neck & tied it to a Saddle & told him they would hang him. He Begged & prayed they would Shoot him, then they tied him to a Tree & gave him a Hundred lashes, then he Begged they would Hang him. Now he is to receive two Hundred more [lashes] which two Morning's will Complete & then to be Tried by a Court-Martial for his Life.

Friday 17th 1777 The Hand of Providence worked wonderfully In favour of America this Day. According to the Agreement of General Burgoyne Yesterday he marched his Army out of his works at Ten O'Clock In Brigades & Paraded their Arms on the Meadow at Saratoga. At Three O'Clock in the Afternoon they Marched through our Army that was paraded on the Right & Left, with a Guard for Boston.

It was a glorious sight to see the haughty Britons march out & Surrender their arms to an Army which but a little before, they despised & called poltroons, they however before the surrender were convinced of their error, having in two engagements previous seen the greatest bravery that ever was displayed, & the most consummate Generalship exercised. The enemy acknowledge the Spirit and bravery of our officers & men, and do not hesitate to Say, that the idea held up to them of the Americans, was false.[24]

## The Great Contradiction

The Americans claimed to be fighting for freedom, yet roughly one-fourth of the population of their nation was enslaved. This contradiction was obvious and troubled some supporters of the Revolution, though the majority of whites accepted slavery as a given and made no effort to alter societal structures. As a consequence, it fell to the British to appear as the liberators of slaves, though never in a systematic fashion. Most famously, John Murray, Lord Dunmore, the last Royal governor of Virginia, issued a proclamation offering freedom to slaves who fought for the British. On November 14, 1775, Dunmore led a force of former slaves at Kemp's Landing in defeating the militia of Princess Anne County, sending shock waves through the colony. Many thousands fled to join the British in hopes of attaining their freedom; more than a thousand served in the Ethiopian Regiment, a great number died of disease, some were sold back into slavery by unscrupulous British officers, and many eventually found freedom in various parts of the British Empire.

At the beginning of the Revolution, a number of African Americans, some of them slaves, fought in the New England armies. But Congress appointed a slaveowner commander of the Continental Army, and on October 8, 1775, George Washington ordered that no blacks were to serve in his army. American units treated runaway slaves as war booty, property to either be returned to its owner or sold for the benefit of the possessor. But some rebels saw the issue differently. In November 1777, Captain Ebenezer Allen's company of the Green Mountain Regiment took a number of British prisoners along Lake Champlain. The British officer had a slave named Dinah Mattis and her two-month-old child (given the child's age, the officer was likely the father). Although the company faced a clear economic incentive to treat Mattis and her child as slaves, Captain Allen and his men discussed the meaning of slavery in a land of liberty and voted unanimously to insure Mattis's freedom. Allen issued Mattis a certificate that stated, "I being conscientious that it is not right in the sight of God to keep slaves—I therefore obtaining leave of the detachment under my command to give her and her child their freedom to pass and repass any where through the United States of America with her behaving as becometh, and to trade and to traffic for herself and child as though she was born free, without being molested by any person or persons." At least these frontier soldiers stood fast to the dignity of their cause.[25]

By 1776, Washington, desperate for men, persuaded Congress to allow him to enlist African Americans. The northern states welcomed the opportunity to fill their quota with blacks, while the southern states had a mixed reaction. Virginia and North Carolina limited enlistment to free blacks, and South Carolina and Georgia refused to allow any blacks to serve. Maryland, however, allowed hundreds of slaves to enlist in return for freedom, a step which resulted in the dramatic growth of its free black population in the aftermath of the war. Some states, including Maryland, paid slaveowners for permitting slaves to volunteer to serve, while others, including most of the New England states, figured that not drafting the slaveowner was a fair exchange.[26]

For some slaves, then, serving in the Continental Army offered a clear path to freedom. Boyrereau Brinch was one of those who enlisted in return for his freedom. Brinch was born along the Niger River, where he was kidnapped as a young boy around 1760 and served as a slave to a British naval officer until he was sold to John Burrell, a farmer in Milford, Connecticut, in 1763. Burrell routinely beat Brinch, often for the most minor transgressions. Brinch thought Burrell a hypocrite, "as he was one of the strongest professors in the church, and as strict in his family devotion as any man I was ever acquainted with."[27] Brinch was sold several times to various owners in the Milford area, most of whom treated him poorly, until finally the widow Mary Stiles, of Woodbury, Connecticut, purchased Brinch. Stiles treated Brinch with kindness and taught him how to read and write, allowing him to record his Revolutionary experiences:

When this lady died I descended like real estate, in fee simple to her son Benjamin Stiles, Esq. About four years after her death, her two sons, Benjamin and David, were drafted to fight in the revolution. I also entered the banners of freedom. Alas! Poor African Slave, to liberate freemen, my tyrants. . . .

I went into Capt. Granger's company, from hence I was drafted into Capt. Borker's company of light infantry, as they wanted six feet men. I then wanted but a quarter of an inch of being 6 feet 3 inches. [Brinch saw action on Long Island and then in New York, both British victories. His fellow soldiers found his name difficult and called him Jeffrey Brace.] . . .

However previous to the evacuation of New York, I was one of a hundred, selected for the purpose of plundering a certain British Store, which was completed without the loss of a single man—but with the gain of seven loads of excellent Provisions.

We were overtaken by the British, after we had marched about a mile towards North Castle. The party that pursued us were 60 light dragoons, whom we saluted so warmly with a well aimed fire: that they were obliged to return for additional force. They again overtook us about 3 miles from New York, but as we had also some new forces, they thought most proper to return without an engagement.

[In the spring 1777] we moved to Hackensack in the Jerseys. Soon after our arrival there, the enemy stole some cattle from our lines. Capt. Granger with twenty chosen men was sent in pursuit of them. . . . I was one of the number. . . . [The command separated and Brinch and two other soldiers] came to a small hill or rise of land over which they must have passed. This rise being covered with bushes, it was thought prudent, that I should wait upon the hither side of the hill while they went over and examined into the fact, whether the cattle were actually in the meadow or not, and at the same time, to keep a look out for the enemy. While I stood there anxiously waiting for their return, I suddenly discovered a man riding up to me not more than eight rods distant on full speed with a pistol in his hand, and ordered me to lay down my arms. . . . I demanded to whom I was to surrender and by what authority he demanded it.—he said I must surrender to him who demanded me in the name of the King his majesty of Great Britain. I then plainly told him that neither him or his King's majesty would get my arms unless he took them by force. He immediately cocked his pistol and fired; I fell flat upon the ground in order to dodge his ball, and did so effectually do it, that he missed me.

I rose, he drew his sword and rode up to me so quick that I had no time to take aim before he struck my gun barrel with his cutlass, and cut it almost one third off—also cut off the bone of my middle finger on my hand. As he struck the horse jumped before he could wheel upon me, again altho' my gun barrel was cut, I fired and killed him, as he fell I caught his horse and sword. He was a British light horseman in disguise.—I mounted immediately, and that instant discovered four men on horse back approaching me from [a] different direction, I fled, passed one man, just before I came to a stone wall. Both of our horses were upon the full run, he fired and missed me. My horse leaped the wall like a deer; they all pursued me. . . .

I made no halt until I arrived within our Camp. When I dismounted tied my horse and went to set up my gun, I found I could not open my hand which was the first time that I discovered that I was wounded. [My] fear and precipitation had turned me almost as white as my fellow soldiers. In consequence of my wounds, I was unfit for duty again for almost three months. . . .

[W]e heard that the enemy were making their way to Stanford, we marched there immediately, and arrived before them. A party marched down into some meadows to watch their motion; on discovering their su-periour force, we fired upon them and ran off fully believing,

> That he who fights and runs away,
> May live to fight another day. . . .

I was in the battle at Cambridge, White plains, Monmouth, Princeton, Newark, Froggs-point, Horseneck where I had a ball pass through my knapsack. All which battles the reader can obtain a more perfect account of in history, than I can give. At last we returned to West point and were discharged; as the war was over.—Thus was I, a slave for five years fighting for liberty.

After we were disbanded, I returned to my old master at Woodbury, with whom I lived one year; my services in the American war, having emancipated me from further slavery, and from being bartered or sold.— My master consented that I might go where I pleased and seek my fortune. Hearing flattering accounts of the new state of Vermont; I left Woodbury, and travelled as far as the town of Lenox, in Massachusetts, where for the first time I made a bargain as a freeman for labor. . . . When I had fulfilled this contract, I travelled to the town of Poultney in Vermont. . . . Here I enjoyed the pleasures of a freeman; my food was sweet, my labor pleasure: and one bright gleam of life seemed to shine upon me. . . . I was fortunes football, and must depend upon her gentle kicks. . . . [I] determined to obtain some property, that I might in some measure enjoy the independence of the freedom I possessed. I purchased by agreement twenty five acres of land of Mr. Craw, which lay in the East Part of the town. . . .

[Brinch married Susannah Dublin and settled in Poultney. The lessons of the Revolution were clear for Brinch.] [I]t is my anxious wish, that this simple narrative, may be the means of opening the hearts of those who hold slaves and move them to consent to give them that freedom which they themselves enjoy, and which all mankind have an equal right to possess.[28]

## Victory

The campaign that led to the victory at Yorktown was the most brilliant in the American Revolution. A master of maneuver, Nathanael Greene drew the British under Lord Cornwallis deeper into the interior while wearing down their men and resources. In March 1781, a frustrated Cornwallis wrote his friend General William Phillips, commanding a British army in Virginia, "I am quite tired of marching about the country in quest of adventures," and decided to try his luck in Virginia. "If we mean an offensive war in America, we must abandon New York, and bring our whole force into Virginia." Cornwallis wrote General Henry Clinton, commander of British forces in America, recommending that he leave New York City with his entire force and join him in Virginia for one final battle with Washington.[29] Not waiting for a response, Cornwallis left Wilmington, North Carolina, for Virginia on April 25, hoping to meet up with first Phillips and then Clinton. He was to get his final battle, but not in the way he expected.

Everything went wrong with Cornwallis's hastily planned operation into Virginia. Phillips died of a fever in May; shortly thereafter Clinton received news that Cornwallis had already left for Virginia without waiting for confirmation, and the commanding general stayed put in New York. Admiral François Joseph Comte de Grasse sailed his fleet from France, meeting no opposition from the British as he crossed the Atlantic. In June, Cornwallis received orders from Clinton that he was to select a secure site for a naval base on the Chesapeake. Cornwallis blundered around Virginia for the next several weeks until finally settling on Yorktown in August to wait for the British navy to pick up his army. Meanwhile, Washington had an excellent ally in the French General Jean Baptiste de Vimeur, Comte de Rochambeau. In August, the two generals worked well together, faking operations against New York to mislead Clinton, while quietly moving their armies south, through New York and Pennsylvania, headed for the Chesapeake.

Washington, who demonstrated formidable organizational skills moving the two armies rapidly south, arrived in Virginia in mid-September. On September

5, de Grasse's fleet defeated the British under Admiral Thomas Graves, who gave up and returned to New York, leaving Cornwallis trapped at Yorktown. In the last days of September, Washington and Rochambeau drew a net around the British army at Yorktown and began besieging Cornwallis's demoralized forces. James Duncan of Philadelphia, who was twenty-five in 1781, was a Princeton graduate preparing for the ministry when he enlisted in Colonel Moses Hazen's regiment, known as Congress's Own. In his diary, Duncan recorded the siege, culminating with the dramatic attack on the British outposts by French and American forces on October 15—the latter commanded by Washington's young aide, Colonel Alexander Hamilton. Duncan clearly took pride in the professional conduct of the Continental Army:

> [September 29, 1781], the allied army moved down toward York . . . and made a short halt about two miles distant from the enemy's outworks when a few shots were fired from the French pieces at some of Tarleton's horse, who immediately dispersed. In the evening we proceeded about half a mile farther and encamped for the night. . . . On the morning of the 30th we had orders to approach the enemy's works. After marching a short distance we were ordered to load, and proceeded within half a mile of the enemy's works on the left.
>
> . . . No sooner was the enemy's works evacuated than they were taken possession of by our pickets, supported by the whole army, who marched up for that purpose, and continued on the lines a great part of the day, although the enemy at certain times fired very briskly from their pieces. About 8 o'clock this morning the French grenadiers attacked and carried a small battery, with the loss of four killed and six wounded. Ten companies were ordered out early this morning for fatigue, of which I had the honor to command one. Until 11 a.m. we were employed in cutting and stripping branches for gabions [baskets filled with earth for fortification purposes]. On being furnished with shovels, spades, pickaxes, etc., we were ordered up to the lines, where we continued inactive until about an hour before sunset. In the meantime, the engineers were employed in reconnoitering the enemy's works, and fixing on proper places to break the first ground. Let me here observe that the enemy by evacuating their works had given us an amazing advantage, as the ground they left commanded the whole town. . . .
>
> October 10.—Last night the men were busily employed in finishing the batteries, and early this morning four more were opened against the enemy. . . .
>
> October 11.—Last night commenced a very heavy cannonade and the enemy returned the fire with no less spirit. Being apprehensive of a storm,

they often fired in every direction. The largest of the enemy's vessels was set on fire by the bursting of a shell or red hot ball from some of our batteries, and communicated it to another, both of which were burnt down. They must have lost a considerable quantity of powder in the last, as there was an explosion which made a heavy report. The whole night was nothing but one continual roar of cannon, mixed with the bursting of shells and rumbling of houses torn to pieces. As soon as the day approached the enemy withdrew their pieces from their embrazures and retired under cover of their works, and now commenced a still more dreadful cannonade from all our batteries without scarcely any intermission for the whole day. . . .

October 13.—Last night we were employed in strengthening the line, and began a French battery and a redoubt. We lost, several men this night, as the enemy by practice were enabled to throw their shells with great certainty. . . .

October 14.—The enemy last night kept up a continual blaze from several pieces of cannon of nine royals and some howitzers. Early in the night the fire was chiefly directed against the French, who were just on our left, but about 10 o'clock our people [began] to erect a battery. They soon discovered us, and changed the direction of their fire. It happened to be our lot to lie in the trenches just in the rear of the battery exposed to all their fire; and now were I to recount all the narrow escapes I made that night, it would almost be incredible. I cannot, however, but take notice of a remarkable and miraculous one indeed. About midnight the sentry called "A shell!" I jumped up immediately to watch the direction, but had no suspicion of its coming so near until it fell in the center of the trench, within less than two feet of me. I immediately flung myself . . . among some arms, and although the explosion was very sudden and the trench as full of men as it could possibly contain, yet not a single man was killed and only two of my own company slightly wounded. . . .

October 15.—I have just said we were ordered yesterday to the trenches. The French grenadiers were ordered out the same time and all for the purpose of storming two redoubts on the enemy's left. Our division arrived at [illegible] a little before dark where every man was ordered to disencumber himself of his pack. The evening was pretty dark and favored the attack. The column advanced. Colonel Guinot's regiment in front and ours in the rear. We had not got far before we were discovered and now the enemy opened a fire of cannon, grape shot, shell and musketry upon us, but all to no effect. The column moved on undisturbed and took the redoubt by the bayonet without firing a single gun. The enemy made an obstinate defense (but what cannot brave men do when determined)? We

had 7 men killed and 30 wounded. Among the latter were Colonel Guinot, Major Barber and Captain Oney. Fifteen men of the enemy were
killed and wounded in the work, 20 were taken prisoners besides Major
Campbell, who commanded. . . . [Manuscript suddenly breaks off][30]

James Thacher of Barnstable, Massachusetts, was studying medicine with his
uncle when the Revolution broke out. Thacher rushed to join the Continental
Army outside Boston in 1775, enlisting as a surgeon's mate, and served throughout the war. After the war, Thacher would become a prominent doctor and
agronomist, the author of numerous books and a member of the American
Academy of Arts and Sciences, dying in 1844. His journal—which he probably
embellished after the war—picks up with the same battle for the British redoubts
that ends Duncan's journal:

[October 15] The siege is daily becoming more and more formidable and
alarming, and his lordship [Cornwallis] must view his situation as extremely critical, if not desperate. Being in the trenches every other night
and day, I have a fine opportunity of witnessing the sublime and stupen-
dous scene. . . . The bomb-shells from the besiegers and the besieged are
incessantly crossing each others' path in the air. They are clearly visible in
the form of a black ball in the day, but in the night, they appear like a fiery
meteor with a blazing tail, most beautifully brilliant. . . . When a shell
falls, it whirls round, burrows, and excavates the earth to a considerable
extent, and bursting, makes dreadful havoc around. I have more than
once witnessed fragments of the mangled bodies and limbs of the British
soldiers thrown into the air by the bursting of our shells; and by one from
the enemy, Captain White, of the seventh Massachusetts regiment, and
one soldier were killed, and another wounded near where I was standing.
About twelve or fourteen men have been killed or wounded within twenty-
four hours; I attended at the hospital, amputated a man's arm, and assisted
in dressing a number of wounds.
    During the assault, the British kept up an incessant firing of cannon
and musketry from their whole line. . . . The other redoubt on the right of
the British lines was assaulted at the same time by a detachment of the
French, commanded by the gallant Baron de Viomenil. Such was the
ardor displayed by the assailants, that all resistance was soon overcome,
though at the expense of nearly one hundred men killed and wounded. . . .
    17th.—The whole of our works are now mounted with cannon and
mortars; not less than one hundred pieces of heavy ordnance have been in
continual operation during the last twenty-four hours. The whole peninsula trembles under the incessant thunderings of our infernal machines;

we have leveled some of their works in ruins, and silenced their guns; they have almost ceased firing. We are so near as to have a distinct view of the dreadful havoc and destruction of their works, and even see the men in their lines tore to pieces by the bursting of our shells. . . .

18th.—It is now ascertained that Lord Cornwallis, to avoid the necessity of a surrender, had determined on the bold attempt to make his escape in the night of the 16th, with a part of his army into the country. His plan was to leave sick and baggage behind, and to cross with his effective force over to Gloucester Point, there to destroy the French legion and other troops, and to mount his infantry on their horses and such others as might be procured, and thus push their way to New York by land. . . . Boats were secretly prepared . . . when, from a moderate and calm evening, a most violent storm of wind and rain ensued. The boats with the remaining troops were all driven down the river, and it was not till the next day that his troops could be returned to the garrison at York.

At an early hour this forenoon General Washington communicated to Lord Cornwallis the general basis of the terms of capitulation, which he deemed admissible, and allowed two hours for his reply. . . . [T]he terms of capitulation are settled, and being confirmed by the commanders of both armies, the royal troops are to march out tomorrow and surrender their arms.

19th.— . . . At about twelve o'clock, the combined army was arranged and drawn up in two lines extending more than a mile in length. The Americans were drawn up in a line on the right side of the road, and the French occupied the left. At the head of the former, the great American commander, mounted on his noble courser, took his station, attended by his aids. At the head of the latter was posted the excellent Count Rochambeau and his suite. The French troops, in complete uniform, displayed a martial and noble appearance, their band of music, of which the timbrel formed a part, is a delightful novelty, and produced while marching to the ground a most enchanting effect. The Americans, though not all in uniform, nor their dress so neat, yet exhibited an erect, soldierly air, and every countenance beamed with satisfaction and joy. The concourse of spectators from the country was prodigious, in point of numbers was probably equal to the military, but universal silence and order prevailed.

It was about two o'clock when the captive army advanced through the line formed for their reception. Every eye was prepared to gaze on Lord Cornwallis, the object of peculiar interest and solicitude; but he disappointed our anxious expectations; pretending indisposition, he made General O'Hara his substitute as the leader of his army. This officer was followed by the conquered troops in a slow and solemn step, with shouldered arms, colors cased, and drums beating a British march. Having arrived at the head of the line, General O'Hara, elegantly mounted, advanced to his excellency the commander-in-chief, taking off his hat, and apologized for the non-appearance of Earl Cornwallis. With his usual dignity and politeness, his excellency pointed to Major-General [Benjamin] Lincoln [to accept the surrender]. . . .

The royal troops, while marching through the line formed by the allied army, exhibited a decent and neat appearance. . . . But it was in the field, when they came to the last act of the drama, that the spirit and pride of the British soldier was put to the severest test: here their mortification could not be concealed. Some of the platoon officers appeared to be exceedingly chagrined when giving the word "ground arms," and I am a witness that they performed this duty in a very unofficer-like manner; and that many of the soldiers manifested a sullen temper, throwing their arms on the pile with violence, as if determined to render them useless. . . . The joy on this momentous occasion is universally diffused, and the hope entertained that it will arrest the career of a cruel warfare, and advance the establishment of American Independence.[31]

## America's First Veterans

Students of the American Revolution are often shocked by the shoddy treatment soldiers received at the hands of an ungrateful public during the war. Revolutionary America felt no obligation to the troops who won their independence, nor, in the two years after Yorktown, did many political leaders find reason to maintain their victorious army. As Washington wrote in January 1783: "The army as usual is without pay, and a great part of the soldiery without shirts; and tho' the patience of them is equally threadbare, it seems to be a matter of small concern to those at a distance. In truth, if one was to hazard an opinion for them on this subject, it would be, that the army having contracted a habit of encountering distress and difficulties, and of living without money, it would be injurious to it, to introduce other customs."[32] Washington attempted not only to win assurances from Congress that his men would receive their promised rewards once a peace treaty was signed, but to get the necessary supplies and pay. He failed at both tasks.

Many Americans feared that the army would rise up against their mistreatment, perhaps even refusing to disband with the end of hostilities. Alexander Hamilton wrote Washington in February 1783 that the real challenge facing them as peace approached was to keep the army, which had every cause for complaint, in check: "It appears to be a prevailing opinion in the army, that the disposition to recompense their services, will cease with the necessity for them; and that if they once lay down their arms, they part with the means of obtaining justice. It is to be lamented that appearances afford too much ground for their distrust. . . . But the difficulty will be, to keep a *complaining and suffering army* within the bounds of moderation." Washington disagreed with his aide, writing back that he had "no great apprehension of its [the soldier's discontent] exceeding the bounds of reason and moderation; notwithstanding the prevailing sentiment in the army is, that the prospect of compensation for past services will terminate with the war." He felt great concern for the soldiers, who faced being decommissioned without any hope for the future, "turned into the world," as he wrote in another letter, "soured by penury and what they call the ingratitude of the public, involved in debts without one farthing of money to carry them home, after having spent the flower of their days, and many of them their patrimonies, in establishing the freedom and independence of their country, and suffered every thing that human nature is capable of enduring on this side of death." However, he placed his faith in reason and justice, which demanded that the soldiers receive their fair recompense: "The States cannot, surely, be so devoid of common sense, common honesty, and common policy, as to refuse their aid, on a full, clear, and candid representation of facts."[33]

After the Treaty of Paris officially ended the war on September 3, 1783, many officers wanted to follow the British example and receive half pay for the rest of their lives. During the crisis of 1780, when it appeared that the Continental Army might disintegrate, Congress had, in fact, voted to grant half pay to officers who remained in the army until the war's end. They would not deliver on that promise, however, nor on promises for pay and land made to the common soldiers.[34]

One of the quirks of America's military history, apparent as early as the Revolution, is that society allows war profiteering, and even rewards its practitioners, while framing any support for veterans as a dangerous step toward establishing an aristocracy or creating a dependent class of citizens. Congress and the states had long dangled promises of future rewards before prospective enlistees, and then yanked back those proffered riches once the war was won. Yet when veterans demanded what they had been promised, they were labeled mercenaries and parasites. The members of the Society of the Cincinnati, whose claims for distinction aroused so much public furor, learned this lesson the hard way. Once the society dropped all claims to special consideration for their service to the country, the public lost interest.

Many returning veterans found only destitution at home. The Massachusetts legislature complained to Congress that homeless veterans created a problem for their state: having received no pay in months and lacking the means to find their way home, many veterans cluttered the streets of Boston begging for aid.[35] Even an officer as notable as Colonel Timothy Bigelow of Worcester died in debtor's prison, and thousands of veterans like him found themselves buried in debt within a year of returning home, many struggling for years to rise from poverty. David Szatmary has suggested a direct connection between the debts accrued by veterans after the war and Shays' Rebellion, the leaders of which were veterans—Luke Day, Daniel Shays, and Joel Billings among others. It is telling in this context that their first target was the Court of Common Pleas, where debt cases were heard. The state of Massachusetts and wealthy Boston merchants responded by funding a private army to put down the rebellion— which, ironically, proved far more of a threat to liberty than had the Continental Army.[36]

The public wanted to forget about their dependence on the Continental Army—and wanted the soldiers to forget as well. At some level, civilians had to know that the soldiers had made the greater sacrifice, but not until 1818 would Congress, moved by images of Revolutionary veterans suffering from dire poverty, finally grant a pension to those who had won the nation's independence. By that time, it was too late for the majority of them.

One of those veterans who lived long enough to claim his small pension did not want the United States to forget all it owed to the common soldier of the Continental Army. Joseph Plumb Martin had survived, but not prospered, in the years after the war. Martin seems to have been inspired to write his narrative by the complaints of many that too much deference was shown to the veterans and too much money wasted on their paltry pensions. There were those, Martin wrote, who appeared content for the veterans "to die on a dunghill," and he asked his readers to imagine what would have happened had the veterans "not ventured their lives in battle and faced poverty, disease, and death for their country to gain and maintain that Independence and Liberty." Though his narrative is far from a fanciful glorification of military service and contains little of romantic heroism, Martin upheld the honor of those who sacrificed so that others might enjoy the benefits of the independence they won:

> When those who engaged to serve during the war enlisted, they were promised a hundred acres of land, each, which was to be in their own or adjoining states. When the country had drained the last drop of service it could screw out of the poor soldiers, they were turned adrift like old worn-out horses, and nothing said about land to pasture them upon. Congress did, indeed, appropriate lands under the denomination of "Soldier's Lands", in Ohio state, or some state, or a future state, but no care was taken that the soldiers should get them. No agents were appointed to

see that the poor fellows ever got possession of their lands; no one ever took the least care about it, except a pack of speculators, who were driving about the country like so many evil spirits, endeavoring to pluck the last feather from the soldiers. The soldiers were ignorant of the ways and means to obtain their bounty lands, and there was no one appointed to inform them. The truth was, none cared for them; the county was served, and faithfully served, and that was all that was deemed necessary. It was, soldiers, look to yourselves; we want no more of you. I hope I shall one day find land enough to lay my bones in. If I chance to die in a civilized country, none will deny me that. A dead body never begs a grave;—thanks for that.[37]

# 2

# The War of 1812

The War of 1812 holds an unusual and contradictory place in American history. Some of the nation's most powerful national icons emerged from this conflict: the national anthem and the glorification of "Old Glory," Jackson at New Orleans and Perry at Lake Erie. The war created a generation of national leaders: Andrew Jackson, William Henry Harrison, Richard M. Johnson, and Winfield Scott. Yet the vast majority of Americans know nothing about this war or the people who fought it; for instance, a 2004 Harris poll found that two-thirds of Americans had no knowledge of their national anthem or its origins.[1] A recent poll of college students beginning a U.S. history survey course found that none of them knew that enemy forces had once set fire to the nation's Capitol. Even historians will often focus on the same set of iconic stories in order to avoid dealing with the generally abysmal performance of U.S. forces against smaller British contingents. Some scholars even promote a mythology that the United States won the War of 1812, that "the British had been beaten again," in what is often called "nothing less than a second Declaration of Independence, the reaffirmation of America's right to exist free of Britain."[2] And to this day, the causality of the war remains obscure.

This sense of confusion is not difficult to understand and was shared by those alive in 1812. Any analysis of the letters, journals, and memoirs of common soldiers who served during the War of 1812 reveals a failure to grasp the war's roots.[3] But then few of their contemporaries understood the conflict either. President James Madison stumbled badly in his message to Congress, as he attempted to explain why the United States had no choice but to declare war on Great Britain because of the impressment of sailors, the violation of neutral rights, and affronts to national honor.[4] Oddly, those areas most directly affected by the impressment crisis, the eastern seaports, proved least supportive of the war. Even more oddly, Britain responded to American diplomatic efforts, repealing the Orders in Council—which restricted neutral trade in Europe—before Madison's declaration of war.[5] News of the revocation did not reach Washington until after Madison's message but before Congress declared war, giving the government the chance to declare victory and save a lot of trouble. Congressional

Democratic-Republicans quashed all proposals to declare peace and set about justifying the war on other grounds, to the confusion of contemporaries and historians.[6] Diplomacy had worked just fine, but the U.S. government preferred to give war a chance.

In addition to clinging to impressment, proponents of war argued that Britain deliberately disrupted the American economy, interfered with American commerce, affronted the nation's honor, armed western Indians and drove them to war, and conspired to restore the United States to its empire; besides, the United States would definitely conquer Canada.[7] This latter justification proved particularly baffling. Opponents of the war, such as Virginia's John Randolph, accused Madison of launching "a war of conquest, a war for the acquisition of territory," unsuited to a republican government.[8] William R. King of North Carolina denied that "this will be a war of aggrandizement, a war of conquest. I am as little disposed to extend the territory [of the United States] as any other individual in this House." However, "I trust if our differences with Great Britain are not speedily adjusted, (of which, indeed, I have no expectation,) we shall take Canada. Yes, sir, by force."[9] While denying any intention of conquering Canada, King gloried in the certainty of it. Put another way, the Democratic-Republicans knew that they wanted a war with Britain, but they were just not sure why, and they struggled to construct an explanatory rhetoric.[10]

## The Militia Myth Cripples the Nation

The oddest aspect of the War of 1812 may in fact be that the United States did so little to prepare for the conflict despite the long certainty that there would be a war. Most political leaders, even those living in the Far West, saw war with Britain as probable for at least five years prior to its declaration. In March 1807, President Thomas Jefferson suggested to Governor William Hull of Michigan Territory that he begin planning an invasion of Canada; late that same year, Hull wrote Secretary of War Henry Dearborn that "differences with England will not be settled, . . . [and] war will be the consequence."[11] Western officials routinely expressed similar sentiments over the intervening years to 1812.[12] Yet when war was finally declared, the western territories and states, as well as the United States itself, were completely unprepared.[13] In many ways the reason for this refusal to prepare for a certain war resulted from mythologies borne of the Revolution. In the popular and Jeffersonian imagination, the United States enjoyed the protection of a vigilant militia that would rush forth to defend the nation's liberty at a moment's notice, as they had done so well in the Revolution.[14] When Jefferson had suggested that Hull prepare to attack Canada, he had spoken entirely in terms of the local militia.[15] On paper the United States could have called upon a militia of half a million men, while Canada's militia totaled forty thousand backed by six thousand British regulars. Once the war started, Britain fielded a small professional army supported by the Canadian militia and Indian allies, while the United States relied on amateurs. Within a few weeks it was obvious that the United States had made a terrible mistake.[16] As one early-twentieth-century historian put it with polite understatement, while there were some glorious moments at sea during the War of 1812, the land "campaigns were distinctly unfortunate."[17]

The invasion of Canada began almost immediately after the declaration of war. The United States planned a three-pronged attack on the frontiers at Montreal, Niagara, and Detroit. What should have been the most important effort, the move toward Montreal, proved a pathetic failure. General Henry Dearborn gathered a formidable army of seven thousand men on the shores of Lake Champlain and then procrastinated for several months, losing two thousand militia as enlistments ran out. When he finally moved on November 16, Dearborn allowed the enemy to escape from their blockhouse on the north end of the lake and then exchanged fire for half an hour with some New York militia on their way to join his command. After this brief encounter, the majority of the militia refused to enter Canada, and Dearborn abandoned the campaign.[18]

The invasion from Detroit ended in complete disaster, and is described in graphic and angry detail by Robert Lucas of Ohio. Lucas came to Ohio near the beginning of the nineteenth century and settled in what is now Scioto County. In April 1812 the government granted him a commission as captain in the regular army, but gave him no command or orders. Impatient to serve, Lucas joined a volunteer company of which his brother John had been elected captain. Though now officially a private, Lucas served informally as a courier and advisor, moving freely between units throughout the invasion. On May 25, General William Hull asked Lucas to take dispatches to Detroit and to assure any Indians he encountered of the peaceful intentions of the U.S. Army:

[May] 27th proceeded on to Dellaware where we prepared for our journey, made inquiry of the situation of the frontier, was informed that the inhabitants was moving off. I endeavored to quiet their fears by assuring them that they would be protected and that men would be sent to their assistance. . . .

28th proceeded on from Dellaware to Sandusky. . . . [L]odged at the home of an Indian by the name of Willy Hermky was treated hospitably by him.

29 . . . accompanied by Willy Hermky. . . . Proceeded on to Negro town got an interpreter. Called all the Chiefs together . . . I read and explained Gnl Hulls address to them, they all appeared to be well pleased

and expressed great friendship and a full determination to adhere to the treaty of Greenville.

[Lucas starts back to Hull's army.] 20th encamped on the head waters of the great Miami, was Surrounded in the night by hostile Indians as was Supposed, we left our fire and lay in the Bushes without fear, the musqueatos and gnats tormented us Severely.

22 . . . came to the main army encamped at Camp Necessity a Disagreeable Muddy place . . . was invited to remain in the generals family [staff] but seeing so many fops and so much parade and no action among them I Chose to attach myself to . . . my Brothers Company.

[July] 4th [As the army approached Detroit] we was informed by Some friendly Indians, that the British intended Crossing over that night and either to attack the army or Detroit. . . . The army was kept under arms all night. . . . We passed the pickets about a half a mile or a mile and explored and watched the roads till day—The general was mistaken, he had Sent on a party of men who he had forgot and instead of going to where they was directed they went a piece and lay in the Bushes at the side of the road, who on our approach instead of making themselves known was alarmed and acted in this imprudent manner by hailing us not like a friend but an enemy. They may thank me for their lives had it not struck me that it might be Some of our men they would Certainly have been killed. . . .

[Hull's army arrived at Detroit on July 6; on July 10 he prepared to invade Canada.] This night was pitched upon to Cross the river, and Considerable Confusion took place with the militia, a number of them refused to Cross the river—Those that refused to Cross was Considered by the army as Cowards. The army was almost prepared to march when by accident, Major Munson was badly wounded, and the Camp thrown into confusion. The Gnl postponed the march till the next day—

11 This day Capt Cunninghams and Capt Rupes Companys refused to Cross the river, but after Some Statement made by the Colonel [Lewis Cass], Cunninghams Company agreed to go. The Genl demanded a list of the names of those that refused to Cross the river. . . . The adjutant rashly abused the whole Company as Cowards Traitors &c. . . . and then arrested Captain Rupe—for ungentlemanly and unofficer like Conduct. . . .

16 This day Col. Cass and Col. James Miller obtained permission to take a Detachment of men for the purpose of obtaining possession of the Bridge at the River Canard within 5 miles of Malden. The Bridge we had been informed was broken and occupied by a British force on the opposite side. The Detachment consisted of . . . about 200 men,—I was permitted

to accompany them as a volunteer. . . . We marched on within 2 or 3 miles of the bridge when we was informed by some of Calvary that the Bridge was guarded by a British force and Some Indians, also that they had artillery at the Bridge. A Sergeant and 12 of Capt Robinsons men was requested to go in front with me as the advanced guard together with the two rangers that had accompanied me, and took a route to Cross the River and Come in upon the Back of the enemy. . . .

We ascended the river about 5 or 6 miles (piloted by two frenchmen that we made go with us) crossed the river. . . . We Descended on the opposite side through a tremendous thicket of Bushes and Prickly ash. . . . [F]iring Commenced by our men across the Creek, and was returned by the British and Commanded our men. . . . We ran through the point of woods to where the British and Indians had been encamped. . . . We fired upon them from the woods, being about 200 yards distant, . . . they retreated in Such haste that we Could not Come up with them. By this time it began to get dark in the evening, we returned not having one man injured. . . . The troops all acted with good Courage but not good Conduct, the fault is generally in the officers.

17 This morning . . . a Horseman returned from the Bridge stating that the whole British army was a coming. . . . The officers then met and held a Council and all insisted upon evacuating the Bridge except Col. Cass and Capt Snelling, who insisted upon maintaining the post as . . . the only obstruction in the way from where the army was encamped to Maldon. . . .

[August] 15th Every thing in confusion as usual. . . . Two [British] officers arrived from Sandwich with a flag of truce. . . . About 2 o'clock we was informed that the British Summoned the fort to Surrender and . . . if it did not surrender that the Garrison and Town would be massacred by the Indians, to this demand an immediate refusal was given. The army was astonished at the insolence of the British knowing our force to be Superior and possessing every advantage over them that we could desire were it properly used—about 4 o'clock 2 vessels hove in Sight below Sandwich point, and their battery played upon the town. The fire was returned and continued without interruption and with little effect till Dark. . . .

16th This morning about daybreak the British renewed their fire upon the fort, and it was returned from our Battery. The roaring of the cannon was tremendous but there was but little injury done, one Shot . . . took off entirely one of Doctor Reynolds legs, and the other partly off, he Died in about a half an hour after. . . . But his comrades was prevented from fighting, by their commander—for the fort was Surrendered about 8 o'clock, the Gnl Capitulated.[19]

Lucas refused to give himself up as a prisoner of war and fled the fort, traveling with a few friends back to Ohio. He reached his home in Portsmouth, Ohio, on September 4, 1812, bitter at what he saw as Hull's incompetence, if not treachery. After surrendering Detroit and his army to General Isaac Brock, General Hull returned to face a court-martial for cowardice. Lucas testified as a witness against Hull, but the general's main accuser was Colonel Lewis Cass, who succeeded Hull as governor of Michigan Territory. The court, ironically presided over by General Henry Dearborn, found Hull guilty and sentenced him to be shot, though recommending mercy. President Madison reprieved the general, who retired to Massachusetts and wrote two books that attempted to justify his actions. Lucas would serve as Ohio's governor from 1832 to 1836, and as the first governor of Iowa Territory from 1838 to 1841.[20]

The third prong of the planned conquest of Canada, along the Niagara frontier, failed twice in rapid succession. American forces prepared slowly, as their commander, General Stephen Van Rensselaer, struggled to encourage the militia to actually do battle with the enemy, while the commander of the regular army forces, General Alexander Smyth, routinely ignored or disobeyed Van Rensselaer's orders. The American delay gave General Brock sufficient time to rush from his nearly bloodless victory at Detroit to Niagara. The secretary to Van Rensselaer, John Lovett of Albany, recorded this frustrating campaign in letters to various friends. Lovett here describes the disastrous Battle of Queenston Heights, at which he was wounded:

John Lovett to Joseph Alexander, Evening of 14th October, 1812.

Dear Alexander,—I told you the dreadful day of battle was at hand. Yesterday was that day in good earnest. . . .

At four o'clock yesterday morning our column of 300 militia, under the command of Col. [Solomon] Van Rensselaer, and one column of 300 regulars, under the command of Lieut.-Col. [John] Christie, embarked in boats to dislodge the enemy from the Heights of Queenstown, opposite the camp. They were to land under cover of a battery of two eighteen-pounders and two sixes. As the fire from this battery was all important, and to be directed by a very scant light, and if illy directed would be fatal to ourselves, General Van Rensselaer did me the very great honor to direct [the artillery]. The river is rapid and full of whirlpools and eddies. The movement was instantly discovered; the shore was one incessant blaze of musketry. . . . In a word, the scene was tremendous.

The boats were a little embarrassed, but Colonel Van Rensselaer made good his landing in a perfect sheet of fire. He had advanced but a few steps when he received a shot in his right thigh, entering just back of the hipbone. . . . Both parties reinforced fast; every battery played its best.

The conflict spread wide and became general over the heights. The enemy gave way and fled in every direction. A large body of them got behind a stone guard-house, in which was mounted a piece of heavy ordnance. . . . We raked them severely, and at the eighth shot tumbled up a heap of men, and I believe dismounted the gun. . . . By . . . ten o'clock, the enemy's fire, except one gun out of reach down the river, was silenced. Victory seemed complete.

. . . Soon after the General got over and was taking a bite of bread and cheese in John Bull's barracks (for he had eaten no breakfast) a detachment of some hundreds of Indians from Chippawa arrived and commenced their attack with great fury, but the rifle and the bayonet scattered the sons of Belial and drove them to the woods. Still the reinforcements moved over very slowly and, in short, stopped. The General returned to accelerate them. . . . But the name of Indian, or the sight of the wounded, or the devil, or something else petrified them. Not a regiment, not a company, scarcely a man would go.

. . . By this time General Brock had got a large reinforcement of regulars on their way from Fort George, . . . formed a junction with the Indians and prepared to renew the attack. The ammunition of the men on the Heights was nearly exhausted, for they had now fought with little intermission for eleven hours. The General sent them some supplies, which I think could scarcely have reached them when, at about half-past four, commenced a furious, obstinate and tremendous conflict. On both sides fixed cannon, flying artillery and roll of musketry. The mountains seemed to shake beneath the stride of death.[21]

The Battle of Queenston Heights, the largest of the war to that date, was a devastating blow to American plans and revealed abundantly the danger of the militia ideology. When General Van Rensselaer asked for volunteers to attack a British schooner at Prescott, only sixty-six men were willing to serve, and the plan was canceled. Van Rensselaer informed General Dearborn that his troops were too ill armed for anything but defensive actions.[22] The militia, Van Rensselaer reported, were grossly unprepared for warfare and sought any excuse to go home: "They are incessantly pressing for furloughs under every possible pretence. Many are without shoes; all are clamorous for pay; many are sick. . . . While we are thus growing weaker our enemy is growing stronger. . . . They are fortifying almost every prominent point from Fort Erie to Fort George. . . . I have no reinforcements of men, no ordnance or munitions of war."[23] Though the federal militia act required New York to supply 13,000 militia, fewer than 2,500 reported for duty. Nonetheless, Dearborn urged Van Rensselaer to seize the initiative before British reinforcements could arrive. The New York commander procrastinated as long as he could, finally leading his forces into the disastrous attack at Queenston Heights.[24] Though he had six thousand troops under his command, counting militia from other states, as well as Smyth's 1,600 regulars at Black Rock near Buffalo, only one thousand crossed the river into Canada, and, according to Winfield Scott, half of those hid until they could surrender. The rest stayed in New York, watching the battle like "spectators in a balloon."[25] The British and their Indian allies lost 21 killed and 85 wounded, with just 22 taken prisoner, while the United States lost between 60 and 100 killed, 170 wounded, and 955 taken prisoner.[26]

General Alexander Smyth's attempt to renew the invasion failed miserably, as the militia rejected his orders and his soldiers offered a $200 reward for the soldier who shot him.[27] The Pennsylvania militia was willing to fight, just not against the British. On November 25, 1812, fifty militia stormed and set fire to Pomeroy's hotel in Buffalo because the innkeeper opposed the war. When locals attempted to put out the fire, the militia drove them back with bayonets. When an artillery company was sent to restore order, the militia attacked them. Two people died in the riot and General Smyth had to detach three hundred of his regulars to protect Buffalo from the militia.[28] After the riot, the two thousand Pennsylvania militia went home; the only action they saw in the campaign of 1812 was against Pomeroy's hotel.[29]

## Fear and Loathing on the Early Frontier

The War of 1812 overlapped a bitter conflict between the United States and a coalition of Native peoples. In 1810 the Shawnee brothers Tecumseh and Tenskwatawa—the latter known as the Prophet—launched their resistance to the expansion of the United States into Native lands in the old Midwest. Tenskwatawa established the center of his cultural resistance at Prophetstown on the Wabash River. Meanwhile, Tecumseh worked to establish an alliance of Native peoples throughout the region and along the Mississippi River. Wherever he went he would ask, "Where today are the Pequot? Where the Narraganset, the Mohican, the Pocanoket and many other once powerful tribes of our people? They have vanished before the avarice and oppression of the white man. . . . In the vain hope of defending alone their ancient possessions, they have fallen in the war."[30] The United States responded with an army commanded by General William Henry Harrison, which, in November 1811, destroyed Prophetstown in the Battle of Tippecanoe.

John Tipton's journal is the only contemporary account of the campaign by a common soldier. Tipton, who was skilled at repairing rifles and served as a scout, was a member of a group of forty-seven militia from Harrison County, Indiana Territory, commanded by a Captain Spencer. As well as providing a sense of life on the frontier, Tipton's journal indicates that mutiny had become common in the militia as a way for soldiers to demonstrate their dissatisfaction. William Henry Harrison, who was also the governor of Indiana Territory, relied heavily on Indian allies in these campaigns, as did most military leaders of the time:

Thursday 12 of September, 1811—Left Corydon at 3 o'clock, march six miles to governor Harrison's mill and encampt.

14th. Marched 3 miles and encampt at half moon spring. Was joined by Capt Baggs with a troop of horse, and in the evening by Col Bartholomew, with 120 of militia from Clark County. . . .

Saturday 21st I cut out a gun and went to Shakertown and got my mare shod, the men was Paraded and marched to the big Prairie and mustered till late and in the time mutinized with some of Capt Heath's men, but marched back at sunset and dismisst in order. . . .

Thursday 26th We crosst the Wabash and fired two Platoons. . . . Dinner, much whisky drank which caused quarreling. . . . [The army spends the next several days marching toward Prophetstown.]

Friday 11. Mounted and went to the Prairie in Company with the light horse to look for indians. . . . After traveling 15 miles came to camp at twelve then Drawd flour whisky and Pickled Pork got brekfast at four in the evening.

Saturday 12th . . . [One] of the Delaware chiefs . . . spoke good English, Plaid Cards with our men and informed [us] that thirty of his young men was coming to join us. I cut a gun and went to shooting.

Tuesday the 15 . . . All the spies came in, nothing seen. I went with another man down to tare holt to look for indians. We had whisky. . . . Returned to Camp, was alarmed at the fire of a gun at 11 o'clock, was ordered to lie with our guns in hand, the wind blew hard, it Began to Rain. . . . One of our men Deserted today while I was out.

Wednesday the 16th Cold cloudy and windy. . . . Dragoons sent after three men that Deserted last night. . . .

Saturday the 19—Musterd as usual. . . . [T]he governor informed us that our ration was reduced to 3/4 of a pound of flour [because] the contractor failing. He also told us that we should have to fight the indians. . . . [I]t stopt Raining and Began to Snow and Blow hard, . . . it was the Disagreeablest night I ever saw. . . .

Monday the 28 . . . Cut out a gun and went to the talk with the [Miami] Indians then came to my tent was ordered to parade the Company for to see a man whipt. We was drawd in a hollow square, . . . the man brought in ordered to [be] stript then pardoned. We [received] money for back ration this day, orders to march tomorrow, this day I got one gallon of whisky.

Thursday the 7 Agreeable to their [the Shawnees'] promise, Last night we ware awakened by the firing of guns and the Shawnies Braking into our tents, a blood[y] Combat Took Place at Precisely 15 minutes before 5 in the morning which lasted two hours and 20 minutes of a continual firing while many times mixed among the Indians so that we Could not tell the indians and our men apart.[31] They kept up a firing on three sides of us. [The Kentuckians fell back, opening the way for the Indians to enter the camp.] . . . Our Lost in killed and wounded was 179 and theirs greater than ours. . . . After the indians gave ground we Buried our Dead.[32]

Expecting the Indians to return to the attack, Harrison led his troops back to their base the next morning. Tipton "got safe Home after a Campaign of 74 days" on November 24. Harrison's troops suffered 62 killed and some 125 wounded; the Indians an estimated 50 killed and 70 wounded. While the smaller Indian force suffered fewer casualties than did the U.S. forces, the Battle of Tippecanoe dealt a serious blow to Tecumseh's efforts to craft an effective Indian federation. Those itching for war with the British, popularly known as the War Hawks, immediately charged that the British were responsible for the conflict, guiding and arming the Indians, and used that accusation as another justification for war.[33]

While Tipton credits Captain Joel Cook with saving the collapsing Kentucky company, Harrison praised Tipton for saving the line when he rallied his men just as they were about to break and run. His cool head under fire probably explains his sudden election to captain. After the war he served as an Indian agent with the Miami and Potawatomi peoples and was a Democratic senator from 1831 to 1839. In 1838, he organized the forced removal of the Potawatomi people from Indiana to Kansas, a cruel and ill-planned enterprise known as the Trail of Death.

When the United States declared war in 1812, Tecumseh immediately allied with the British in Canada, soon followed by a number of other Native peoples who hoped that the empire might halt the aggressive expansion of the United States. The ensuing war on the frontiers was often a game of shadows, of militia companies moving to defend settlements against imagined Indian attacks or fleeing in terror at word of Indians in the woods—as indicated in the accounts of both Lucas and Lovett. But the war could also be savage, as when the Red Stick Creeks, inspired by Tecumseh, slaughtered some four hundred settlers, fellow Creeks, and militia at Fort Mims in August 1813. Andrew Jackson, commanding U.S. regulars, Tennessee militia, and a large contingent of Indian allies, responded in kind at the Battle of Horseshoe Bend the following March, killing an estimated eight hundred Creeks.[34]

Though the U.S. Army relied on a large number of Indian allies, persistently hostile relations with the Native peoples played a role in all the western campaigns. Robert Lucas had initially set off for the Michigan frontier on just such a mission in search of Native allies. But militia companies often aggravated these delicately balanced relations with precipitate actions. One of the worst offenders in this regard was the Kentucky militia. Elias Darnell's journal provides an honest assessment of, as its long title puts it, "the Hardships, Sufferings, Battles, Defeat, and Captivity" of the Kentucky volunteers, who begin the war puffed up by tales of their own virtue and heroism and end it running for their lives. Darnell volunteered in 1812 as a private in a Kentucky regiment that set out to reinforce General Hull's army at Detroit. On the march north, word arrived that Hull had surrendered. General William Henry Harrison, the hero of Tippecanoe, quickly claimed command and ordered Darnell's regiment to the relief of Fort Wayne, which "was in great danger of being taken by the Indians and British; he said that we were under the necessity of making a forced march to their relief." They spent the next several weeks burning the fields and houses in every Indian village they encountered, most of which had been friendly until that moment, and eating their "good corn."[35] Such destruction was a time-honored aspect of U.S. military strategy and had worked extremely well in destroying Indian resistance during the Revolution. As Darnell imagines the future uses of the area traversed by his army, he reflects well the hostile attitude of many whites toward the Native population. Along the way, Darnell discovers the unexpected dangers of garrison duty, as disease claims more lives than battle:

12th. We continued our march towards Fort Wayne with as much caution as the nature of our hurrying would admit. . . . In a certain well-known swamp, through which we had to pass, we thought probably the enemy would harbor . . . we were then alarmed. . . . This alarm and the one the night preceding seemed to shake the boasted valor of some of our bravest heroes.

This day's march was twenty miles to Fort Wayne. . . . Our arrival at this fort gave great joy to the inhabitants, who were one company of regular troops and a few families. The Indians had closely invested the fort for several days, and burned the United States factory [trading post] and all the other valuable houses which were not inside of the stockading. Three of our men who were caught out of the fort were killed by the Indians. The Indians encamped about the fort two weeks before they made the attack on it, and were admitted in by Captain Ray, the commanding officer of the garrison, who would have surrendered to the savages, had it not been for his lieutenant, who defended the fort with great bravery. Three Indians were killed and a few wounded. Captain Ray was arrested and would have been broken had he not resigned. The fort was well provided for a siege, having in it one hundred men, plenty of provisions, ammunition, four small pieces of cannon, and a good well of water. . . .

14th. . . . General [John] Payne was instructed to destroy the Miami towns at the forks of the Wabash. . . . [We] marched twenty-three miles to an Indian town at the forks of the Wabash; we found the town evacuated; we pulled down some of their houses and built up fires and encamped; we had plenty of roasting ears of the best kind.

16th. We marched through their towns, four in number, in the bounds of three or four miles, in which there were fresh signs of Indians. Their houses were all burnt by the orders of General Harrison. [Payne's troops turned back toward Fort Wayne.] . . .

19th. [Command was transferred to General James Winchester.] . . . Gen. Winchester being a stranger, and having the appearance of a supercilious officer, he was generally disliked. His assuming the command almost occasioned a mutiny in camp; this was prevented by the solicitations of some of the officers to go on. . . .

October 4th. [Harrison is made commander of all U.S. forces in the Northwest and rejoins the army at Fort Defiance.] There has been great murmuring in camp, on account of the scarcity of provisions, which threatened a dissolution of this army.

7th. . . . A majority of the mounted men who were ordered to the rapids, and drew ten days' provisions for that expedition, refused to march under Gen. [Edward] Tupper; of course the contemplated expedition failed, and they returned home, as their thirty days were nearly expired. . . .

[November] 4th. . . . The weather is very rainy, which makes our situation extremely unpleasant. . . . Four of this army have gone to the silent tomb to-day, never more to visit their friends in Kentucky; the fever is very prevalent in camp; nearly every day there is one or more buried.

10th. . . . I trust this country was designed for a more noble purpose than to be a harbor for those rapacious savages, whose manners and deportment are not more elevated than the ravenous beasts of the forest. I view the time not far distant, when this country will be interspersed with elegant farms and flourishing towns, and be inhabited by a free and independent people, under an auspicious republic. . . .

[January 18, 1813] . . . We proceeded on with no other view than *to conquer or die*. When we advanced in sight of [Frenchtown on the Raisin River], and were about a quarter of a mile from it, the British saluted us by the firing of a piece of cannon; they fired it three times, but no injury was sustained. During this time we formed the line of battle, and, raising a shout, advanced on them briskly; they soon commenced the firing of their small arms, but this did not deter us from a charge; we advanced close and let loose on them; they gave way, and we soon had possession of the village without the loss of a man! Three were slightly wounded. Twelve of their warriors were slain and scalped, and one prisoner taken before they got to the woods. . . .

During this time a heavy fire was kept up on both sides; at length, after a battle of three hours and five minutes, we were obliged to stop the pursuit on account of the approach of night, and retire to the village. . . . Our loss in this action was eleven killed and fifty wounded.[36]

The next morning the British under Colonel Henry Proctor counterattacked, taking the unprepared Americans by surprise and capturing General Winchester, who surrendered his entire command. Darnell and the other Kentuckians were paroled by the British on February 10, 1813, and allowed to return home on condition that they not take up arms against Great Britain.

## Fighting an Unpopular War

The War of 1812 was notably unpopular, even among the troops engaged in the conflict. Civilians voiced their resistance in a number of protests and their vote, which led to the temporary revival of the Federalist Party. Soldiers indicated their opposition to the war by mutinies, desertion, and more subtle forms of protest. It must be emphasized, however, that many of these protests were directed at the conduct of particular officers, rather than at the war itself. The most typical method of resistance, and the most difficult to punish, was sluggish marching; troops would deliberately slow to a stately crawl, often driving officers to give in to their demands for more food, better quarters, or even a less aggressive campaign against the enemy.[37] Creative acts of resistance to military authority took many forms; for instance, when General Tupper ordered his troops to stop firing their guns in celebration of Christmas Eve, the soldiers immediately began an erratic fire that lasted until dawn.[38] Officers found that command required constant negotiation. As Tipton recorded, when the officers took two companies on a march the men deemed excessive, they "mutinized" until the commanders promised that they would return to camp.[39]

The opposition to the war spilled over into ministerial sermons given to troops and militia. When President Madison called for a day of prayer in support of the war effort, the Reverend Jacob Catlin reminded his congregation that those who live by the sword shall die by the sword—hardly encouraging to enlistments.[40] In a sermon delivered to the Massachusetts militia, the Reverend James Flint called on the assembled men to give thanks that they were not being led by "some cowardly minion of President Madison, into the wilds of Canada, there to perish by disease, or to whiten the plains of battle with your bones."[41] Other ministers warned of the danger a military establishment posed to the nation. Ralph Waldo Emerson's father, the Reverend Brown Emerson, charged that the military was a school for "profaneness, blasphemy, [and] debauchery" in which soldiers lost "every spark of kindness and mercy" and became accustomed to violence. In a theme that would recur in American history, Emerson charged that veterans brought their ill habits and brutal natures back to civilian life, so that society would continue to pay the price of war.[42] It's little wonder that John Patterson, from western Pennsylvania, worried over his neighbor's response to his enlistment; "I hope that you will pray for me—and i hope that the friends will not dispise you or me because i am a souldier."[43]

In the War of 1812, dissatisfaction with pay and food occasionally led to outright mutiny. Andrew Jackson twice threatened to fire cannon on his starving infantry when they tried to head home, successfully keeping his men in line.[44] Many other mutinies disrupted Americans forces; and, as Darnell's diary indicates, threatened mutinies were common and effective. John Lovett briefly described "a daring mutiny" that had broken out in General Daniel Miller's militia brigade on November 1, 1812, when one hundred men stacked their arms and headed home. [45] Miller did nothing to stop these men, but promised better conditions to those who stayed.[46] General Alexander Smyth responded more aggressively, holding courts-martial, executing five men for desertion, and removing Miller and several other officers from their commands. There were several additional mutinies among the New York militia during the war,[47] leading General George Izard to write the secretary of war in 1814 that the "disorganized, unarmed militia" of New York threatened the morale of his regulars. The New York militia, he wrote, consisted of "between four and six thousand, without guns, mutinous, and determined to move off (as they came,) *en masse*" if Izard did not issue them their discharge pay in advance.[48] Captain Samuel White, of the notoriously unreliable Pennsylvania militia, describes a mutiny among his men that included half the regiment. White, like many contemporaries, also presents a neat reversal of events in his opening sentence by describing the United States as invading Canada in self-defense:

> To repel the inroads of the British on the northern frontier, . . . the governor of the state of Pennsylvania ordered out the militia to the number of one thousand. . . . The detachment of the troops to which I belonged, rendezvoused at Gettysburg, on the 28th of February, 1814, and departed from that place on their march to Erie, on the tenth day of March following. . . .

About this time it was made known in camp that an expedition to Long Point was projected, and that volunteers to the number of five hundred stepped forward to assist the regular forces amounting to about four hundred men.

When we reached Dover, we found it deserted by all but a few women, who had white clothes hanging upon broomsticks suing for peace. . . . Every possible respect was paid to the women and children, and the best part of the furniture in the houses which were destroyed, was even carried out by the troops previous to their being set on fire.

Before we had embarked on the expedition, my company had drawn rations for three days, every pound of which had been left on the shore in consequence of the badness of its quality, so that the poor fellows had nothing but bread to eat for that time. . . . In the evening we completed our landing, and arrived in safety at our camp in Erie.

Next day we learned that a general order had been given for our march to Buffalo, and that preparations for that purpose had been commenced by Col. Fenton, when they were checked for some time by the presentation of a mutinous paper by some of the men selected for that purpose, which paper had been signed by half, if not more, of the privates in the regiment. This instrument set forth that they had determined not to march from camp, until they had received the amount of pay due them for their services, alleging as their apology, that many of them were much at a loss for shoes and other cloathing. In this situation, undecided as to what course we should pursue, we remained for several days. . . .

But the spirit of mutiny was still alive, and secret resolutions were formed amongst the disaffected, to obey no orders until the terms for which they held out were complied with, and on the following day when according to the orders, at the third roll of the drum the tents should have fallen, a number remained standing, and those who were willing to obey orders, had to be detached for the purpose of pulling them down, which however, they were permitted to do, unmolested. . . .

The order was now passed to form line, and prepare to march; the peaceable portion of the men immediately fell into rank, leaving a number strolling about, as if undecided what course to pursue.

White and Major William L. Marlin had found it necessary to threaten their troops with artillery to get them to march to Buffalo, though they lost several along the way to desertion. Once in Buffalo, the militia joined with two brigades of regulars commanded by General Jacob Brown. White admired the fact that Brown kept his plans to himself—in part to avoid spies learning of his intentions, and also to prevent a large segment of the militia from deciding to return home. Brown announced his intention to move on Fort Erie on July 2, moving out the next morning. His mixed force of regulars and militia performed well at the Battle of Chippewa on July 5, 1814. According to White, the Americans stumbled into battle when Brown asked for volunteers to beat off the Indians hanging around their flanks. After a brief exchange of fire, the Indians retreated, pursued by the Americans, who fell right into the British trap as the regulars opened up with artillery. Brown responded by ordering his whole command to the attack:

> The army consisting of two brigades, were landed on the opposite shore without the least opposition. The first brigade under the command of Gen. [Winfield] Scott, and the artillery corps commanded by Major Hurdman, landed nearly a mile below whilst Gen. Ripley with the second brigade made the shore about the same distance above. Thus the fort was soon completely invested. Several pieces of ordnance and some military stores were found in the fort. . . .
>
> The necessary arrangements for the preservation and garrisoning the Fort Erie, being concluded, Gen. Brown determined to march forward on the following day, and attack the enemy who lay entrenched in his works upon the plains of Chippewa. To this resolution, considered of a desperate and dangerous character, the General was doubtless urged by the necessity which he felt existed, to redeem the reputation which had been lost by the events of former campaigns. . . .
>
> At four o'clock [on July 5] we came in view of the encampment of our regular troops, and halted. We had not been many minutes at rest before a requisition was made for volunteers to turn out and drive off the hostile Indians who had been firing on our pickets.
>
> . . . Orders were issued that every white man who went out under Gen. Porter should leave his hat, and go uncovered. The [allied] Indians tied up their heads with pieces of white muslin, and it was really diverting to see them making their preparations for battle. After having tied up their heads, which process must have consumed at least fifty yards of fine muslin, they painted their faces, making red streaks above their eyes and foreheads—they then went to old logs and burnt stumps, and spitting upon their hands rubbed them upon the burnt part, until they were perfectly black, when they drew their fingers down their cheeks leaving large black streaks—after this preparation they were ready for action or march.
>
> We proceeded in single file through a lane to our left, and in the course of half an hour came in contact with the enemy, who were posted in the woods on our right, and completely concealed from our observation. Immediately upon our entering a long narrow path, they opened upon us

with a pretty brisk fire—we faced to the right and pressing forward put them to rout. They continued their flight and we pursued them, keeping up a smart fire, . . . until they drew us into rather a perilous situation. The whole British army had crossed the bridge at Chippewa, and drawn up their forces under cover of a piece of woods, near the Niagara river, and running parallel with the Chippewa creek, directly across the creek, where the British batteries commanded the same position. Driving the Indians rapidly through the woods, we at length came in full contact with the British regular line, which in conjunction with the batteries, opened a most tremendous fire.[49]

It was difficult enough to deal with citizen-soldiers, who expected respect for their rights as Americans; the militia tended to see themselves as primarily citizens, and soldiering a weekend activity to be set aside at any time. It is little wonder that army officers often found the militia more trouble than they were worth. By the end of 1812, most rational observers agreed with the editor of the *National Intelligencer*: "Every day's experience tends to force on our minds a conviction that we are unwilling to receive, that the volunteer militia are not precisely the species of force on which to rely for carrying on war, however competent they may be to repel invasion."[50] Some members of the militia did attempt to defend their performance—after the war.

The most notorious failures of America's militia occurred at the battles around Washington, D.C., in 1814. The government, rejecting military advice and any standard of reason, made no plans to protect the capital until six weeks before it fell. On July 1, 1814, the cabinet wrote out "a programme of defense" that imagined an army of some 100,000 militia ringing the capital, and called on the governors to send militia immediately. Falling for his own paper fortress, the secretary of war sent 500 regulars from Washington to the northern frontier, leaving just 330 regulars for the capital's defense. At the approach of the British troops, 11,000 militia responded to the call for help—the majority of militia refused to turn out, probably testifying more to their opposition to the war than to cowardice.[51] In numbers, at least, they enjoyed a slight superiority over the British army of 4,370 mixed troops. The British also lacked cavalry and heavy artillery, were worn from several months aboard ship, and marched forty miles through August humidity.[52] British Lieutenant George Gleig wrote, "I do not recollect a period of my military life during which I suffered more severely from heat and fatigue."[53] But, as a later American military scholar summarized the situation for the United States, "Our so-called army, except Barney's seamen and Peter's regulars, was a heterogeneous mass without order or discipline, and had scarcely one officer with the least knowledge of actual warfare."[54]

The Americans began the campaign by blowing up their own fleet in the Chesapeake. Allen McLane, a Revolutionary War veteran, described the British advance on August 22: "the enemy was advancing from Nottingham, in two columns on the road leading to Upper Marlboro, and on the water in open boats, . . . and that the people between the rivers had not appeared disposed to fight, for it was very common to see a white cloth stuck on a pole at a house, a signal of submission." McLane found "the roads crowded with men in arms running from the enemy to secure their property, . . . none disposed to fight, or obstruct the roads, &c., all panic-struck."[55] The British contemptuously targeted the militia in battle, confident that they would break and run. British soldiers described battles in North America as "scaring the militia."[56]

The future novelist John Pendleton Kennedy was an eighteen-year-old private in the Baltimore militia when called to the defense of Washington in August 1814. In his memoir, Kennedy recalls the march as a delightful excursion punctuated by an encounter with the British he would rather forget. His experience of battle proved a quick and largely ignoble affair. His company, like most others at the Battle of Bladensburg, fled when fired upon, making "a fine scamper of it":

> As for me,—not yet nineteen,—I was too full of the exultation of the time to think of myself;—all my fervor was spent in admiration of this glittering army.
>
> . . . By sundown we reached Elk Ridge Landing, and there turned in upon the flat meadow ground that lies under the hills upon the further bank of the Patapsco, to pitch our tents for the night. Camp-kettles were served out to us and our rations of pork and hard bread. We formed our messes that evening, and mine, consisting of six members, who were consigned to one tent, was made up of pleasant companions. The company consisted of gentlemen of good condition and accustomed to luxurious life, and the idea of a supper of fat pork and hard biscuit was a pleasant absurdity which we treated as a matter of laughter. We had our own stores in the wagon to rely upon when we could get at them, and a short, active negro man [named Lige] as a servant for the mess. . . .
>
> [Lige acquired] coffee and chocolate, good bread and ham in abundance. At the regulation hour, the members of the mess who were not detailed for guard duty—some four of us—crept into our tent and arranging our blankets into a soft bed, laid down and fell into a hearty sleep, which was only broken by the reveille the next morning. This was my first night of a regular campaign.
>
> The next day we marched from the Landing to Vansville, about twenty miles,—halting an hour or so at Waterloo, then McCoy's tavern, where we got dinner. . . . The day was hot, and portions of the road in deep sand. It was a great trial. We were in winter cloth uniform, with a most absurd

helmet of thick jacked leather and covered with plumes. . . . But we bore it splendidly, toiling and sweating in a dense cloud of dust, . . . and taking all the discomforts of this rough experience with a cheerful heart and a stout resolve.

. . . I was too much excited by the novelty and attraction of my position and by the talk of my comrades in the tent, to get asleep much before midnight. About an hour after this—one o'clock—we were aroused by the scattered shots of our pickets, some four or five in succession, in the direction of the Marlborough road, and by the rapid beating of the long roll from every drum in the camp. Every one believed that the enemy was upon us, and there was consequently an immense bustle in getting ready to meet him. . . . Some got the wrong boots, others a coat that didn't fit, and some could not find their cross-belts. There was no time allowed to rectify these mistakes. I, luckily, was all right, except that I sallied out in my pumps. We were formed in line and marched off towards the front, perhaps a mile, and when we came to a halt, we were soon ordered to march back again to camp.

What was the cause of this sudden excursion and quick abandonment of it I never learned. But it was evident there was a false alarm. On our return march our attention was called to the sudden reddening of the sky in the direction of the lower bridge of the eastern branch, by which the river road from Marlborough crossed to Washington. The sky became more lurid every moment, and at last we could discern the flames. A despatch which reached us when we got back to camp, and had just laid down again to sleep, brought us information that Winder had crossed the bridge and then burnt it to impede the march of the enemy . . . we were ordered forthwith to break up our camp and march towards Washington. Here was new excitement—every thing was gathered up in a few moments.

Descending into the village we crossed the bridge and moved toward Washington; but after making about two miles at a very slow pace, we found ourselves brought to a halt, and after this we loitered, as slow as foot could fall, along the road, manifestly expecting some order that should turn us back towards the village we had left. . . . The burning of the bridge lighted up the whole southern sky, but it had no power to attract our gaze.

When I awoke I was lying on my back with the hot sun of a summer morning beaming upon my face. Our orders then were to march back to Bladensburg. Soon we had the famous "trial of souls"—the battle of Bladensburg. The drafted militia ran away at the first fire, and the Fifth Regiment was driven off the field with the bayonet. We made a fine scamper of it. I lost my musket in the melee while bearing off a comrade, James W. McCulloch, afterwards the cashier of the Branch Bank of the U.S. in

Baltimore, whose leg was broken by a bullet. The day was very hot, and the weight of my wounded companion great, and not being able to carry both, I gave my musket to a friend who accompanied me, and he, afterwards being wounded himself, dropped his own weapon as well as mine.[57]

At the "disgraceful action" at Bladensburg on August 24, 1814, American forces moved, without cover, in three straight lines toward the British, who had three light artillery pieces. Two militia regiments ran the instant the British fired some harmless rockets, most of the remaining Americans soon followed their example, and only Commodore Joshua Barney's sailors held the British off long enough for most of the Americans to get away.[58] Lieutenant Gleig provided a perfect summary of the battle: "When two lines oppose each other, very little depends upon the accuracy with which individuals take aim. It is then that the habit of acting in concert, the confidence which each man feels in his companions, and the rapidity and good order in which different movements can be executed, are alone of real service."[59]

After the defeat at Bladensburg, there was nothing to prevent the small British army from taking the capital. The troops at Fort Washington fled "on the discharge of the first shell of the enemy."[60] Dolly Madison stood on the roof of the White House "turning my spy-glass in every direction, and watching with unwearied anxiety," she wrote on August 23, 1813. "I can descry only groups of military, wandering in all directions, as if there was a lack of arms, or of spirit to fight for their own fireside."[61]

## The War at Sea

Though the supposed cause of the war—the impressment of American sailors—was at sea, Congress refused to build up the U.S. Navy and declared war with just 16 men-of-war pitted against a British navy of 254 men-of-war and nearly 800 smaller vessels. The U.S. Navy experienced a few brilliant victories at sea during the War of 1812, particularly in the Great Lakes and on Lake Champlain, but was mostly limited to harassing the superior British force. For instance, in August 1812, the *Constitution*, commanded by Captain Isaac Hull, sank the *Guerriere*, and then in December the same ship—now commanded by Captain William Bainbridge—defeated the *Java*. In September 1813, Commodore Oliver Hazard Perry's small fleet defeated the British squadron on Lake Erie; the following year, Captain Thomas Macdonough halted the British invasion from Canada with a brilliant victory over their Lake Champlain fleet.

But the British navy also enjoyed a number of victories in the Atlantic and maintained a stringent blockade of most American ports, occasionally putting into individual harbors, such as at Essex, Connecticut, in 1814, where they burned twenty-seven ships. The United States enjoyed a number of victories in single-ship combats, but their greatest success came with privateers—some 500 American privateers captured 1,300 British merchant ships during the war.[62]

Samuel Leech was in many ways a typical sailor of the early nineteenth century, serving in both the British and American navies, though he made his preference clear at the war's end. Leech was the child of servants, his mother working for the Duchess of Marlborough. In 1810, the duchess arranged for thirteen-year-old Leech to serve aboard the *Macedonian*, a British frigate commanded by the duchess's brother, William FitzRoy, who was soon thereafter removed from command for profiting from the ship's stores. On October 25, 1812, not far from the island of Madeira, the 38-gun *Macedonian*, now under Captain John Surnam Carden, encountered the 44-gun *United States*, commanded by Stephen Decatur, in one of the era's epic sea battles. Leech offers a rare view of naval combat from the perspective of a common sailor—with whom Leech's sentiments clearly lie. Though his description comes from the British side of the conflict, Leech would soon become an American sailor:

At Plymouth we heard some vague rumors of a declaration of war against America. More than this, we could not learn, since the utmost care was taken to prevent our being fully informed . . . because we had several Americans in our crew, most of whom were pressed men. . . . These men, had they been certain that war had broken out, would have given themselves up as prisoners of war, and claimed exemption from that unjust service, which compelled them to act with the enemies of their country. This was a privilege which the magnanimity of our officers ought to have offered them. They had already perpetrated a grievous wrong upon them in impressing them; it was adding cruelty to injustice, to compel their service in a war against their own nation.

But the difficulty with naval officers is, that they do not treat with a sailor as with a man. They know what is fitting between each other as officers; but they treat their crews on another principle; they are apt to look at them as pieces of living mechanism, born to serve. . . .

[Leech sights the *United States*.] A strange noise, such as I had never heard before, next arrested my attention; it sounded like the tearing of sails, just over our heads. This I soon ascertained to be the wind of the enemy's shot. . . . The roaring of cannon could now be heard from all parts of our trembling ship, and, mingling as it did with that of our foes, it made a most hideous noise. By-and-by I heard the shot strike the sides of our ship; the whole scene grew indescribably confused and horrible; it was like some awfully tremendous thunder-storm, whose deafening roar is attended by incessant streaks of lightning, carrying death in every flash, and strewing the ground with the victims of its wrath: only, in our case, the scene was rendered more horrible than that, by the presence of torrents of blood which dyed our decks.

. . . The cries of the wounded now rang through all parts of the ship. These were carried to the cockpit as fast as they fell, while those more fortunate men, who were killed outright, were immediately thrown overboard. As I was stationed but a short distance from the main hatchway, I could catch a glance at all who were carried below. . . . I saw two of these lads fall nearly together. One of them was struck in the leg by a large shot; he had to suffer amputation above the wound. The other had a grape or canister shot sent through his ankle. . . . Two of the boys stationed on the quarter deck were killed. . . . A man, who saw one of them killed, afterwards told me that his powder caught fire and burnt the flesh almost off his face. In this pitiable situation, the agonized boy lifted up both hands, as if imploring relief, when a passing shot instantly cut him in two.[63]

Taken prisoner by the British in 1814, Leech insisted on an American identity and refused to rejoin the British navy, instead plotting with his fellow prisoners to escape their prison in Cape Town, seize a British ship, and sail to the United States. The plot was discovered and, shortly thereafter, the war ended. Leech settled in Massachusetts after the war and became an American citizen.

## Claiming Victory

The War of 1812 is largely remembered for the victory at New Orleans, which famously came after the war had ended. Neither side could truly claim victory in this pointless war: the United States failed in its attempts to seize Canada, and there was no way that the British could hope to conquer the United States. As the Duke of Wellington said in 1814, "I do not know where you could carry on . . . an operation which would be so injurious to the Americans as to force them to sue for peace, which is what one would wish to see."[64] After all, not even burning their capital appeared to affect the Americans in any meaningful way. The only significant strategic consequence of the War of 1812 for the United States was the defeat of Indian forces in both the Northwest and Southwest—but most contemporaries viewed these victories as tangential to the main conflict with Great Britain.[65]

. The Treaty of Ghent, which officially ended the war with no significant changes from where relations between Britain and the United States stood in 1812, was signed on December 24, 1814. Just over two weeks later, on January 8, 1815, 5,000 British regulars commanded by General Sir Edward Pakenham attacked New Orleans, which was defended by roughly 4,700 troops under the command of General Andrew Jackson. The defenders included regular troops, free black volunteers, the Baratarian pirates, and militia from Kentucky, Tennessee, and Louisiana. Pakenham's attack was a disaster from the beginning, as his men marched along the east bank of the Mississippi fully exposed to Jackson's artillery, which poured a relentless fire of grapeshot and canister on the advancing regulars. The British suffered 2,400 casualties and prisoners taken, while the Americans lost some 70 men. Even though it had no impact on the actual war, Americans hailed their great victory at New Orleans as proof of their military superiority, elevating Jackson to heroic stature.

Howell Tatum of North Carolina had served during the American Revolution and had been taken prisoner at Charleston in 1780. After the war he moved to Tennessee, where he came to know Andrew Jackson. In 1814 Tatum volunteered to serve as Jackson's topographical engineer and kept a journal during the campaign around New Orleans, which he submitted to the secretary of war in February 1815. Many of the details in Tatum's account are validated by the memoir of Jackson's chief engineer, Arsène Lacarrière Latour. For instance, Latour quotes General Jackson as complaining, "Hardly one third of the Kentucky troops, so long expected, are armed, and the arms they have are not fit for use."[66] Tatum noted the same deficiency in the Kentucky militia. Given the poorly armed militia, both engineers credit artillery with determining the outcome of the battle:

January 1, 1815 . . . In the course of the week, commencing with this day (Sunday) several skirmishes of small consequence took place between small parties of our sharp shooters and the enemy's Guards, as our partizens were endeavoring to reconnoitre the Batteries, and the ground in their rear.

. . . The Kentucky requisition, under Maj. General [John] Thomas arrived on the 4th and were encamped between Madame Plarnasse and Madame Dupree's Canals. These Troops, as well as the Local Militia, were very badly armed. Many of the arms brought by these Kentucky Troops were unfit for service, and many of the men were destitute of any, nor could they be obtained at this place, as the arsenal had been exhausted in supplying those who had previously arrived.

. . . Information was received early this week that several of the Enemy's armed Vessels were ascending the Mississippi and were approaching near the Fort of St. Phillips. . . . Shortly after receiving this Information the attack on that Fort was distinctly heard at the lines. . . . The Bombardment appeared to be incessant and created considerable anxiety for the fate of the post, although the utmost confidence was placed in the bravery & Talants of the Commanding officer (Maj. [Walter H.] Overton) and the bravery and activity of the officers & soldiers under his command. . . .

On Saturday (the 7th) in the morning Commodore [Daniel Todd] Patterson (ever on the alert) advised the Commanding General that the enemy had opened Villery's Canal to communicate with the river, and had passed a number of Armed Barges through it into the Mississippi. The Idea was immediately conceived that an attack was premeditated against the lines & batteries on the right bank of the river, and that a simultaneous attack would be made to storm the lines on the left.

. . . Two detachments were ordered to be sent from the lines on the right bank, at night-fall, to different points below the line, to meet and repel the enemy at the landing, and prevent it, if possible. 400 men were ordered to reinforce that line, from General Thomas' Command of Kentuckians and that they should be well armed from the balance of that corps and such arms as could be gotten at the arsenal in New Orleans. It has since appeared that only from 170 to 180 men of this force were sent over, as arms could only be procured for that number. . . .

Sunday, Jany 8th, 1815 At the dawn of day the enemy were discovered (by the Piquet guards) to be advancing in force against our lines. . . . The enemy were broken three . . . times, halted, closed column and advanced again and finally entered the canal with their front platoons. Such destruction of men, for the time it lasted, was never before witnessed.

. . . At the commencement of this attack the Kentucky Regiment (in the rear of General Carrolls division) advanced and took cover under the line. A part intermixed with Carrolls men and fought bravely.

The column of the enemy on the Levey & road, advanced rapidly and entered the Fosse [ditch] under the face of the Demi-Bastion, mounted over the parapet and gained entire possession of that advance work. The commander & party retreating behind our lines in a state of confusion disgraceful to its commander. The enemy were now open to the fire of Captain [Thomas] Beal's company of Riflemen, by whom every officer & man that entered this work was killed, wounded & taken—not one escaped. . . . The whole time from the commencement to the close of this action, 45 minutes.

The scene exhibited on the field of action, in front of the line of defence, where the columns advanced & retired, was truly distressing to a feeling mind. The column that had retired from before General Carrolls division & the before mentioned batteries appeared to have left behind them, in advance of the first ditch (a distance of about 20 chain from the line) upwards of 500 dead bodies. . . . On the Levey nearly one hundred were killed.

Shortly after the firing had ceased, numbers of those that were supposed to have been killed, began to rise and solicit assistance. They were severely wounded. Arms, Legs & thighs had been shattered, in great abundance, by our Grape & ball, as well as by our rifles & musquets.

The relief solicited was most liberally furnished. The militia, in great numbers were sent to assist them into the lines, with such of the 44th Infantry as lay contiguous to the scene of action. They brought those that could not walk, with assistance, on their backs and on a few planks placed along a few scaling ladders, the enemy had left on the field.

Shortly after the firing had finally ceased on the left bank, and the enemy retired beyond our reach, a heavy firing was heard from the right. It was soon seen that the enemy had attacked and driven General Morgans Command from their line of defence, and that they were retreating with great speed and confusion, up the river, and pursued by the enemy.

Having never seen an official report of the transactions on the right bank (on this occasion) renders me incapable of giving anything like a correct statement of the causes that led to this disaster.[67]

From the start of the war, the United States fooled only itself in believing that an unprepared army of volunteers and militia could defend the country, let alone launch offensive operations. The War of 1812 thus should have laid to rest once and for all the myth of the militia and made clear America's need for a professional army.[68] But then, the new regular troops often appeared little better—not yet trained and mostly poorly armed. Captain William King wrote that the Twelfth and Fourteenth regiments lacked arms and other equipment, while those guns they had were in "infamously bad order" and the troops were "ignorant of their duty." And then, the worst insult, he compared them to militia: "They are mere militia, and, if possible, even worse; and if taken into action in their present state, will prove more dangerous to themselves than to their enemy."[69]

The troops' inexperience proved a real detriment to the American war effort. Even officers who had previously served proved rusty,[70] and most of the men had little or no experience with firearms and an unfortunate tendency to shoot one another: "This day one of Capt. Bradford's corporals was accidentally shot by one of his men through the leg."[71] In 1812 one of the Kentucky volunteers "was accidentally shot through the head by one of the mounted riflemen," and a few days later another Kentuckian "wounded a man as he was feeding his horse, believing him to be an Indian." Such incidents happened far too often for the comfort of those practicing in the use of firearms.[72] And occasionally they shot themselves. As one private wrote his wife, "I received an accident by my own gun going off" during a false alarm; it tore off part of his finger.[73]

Untrained soldiers could be trained, with sufficient time and effort, but the troops themselves generally hated it.[74] Unfortunately for the Americans, few commanding officers were willing to risk the resultant unpopularity of actually requiring regular drill. Winfield Scott, who would write the army's official training manual after the war, made the most concerted effort to train his troops, and with the most positive results. At the Battle of Chippewa, the U.S. forces behaved with greater coolness under fire than they had yet demonstrated. Major Thomas Jesup's forces "hotly pressed by the British right screened by a log fence, advanced upon its flank in face of a deadly fire, coolly marching with arms at a support, and then, charging with the bayonet, routed everything before him."[75] One of the British officers later stated, "It was clear enough that we had something besides militiamen to deal with."[76]

Unfortunately, the Battle of New Orleans undermined many of the lessons that could have been learned from the War of 1812, allowing one-time critics of the militia and volunteer troops to return to prewar rhetoric. Thus the Philadelphia *Aurora*, which had often made clear its disgust with the poor performance of untrained troops, now trumpeted the victory of "raw militia, hastily collected together from the adjoining country, and commanded by farmers and planters."[77] That the editor knew better was irrelevant; the rhetoric was not. Restoring the vision of a glorious militia not only saved face for the Jeffersonians, it also allowed them to prevent the expansion of the U.S. Army. Senator George M. Troup, who had called for a larger standing army during the war, set the tone with his praise for "the farmers of the country triumphantly victorious over the conquerors of Europe." Suffering conveniently from amnesia, he insisted that the war proved that militia could beat regulars and called for a standing army of just ten thousand men.[78] The Democratic-Republicans were operating in a fantasy world; some members of the House reversed themselves mid-debate. Thus Joseph Desha, who had declared the militia a waste of money, suddenly called for reducing the army to six thousand, declaring the militia "better security than ten, or even fifty thousand regulars. . . . We have boasted that a well organized militia was the bulwark of our liberty, and recent circumstances have proved it to be a fact."[79]

John C. Calhoun worked hardest to return Congress to reality, reminding them that "it is easier to keep soldiers than to get them."[80] Nonetheless, Desha's reduction won by a wide margin in the House, which eventually compromised with the Senate for an army of ten thousand.[81] Yet at the same time, the majority of the states allowed the militia system to die.[82] The result was a reduction in both the standing army and the near demise of the militia.

And after initial jubilation over Jackson's victory at New Orleans, the public quickly turned its attention elsewhere, once more reneging on promises to veterans. Public indifference to the memory of the War of 1812 is reflected in the startling paucity of memoirs to emerge from it; few people cared to read about the string of American defeats or their handful of victories. The war and its veterans faded quickly from view, though the archives contain numerous personal accounts. Just as with the American Revolution, celebrations of victory did not translate into support for veterans, who would still be fighting Congress for promised pensions forty years later.

Congress did, however, increase appropriations for West Point, and over the next thirty years created a very credible officer corps. The realities of the War of 1812 made it abundantly clear to those with any interest in the military that the United States would at the very least need a well-trained pool of officers in case of future war. It was primarily West Point graduates who led the United States to victory in the Mexican War and who led the two sides in the Civil War.[83]

# 3

# The Mexican War

As the first successful war of conquest by the United States against a foreign country, the Mexican War divided the nation and its soldiery. For many North Americans, invading Mexican territory was the fulfillment of Manifest Destiny; to others, including the young lieutenant Ulysses S. Grant and a new member of the House of Representatives from Illinois named Abraham Lincoln, the war was a grotesque violation of international law undertaken for the benefit of the slave states. President James K. Polk's government conducted the war on a voluntary basis, though taking the unusual view that volunteers did not actually have to enlist in the U.S. military; rather, they could just show up and be given federal arms. The early stages of the war had their peculiar moments as undisciplined troops went searching for Mexicans to fight and territories to conquer. Eventually generals Zachary Taylor and Winfield Scott imposed order on their armies and won repeated victories over Mexican forces, with Scott's army capturing Mexico City itself. Many of the surviving letters and diaries demonstrate the curiosity of these volunteers in encountering a culture so different from their own; surprisingly, there is very little contempt and a great deal of respect for their Spanish-speaking opponents.[1] An undisguised war of conquest, the Mexican War introduced the United States to the advantages of armed aggression, training an entire generation of officers who would command both sides in the Civil War.[2]

As had consistently been the case in its brief history, the United States entered the war with a small, ill-prepared, and largely demoralized army. Though its officer corps was outstanding, the army was held in low repute by the public, which clung to its suspicion of a standing army as a threat to democratic institutions, and had difficulty filling its few units with qualified recruits. In the thirty years after the end of the War of 1812, most members of Congress continued to act on the long-standing notion that a large army would quickly turn on the government, setting up some tin-pot Caesar as dictator. This fear of their own soldiers mixed easily with contempt, especially when so many soldiers were Irish Catholic immigrants. Critics of the military saw men of loose morals and debased character, and even suggested that many respectable men who had fallen on hard times enlisted under false names so as to spare their families from shame. It is little wonder that in 1826 desertions equaled one-half of the year's enlistments. In 1831, Secretary of War Lewis Cass informed Congress that of the 5,000 men in the army, 1,200 had deserted in 1830, at a cost to the army of at least $100,000. This pattern would hold into the late 1840s, as one-tenth of Winfield Scott's army deserted in Mexico—contrary to many accounts, Catholics accounted for just 5.3 percent of these desertions.[3]

In the years from 1815 to 1846, the army essentially functioned as a frontier police force, while the navy protected maritime trade. Facing no foreign invasion, the United States continued its westward expansion in the face of no enemy more powerful than the Native peoples. Even while giving lip service to the militia as the bulwark of liberty, in Justice Joseph Story's famous phrase, the public routinely mocked the militia and the drunken revels of annual musters. No serious observer of military affairs believed that the militia could be relied upon. Repeatedly during this period, political and military leaders promoted militia reform, but were roundly ignored by Congress.

However, largely as a result of some modest reforms implemented by Secretary of War John C. Calhoun between 1817 and 1825, the officer corps became an acceptable career for ambitious young men, and even a source of social mobility for many. The appointment of Captain Sylvanus Thayer as superintendent of West Point in 1817 further strengthened the officer corps. Thayer established the four-year curriculum with an emphasis on mathematics and engineering, resulting in a solid, reliable cadre of young officers who would lead the army through the Civil War. However, the government prevented true professionalism by making the military the servant of economic development; the army oversaw the dredging and expansion of harbors and surveyed the routes of roads and railroads, while the navy mapped and charted waterways to aid navigation. American business got in the habit of relying on the military for key services.

The path to the Mexican War followed directly from the annexation of Texas in 1845. Because Texas—unlike Mexico—allowed slavery, President John Tyler could not get the necessary two-thirds vote in the Senate required for the annexation treaty. Undeterred, Tyler submitted Texas statehood to Congress as a joint resolution of both houses, which only required a majority vote. This tactic worked and Texas entered the Union in December 1845. Tyler's successor, James K. Polk, had been elected president on the basis of an aggressive expansionist policy that sought to fulfill the claimed Manifest Destiny of the United States to expand across North America. Polk did not simply want to secure Texas to the Union; he also sought to add New Mexico and California, casting a lustful eye on the magnificent harbor at San Francisco.[4]

Seeking to provoke Mexico, Polk sent a force under the command of Major General Zachary Taylor to Texas. In March 1846, Taylor crossed the Nueces River, which Mexico claimed as its border, and advanced to the Rio Grande, which Polk asserted was the border between the two nations. Mexico charged the United States with invading their territory, and in April a Mexican contingent attacked a U.S. scouting party. The war was on.[5]

## War and Politics

Like the War of 1812, the Mexican War divided the country along political and, to a degree, sectional lines. The Democratic Party favored the war, while the Whigs insisted that the United States had no moral or legal grounds for violating Mexican sovereignty (most modern scholars agree with the Whigs that the Nueces was the international border).[6] Those opposed to slavery, particularly in the Northeast of the country, charged that the war had been launched to expand slave territory and tip the precarious national balance toward slavery; not surprisingly, proponents of slavery almost unanimously favored the war, seeing fresh territories for exploitation. However, once American troops had entered combat against Mexico, most antiwar Whigs thought they had little choice but to support the war effort in order to avoid being labeled unpatriotic.[7]

Suspicion of the actual motivation for the war seeped into the military, and many officers doubted the official reason for the war as a response to Mexican aggression. This perspective is best expressed in the private writings of Ethan Allen's grandson, Ethan Allen Hitchcock. An unusual career soldier, Hitchcock saw a life in the military as an opportunity to study, a sort of interminable graduate school. As a consequence, he became America's leading scholar on alchemy and Swedenborgianism, writing seven books on philosophical and literary subjects. He was also a highly competent commander who was widely respected within the army and eventually rose to the position of inspector general. But he was a soldier with a conscience, deeply troubled by the war against Mexico. His diary provides a unique insight into the complexities of service in a democracy, as he struggles to balance politics and service while remaining true to his personal morality:

Nov. 28 [1844] We have certain intelligence that J. K. Polk is elected President over Henry Clay. . . . I look upon this as a step towards the annexation of Texas first, and then, in due time, the separation of the Union. . . .

Fort Jesup, La., June 30, 1845. Orders came last evening by express from Washington City directing General Taylor to move without any delay to some point on the coast near the Sabine. . . . I have scarcely slept a wink, thinking of the needful preparations. . . . Violence leads to violence, and if this movement of ours does not lead to others and to bloodshed, I am much mistaken. . . .

[Aug. 1845] I am now here, however, with two companies of the 3rd Infantry—K and G,—the first troops occupying the soil of Texas. Corpus Christi is a very small village at the head of the bay. Our arrival is hailed with satisfaction.

Yet the regiment was now clearly in Mexico, according to all the treaties, agreements, and maps which had fixed the frontier. Corpus Christi was a settlement of a few houses on the west banks of the Nueces River, thitherto claimed by Mexico and conceded by Texas to be the boundary. . . .

29th Aug. Received last evening . . . a map of Texas from the Quartermaster-General's office, the latter being the one prepared by Lieutenant [William] Emory; but it has added to it a distinct boundary mark to the Rio Grande. Our people ought to be damned for their impudent arrogance and domineering presumption! It is enough to make atheist of us all to see such wickedness in the world, whether punished or unpunished. . . .

[Sept. 8] General Taylor talks, whether sincerely or not, of going to the Rio Grande. This is singular language from one who originally and till very lately denounced annexation as both injudicious in policy and wicked in fact! The "claim," so-called, of the Texans to the Rio Grande, is without foundation. The argument of Mr. [Sam] Walker [of Texas] passes by the treaty of 1819, by which the United States gave up all west and south of the Sabine, either saying nothing about it or presuming that it was not valid. Yet we took possession of Florida under that treaty. . . . The treaty of 1819 fixed the boundary, and since then Texas has been to the United States as much a foreign country as Yucatan, and we have no right whatever to go behind the treaty. . . .

C. C. [Corpus Christi], Sept. 20. General Taylor came into my tent this morning and again, as frequently of late, he introduced the subject of moving upon the Rio Grande. I discovered this time more clearly than ever that the General is instigated by ambition—or so it appears to me. He seems quite to have lost all respect for Mexican rights and [is] willing to be an instrument of Mr. Polk for pushing our boundary as far west as possible. . . .

2d Nov. Newspapers all seem to indicate that Mexico will make no movement, and the government is magnanimously bent on taking advantage of it to insist upon "our claim" as far as the Rio Grande. I hold this to be monstrous and abominable. But now, I see, the United States of America, as a people, are undergoing changes in character, and the real status and principles for which our forefathers fought are fast being lost sight of. . . .

[March 1846] As to the right of this movement, I have said from the first that the United States are the aggressors. We have outraged the Mexican government and people by an arrogance and presumption that deserve to be punished. . . . I know of nothing Mexico has done to deserve censure. Her people I consider a simple, well disposed, pastoral race, no way inclined to savage usages. . . .[8]

My heart is not in this business; I am against it from the bottom of my soul as a most unholy and unrighteous proceeding; but, as a military man, I am bound to execute orders. . . .

[May 20] The President gives a history ("his-story") of our intercourse with Mexico for the last twenty years, in which he would make it appear that we have been the most injured, patient, and forbearing people in the world! . . .

10th Nov. I am very much disgusted with this war in all of its features. . . . In the present case, I not only think this Mexican war unnecessary and unjust as regards Mexico, but I also think it not only hostile to the principles our own government—a government of the people, securing to them liberty—but I think it a step and a great step towards a dissolution of our Union. And I doubt not that a dissolution of the Union will bring on wars between the separated parts.[9]

Convinced that the war was fought for the benefit of slaveowners, Hitchcock often thought of resigning his commission. He would eventually do so, but, as we shall see in chapter 5, for very different reasons.

## Professionals and Enthusiasts

Unlike in the War of 1812, the military had a clear strategic vision, moving to seize Mexican territory as quickly as possible. The government had already placed agents and an "exploratory party" under the command of John C. Fremont in California, with U.S. naval units off the coast. These forces almost immediately seized control of California. Two days after the declaration of war in May 1846, Colonel Stephen Kearny set off from Fort Leavenworth with a small army to capture New Mexico, which fell to the United States in September. Once Taylor's army moved into Mexico's northeastern provinces, Polk intended to present Mexico with a fait accompli: with the United States in possession of so much of its northern territory, the Mexican government would have no choice but to negotiate an end to the war.[10]

At the war's start, the Mexican army, with 32,000 men, outnumbered the U.S. Army four to one. While Mexico had more troops, interior supply lines, and an excellent light cavalry, the United States could draw upon a much larger population base, carried superior arms, and benefited enormously from its first-rate field artillery—the latter repeatedly proving decisive in battle. The first major battle came on May 8 at Palo Alto, just north of the Rio Grande. Taylor's infantry barely figured in the battle as his artillery decimated the Mexican attack. The following day the Mexicans were again soundly beaten, at Resaca de la Palma, and Taylor crossed the Rio Grande, seizing the Mexican city of Matamoros. Heavily reinforced, Taylor moved inland to take Monterrey, the capital of Nuevo León, which fell to U.S. forces after three brutal days of battle. Meanwhile John Wool's forces seized much of Chihuahua. At this point, with California, New Mexico, and several others of Mexico's northern provinces in U.S. hands, Polk expected Mexico to sue for peace. However, the Mexicans refused to give in, leading Polk to approve General Winfield Scott's plan to take Mexico City itself.[11]

At this point Polk made a serious miscalculation. The former dictator of Mexico, General Santa Anna, lived in exile in Cuba. He assured Polk that if allowed to return to Mexico, he would negotiate a quick end to the war. Polk had the navy let Santa Anna through its blockade, whereupon the general immediately announced that he had returned to save his homeland from U.S. aggression. By the end of the year, he commanded both the army and the presidency of Mexico and vowed to expel the *Norte-americanos*.[12]

Almost immediately after Congress approved Polk's declaration of war, the question arose of who exactly would do the fighting. Congress expanded the U.S. Army from eight to fifteen thousand troops, hardly a sufficient force for a war of conquest, but all the antiwar Whigs were willing to allow. While politicians continued to praise the militia as the bulwark of American liberty, and many insisted that the country should once more turn to this fantasy force, most states had allowed the militia to atrophy. Therefore, to supplement the army, President Polk bypassed the militia and called for fifty thousand volunteers, who would act for specific periods in their own units. Most of these volunteer companies came from the southern states, where war fever ran highest. Some of these companies, such as the Mississippi Rifles under the command of Colonel Jefferson Davis, would demonstrate ability on the battlefield, while most would create a stream of problems for the regular army and head back home as soon as possible.[13]

In the War of 1812, members of the regular army held the militia in contempt, especially as Congress had consistently kept military budgets small in deference to the militia myth. In the Mexican War, professional soldiers instead had to contend with the volunteers, units hastily raised in the enthusiastic first flush of Polk's declaration of war. Particularly annoying to the army's officer corps was the fact that so many officers of the volunteer units had no military experience but gained their office through political influence or by election; junior officers found it galling to be outranked by local politicians—known as "Mustang Generals"—lacking the most rudimentary knowledge of warfare. The majority of volunteers had no military training and, in the opinion of both Generals Taylor and Scott, were often more of a hindrance than help. As one young lieutenant, George Gordon Meade, who would later command the Union army at Gettysburg, wrote from Matamoras in northern Mexico early in the war:

> I believe with fifteen thousand regulars, we could go to the City of Mexico, but with thirty thousand volunteers the whole nature and policy of the war will be changed. Already are the injurious influences of their presence perceptible, and you will hear any Mexican in the street descanting on the good conduct of the "tropas de ligna," as they call us, and the dread of the "volontarios." And with reason, they (the volunteers) have killed five or six innocent people walking in the streets, for no other object than their own amusement; to-be-sure, they are always drunk, and are in a measure irresponsible for their conduct. They rob and steal the cattle and corn of the poor farmers, and in fact act more like a body of hostile Indians than of civilized whites. Their own officers have no command or control over them, and the General has given up in despair any hope of keeping them in order. The consequence is they are exciting a feeling among the people which will induce them to rise en masse to obstruct our progress, and if, when we reach the mountains, we have to fight the people as well as the soldiers, the game will be up with us.[14]

As with most wars, the reality of service matched neither the fears of opponents nor the desires of supporters. Those who rushed to war tended to be disappointed by the daily grind of army life. The enthusiastic twenty-year-old volunteer Benjamin Franklin Scribner is fairly typical, except in having kept a fascinating and thorough journal that expresses the conflicting feelings of a volunteer who expected romance and found tedium and hardship. Scribner joined the Spencer Greys, a volunteer company from New Albany, Indiana, and discovered little glory in the midst and as a consequence of battle:

Camp at Agua Nueva, February 12th [1847]

We arrived at this place, on last Saturday, to join General Taylor and [Brigadier General John E.] Wool, who recently concentrated their forces here. . . . It is quite cold in this elevated situation, and we have suffered exceedingly. . . .

Recently I became sergeant. . . .

28th.— . . . Traveling about sixteen miles, we arrived at Buena Vista. After pitching our tents, we lay down supperless, for we had neither wood nor provisions. . . .

We had scarcely finished our breakfast, when the long roll was beaten, calling us all to arms, as our picket guard had just arrived with the intelligence that the Mexican army was approaching. . . .

Before hostilities commenced, a flag of truce was sent by Santa Anna with dispatches to General Taylor, stating that he was here with twenty thousand men, and to save loss of blood, demanded immediate capitulation. General Taylor is said to have replied, "If you want us, come and take us!" It looked almost like madness, with an army of four thousand five hundred men, and sixteen small pieces of cannon, to compete with a force, which all our prisoners, and Santa Anna himself, agree in being twenty thousand men, and seventeen pieces of cannon—of which eight were sixteen and twenty-four pounders. What a fearful difference! Yet that small army of raw, inexperienced volunteers not only struggled against twenty thousand strong of the flower of the Mexican army, commanded by one of the ablest generals in the world, but obtained a complete victory. This I hold to be one of the greatest achievements upon record.

At sunrise, on the following day, the roaring of the enemy's cannon announced the commencement of hostilities. A heavy fire was opened upon our riflemen upon the mountain, but they returned it in a handsome style. They were reinforced by a part of the 2d Illinois regiment and Kentucky cavalry, but still the odds were greatly against them. The whole mountain side, as far as the eye could reach, glittered with the enemy's bayonets and lances.

It was about nine o'clock in the morning when our regiment and a battery of three pieces, commanded by Lieut. O'Brien, marched out towards the battery which had been playing against us during the night and morning. . . . [B]efore our line was formed, they had fired two rounds, which we soon returned in right good earnest.

I was at my post in the rank of file closers, and was urging the men to form in their proper places, when Captain Sanderson cried out, "Never mind, Frank, fire away!" which I did, with all possible haste. About this time the battery on our left opened upon us a deadly fire of grape, which raked our flank with terrible effect; still we stood front to front, and poured our fire upon the infantry, which did us but little injury, as they shot too high. But the battery on our left galled us exceedingly. It appeared as if we had purposely halted in their exact range, and the whole atmosphere resounded with the whizzing shot that came with increasing precision. Apollos Stephens was the first of the Greys to fall. He received a grape shot in the head, and fell back almost into my arms. . . . I was loading when he fell, and compressing my lips, and smothering my emotions, I stepped over him and fired. Our captain was the next to fall, exclaiming "I've got it, boys!" A grape shot had struck his scabbard, which saved his life. Being ready to fire again, I stepped into a vacant place in the ranks, where I continued to load and fire without noticing anything around. The only thought I remember to have had was, "What a wonder I did not receive Captain Sanderson's shot, as I was next to him on the same line! so the ball must have passed me before it struck him." All was hurry and excitement, each working hard and doing his best. . . .

We had fired about twenty-one rounds, when I heard some one say, "They are all retreating!" and turning, I saw that the right wing [of the U.S. forces] had gone, and the left starting. But several who had not heard Colonel Bowles' order to retreat, cried out, "Halt, men! for God's sake, stop!" At this, many of us hesitated; but the retreat was general, and the enemy fast advancing upon us, led on by a large force of lancers. At length, Lieutenant Cayre, then in command, remarked, "It's no use, boys, to stay here alone; let us retreat!" which we did, with the balls raining around us, and the lancers at our heels. We rallied, by order, on the brow of the ridge. . . . Here many of us met the Mississippi regiment of riflemen, who had just arrived from their quarters in town.[15]

Scribner had survived the fiercely contested Battle of Buena Vista, where for two days in February 1847, Santa Anna's fifteen thousand troops battled Taylor's five thousand men. Taylor's brilliant maneuvering and his artillery drove off Santa Anna, who suffered 2,000 casualties to Taylor's 750. Many modern military historians feel that Taylor made an unnecessary gamble at Buena Vista, rising to the White House on the basis of many needless deaths.[16] The rest of Scribner's journal indicates that he felt keenly the loss of so many friends, and he returned home to New Albany as soon after the battle as he could get permission, publishing his journal that same year. He settled down and became a druggist, attaining little distinction until 1861, when he recruited the Thirty-eighth Indiana Volunteers, acting as their colonel and seeing action in Kentucky and Tennessee. After this war he wrote a memoir of his experiences, returning to the druggist's life until his death in 1900.[17]

Where Scribner perceived the war as a series of tragedies punctuated by a few hours of transcendent terror and glory, one young Philadelphian found the war a bit of a lark, presenting his observations of the troops' complete lack of discipline with good humor. Twenty-year-old George B. McClellan, future commander of the Army of the Potomac, graduated second from the famous West Point class of 1846.[18] McClellan went straight from West Point to Taylor's army in northern Mexico as a second lieutenant of engineers, where he echoed many of Meade's sentiments about the volunteers. Both men found the volunteers guilty of serious violations of military and civil law, to the point that they endangered the war effort, but McClellan consistently insisted that nothing better could be expected from men lacking military training and professional officers. Except for the first paragraph, which is from a letter to his mother, the following are entries from McClellan's diary:

[From a letter to his mother:] Camp off Camargo, Mex., November 14, 1846. The people are very polite to the regulars . . . but they hate the volunteers as they do old scratch [the devil] himself. . . . You never hear of a Mexican being murdered by a regular or a regular by a Mexican. The volunteers carry on in a most shameful and disgraceful manner; they think nothing of robbing and killing the Mexicans.

December 5, 1846. . . . I have seen more suffering since I came out here than I could have imagined to exist. It is really awful. I allude to the sufferings of the Volunteers. They literally die like dogs. Were it all known in the States, there would be no more hue and cry against the Army, all would be willing to have so large a regular army that we could dispense entirely with the volunteer system. The suffering among the Regulars is comparatively trifling, for their officers know their duty and take good care of the men. . . .

December 25th. . . . At last we reached our camp at a dirty, muddy lake—ornamented by a dead jackass. Pat [General Robert Patterson] ensconced himself in the best place with Tennessee horse as a guard, put Gibson "in battery" on the road, with us on his left flank—a large interval between us and the Tennessee horse—a similar one between Gibson and the Illinois foot. Gibson had orders to defend the road. How he was to be informed of the approach of the enemy "this deponent knoweth not," such a thing as a picket was not thought of. . . .

For our Christmas dinner we had a beefsteak and some fried mush. . . . December 30th. . . . [T]he Major commanding the rear guard (Waterhouse, of the Tennessee Cavalry) was told by a wagonmaster that the advanced guard was in action with the Mexicans. The men, in the rear guard, immediately imagined that they could distinguish the sound of cannon and musketry. The cavalry threw off their saddle bags and set off at a gallop—the infantry jerked off their knapsacks and put out—Major and all deserted their posts on the bare report of a wagonmaster that the advance was engaged. A beautiful commentary this on the "citizen soldiery."

December 31st. . . . I have some indistinct ideas of my last *sensible* moments being spent in kneeling on my bed, and making an extra eggnog on the old mess chest. I dont recollect whether I drank it or not, but as the pitcher was empty the next morning, I rather fancy that I must have done so.

January 1st, 1847. . . . Smith had been informed the preceding day by Winship (General Pillow's Adjutant General) that the road we took was the right one to Victoria. We quickly discovered the magnitude of our mistake, for we got amongst the Volunteers, and the lord deliver us from ever getting into such a scrape again. Falstaff's company were regulars in comparison with these fellows—most of them without coats; some would have looked much better without any pants than with the parts of pants they wore; all had torn and dirty shirts—uncombed heads—unwashed faces—they were dirt and filth from top to toe. Such marching! They were marching by the flank, yet the road was not wide enough to hold them and it was with the greatest difficulty that you could get by—all hollowing, cursing, yelling like so many incarnate fiends—no attention or respect paid to the commands of their officers, whom they would curse as quickly as they would look at them. They literally straggled along for miles.[19]

## The Road to Mexico City

With one exception, the campaigns of the Mexican War, even Taylor's, replicated the amateur approach to combat evident in the War of 1812. Winfield Scott's campaign to capture the port of Veracruz and move on from there to take the Mexican capital was a very different matter, a triumph of professional standards and, in the view of most military historians, a masterpiece of meticulous planning and bold initiative. The amphibious landing of his army near Veracruz on March 7, 1847, demonstrated this modern mastery. The landing was perfectly synchronized in boats specifically designed for the task with stores needed immediately stockpiled in such a way as to be the first items off-loaded (what is today called combat-loaded). The journal of one lieutenant provides a vivid portrait of this operation.

Unlike Scribner, the eager volunteer, or McClellan, the cynical recent West Point graduate, Francis Collins offers the less impassioned perspective of a young professional. Born in Lowville, New York, in 1820, Collins graduated from West Point in 1845, just in time for the war. In October 1846, he set off for Mexico as a second lieutenant of artillery assigned to the command of the same general McClellan gleefully maligned, Major General Robert Patterson, who "did not belong to the regular army but was appointed for the war by President Polk, and was one of the poorest of his appointments."[20] Once the army seized the Mexican town of Tampico, Collins requested and received a transfer to the Illinois Volunteers led by Brigadier General James Shields, whom he expected to mold into a competent commander: "This appointment was much more agreeable to me than doing duty with my company, which I never much liked." Like many professional soldiers, Collins did not always respect his volunteer colleagues, but he held his commanding officer, General Winfield Scott, in the highest esteem:

Feb'y. 19. General Scott arrived here to-day from Brazas, Santiago, where he has been for sometime past perfecting his arrangements for a descent on Vera Cruz. He declares martial law in force throughout all the Mexican provinces of which we have possession. He comes here for the purpose of organizing troops near here under the command of Gen'ls Patterson, Twiggs, Pillow, Quitman, and Shields, about six thousand strong. . . .

27 Feb'y. Arrived at Lobos Island. There are about forty transports here ladened with troops and stores. . . . This island is . . . about one mile and a half in circumference, and much of it covered with a dense growth of chapperel that is a thicket of bushes and small trees interlaced with vines etc. None of the troops have been disembarked on the island except those on the transports where disease began to make its appearance, which is confined entirely to "volunteers." They have embarked in this campaign in anticipation of a grand frolic, but . . . I think they will find more reality and less romance in it than they thought, and will wish themselves comfortably at home again. . . .

30 Feb'y. During the past few days many more transports have arrived with troops and still they come. . . . General Scott is busily engaged in perfecting the organization of his army and orders emanating from him are hourly circulating through the fleet. . . .

2 March. Today at Twelve o'clock the old Massachusetts fired her signal, and immediately after came ploughing through the fleet, giving the lead for Vera Cruz. . . . Shouts and cheers, and martial music, peal upon

peal, burst from the ten thousand throats, as the old chief [Scott] towering high, with uncovered head, stood on the deck as his ship passed along,
dashing the spray from her bows, as if knowing her charge to many victories. Never did I witness on any other occasion so much enthusiasm.
Proud should be the man and confident, who commands such hearts! In
a very short time every sail was set, and an hundred ships with a good
breeze were under way for the appointed destination. It was indeed a magnificent sight and one long to be remembered.

9 March. . . . In about two hours all arrived in position under shelter of
the small island of Sacrificios which lies about three miles south of Vera
Cruz, and one fourth of a mile from the coast. Behind this island the
ships had a safe anchorage, and were able to approach within a quarter of
a mile to the land. Under the most favorable circumstances the descent of
an Army on an enemy's coast is a most delicate operation. In this case it
was to be made on the most dangerous coast in the world, within view of
a strongly fortified and garrisoned city, and almost under its guns. It was
to be accomplished, too, by means of surf boats capable of carrying about
seventy men each, which were to be impelled through the beating surf. It
must necessarily, therefore be a slow operation, and of course, if any
opposition was offered, a hazardous one, since, packed as we were in the
small boats it was impossible to make any resistance. . . . [The Mexicans
stayed within their fortifications.]

Our camp fires soon extended more than a mile along the coast. After
our suppers, from what chanced to be in our haversacks, we lay down on
the sand to get a little sleep or at any rate rest from the fatigues and excitement of the twelve hours past. . . .

10th March. We did not get much rest last night. Our picket-guards
came in contact with the guards of the enemy two or three times during
the night. As each time it resulted in the exchange of a few shots, our entire
camp was as often roused to arms. Our sleep and rest was the only thing
damaged by the collisions.

At the break of day this morning the drums beat to arms, and in a short
time the whole army, about thirteen thousand in numbers, was in motion,
advancing towards the city of Vera Cruz. On the level beach and all
together, the eye could take in the whole army at a glance. It was a very
stirring military scene.

11 March. . . . At an early hour today our division began to move forward towards the north side of the city for the purpose of extending the
investment. The enemy has kept his batteries playing upon us continu-
ously during the day, both from the city and castle; but as we took a route
bending around the city, well-protected most of the time by a low range of

sand hills, our loss has not been great. Captain Albertus of the Second regiment killed . . . [when] our division was at a halt, waiting for the removal of some obstructions in front. Availing himself of this opportunity he had seated himself on a log, and was reading a letter which he had received a short time before from home; while thus engaged a cannon ball took his head off.

A body of about three hundred Lancers have hung on our flanks and along our line of march to annoy us and impede our progress, but they have not succeeded very well in their object. . . . The numerous difficulties and obstructions which have impeded our progress, and the annoyance which we have received from the enemy's guns have made the day's advance of three or four miles very fatiguing.

12 March. Our division has remained in camp to-day waiting for some reconnoitering parties to report the nature of the country. Although we are encamped within range of the guns of the city and castle they have not molested us, thanks to some low sand hills behind which we are sheltered. In the place of cannon balls, however, there has been a terrible "Norther" raging all day, and it would be difficult to decide which were the worse of the two. These northers frequently come upon us very suddenly and continue to blow with unceasing violence, sometimes for forty-eight hours. During such times the sand drifts about like snow in northern latitudes. It fills one's hair, eyes, nose and mouth; the finer sand gets into the pores of the skin, often causing painful irritation. At these times, too, we suffer much from cold. The destitute classes of the natives wrap their blankets, or "panchos" close around them, and squatting down in some corner when the wind in its greatest force is broken, they will hardly move for anything less than to save their lives.

22 March. . . . Some of our batteries being in position and ready for action General Scott summoned the city to surrender. The Governor General in command replied in a courteous manner, that he had been entrusted with the defense of the town and castle, and had been furnished with the necessary means to do it; and that he was prepared to make use of those means as long as he was able. On receiving this reply, one of our batteries composed of seven heavy mortars opened a fire on the city. It was about six o'clock in the evening. The shells seem to have done great execution. The crashing, rumbling report which they make as they fall through the roofs of the buildings, bursting and scattering death and destruction around is truly terrible. The screams and yells of the populace, whether in defiance or fear could be distinctly heard, and now while I write do I hear them. . . .

25 March. . . . To-day we received intelligence that there is a force of about two thousand Mexicans in our rear. . . . Colonel [William S.] Harney of the Second Regiment Dragoons was sent out with a small force of cavalry to reconnoitre, and if expedient to attack them. He found them posted for a fight at the stone bridge of Moreno. The bridge being fortified, Harney sent back to camp for some artillery. Lieutenant Judd of the Third Artillery was sent to his assistance. It did not take long to demolish the enemy's barricades, and he was soon after driven from his position and pursued to the village of Madeline, about six miles from the bridge. . . .

26 March. This morning there was a spirited cannonading on both sides. It did not last long, however, and since it ceased all has been quiet. . . . White flags have been passing to and from the city during the day. It is thought that unless the place surrenders soon it will be taken by storm. If this takes place it will be attended with great destruction of life.

27 March. All is quiet to-day. Negotiations are still pending.

Evening. Terms of capitulation have been agreed on; the Bravos Mexicanoes have surrendered into our hands the city of Vera Cruz and the Castle of San Juan de Ulloa.[21]

Scott conducted the siege of Veracruz according to the highest military standards, minimizing casualties and capturing the city quickly. Writing a few days later, Collins credited the success of the U.S. forces at Veracruz to their mastery of "scientific warfare." He was convinced that the same skill would lead to the conquest of Mexico, a certainty borne out as he took part in Scott's brilliant campaign aimed at the capture of Mexico City itself.[22]

After the capitulation of Veracruz in March 1847, Santa Anna rushed back south, gathering an army of 25,000 to confront Scott's 15,000 troops. Even though the mountainous terrain gave Santa Anna every defensive advantage, he was repeatedly outmaneuvered and outfought by Scott. At Cerro Gordo on April 17 and 18, Scott smoothly turned Santa Anna's flank, driving the Mexicans in disarray from the field. A few days after this battle, at Jalapa, Scott lost seven regiments of volunteers who went home, as E. Kirby Smith wrote, to boast of their courage. With his remaining 11,000 men, Scott cut himself off from his lines of communication and continued his march west. Even the Duke of Wellington declared that "Scott is lost!"[23]

Scott made intelligent use of his young officers, relying on their engineering, artillery, and leadership skills to defeat the well-entrenched Mexicans again and again: at Perote, Puebla, Lake Chalco, San Augustin, Contreras, Churubusco, Molino del Rey, Chapultepec, and, finally, Mexico City itself.[24] One of these capable junior officers was Captain E. Kirby Smith, whose father served in the War of 1812 and grandfather in the American Revolution. A member of the regular army, Smith fought under General Taylor at Palo Alto and Resaca de la Palma, then returned home owing to the death of his father. After taking care of family matters, he rushed back to Mexico in time to join Scott's expedition, taking part in all operations from Veracruz to Mexico City. In long, thorough letters to his wife, Smith described the campaign in detail. At a time when letters were often published in newspapers as though they originated with correspondents, Smith emphatically insisted that these letters must remain private: *"Not a word I write must get into the papers."* Smith's description of the siege of Veracruz, not included here, closely matches that of Francis Collins, even to the decapitation of Captain Albertus by a cannonball. Like many soldiers, he had his doubts about the morality of the war, but felt that his concerns must be put aside once Congress declared war and worried in his letters that the Whig Party's opposition to the war undermined the military effort and emboldened the Mexicans. Also like many professional soldiers, Smith considered the volunteers overrated and the regulars routinely underappreciated:

Camp at Brasos St. Iago, February 17, 1847. . . . This large Depot is now the scene of the most utter confusion imaginable. Quarter-masters, wagon-masters, wharf-masters and government agents of all descriptions running about as if mad, while orders upon orders and counter-orders are constantly issued. . . . Enter sergeant with a large bundle of papers under each arm.

*Officer*: What have you under your right arm?

*Sergeant*: Orders.

*Officer*: And what under your left?

*Sergeant*: Counter-orders. . . .

[March 29] . . . [A]t one o'clock at night a Dragoon rode into our bivouac with a note from Colonel [Ethan Allen] Hitchcock saying that General Scott had just approved the Articles of Capitulation. Huzza! Huzza! the city and the strong castle of San Juan have surrendered! . . .

April 17, 1847. . . . We arrived at Alvarado, which is near the mouth of the river, just at sunset. . . . It is much like other Mexican towns,—a large church, a few decent houses owned by the rich, the residue mean and dirty, filled with ticks, fleas, vermin, idleness, and licentiousness. . . .

The march . . . was most horrible,—the men without bread, and had to be up all night watching the horses. We have just arrived. I am completely worn out and have just seen the villainous order of promotions and brevets in which the Fifth is entirely neglected. I am utterly disgusted with the service and were it not for you and the dear children would resign at once, but for your sakes I must continue to endure. . . .

Jalapa, April 25, 1847. . . . I am now sitting on the ground writing on the top of a box. . . . We are to march to Perote, forty miles from here, tomorrow, to join General [William J.] Worth, to whose division we belong. . . .

We were occasionally shocked by the sight of some poor soldier who had been shot by the wayside and whose unsepulchered remains were rotting on the ground. The road began to be strewed with the offensive bodies of dead horses and cattle, and the fragments of broken wagons, etc., which are ever scattered behind an army. We marched on steadily until about two in the morning, when after descending a very long steep hill down which the road winds we halted at the town of Plan del Rio, four miles from the battle field of Cerro Gordo. Every hut, every place of shelter was found filled with the wounded.

We had marched after sunset eighteen miles, and as soon as we halted the weary men dropped on the rugged, dirty earth, the officers promiscuously scattered among them. I was officer of the day and as soon as I had posted a few sentinels I lay down in the very dust and dirt of the road with no bed or covering but my cloak, and in spite of the groans of the wounded and the shrieks of those who were suffering from the knives of the surgeons, I slept soundly for three hours.

In the morning I visited those of my friends who were wounded, among whom is Poet Patten, all his left hand but the forefinger and thumb having been carried off by a grape shot. He was doing well and is very cheerful. I consoled him with the fact that though he could no longer play the guitar he might write better poetry than before.[25]

. . . The battle of Cerro Gordo is not likely to terminate the war as we supposed. The Mexicans appear determined never to give up even if we should take every town and fortress in the nation. What a stupid people they are! They can do nothing and their continued defeats should convince them of it. They have lost six great battles; we have captured six hundred and eighty cannon, nearly one hundred thousand stand of arms, made twenty thousand prisoners, have possession of the greatest portion of their country and are fast advancing upon their Capital which must soon be ours,—yet they refuse to treat! . . .

May 5. . . . My opinion of volunteers and the whole volunteer system is not changed in the least. They are expensive, unruly, and not to be relied upon in action. Their conduct towards the poor inhabitants has been horrible, and their coming is dreaded like death in every village in Mexico, while the regulars are met by the people almost as friends. A portion of them (the volunteers) have fled in every action in which they have been engaged and they can never succeed unless supported by the line. At Monterey, Buena Vista, and Cerro Gordo portions of them ran. General

Taylor says in a letter that at Buena Vista, had they not been turned back by the enemy who had got to his rear, many more than did would have entirely fled the battle field. [General Gideon] Pillow's Brigade of volunteers were defeated at Cerro Gordo, and he requested the General to send him a few regulars, if only one company, to support and set an example to his men. The first instance is yet to occur in this war in which a regular has abandoned his post or been defeated. Portions of the volunteers have fought most gallantly, but when they will fight, and when they won't, can only be determined by experiment. I am aware that these opinions would be considered almost treasonable in the United States, but here they are the sentiments of all the regulars and of a large number of the volunteer officers in the field. . . .

May 9. . . . I have learned in common with many other poor fellows that it is not he who patiently does his duty, or who in the hour of danger is in the front of the battle, who gains the laurel or the more vulgar reward of government patronage. It is too frequently the sycophant who flatters the foibles of his commanding officer, he who has political family influence, or whom some accident makes conspicuous, who reaps all the benefits of the exposure and labors of others. The long list of brevets, most outrageously unjust as they are, many of them double, is a register of evidence to the facts that success is a lottery and that government rewards are by no means dependent on merit. How tired and sick I am of a war to which I can see no probable termination! How readily would I exchange my profession for any honest, mechanical employment, were it possible to do so! . . . Why do I grumble or let you know how miserable I am? Think not I am always so. It is not often that I suffer my mind to dwell on these matters, or yield to any despondency. . . . [T]he "Mohawks" . . . are tired of the war and are going home to boast of their deeds of arms. . . .

August 12. We marched from Rio Frio at six. . . . The broad, excellent road ran through a dense pine and cedar forest. In two hours we reached the summit of the mountain, ten thousand seven hundred feet above the sea. On our right and left were still loftier mountains towering high above us in the clouds. . . . The road plunged rapidly toward the plain and after descending a few miles the great valley of Mexico broke upon our view, a most glorious spectacle, which we beheld from the same point where Cortes first gazed upon it. Far to the right scarcely perceptible was the great city, and all over the vast plain spread out before us like a map were lakes, towns, haciendas, and large cultivated fields. We dipped into the valley by a winding road so steep as to be barely practicable for our wagons. . . .

August 13, Chalco. . . . It is reported that the Mexicans have between thirty and forty thousand troops to oppose our weak ten thousand. Our task is truly desperate, and many of us will, of course, be sacrificed before we take the city. . . .

August 15. It has been decided to abandon entirely the route by El Peñon and advance by the road to the left of Lakes Chalco and Xochamilco. We go to victory or death,—we can only be defeated by annihilation. Our spirits and courage are good, we have confidence in ourselves, and confidence in our generals.

[August 17] . . . We entered the beautiful town of San Augustine about four in the afternoon. . . . We advance again tomorrow and shall meet more serious opposition which must increase every step to the city. "One leg" [Santa Anna] vows to defend the Capital to the last extremity. I picked up a curious proclamation signed by him, written yesterday, to induce our men to desert. I shall enclose it in this. . . .

Tacubaya, August 22, 1847. I hardly know how to commence a description of the events of the last three days. My brain is whirling from the long continued excitement and my body sore with bruises and fatigue—but I will try to get into my usual humdrum style and record things as they happened. On the nineteenth we still lay near San Antonio. In the morning a force composed of [General David E.] Twiggs' and Pillow's divisions was ordered far to the right on the San Angel road. Quitman held San Augustine and we kept the enemy in check at San Antonio. . . . We . . . took no pains to conceal our march among the lava crags and ravines as before, but showed ourselves to the enemy wishing them to believe we still threatened their position at San Antonio. About twelve [of] the enemy's guns at Contreras, or San Magdalene, opened fire upon Twigg's and Pillow's advancing column. . . .

The firing soon became tremendous—every flash and every peal was plainly perceptible to us, where we lay in reach of the guns of San Antonio. Soon the crash of small arms mingled with the incessant roar of artillery, the firing continuing for hours without our being able to perceive that our forces gained an inch. . . . I then learned . . . that our operations were entirely for position . . . —that the ground was broken, utterly impracticable for cavalry or field artillery, and that at daybreak the enemy's fortifications were to be assaulted by our infantry.

Early on the morning of the twentieth, the attack was made and the works carried at the point of the bayonet, scarcely a gun being fired. We took fifteen hundred prisoners and twenty-two pieces of artillery among which were the guns captured by Santa Anna at Buena Vista. As soon as the result was known to General Worth, the Second Brigade of his division with our battalion were put in motion to endeavor to turn the position at

San Antonio. For two hours we ran over the rocks moving by a flank, the enemy in a heavy column marching parallel to us and almost in gun shot, until the head of the Fifth Infantry pierced their line and the fight began at a quarter before twelve.

It will be entirely impossible for me to give any lucid description of this terrible battle. It extended over a large space and I could see but little of it, being too hotly engaged to notice much beyond the sphere of my own duties. The point where our troops pierced the retreating column of the enemy was on the road from San Antonio to Mexico near a hacienda where the left of their line of defences terminated. . . . It was soon seen as we rushed along the road that the enemy were only retreating to a fortified position which constituted their second line of defences at Churubusco.

. . . We had advanced on the road less than a mile when we were ordered into the fields to assault the right of the enemy's position,—I am speaking of our battalion. . . . The escopet [carbine] balls were whistling over our heads, though at long range, and occasionally a cannon ball sang through the corn as it tore its path along in our front.

At this time the battle was fiercely contested on our left and front. . . . Immediately in front of us, at perhaps five hundred yards, the roll of the Mexican fire exceeded anything I have ever heard. The din was most horrible, the roar of cannon and musketry, the screams of the wounded, the awful cry of terrified horses and mules, and the yells of the fierce combatants all combined in a sound as hellish as can be conceived. . . .

We soon came out of it into a crossroad near some small houses, where we were exposed to a dreadful cross fire, which could scarcely be resisted. Many had fallen and the battalion was much scattered and broken. The grape round shot and musketry were sweeping over the ground in a storm which strewed it with the dead and dying. I found it extremely difficult to make the men stand or form, but finally succeeded with my own company which was at once ordered to charge under my brave Lieutenant Farrelly. . . . My men were just formed and I had ordered the charge which I was about to lead, when the dreadful cry came from the left and rear that we were repulsed. A rush of men and officers in a panic followed, running over and again breaking my little command. I, however, succeeded in disentangling them from the mass, composed of a great portion of the Eighth, Sixth, and Fifth Infantry, with some artillery. I shouted that we were not repulsed—to charge—and the day would be ours. Our colonel, C. F. Smith, now joined us, and the cry throughout was: "Forward!"

Up to this time we were not aware that the other divisions of the army were engaged, but we now learned that Twiggs and others were pressing them on the left and had been fighting them an hour or more. Before this we had discovered we were under the fire of two forts. . . . Now as the whole army shouted and rushed to the assault, the enemy gave way, retreating as best they could to Mexico [City]. They were pursued by all, hundreds being shot down in the retreat, our Dragoons charging after them to the guns at the gate of the city, where they were stayed by a tremendous discharge from the battery covering the entrance. . . .

It was a wonderful victory and undoubtedly the greatest battle our country has ever fought, and I hope will bring peace. At all events, the great city is at our mercy, and we could enter it at any hour.

On the morning of the twenty-first I was ordered to take charge of some funeral parties collecting and burying the dead. This was a sad, a solemn service—though in our haste we performed no burial rites— paid no honors—but laid our dead in the earth in the bloody garments in which they died, most of them on the spot where they fell. . . . At the convent, around which one fortification is constructed, I saw the Mexican prisoners and some fifty of our deserters who were taken in arms against us. . . .

September 7. . . . General Scott declared the truce terminated in consequence of the frequent violations of its articles by Santa Anna. . . . In the sixteen days during which he has been flattering us with the hopes of peace he has been actively collecting his scattered forces, and with all his energies preparing to renew the combat. He has now twenty-two thousand men under arms and the Capital placed in such a state of defence that the enemy loudly boasts we cannot take it. Fatal credulity! How awful are its consequences to us! By it, the fruits of our glorious and incomparable victory are entirely thrown away. . . .

I have just learned that the plan of attack is arranged. . . . I firmly trust and pray that victory may crown our efforts though the odds are immense.

I am thankful that you do not know the peril we are in. Good night.[26]

The morning after this last letter, Ephraim Kirby Smith was shot in the face and died during the battle at Molino del Rey. Mexico City fell to Scott's army on September 13, 1847. Smith's brother, Edmund Kirby Smith, served as a general in the army of the Confederacy.

## The War's End

The stunning successes of the U.S. Army, outnumbered at every battle, shattered the Mexican will to continue the war, and peace negotiations began a few weeks later. The Treaty of Guadalupe-Hidalgo, signed in February 1848, gave the United States a massive extent of western lands—and a major political crisis as the question of slavery in these territories would tear the country apart.[27] As Ralph Waldo Emerson predicted in 1846, the acquisition of Mexican territory "will be as the man [who] swallows the arsenic, which brings him down in turn. Mexico will poison us."[28]

Once more, at the war's end, Americans returned to the militia myth. In the campaign biography he wrote for Franklin Pierce in 1852, Nathaniel Hawthorne ignored both the widespread opposition to the war and the military's reliance on its regular forces to promote the Mexican War as a people's war: "There is nothing in any other country similar to what we see in our own, when the blast of the trumpet at once converts men of peaceful pursuits into warriors. Every war in which America has been engaged has done this; the valor that wins our battles is not the trained hardihood of veterans, but a native and spontaneous fire; and there is surely a chivalrous beauty in the devotion of the citizen soldier to his country's cause, which the man who makes arms his profession, and is but doing his regular business on the field of battle, cannot pretend to rival. Taking the Mexican War as a specimen, this peculiar composition of an American army, as well in respect to its officers as its private soldiers, seems to create a spirit of romantic adventure which more than supplies the place of disciplined courage."[29] One hopes the experience of volunteers and regulars recorded above give the lie to Hawthorne's romantic effusions.

During the Mexican War, 1,500 Americans died in battle, and an additional 10,800 died from disease. Though these numbers pale in comparison to the Civil War, these deaths amount to 153.5 deaths per 1,000 participants a year, exceeding the rate for the Civil War of 98 per 1,000.[30] It had proven a rapid, violent war, one that glorified American conquest and appeared to prove the reality of Manifest Destiny. As the public temporarily celebrated this great success, politicians who had opposed the war, like Abraham Lincoln of Illinois, thought their political careers at an end. But as it became evident that the acquisition of new territories meant the likely expansion of the institution of slavery, a great proportion of the public in the northern states came to feel that they had been manipulated into the war for the benefit of powerful vested interests.

A young lieutenant in the Mexican War would best express the conflict's impact on the United States when he wrote his memoirs forty years later. In describing his plans prior to the advent of war, Ulysses S. Grant sounds a lot like the studious Ethan Allen Hitchcock:

[It] was never my intention to remain in the army long, but to prepare myself for a professorship in some college. Accordingly, soon after I was

settled at Jefferson Barracks, I wrote a letter to Professor Church—
Professor of Mathematics at West Point—requesting him to ask my designation as his assistant, when next a detail had to be made. Assistant
professors at West Point are all officers of the army, supposed to be selected for their special fitness for the particular branch of study they are
assigned to teach. The answer from Professor Church was entirely satisfac-
tory, and no doubt I should have been detailed a year or two later but for
the Mexican War coming on. Accordingly I laid out for myself a course of
studies to be pursued in garrison, with regularity, if not persistency. I reviewed my West Point course of mathematics during the seven months at
Jefferson Barracks, and read many valuable historical works, besides an
occasional novel. . . .

There was no intimation given that the removal of the 3d and 4th regiments of infantry to the western border of Louisiana was occasioned in
any way by the prospective annexation of Texas, but it was generally
understood that such was the case. Ostensibly we were intended to prevent
filibustering into Texas, but really as a menace to Mexico in case she appeared to contemplate war. Generally the officers of the army were in-
different whether the annexation was consummated or not; but not so all
of them. For myself, I was bitterly opposed to the measure, and to this day
regard the war, which resulted, as one of the most unjust ever waged by a
stronger against a weaker nation. It was an instance of a republic following the bad example of European monarchies, in not considering justice
in their desire to acquire additional territory.

Texas was originally a state belonging to the republic of Mexico. . . .
An empire in territory, it had but a very sparse population, until settled by
Americans who had received authority from Mexico to colonize. These
colonists paid very little attention to the supreme government, and introduced slavery into the state almost from the start, though the constitution
of Mexico did not, nor does it now, sanction that institution. Soon they
set up an independent government of their own, and war existed, between
Texas and Mexico, in name from that time until 1836. . . . Before long,
however, the same people—who with permission of Mexico had colo-
nized Texas, and afterwards set up slavery there, and then seceded as soon
as they felt strong enough to do so—offered themselves and the State to
the United States, and in 1845 their offer was accepted. The occupation,
separation and annexation were, from the inception of the movement to
its final consummation, a conspiracy to acquire territory out of which slave
states might be formed for the American Union.

Even if the annexation itself could be justified, the manner in which the
subsequent war was forced upon Mexico cannot. The fact is, annexationists

wanted more territory than they could possibly lay any claim to, as part of the new acquisition. . . . The Southern rebellion was largely the outgrowth of the Mexican war. Nations, like individuals, are punished for their transgressions. We got our punishment in the most sanguinary and expensive war of modern times.[31]

# 4

# The Civil War

The Civil War has been called America's Iliad, the nation's defining moment, the Great Divide, and scores of other glorifying names. For the soldiers in the field, it was the ultimate horror. The Civil War proved distinctive in one highly significant particular: soldiers encountered mass death. In prior American wars, even in the bloodiest battles, American soldiers might have seen dozens of their comrades fall in battle. During the Civil War, they saw thousands torn apart by bullets and cannon, heard the screams of the maimed, saw piles of amputated limbs, and were surrounded by the stench of death. At the hotly contested Battle of Guilford Courthouse during the Revolution, 261 Americans were killed and wounded compared to 532 British; in the climactic Battle of Chapultepec leading to the capture of Mexico City during the Mexican War, the United States suffered 860 casualties, with Mexican losses approximately twice that number; at Antietam, 6,000 Americans died, with another 16,000 wounded. Of course, in the Civil War, Americans fell on both sides.

## Confronting the Slaughter

The average soldier was completely unprepared for the nature of battle in the Civil War. Most had been raised on heroic tales of the American Revolution, the Battle of New Orleans, and Scott's campaign in Mexico. Now they were not only confronting fellow Americans, but doing so in a kind of battle that proved more horrific than anyone had yet imagined. Technological advances in arms production—most particularly rifled muskets and ordnance—shifted the battlefield advantage to the defensive position and made the traditional Napoleonic tactics of headlong charges not just obsolete but suicidal. The enhanced firepower of modern armies rendered attacks on well-entrenched troops a form of senseless slaughter, as the Battle of Fredericksburg convincingly demonstrated. Soldiers struggled to describe what they faced, and to explain why they fought on.[1]

Even near the end of his long life, Oliver Wendell Holmes Jr. recalled April 12, 1861, as the decisive moment in his life. When he heard that South Carolina volunteers had bombarded Fort Sumter, Holmes, then a student at Harvard, quit college and enlisted. The son of one of the most prominent medical and literary figures in America, Holmes could have easily avoided combat and maintained his patriotic credentials with a staff job of some kind. Instead, he insisted on the infantry, becoming a lieutenant in the Twentieth Massachusetts Volunteer Infantry.

His diary and letters home express the experience of many young men who marched to war singing "John Brown's Body," only to find carnage rather than heroism, and despair in the place of glory.[2] Thrice wounded in battle—the second time at Antietam—Holmes had seen enough of war by the summer of 1863, writing his parents that he wanted somehow to return to civilian life. It is probable that the senior Holmes used his influence to get his son a discharge in 1864, allowing the young veteran to enroll in Harvard Law School.

The First Battle of Bull Run, in July 1861, made evident to both sides that the war would not be a brief affair. The commander of the Union's Army of the Potomac, Mexican War veteran General George B. McClellan, worked to transform his inexperienced volunteers into a professional army. Moving cautiously, but hoping for a demonstration of the army's ability, McClellan sent General Charles P. Stone into Virginia. On October 21, 1861, at the Battle of Ball's Bluff near Leesburg, Colonel Edward Baker's Massachusetts troops met the Confederates. The Union forces fell apart when Baker was killed, precipitously fleeing back to the Potomac, where they came under fire from Confederate troops on the bluff above the river. This second defeat for the Union led to bitter public recrimination, a congressional inquiry, and the imprisonment of General Stone—a precedent that haunted Union officers, who often refused to make bold moves for fear of ending up like Stone, an imprisoned scapegoat. This extract from Holmes's diary describes the battle from his perspective, while giving a sense of the war's standards of medical care, which often aggravated injury and increased the death rate:

I was hit at 4½ P.M., the heavy firing having begun about an hour before, by the watch—I felt as if a horse had kicked me and went over—1st Sergt Smith grabbed me and lugged me to the rear a little way & opened my shirt and ecce! The two holes in my breasts & the bullet, which he gave me—George says he squeezed it from the right opening—Well—I remember the sickening feeling of water in my face—I was quite faint— and seeing poor Sergt Merchant lying near—shot through the head and covered with blood—and then the thinking begun . . . —Shot through the lungs? Let's see—and I spit—Yes—already the blood was in my mouth. . . . What should I do? Just then I remembered and felt in my waist coat pocket—Yes there it was—a little bottle of laudanum which I had brought along—But I won't take it yet; no, see a doctor first—It may not be as bad as it looks—At any rate wait till the pain begins.[3]

Holmes became one of the great legal scholars of his day, serving on the U.S. Supreme Court from 1902 to 1932. But the Civil War never left his thoughts. His military service formed the basis for his intellectual development, the slaughter he witnessed engendering a deep skepticism of human nature. Scholars generally hold that the Civil War hardened Holmes, toughening his attitude toward people and life. Yet underneath the surface gruffness lived a powerful emotional tie of fraternity borne of shared sacrifice. In his famous "The Soldier's Faith" speech, delivered on Memorial Day, 1884, to the Keene, New Hampshire, Grand Army of the Republic post, Holmes praised the sense of duty that had driven his generation to war: "Through our great good fortune, in our youth our hearts were touched with fire." The "brotherhood" he found in the Twentieth Massachusetts was among the most profound experiences of his life; he called on his listeners to never forget those young men who had been their brothers. Military service in time of war formed the "closest tie which is possible between men—a tie which suffering has made indissoluble for better, for worse."[4] Upon Holmes's death in 1935, his executors found in his safety deposit box two musket balls wrapped in paper. There was a note: "These were taken from my body in the Civil War."[5]

Leander Stillwell of Jersey County, Illinois, was just seventeen when the war started. Ignoring his father's objections, he felt it his duty to join the Union army, leaving a useful narrative of public sentiment at the war's start, the perspective of the new recruit, and a vivid description of the Battle of Shiloh. In addition to keeping a diary, Stillwell wrote home every week, and his parents kept the letters. Together these documents formed the basis for Stillwell's memoirs. In a short preface, he wrote, "This is simply the story of a common soldier who served in the army during the great war, and who faithfully tried to do his duty":

On our arrival [at Pittsburg Landing] we were assigned to the division of General B. M. Prentiss, and we at once marched out and went into camp. About half a mile from the landing the road forks, the main Corinth road goes to the right, past Shiloh church, the other goes to the left. These two roads come together again some miles out. General Prentiss' division was camped on this left-hand road at right angles to it. Our regiment went into camp almost on the extreme left of Prentiss' line. There was a brigade of [William T.] Sherman's division under General [David] Stuart still further to the left . . . and between the left of Prentiss' and General Stuart's camp there were no troops. I know that, for during the few days intervening between our arrival and the battle I roamed all through those woods on our left, between us and Stuart, hunting for wild onions and "turkey peas."

The camp of our regiment was about two miles from the landing. The tents were pitched in the woods, and there was a little field of about twenty acres in our front. . . . [On] April 6, 1862, . . . we had "turned out" about sunup, answered to roll-call, and had cooked and eaten our breakfast. We had then gone to work, preparing for the regular Sunday morning inspection, which would take place at nine o'clock. The boys were scattered around the company streets and in front of the company parade grounds, engaged in polishing and brightening their muskets, and brushing up and cleaning their shoes, jackets, trousers, and clothing generally. It was a most beautiful morning. The sun was shining brightly through the trees, and there was not a cloud in the sky. It really seemed like Sunday in the country at home. . . . I listened with delight to the plaintive, mournful tones of a turtle-dove in the woods close by, while on the dead limb of a tall tree right in the camp a woodpecker was sounding his "long roll" just as I had heard it beaten by his Northern brothers a thousand times on the trees in the Otter Creek bottom at home.

Suddenly, away off on the right, in the direction of Shiloh church, came a dull, heavy "Pum!" then another, and still another. Every man sprung to his feet as if struck by an electric shock, and we looked inquiringly into one another's faces. "What is that?" asked every one, but no one answered. Those heavy booms then came thicker and faster, and just a few seconds after we heard that first dull, ominous growl off to the southwest, came a low, sullen, continuous roar. There was no mistaking that sound. That was not a squad of pickets emptying their guns on being relieved from duty; it was the continuous roll of thousands of muskets, and told us that a battle was on.

. . . Then ensued a scene of desperate haste, the like of which I certainly had never seen before, nor ever saw again. I remember that in the midst of this terrible uproar and confusion, while the boys were buckling on their cartridge boxes, and before even the companies had been formed, a mounted staff officer came galloping wildly down the line from the right. He checked and whirled his horse sharply around right in our company street, the iron-bound hoofs of his steed crashing among the tin plates lying in a little pile where my mess had eaten its breakfast that morning. The horse was flecked with foam and its eyes and nostrils were red as blood. The officer cast one hurried glance around him, and exclaimed: "My God! this regiment not in line yet! They have been fighting on the right over an hour!" And wheeling his horse, he disappeared in the direction of the colonel's tent.

I know now that history says the battle began about 4:30 that morning; that it was brought on by a reconnoitering party sent out early that morning by General Prentiss; that General Sherman's division on the right was early advised of the approach of the Rebel army, and got ready to meet them in ample time. I have read these things in books and am not disputing them, but am simply telling the story of an enlisted man on the left of Prentiss' line as to what he saw and knew of the condition of things at about seven o'clock that morning.

Well, the companies were formed. . . . The command was given: "Load at will; load!" . . . All this time the roar on the right was getting nearer and louder. Our old colonel rode up close to us, opposite the center of the regimental line, and called out, "Attention, battalion!" We fixed our eyes on him to hear what was coming. . . . "Gentlemen," said he, in a voice that every man in the regiment heard, "remember your State, and do your duty today like brave men."

And there we stood, in the edge of the woods, so still, waiting for the storm to break on us. I know mighty well what I was thinking about then. . . . I am not ashamed to say now that I would willingly have given a general quit-claim deed for every jot and tittle of military glory falling to me, past, present, and to come, if I only could have been miraculously and instantaneously set down in the yard of that peaceful little home, a thousand miles away from the haunts of fighting men.

. . . After the battle of Shiloh, it fell to my lot to play my humble part in several other fierce conflicts of arms, but Shiloh was my maiden fight. It was there I first saw a gun fired in anger, heard the whistle of a bullet, or saw a man die a violent death, and my experiences, thoughts, impressions, and sensations on that bloody Sunday will abide with me as long as I live.[6]

Stillwell saw action at Corinth, Vicksburg, and Mufreesboro, rising to the rank of first lieutenant and serving until the end of the war. In 1866, he enrolled in the Albany Law School in New York, then moved to Kansas, where he served as a judge from 1883 until 1907.

In the first two years of the Civil War, young men enlisted for a variety of reasons, though it seems fair to say that most probably followed the same route as did Leander Stillwell.[7] Adherence to a specific cause, rather than a general notion of patriotism, drove Chauncey H. Cooke. Born in Columbus, Ohio, in 1846, Cooke moved with his family to Wisconsin in 1856. His father Samuel, a farmer, was an ardent abolitionist, a belief that he passed on to his son, who enlisted in the Twenty-fifth Wisconsin Infantry in September 1862, at the age of sixteen. Cooke fought in order to put an end to slavery, and his letters indicate how that commitment sustained him at the siege of Vicksburg. During his service, Cooke discovered his own country, seeing the United States through fresh eyes and wondering at the strange class and racial structure of the South:

Haines Bluff, June 8, 1863. 25th Wis. Vol.

Dear Father And Mother: . . . While we lay at Satartia the boys went wild raiding and foraging the country for anything they could eat or wear or destroy, and it was all right, for every white man and woman was ready to shoot or poison us. The negroes were our only friends, and they kept us posted on what the whites were doing and saying. Their masters told their slaves that the Yankees had horns, that they eat nigger babies, and that they lived in the North in houses built of snow and ice, and that the Yankee soldiers were fighting to take the niggers back north where they would freeze to death. It is a fright what stories the whites tell their slaves. The younger ones know better and laugh when they speak of it, but some of the real black ones just from Africa look nervous and scared when the boys [Union troops] crowd around them to tease and play tricks on them. They seem to know what the boys want. They bring in chickens, turkeys, eggs, molasses, sugar corn pones, smoked meat, and honey. The boys don't treat them right. They cheat them out of a lot and their excuse is they stole the stuff from their white masters. The poor black creatures never get mad but just smile and say nothing.

The day before we left Satartia some of our boys raided a big plantation, took everything in sight, and came into camp with a mule team and wagon loaded with a fancy piano. They put the piano on board a steamboat and blindfolding the mules, which were wild, turned them loose in camp. It was a crazy thing to do. There was some bee hives in the wagon full of honey and bees. The mules ran over some tents nearly killing a lot of soldiers and scattering bees and boxes along the way. It was fun all right for some of the boys got badly stung. . . .

Your son, Chauncey.

Snyder's Bluff, Miss. Hd. Quarters 25th. Wis. Vol. Inft.

Dear Father: Since my last letter we have moved our position to within eight miles of Vicksburg. Yesterday eleven regiments of [Ambrose] Burnside's corps landed. The old fellow himself with his well-known side whiskers came also. His men think he is pretty near a god. The hills and valleys for miles and miles are literally white with tents, and the music of bands from morning till night is ringing in our ears. I think it would be safe to say there are not less than twenty-five thousand tents within a circumference of eight miles. Clouds of dust from moving troops fill the air in every direction. . . .

Rumor is still in the air that the Rebel General [Joseph E.] Johnston is maneuvering to cut his way through to help General [John C.] Pemberton in Vicksburg. . . . I am sure a hundred thousand rebels could not break our lines at this point. We have three lines of heavy fortifications with batteries every eighty rods. Several thousand spades are kept constantly busy strengthening the lines. Our regiment was out yesterday on spade duty. . . . One hundred negroes will shovel as much dirt as a thousand yankee soldiers, and sing plantation songs all the time. I went out a mile yesterday on the second line to see them work and hear them sing. Most of their songs are love songs, and it's always something about the cotton and the canefields.

Rules are mighty strict and getting stricter everyday. Our main work is to clean and polish up our guns, and to see that our cartridge and cap boxes are kept dry. We have inspection of arms every day at ten o'clock. Every gun is examined and woe to the soldier whose gun is not in order. We know not at what hour, day, or night the roll of the drum will call us into line of battle.

I noticed in a copy of the Alma Journal you sent me that the people of Gilmanton had been subscribing funds for the U. S. Sanitary commission. The object is a noble one and I am glad the Gilmanton folks have gone into their pockets to help it. . . . This sanitary commission is a soldier's home or stopping place, wherever a soldier happens to be, in any town in the north. He is given a bed and meals free of charge and medicine and care if he is sick. . . .

I am glad that sister D. secured a school. She don't write me so often any more. What's the matter with her? If the folks at home could know what happy fools it made of us to get letters, they would write more of them and longer ones. I have half a mind to confess that I have had the blues for a couple of days. I have had a touch of intermittent fever. Hundreds of the boys are under the care of the doctor for chills and fever. We are drinking water a little better than poison. . . . The cannonading about Vicksburg is fiercer than ever. Last night the doctor gave me some infernal stuff for my fever that kept me awake. It must have been midnight before I got to sleep. I lay with the flap of my tent thrown back watching the shells from a hundred mortars, making a fiery half-circle as rising like a flaming rocket, they circled and fell into the city; then followed the explosion. How can those people sleep? I should think the people of that city would be perishing for sleep. There has not been an hour the three weeks past but shells have been bursting in every part of the city.

There was a bunch of about fifty rebs passed our camp yesterday taken at Vicksburg in a charge upon our works. . . . They tell awful tales of hunger and want of sleep in Vicksburg. It takes half the people all the time to put out the fires started by our shells and they have no flour and only horse and mule meat. . . .

A victory here and the surrender of Pemberton would open the Mississippi to the Gulf, then hurrah for Virginia and a healthier climate. . . . Love to all, Your son, Chauncey.

Snyder's Bluff, Miss., July 15, 1863. 7th Hd. Quarters 25th Vol.
Dear Brother: I have for many days thought of writing to you, first because I like you and second because you are not writing to me as often as you ought.

Since the surrender of Vicksburg on the fourth of this month there has been all sorts of rumors as to our future movements. The late battles won by the Army of the Potomac along with the victory over Pemberton here at Vicksburg somehow make us boys feel that the end of the war is near. O, if you could have seen and heard what I have these ten days past. Pemberton had nearly thirty thousand all surrendered to Grant on the 4th of this month. And they were glad to be prisoners and paroled to go to their homes. They cursed the war and called it a nigger war. I heard lots of them say, that they had never owned a nigger, that they were fooled and wished they had stayed at home. The bombardment of Vicksburg the night of the surrender was fearful. The clouds above the city looked blood-red as if they were all on fire. The thunder of the cannon for two or three nights and the rumor of surrender kept us awake. . . .

Some of the boys went down to the city of Vicksburg today. They said it was a pretty nice place, but it was badly shot up. Nearly half the town had been burned and the streets were torn up by our shells. . . . The darkies were filling up the town and grinning and showing their white teeth at every corner. Grey headed niggers and pretty quadroons begged the soldiers for money and blessed Abraham Lincoln for sending them south to make them free. Most of the boys hate the blacks and say hard things about them. I never can forget what father told me at Mr. Fuller's place. . . . He said if you ever get a chance, my boy, take good aim and shoot twice to free the black while shooting once for the Union.

I don't dare say anything like this to the boys, because they would laugh at me. But I have read enough to know that Phillips was right and Garrison was right and he [Cooke's father] thought as they did.[8] And I thought for days after going to La Crosse of the tears I saw in his eyes as he asked me always to remember the slave. . . .

I am writing this upon my back. The doctor gave me something for my fever that makes my head whirl. When he came to my tent this morning

I asked him if I was very sick. When I told him I was seventeen he said, "you ought to have been thrashed and kept at home two years longer." I told the doctor that he looked sick himself, and he admitted he was not feeling well. . . .
Your brother, Chauncey.

Snyder Bluff, Miss., July 19, 1863. 25th Regt. Wis. Vol. Inft.
Dear Sister:

I got your much valued letter containing your likeness nearly two weeks ago. . . . Just two weeks ago I was taken with the chills the day after the fall of Vicksburg. But I ain't alone, there are thousands along this river of death, that's what the boys have named the Yazoo, that are on their backs just like me.

The doctor has knocked the chills for the time at least, though they have made me weak. Dan Hadley and Bill Anderson look in on me once in a while to see that I want for nothing. All the other boys that are well have their patients too. Every fellow has his chum to wait on him. . . .

The black freedmen are coming in from the country by the thousand and going north to enlist. Several men from our regiment have offered to go as officers in the black regiments. They are doing with the slaves just what General [John C.] Fremont asked Lincoln to do at the beginning of the war. This is, set the blacks free and make soldiers of them. . . . Sorry I offended pretty Maggie Cass when I wrote her the black people were human beings and had souls. So she says she won't write me any more? Well unless I run against a rebel bullet or a hard dose of Yazoo fever I'll try and outlive her scorn. . . .
Your brother, Chauncey.

[Chauncey's regiment joined Sherman's army for the march into Georgia.]

May 10th, 1864. Dear Folks At Home: I send you my diary for three days of hard marching and rather hard fare.

May 6th. We had hardly time to swallow our coffee when we were ordered to fall in and march this morning before daylight. We marched out 12 miles thru the Chickamauga battle ground. For ten miles of the way the woods were scarred and limbed and many trees cut in two by solid shot. All the way little mounds showed where the boys fell and were buried. The battle ground is generally level and covered with timber. The heavy shot has mowed fearful paths on all sides thru the tree tops. Camped a little before sunset at Gordon's Mills. Am sitting with my feet in some spring water writing these notes. Several of the boys are with me bathing their blistered feet.

May 7th. Broke camp and began our march at sunrise thru a rough mountainous country, expecting the enemy to attack any minute. Cannonading is heard on our left. Met a lot of poor whites leaving the country. They are a wretched looking lot. They say we are the first Yanks they ever saw. The horses and cattle and pigs, like the people driving them, are the sorriest things I ever saw. The wagons were driven by the women, and the men, with long-barreled guns and five to ten children, all white haired, followed behind driving the cattle and a sheep or two and sometimes a pig. These were all mountain people, the clay eaters and best shots in the rebel army. Some of the boys asked them what they were fighting for, and they answered, "You Yanks want us to marry our daughters to the niggers." Poor ignorant devils.[9]

Cooke's Twenty-fifth Regiment took part in Sherman's campaign against Atlanta, and then the march to the sea. Cooke served until the war's end and was discharged due to illness on May 15, 1865. After the war he went to the University of Wisconsin and became a teacher in freedmen's schools in Texas, returning in the 1870s to Wisconsin, where he died in 1919.

Men on both sides may have fought for a number of reasons, but the cynical Warren Lee Goss felt it all came down to survival. Looking back on the war as "campaigning to no purpose," Goss recalled an encounter with one Confederate POW:

Near New Kent Court-House, a little settlement of two or three houses, we came upon several Confederate sick. One of them was full of fighting talk. I asked him what he was fighting for. He said he didn't know, except it be "not to get licked!" . . . I could not argue with a prisoner, and a sick man at that, on equal terms; so I replenished his canteen, and induced one of my comrades to give him some of his rations. From the number of interviews held at different times with our Confederate prisoners, I gathered the general impression that their private soldiers knew but very little about the causes of the war, but were fighting "not to get licked," which is so strong a feeling in human nature that I may say it will account for much hard fighting on both sides.[10]

## Prisoners of War

Americans took one another prisoner in record numbers in the Civil War, though neither side prepared adequately to care for these men. Both sides treated prisoners of war horribly, with prisons north and south turning into death camps. The death rate accelerated in 1864 as General Ulysses S. Grant put an end to prisoner exchanges as part of his policy of bleeding the Confederacy of its man-power. The Confederates, suffering a terrible food shortage, often allowed pris-oners to slowly starve to death. Given horrendously overcrowded conditions, only disease flourished in the prison camps. Of 194,000 Union soldiers held in Confederate camps, 36,400 died in captivity; 30,150 of the 220,000 Confeder-ates captured died in prison camps. The conditions sank beneath inhumane; one Union POW called his prison camp "the closest existence to hell on earth."[11] Alexander G. Downing of the Eleventh Iowa Volunteers felt completely justi-fied in destroying the property of slaveowners during Sherman's march to the sea, especially after his regiments stumbled upon a Confederate prison camp in Georgia:

> At Millen there was located one of those hell-holes, a rebel prison, where the rebels kept about thirteen hundred of our men as prisoners. They rushed them off on the train for Charleston, South Carolina, just before our army arrived. I never saw a feed-yard looking so filthy and forsaken as this pen. We burned everything here that a match would ignite.[12]

John L. Ransom of the Ninth Michigan Cavalry was taken prisoner in Ten-nessee in November 1863, at the age of twenty. Originally held at the Belle Isle prison camp outside Richmond, Ransom was sent to the notorious Anderson-ville prison in southern Georgia, where he battled to stay alive as disease swept through the camp. With almost no food, he was preyed upon by other Union prisoners and was threatened with being shot should he pass the "dead line":

> Dec. 3. [1863] Rumors of exchange to be effected soon. Rebels say we will all be exchanged before many days. It cannot be possible our government will allow us to remain here all winter. [Union] Gen. [Neal] Dow is still issuing clothing, but the rebels get more than our men do of it. Guards nearly all dressed in Yankee uniforms. In our mess we have established regulations, and any one not conforming with the rules is to be turned out of the tent. Must take plenty of exercise, keep clean, free as circum-stances will permit of vermin, drink no water until it has been boiled, which process purifies and makes it more healthy, are not to allow our-selves to get despondent, and must talk, laugh and make as light of our affairs as possible. Sure death for a person to give up and lose all ambition. Received a spoonful of salt to-day for the first time since I came here. . . .
> Jan. 26 [1864]—Ninety-two squads of prisoners confined on less than six acres of ground—one hundred in a squad, making nine thousand two hundred altogether. The lice are getting the upper hand of us. The ground is literally covered with them. Bean soup to-day and is made from the

following recipe, (don't know from what cook book, some new edition): Beans are very wormy and musty. Hard work finding a bean without from one to three bugs in it. They are put into a large caldron kettle of river water and boiled for a couple of hours. No seasoning, not even salt put into them. It is then taken out and brought inside. Six pails full for each squad about a pint per man, and not over a pint of beans in each bucket. The water is hardly colored and I could see clear through to the bottom and count every bean in the pail. The men drink it because it is warm. There is not enough strength or substance in it to do any good. . . .

Jan. 27. More prisoners came to day and say there is to be no general exchange during the war. . . . Very still among the men, owing to the bad news hardly a word spoken by anybody. . . . I this morning looked into a tent where there were seventeen men and started back frightened at the view inside. . . . They were all old prisoners nearly naked, very dirty and poor, some of them sick lying on the cold ground with nothing under or over them, and no fire; had just been talking over the prospect ahead and all looked the very picture of despair, with their hollow eyes, sunken cheeks and haggard expression. . . .

Andersonville, Ga., March 14—Arrived at our destination at last and a dismal hole it is, too. We got off the cars at two o'clock this morning in a cold rain, and were marched into our pen between a strong guard carrying lighted pitch pine knots to prevent our crawling off in the dark. I could hardly walk have been cramped up so long, and feel as if I was a hundred years old. . . . The rain has wet us to the skin and we are worn out and miserable. Nothing to eat to-day. . . .

April 12. . . . Insects of all descriptions making their appearance, such as lizards, a worm four or five inches long, fleas, maggots, &c. There is so much filth about the camp that it is terrible trying to live here. New prisoners are made sick the first hours of their arrival by the stench which pervades the prison. Old prisoners do not mind it so much, having become used to it. . . . Everybody sick, almost, with scurvy, an awful disease. . . . Hendryx has a very sore arm which troubles him much. Even he begins to look and feel bad. James Gordan . . . was killed to day by the guard. . . . [The creek] runs very near the dead line, and guards take the occasion to shoot parties who put their hands on the dead line in going across. Some also reach up under the dead line to get purer water, and are shot. Men seemingly reckless of their lives. New prisoners coming in and are shocked at the sights.

April 13. Jack Shannon, from Ann Arbor, died this morning. The raiders are the stronger party now, and do as they please; and we are in nearly as much danger now from our own men as from the rebels. Capt. Moseby, of my own hundred, figures conspicuously among the robberies, and is a terrible villain. During the night someone stole my jacket. . . . I do quite a business trading rations, making soup for the sick ones, taking in payment their raw food which they cannot eat. Get many a little snack by so doing.

April 14. At least twenty fights among our own men this forenoon. It beats all what a snarling crowd we are getting to be. The men are perfectly reckless, and had just as soon have their necks broken by fighting as anything else. . . . Van Tassel, a Pennsylvanian, is about to die. Many give me parting injunctions relative to their families, in case I should live through. Have half a dozen photographs of dead men's wives, with addresses on the back of them. Seems to be pretty generally conceded that if any get through, I will. Not a man here now is in good health. An utter impossibility to remain well. Signs of scurvy about my person. Still adhere to our sanitary rule. . . . Those who have stood it bravely begin to weaken. . . .

July 6. Boiling hot, camp reeking with filth, and no sanitary privileges; men dying off over a hundred and forty per day. . . . Mike Hoare is in good health; not so Jimmy Devers. Jimmy has now been a prisoner over a year, and poor boy, will probably die soon. Have more mementoes than I can carry, from those who have died, to be given to their friends at home. . . . Hope I shan't have to turn them over to some one else. . . .

July 8. Oh, how hot, and oh, how miserable. The news that six have been sentenced to be hanged is true, and one of them is Moseby. The camp is thoroughly under control of the police now, and it is a heavenly boon. Of course there is some stealing and robbery, but not as before. Swan of our mess, is sick with scurvy. I am gradually swelling up and growing weaker. But a few more pages in my diary. Over a hundred and fifty dying per day now, and twenty-six thousand in camp. Guards shoot now very often. Boys, as guards, are the most cruel. It is said that if they kill a Yankee, they are given a thirty days furlough. . . . The swamp now is fearful, water perfectly reeking with prison offal and poison. Still men drink it and die. . . . The place still gets worse. . . . The prison is a success as regards safety; no escape except by death, and very many take advantage of that way. . . . Have taken to building air castles of late, on being exchanged. Getting loony, I guess, same as all the rest.

July 9. Battese brought me some onions, and if they ain't good then no matter; also a sweet potato. One half the men here would get well if they only had something in the vegetable line to eat, or acids. Scurvy is about the most loathsome disease, and when dropsy takes hold with the scurvy, it is terrible. I have both diseases but keep them in check, and it only grows worse slowly. My legs are swollen, but the cords are not contracted much, and I can still walk very well. Our mess all keep clean, in fact are obliged to or else turned adrift. We want none of the dirty sort in our mess. . . . A guard told me to day that the Yanks were "gittin licked," and they didn't want us exchanged; just as soon we should die here as not; a Yank asked him if he knew what exchange meant; said he knew what shootin' meant, and as he began to swing around his old shooting iron we retreated in among the crowd. . . .

July 10. Have bought of a new prisoner quite a large . . . blank book so as to continue my diary. Although it's a tedious and tiresome task, am determined to keep it up. Don't know of another man in prison who is doing likewise. Wish I had the gift of description that I might describe this place. Know that I am not good at such things, and have more particularly kept track of the mess which was the Astor House Mess on Belle Isle, and is still called so here. Thought that Belle Isle was a very bad place, and used about the worst language I knew how to use in describing it, and so find myself at fault in depicting matters here as they are. At Belle Isle we had good water and plenty of it, and I believe it depends more upon water than food as regards health. We also had good pure air from up the James River. Here we have the very worst kind of water. Nothing can be worse or nastier than the stream drizzling its way through this camp. And for air to breathe, it is what arises from this foul place. On all four sides of us are high walls and tall trees, and there is apparently no wind or breeze to blow away the stench, and we are obliged to breathe and live in it. Dead bodies lay around all day in the broiling sun, by the dozen and even hundreds, and we must suffer and live in this atmosphere. It's too horrible for me to describe in fitting language. . . . Only those who are here will ever know what Andersonville is.[13]

Andersonville held 49,485 Union soldiers during the war, 13,000 of whom died. Its commandant, Henry Wirz, was the only Confederate convicted of war crimes, and was hanged in November 1865. After the war, Ransom returned to his home in Jackson, Michigan, where he slowly recovered and became a printer. He published his diary in 1881, shortly after he moved to Chicago, where he lived until his death in 1919.

John V. Hadley, who would later serve on the Indiana Supreme Court, was a young corporal when wounded at the Second Battle of Bull Run, earning a field promotion to lieutenant. Hadley's Seventh Indiana served at Chancellorsville, Gettysburg, and the Wilderness. Wounded and taken prisoner in the latter battle, Hadley was sent to a prison camp near Columbia, South Carolina, where he experienced hardships and cruelty similar to what Ransom had encountered at Andersonville:

The spring was within twenty feet of the dead-line, and it was no violation of orders to go to it at any time of the day or night. A German Captain, of the Forty-fifth New York, went to the spring for water at dusk on the seventeenth day of June, and was just beginning his return, when the guard nearest the point, without saying a word, or having a word said to him, deliberately shot him through the body, and he died an hour afterward.

A written appeal to the [Confederate] authorities to investigate the matter was answered, so it was reported, by promoting the homicide to be a sergeant, and giving him a thirty days' furlough. News of the reward was freely circulated among us—under pretense of the officer's having crossed the dead-line—as an example of reward to vigilant sentinels, and a caution to indiscreet prisoners. . . .

The Confederates . . . had a pack or two of these trained dogs at Columbia, which they tried to make as fierce and terrible as possible. They would keep them tied up through the day, and at evening bring them out upon the lawn before us, jumping and howling around their keeper for their food. It was these dogs that kept more prisoners within the guard-line than the six pieces of artillery trained on the camp; for if one should go out and the dogs find his trail, he was sure to be caught, and apt to be torn to pieces.

One night in October, a lieutenant escaped. He was out five days when a two-horse wagon came rattling over the stones toward the camp and drove over the deadline. Two guards got in, and two stood by and lifted out the body of the lieutenant. Life was still in it, but the gash in the side, and the horrible mangling of the throat and face, showed that it would soon depart. His captain brother, bending over him, piteously asked:

"Harry, what's the matter?"

Only a whisper answered: "Dogs. Don't tell mother how it was."

Next morning, soon after daylight, they carried the young man a hundred yards to the north of the camp and buried him.[14]

Hadley wrote that being a prisoner destroyed his sense of hope, and that for a long time he wished the bullet that wounded him had proved fatal. Haunted by his experiences as a prisoner of war, Ransom fell into a deep depression for years after the war. Abner Small of Maine, held for seven months by the Confederates at Libby prison in Richmond, described his time there as "that long night of systemic cruelty." More than thirty years after the war, those memories brought nightmares and remained "an ever-present horror, a thing of the past living in the present and reaching out into the future, to sting with its poison every hour of life until death brings welcome relief."[15]

## A Diversity of Soldiers

In the first flush of enthusiasm for the war, tens of thousands enlisted to preserve the Union. But as casualty lists lengthened, it became ever more difficult for the Union to find men, and tens of thousands of soldiers deserted in 1862.[16] It was obvious that on pay of just $13 per month, few men initially enlisted for economic reasons, although the government also offered bounties. As the steady carnage of war continued, the Confederacy turned to conscription in April 1862, followed by the Union in March 1863. The rich were able to exploit a huge loophole in the draft by paying a $300 commutation fee or buying a substitute. Prosperous young men like James Mellon, Jay Gould, and John D. Rockefeller found their patriotism enhanced by paying someone else to fight while they worked on creating their fortunes. Bribery and connections also worked to get one's name removed from conscription rolls. Jonathan Brough, the governor of Ohio, discreetly noted that conscription officials "are manifesting outward tokens of worldly means not derived from salaries." He estimated that half of them were taking bribes.[17]

Opposition to the draft was endemic. More than 200,000 conscripted men did not show up for duty, while another 160,000, or 31 percent of all Union draftees, received medical exemptions. Many seeking to avoid the draft headed out west, certain that the federal government would never find them in distant California. An estimated 90,000 draft evaders fled into Canada. Many of those drafted deserted as soon as possible, generally discovering support in their home communities. The antidraft riot in New York City, in July 1863, deservedly captures a great deal of attention, especially for its racist violence, but it was only the largest of dozens of similar instances. With resistance to the draft widespread and increasing, Congress abolished the commutation fee in July 1864, though the wealthy could still purchase a substitute.[18]

The United States benefited enormously from the presence of some four million slaves in the Confederacy. Not only were the Confederate states unable to call upon the military services of black adult males, but they also had to divert white forces to control these slaves. Thousands of slaves took part in what W.E.B. DuBois called "the general strike" against the Confederacy, leaving their plantations and heading to Union lines, depriving the South of their labor.[19] In addition, the Union garnered intelligence,[20] supplies, aid to lost and escaped soldiers, and the enlistment of thousands of African Americans.[21] Slaveowners had long claimed that they could rely on the loyalty of their slaves, yet when the opportunity came to express their choice, Southern African Americans voted with their feet, their assistance, and their lives for freedom. To no surprise, Southern racists continually expressed shock over what they saw as betrayal by the same people they had mistreated and tortured for generations.

From the first days of the war, African Americans had demonstrated their willingness to serve their country. When Abraham Lincoln called for volunteers in April 1861, blacks in Boston, Providence, New York, Philadelphia, and Washington organized units and announced their readiness to march.[22] In fact, the first volunteer to shed blood in the war was a runaway slave, Nicholas Biddle, who was attacked by a pro-Confederate mob as his working-class unit from Pennsylvania marched through Baltimore on April 18.[23] But at every turn, whites responded with hostility to black enthusiasm to serve. Local officials ordered them to cancel their musters, editors and officers mocked their efforts, and the president of the United States proclaimed them incapable of making good soldiers: "If we were to arm them, I fear that in a few weeks the arms would be in the hands of the rebels."[24]

Enslaved men and women served the United States even before the government would accept their aid. Slaves frequently warned Union soldiers of Confederate ambushes and served as guides.[25] P.H. Aylett, the Confederate district attorney for Richmond, sought to make an example of Tom Heath, "a freeman of color," who "acted as a guide to the enemy during the recent raid of General Kilpatrick and Colonel Dahlgren. . . . The crime with which he is charged is one of such frequent occurrence that an example should be made of Heath. It is a matter of notoriety in the sections of the Confederacy where raids are frequent that the guides of the enemy are nearly always free negroes and slaves."[26] Some contributions were even more material, as when the heroic Robert Smalls, a sailor and a slave, brought the steamer *Planter*, loaded with ammunition and artillery, out of Charleston harbor to the blockading federal fleet in 1862. As he came alongside the *Onward*, Smalls jauntily shouted to a surprised Captain [Edward] Nichols, "Good morning, sir! I've brought you some of the old United States guns, sir!" Smalls served with distinction during the war, eventually becoming captain of the *Planter* when its white commander deserted his post under enemy fire. After the war the free people of South Carolina elected Smalls to Congress.[27]

The attitude of Southern whites to the idea of African American soldiers was well expressed by Confederate General Howell Cobb. "You cannot make soldiers of slaves, nor slaves of soldiers," he insisted. "If slaves will make good soldiers our whole theory of slavery is wrong."[28] Among most Northern whites the variation of this view in the first year of war seems to have been, "if blacks make good soldiers, then our racist theories are wrong." Initially, white public opinion—as indicated by the words and actions of Congress, leading editors, and President Lincoln—firmly opposed the idea of black soldiers serving in the Union army. The response of slaves was well expressed by a Florida slave asked by a Union lieutenant about his willingness to serve: "Just put the guns into our hands, and you'll soon see that we not only know how to shoot, but who to shoot. My master wouldn't be worth much if I was a soldier."[29] Frederick Douglass, two of whose sons served in the army, understood full well the meaning of military service for all African Americans: "Once let the black man get upon his person the brass letters U.S., let him get an eagle on his button, and a musket on his shoulder, and bullets in his pocket; and there is no power on earth . . . which can deny that he has earned the right of citizenship in the United States."[30] Black soldiers gave an eloquent response to those who questioned their ability to fight at Port Hudson, Milliken's Bend, James Island, and Fort Wagner in 1863.[31]

As much as Lincoln tried to keep the Civil War a white man's war, the realities of the conflict soon overwhelmed his racial biases. By the end of 1862, the Union desperately needed any men they could get, and the government turned with reluctance to immigrants and African Americans. The Emancipation Proclamation is justly famous for taking the first step to the legal extinction of slavery in the United States, but is less well known for declaring that blacks would now "be received into the armed service of the United States"— just in the nick of time for the Union.[32] Some 200,000 blacks enlisted before the war ended, an estimated 80 percent of whom came from the South, while an estimated 70 percent of the African Americans of military age in the North served.[33]

White soldiers did not hesitate to express their sense of racial superiority and generally refused to serve with blacks, and there is some evidence that several thousand deserted rather than fight for emancipation. However, many grudgingly agreed with the logic of one Indiana sergeant who wrote that he would do "anything to beat the South," even accept black troops.[34] The government accommodated their racism by organizing segregated units, with black troops serving under white officers. Jefferson Davis responded to black troops by issuing his own proclamation ending the status of free blacks within the Confederacy and promising that captured black Union soldiers would be sold into slavery and their white officers executed for leading a slave rebellion.[35] Racists north and south battled strenuously against that arc of history that bends toward justice, as African Americans battled for their freedom.

Black troops first saw combat on May 27, 1863, at Port Hudson on the Mississippi, where the Louisiana Native Guards won the respect of a number of white soldiers with their bravery under fire. A white lieutenant described the operation and his change of heart:

My Co. was apparently brave. Yet they are mostly contrabands [runaway slaves], and I must say I entertained some fears as to their pluck. But I have now none—The moment the order was given, they entered upon its execution. Valiantly did the heroic descendants of Africa move forward

cool as if Marshaled for dress parade, under a most murderous fire from
the enemies guns, until we reached the main ditch which surrounds the
Fort. . . . In the charge we lost our Capt. and Colored sergeant, the latter
fell wrapped in the flag he had so gallantly borne. Alone we held our position until 12 o'clock when we were relieved.

At two o'clock P.M. we were again ordered to the front where we made
two separate charges each in the face of a heavy fire from the enemies Battery of seven guns—whose destructive fire would have confuse[d] and
almost disorganized the bravest troops. But these men did not swerve, or
show cowardice. I have been in several engagements, and I never before
beheld such coolness and daring—Their gallantry entitles them to a special praise. And I already observe, the sneers of others are being tempered
into eulogy.[36]

A few days later, Captain M.M. Miller of the Ninth Louisiana Colored
Regiment described the Confederate attack on Union positions at Milliken's
Bend north of Vicksburg in a letter to his wife back home in Illinois:

We were attacked here on June 7 [1863], about three o'clock in the morning, by a brigade of Texas troops, about two thousand five hundred in
number. We had about six hundred men to withstand them, five hundred
of them negroes. I commanded Company I, Ninth Louisiana. We went into
the fight with thirty-three men. I had sixteen killed, eleven badly wounded,
and four slightly. I was wounded slightly on the head, near the right eye,
with a bayonet, and had a bayonet run through my right hand, near the
forefinger; that will account for this miserable style of penmanship.

. . . I never felt more grieved and sick at heart, than when I saw how my
brave soldiers had been slaughtered,—one with six wounds, all the rest
with two or three, none less than two wounds. Two of my colored sergeants were killed; both brave, noble men, always prompt, vigilant, and
ready for the fray. I never more wish to hear the expression, "The niggers
won't fight." Come with me, a hundred yards from where I sit, and I can
show you the wounds that cover the bodies of sixteen as brave, loyal, and
patriotic soldiers as ever drew bead on a rebel. . . .

It was a horrible fight, the worst I was ever engaged in,—not even
excepting Shiloh. The enemy cried, "No quarter!" but some of them were
very glad to take it when made prisoners.

. . . My wound is not serious but troublesome. What few men I have
left seem to think much of me, because I stood up with them in the
fight. I can say for them that I never saw a braver company of men in
my life.[37]

Miller was not the only white officer to recalibrate his judgment of blacks based on their military service. A naval captain who had opposed the use of black troops found his views transformed by the experience of battle. When a uniformed black soldier was insulted by a fellow passenger on a street car, the captain stood up and addressed the soldier: "Come here, my good fellow! I've been fighting along side people of your color, and glad enough I was to have 'em by my side. Come and sit by me."[38] And for those African Americans who wore the uniform, military service granted a self-respect few had previously known.

The courage of the Fifty-fourth Massachusetts Regiment at James Island and Fort Wagner removed any doubts that black troops could perform as well as whites. Under their commander, Robert Gould Shaw, the Fifty-fourth repulsed a Confederate attack on James Island, south of Charleston, on July 16, 1863. Corporal James Henry Gooding realized that the attitudes of his white comrades had changed when "a regiment of white men gave us three cheers as we were passing them."[39] In a daring, and probably foolhardy, direct assault on the Confederate stronghold of Fort Wagner on Charleston harbor, the six hundred men of the Fifty-fourth suffered 40 percent casualties, including the death of Colonel Shaw. Sergeant William Carney, with wounds in his head, chest, leg, and arm, retrieved the flag and carried it back with the survivors, becoming the first of twenty-nine black soldiers to receive the Congressional Medal of Honor during the Civil War.[40]

As an indication of the increased reputation of black troops, Confederate troops occasionally demonstrated due respect. The African American journalist Thomas Morris Chester described a truce between Confederate and black Union troops: "Immediately in our front, an arrangement has been entered into, in which the enemy has agreed to discontinue firing on this part of the picket line. The rebels and our colored soldiers now converse together on apparently very friendly terms, and exchange such luxuries as apples, tobacco, and hard tack, by throwing them to each other."[41] But then there was Fort Pillow. On April 12, 1864, Confederate troops overwhelmed the Union garrison, which they outnumbered four to one, killing some two hundred black troops and their white commander, Major William Bradford, after they had surrendered. With twisted logic, General Nathan Bedford Forrest insisted that the slaughter of his prisoners should "demonstrate to the Northern people that negro soldiers cannot cope with Southerners." It is perhaps not surprising that Forrest went on to found the Ku Klux Klan.[42]

Many Confederate officers ordered their troops to take no black prisoners, and there were numerous reports of black troops executed after surrendering.[43] On many other occasions, Confederate soldiers refused to carry out such orders. General Edmund Kirby Smith, whose brother had died in the Mexican War, was outraged when he heard that his forces were taking black prisoners.

"I have been unofficially informed," he wrote General R. Taylor on June 13, 1863, "that some of your troops have captured negroes in arms. I hope this may not be so, and that your subordinates who may have been in command of capturing parties may have recognized the propriety of giving no quarter to armed negroes and their officers."[44] Even if they were taken prisoner, black troops were treated even more harshly than were white prisoners—35 percent of all black POWs died in Confederate prison camps, double the rate for white POWs. Of course, such policies, well known among Union troops, led black troops to fight with ferocity and to treat Confederate POWs with animosity. On a few occasions, shouting "Remember Fort Pillow," black soldiers killed surrendering rebels.[45]

By September 1864, Lincoln, too, had completely changed his mind as to the utility of black troops, though for entirely practical reasons: "Any different policy in regard to the colored man deprives us of his help, and this is more than we can bear. . . . This is not a question of sentiment or taste, but one of physical force, which may be measured and estimated as horse-power and steam-power are measured and estimated. Keep it, and you can save the Union. Throw it away, and the Union goes with it."[46] Many a common soldier agreed with the president. As an Iowa private wrote his wife, "they will stop Bullets as well as white people."[47]

Many black women bore an extra burden during the war, as they remained in slavery—and not just in the Confederate states—while their husbands served. In one of the many bitter ironies of the Civil War, many black soldiers had wives and families enslaved in the border states while they fought for freedom in the Union army.[48] Patsey Leach of Kentucky, whose husband had fled slavery to serve in the army and died in battle, described the conduct of her "master," Warren Wiley:

He [Wiley] knew of my husbands enlisting before I did but never said anything to me about it. From that time he treated me more cruelly than ever whipping me frequently without any cause and insulting me on every occasion. About three weeks after my husband enlisted a Company of Colored Soldiers passed our house and I was there in the garden and looked at them as they passed. My master had been watching me and when the soldiers had gone I went into the kitchen. My master followed me and Knocked me to the floor senseless saying as he did so, "You have been looking at them darned Nigger Soldiers[.]" When I recovered my senses he beat me with a cowhide[.]

When my husband was Killed my master whipped me severely saying my husband had gone into the army to fight against the white folks and he my master would let me know I was foolish to let my husband go[;] he would "take it out of my back," he would "Kill me by piecemeal" and he hoped "that the last one of the nigger soldiers would be Killed[.]" He whipped me twice after that using similar expressions[.] The last whipping he gave me he took me into the Kitchen tied my hands tore all my clothes off until I was entirely naked, bent me down, placed my head between his Knees, then whipped me most unmercifully until my back was lacerated all over, the blood oozing out in several places so that I could not wear my underclothes without their becoming saturated with blood. The marks are still visible on my back. On this and other occasions my master whipped me for no other cause than my husband having enlisted.

When Wiley threatened to whip her until she died, Leach took her baby child and fled, leaving her four older children behind. In March 1865, she appealed to the government, in whose cause her husband had died, for aid in retrieving her remaining children from Wiley. That same month Congress finally voted to free the wives and children of African American soldiers.[49]

Women constituted another group of Americans that, after initially being denied the right to serve their nation, found respect during the war. At the war's start, many men hoped to keep women out of the conflict for fear they would sully its masculinity. Many women sought to help by nursing, but even here there were men blocking their way. In August 1861, Frederick Law Olmsted wrote Henry Bellows, "Even the care of the sick & wounded in war is not a feminine business. It must have masculine discipline."[50] Olmsted and Bellows organized the U.S. Sanitary Commission and insured that it remained dominated by men, though women responded by organizing the New England Women's Auxiliary Association.[51] Hundreds of women, most famously Clara Barton, played an essential role in the war effort as government staff workers and nurses. Other women demanded an even more active position in the war.

There is a great deal of speculation about the number of women who served during the war by disguising themselves as men, but little more than anecdotal evidence.[52] Mostly only hints remain, such as these two passages from Pennsylvania muster rolls:

46th Pennsylvania, Company D: Charles D. Fuller, detected as being a female; discharged.

126th Pennsylvania, Company F: Sergeant Frank Mayne; deserted Aug. 24, 1862; subsequently killed in battle in another regiment, and discovered to be a woman; real name, Frances Day.[53]

While many of these women were discovered during the war, especially as a result of being wounded in battle, others preserved their secret, often known to only a few fellow soldiers. For instance, Sarah Rosetta Wakeman left her family's farm to serve with the 153rd New York Volunteers as Lyons Wakeman. She wrote her family regularly, and while several friends knew of her subterfuge, she was never exposed. Wakeman left home because she did not want to be a burden on her family. She hoped that after the war she could own a farm out in Wisconsin. Confident that she would make a good soldier, she asked her parents not to worry: "I don't want you to mourn about me for I can take care of my Self and I know my business as well as other folks know them for me. I will Dress as I am a mind to for all anyone else [cares], and if they don't let me Alone they will be sorry for it."[54]

Wakeman felt "tough as a bear" serving in the Union army, and had a good time being a soldier, making friends and taking pride in her abilities. She respected the men with whom she served and had only been bothered once, and she gave that fellow "three or four pretty good cracks," knocking him to the ground.[55] Wakeman proved herself in battle during General Nathaniel Banks's miscarried Red River campaign of 1864.[56] The 153rd performed brilliantly in the battles of Pleasant Hill and Monett's Bluff. Wakeman described the former battle in a letter to her family, sounding much like any other soldier:

> Our army made an advance up the river to pleasant hill about 40 miles. There we had a fight. The first day of the fight our army got whip[ped] and we had to retreat about ten miles. The next day the fight was renewed and the firing took place about eight o'Clock in the morning. There was a heavy Cannonading all day and a Sharp firing of infantry. . . . I had to face the enemy bullets with my regiment. I was under fire about four hours and laid on the field of battle all night. . . .
>
> I feel thankful to God that he spared my life and I pray to him that he will lead me safe through the field of battle and that I may return safe home.[57]

Unfortunately, Wakeman became ill during the retreat and died in a New Orleans hospital on June 19, 1864. Even in death her true identity remained hidden, as her tombstone in the Chalmette National Cemetery reads "Lyons Wakeman." But her family preserved her letters and service records, which finally came to light in the 1990s.

Another woman soldier, Sarah Emma Edmonds, had one of the most exceptional military careers. Born in New Brunswick, Canada, the teenage Edmonds fled her abusive father for Michigan in the 1850s. When the war began, she went to Washington, disguised herself as a man under the alias Frank Thompson, and on April 25, 1861, volunteered as a "field nurse" with the Second Michigan Volunteers, and aided wounded soldiers while under fire during the Battle of Bull Run.[58] Her true identity was known only to a childhood friend, Lieutenant James Vesey, and to the regimental chaplain. During the Peninsular campaign the chaplain recommended her services as a spy, and she went on eleven spy missions behind Confederate lines disguised as a black man and woman, a white Southern boy, and an Irish woman. Edmonds discovered that the Confederates' contempt for slaves often led to significant indiscretions, while the blacks themselves often saw through her disguise and aided her in numerous ways:

> Do my friends wish to know how I felt in such a position and in such a costume? I will tell them. I felt just as happy and as comfortable as it was possible for any one to be under similar circumstances. I am naturally fond of adventure, a little ambitious and a good deal romantic, and this together with my devotion to the Federal cause and determination to assist to the utmost of my ability in crushing the rebellion, made me forget the unpleasant items, and not only endure, but really enjoy, the privations connected with my perilous positions. Perhaps a spirit of adventure was important—but patriotism was the grand secret of my success. . . .
>
> [In 1862] I passed through the enemy's lines in company with nine contrabands [slaves], men, women, and children. . . . I had no difficulty whatever in getting along, for I, with several others, was ordered to head-quarters to cook rations enough, the rebels said, to last them until they reached Washington.
>
> The officers generally talked in low tones, but would sometimes become excited, forget that there were darkies around, and would speak their minds freely. When I had been there a few hours, I had obtained the very information which I had been sent for. I had heard the plan of the morrow discussed, the number of troops at several important points, and the number expected to arrive during the night; and this, too, from the lips of the commanding general and his staff. . . .

At the Battle of Antietam, Edmonds encountered another disguised woman soldier:

> In passing among the wounded after they had been carried from the field, my attention was attracted by the pale, sweet face of a youthful soldier who was severely wounded in the neck. The wound still bled profusely, and the boy was growing faint from loss of blood. I stooped down and asked him if there was anything he would like to have done for him. The soldier turned a pair of beautiful, clear, intelligent eyes upon me for a moment in an earnest gaze, and then, as if satisfied with the scrutiny, said

faintly: "Yes, yes; there is something to be done, and that quickly, for I am dying."

Something in the tone and voice made me look more closely at the face of the speaker, and that look satisfied me that my suspicion was well founded. . . . I administered a little brandy and water to strengthen the wounded boy, for he evidently wished to tell me something that was on his mind before he died. . . . "I can trust you, and will tell you a secret. I am not what I seem, but am a female. I enlisted from the purest motives, and have remained undiscovered and unsuspected. . . . I have performed the duties of a soldier faithfully, and am willing to die for the cause of truth and freedom. My trust is in God, and I die in peace. I wish you to bury me with your own hands, that none may know after my death that I am other than my appearance indicates."

. . . I remained with her until she died, which was about an hour. Then making a grave for her under the shadow of a mulberry tree near the battle-field, apart from all others, with the assistance of two of the boys who were detailed to bury the dead, I carried her remains to that lonely spot and gave her a soldiers burial, without coffin or shroud, only a blanket for a winding-sheet. There she sleeps in that beautiful forest.[59]

## Keeping the Faith

After the first year of war, veteran soldiers understood that commanders on both sides were intent on slaughter. "Our poppy cock generals kill men as Herod killed the innocents," wrote one Union soldier.[60] No battle so well represented this pointless killing of troops as Fredericksburg, in December 1862. General Ambrose Burnside sent the Army of the Potomac across the Rappahannock River under fire and then over open fields against entrenched Confederate positions on the heights west of town. Improved artillery and rifled muskets had changed the nature of warfare since the Mexican War, and the Union forces were mowed down in waves, taking more than twelve thousand casualties. After visiting the battlefield, Pennsylvania governor Andrew Curtin told President Lincoln, "Mr. President, it was not a battle, it was a butchery."[61]

Officers who sought to protect their men from the worst ravages of battle, such as General James B. McPherson, won the affection of their troops, while those thought to be particularly callous about their men's safety often became targeted by their own troops. Soldiers of the Sixth New Hampshire Regiment shot at their commander, General Thomas Williams, on several occasions. It is possible that Williams did not heed the warning, as he was killed by a gunshot at the Battle of Baton Rouge.[62] It is impossible to know how many officers were killed by their troops; but at least a few instances can be verified, as when a sergeant from an Illinois regiment murdered his captain and bluntly stated, "I killed him. The company wanted him killed. . . . I killed the son of a bitch and I was the only man in the company who had the heart to do it."[63]

Reading the letters and diaries from the Civil War leaves little doubt that what kept these soldiers going in the midst of such carnage was their camaraderie. How else can we explain the way soldiers on both sides stood their ground before the most terrible slaughter? They may have joined for many reasons—conviction that the cause was just, a sense of duty, a desire for glory, because family and neighbors had done so—but, as Oliver Wendell Holmes indicated, they quickly came to place their faith in one another. They supported and inspired one another, and often acted to avenge the loss of a close friend. Private Oliver Norton of Pennsylvania describes his feelings at Gaines' Mill when his two messmates are wounded:

Harrison's Landing, James River, Va., Saturday, July 26, 1862.

Dear Brother and Sister:—You ask me how I felt when the battle commenced, if I feared I should fall, etc. That is a very hard question to answer. In the fight at Gaines' Mill I had lain in the woods almost all day waiting for them before I saw a rebel. They had been shelling us all the time, and occasionally a shell would burst within a few feet of me and startle me a little, but we had so strong a position and felt so certain of driving the rebels off that I was anxious to have them come on. . . . "Come on," we thought, "we'll show you how freemen fight," but when they attacked us so unexpectedly in the rear, my feelings changed. Surprise at first and a wonder how they could get there, and then, when the truth flashed through my mind that they had broken through our lines, a feeling of shame and indignation against the men who would retreat before the enemy. Then, when the colonel was killed and Henry and Denny wounded, I felt some excited . . . a kind of desperation seized me. Scenes that would have unnerved me at other times had no effect. I snatched a gun from the hands of a man who was shot through the head, as he staggered and fell. At other times I would have been horror-struck and could not have moved, but then I jumped over dead men with as little feeling as I would over a log. The feeling that was uppermost in my mind was a desire to kill as many rebels as I could. The loss of comrades maddened me, the balls flew past me hissing in the air, they knocked my gun to splinters, but the closer they came they seemed to make me more insensible to fear. I had no time to think of anything but my duty to do all I could to drive back the enemy, and it was not duty that kept me there either, but a feeling that I had a chance then to help put down secession and a determi-

nation to do my best. My heart was in the fight, and I couldn't be anywhere else. I told you it was hard to describe one's feeling in a battle, and
it is. No one can ever know exactly till he has been through it.[64]

In camp the soldiers relieved the strain with cards, singing, storytelling, and
games of baseball.[65] Letters often make the connection between these familiar
events and the longing for the routines of home. The letters and diaries contain
humor, but are generally tinged with bitterness as the war continues. Abner
Small's account of a religious service by several chaplains in northern Virginia
during the spring of 1863 carries the hint of a smirk:

> They were eloquent in their appeals to patriotism, and pictured in glow-
> ing colors the glory that would crown the dead. . . . They besought us to
> stand firm, to be brave; God being our shield, we had nothing to fear.
>     Whoosh! Suddenly interrupting, there came a great rushing sound.
> Crash! A great crackling and bursting rent the air. The explosions of shells,
> the screams of horses, and the shouted commands of officers were almost
> drowned out by the yells and laughter of the men as the brave chaplains, . . .
> their coattails streaming in the wind, fled madly to the rear over stone
> wall and hedges and ditches, followed by gleefully shouted counsel: "Stand
> firm; put your trust in the Lord!"[66]

The camaraderie of service led soldiers to be very forgiving of one another
and accept even serious personal flaws. Even cowardice could cut both ways—
evoking anger and contempt when comrades lost their lives as a consequence of
battlefield terror, but also sympathy for the way fear could overtake anyone in
the noise and chaos of armed conflict. Robert Burdette of Illinois had mixed
feelings for a messmate who performed well in every military duty but battle.
He would march into combat with the rest, but once those around him began
to fall, he turned and fled. "This man was a coward," Burdette wrote, but "a
good coward." Burdette could not judge such a man, lest he be judged; he could
only ask, "Who are the cowards?":

> I remember a coward whom I knew in the army. A good coward. In all
> other respects, a good soldier. . . . A manly voice; an intelligent mind.
> A cheery comrade; rather quiet. Never shirked a duty in camp or on the
> march. Neat in his dress; excellent in drill. Gun and accouterments al-
> ways bright and clean. In scant-ration times, always ready to divide what
> was left in his haversack or canteen, taking the smaller portion himself.
> Vigilant on camp-guard, though I soon observed that he was never detailed

for picket duty, where a man may have to stand vedette—away out by himself, with his own responsibilities—a very lonely post of the highest importance.

This man was a coward.

He knew it. He was ashamed of it. He tried to overcome his cowardice. The regiment never went into battle that he didn't start in with his company. If his number brought him into the front rank, there he stood. He rammed down his cartridge with a look of resolution on that uncertain mouth, and he "fixed bayonets" with the air of a man who is going to reach somebody with it, in spite of the modern military axiom that "bayonets never cross." He lifted the hammer twice or thrice to be certain that the cap was good and fast on the nipple. He tightened his belt a hole or two, as a man who knows there is going to be hot work and no dinner-hour. He shook his canteen at his ear to be sure there was a good supply in case he was wounded. He made all the preparations of an experienced, "first-class fighting man" who intended to volunteer when a forlorn hope was called for some desperate duty, on which only picked men would be taken. . . .

And his comrades stood by him and helped him, for his reputation was known, his weakness and his good points. A sergeant fixed one eye exclusively on him. His nearest comrade touched elbows with a little ejaculation to "play the man." The captain paused behind him as he walked down the line and whispered to him. The lieutenant caught his eye and nodded encouragement. Unconsciously we all seemed to be leaning a little closer to him. Then the order translated the bugle with a shout, the flag fluttered and the line moved forward; a rain of shots told that our skirmishers had found them, and just as we were ready to dash forward like dogs of war the man nearest the coward stopped, choked, coughed up a stream of blood and fell sidewise.

And the coward ran away.

Broke from his file-closer who tried to stop him; tore loose from the corporal who clutched his arm; threw down his gun; dodged the sergeant who lunged fiercely at him with his bayonet; out-stepped the lieutenant who ran after him; ignored the wrathful shout and threatening revolver of the colonel, and was safely gone. That was as far as ever we could see him. Back to the rear he raced. Past the supporting lines; back into the ruck and rabble of other cowards and the demoralized horde of camp-followers that make the rear of the fighting line a pandemonium of fear and misrule and confusion, despite the good soldiers held there on duty. He ran away.

Sometimes shame kept him away from the regiment for a day or two, or even three. But he always came back with a wild excuse for his disappearance which we all knew, himself included, was a foolish lie, and resumed his duties.

In the first instance he suffered for it. The regiment resented it. His company felt disgraced. But insensibly our attitude toward him changed. Cowardice is one of the most serious offenses in the army. It is punishable by extreme measures—even death. I have seen men "drummed out" of the service for it. But no charges were ever brought against this man. He was never punished. And being a young soldier when I joined the regiment, I used to wonder why. . . . I now wonder if the man was a coward, after all!

For the cowards all ran away before the battle, when they didn't have to run. . . . They stayed away. They played sick the day before. They fell out of the marching ranks when we began to double quick. They stopped at the fence when the regiment suddenly deployed into line to tie up a shoe that was already so knotted they couldn't untie it. . . . There were scores of ways of keeping out of a battle without actually suffering the charge of cowardice. . . .

But this man went in every time. . . . A braver man, up to that point, than any of the rest of us. He started in, and he would have stayed through but for that awful smear and sickening smell of hot blood. . . . God never intended that man should kill anybody. . . .

The coward served through the war, and when the regiment marched home to welcome and honors, I think one of the bravest men that went with them was the coward. I know he was beaten in every fight he went into, but he went in. And he fought. And such fighting! Much we knew about it, we laughing, shouting, devil-may-care schoolboys playing with firearms!

What is a coward, anyhow? Cravens, and dastards, and poltroons, we know at sight. But who are the cowards? And how do we distinguish them from the heroes? How does God tell?[67]

Burdette clearly understood that war evoked different qualities in those who served, and that generalizations lay with those sitting quietly at home, reading the newspapers. The Civil War soldier was surrounded by mayhem and death. Some came to accept and live with it, while others became overwhelmed by the burden; some men saw only enemies on the other side, while many arrived at a deep empathy for those who had fallen due to their sense of duty. David L. Thompson of the Ninth New York Regiment walked the Antietam battlefield in the evening following the carnage:

All around lay the . . . dead—undersized men mostly . . . with sallow, hatchet faces, and clad in "butternut" [the Confederate uniform]. . . . As I looked down on the poor, pinched faces, worn with marching and scant fare, all enmity dried out. There was no "secession" in those rigid forms, nor in those fixed eyes staring blankly at the sky. Clearly it was not "their war." . . . Darkness came on rapidly, and it grew very chilly. As little could be done at that hour in the way of burial, we unrolled the blankets of the dead, spread them over the bodies, and then sat down in line, munching a little on our cooked rations in lieu of supper, and listening to the firing, which was kept up on the right, persistently. . . . Drawing our blankets over us, we went to sleep, lying upon our arms in line as we had stood, living Yankee and dead Confederate side by side, and undistinguishable.[68]

Late in the war another New Yorker, Rice Bull, described how he came upon "fifteen unburied Confederate soldiers lying where they had fallen. It was not a pleasant sight to me, even though these men had been our enemies. I thought when I saw them, of the sorrow and grief there would be in fifteen homes somewhere; and for what had these young lives been sacrificed?"[69]

## Coming Home

For most of the country, the war had served its awful and glorious purpose: to preserve the United States as the land of freedom. While civilians had made many sacrifices for the war effort, the soldiers paid the heaviest price of all, with many scores of thousands killed, wounded, and maimed. On March 4, 1865, Abraham Lincoln ended his Second Inaugural Address with a call for the nation to help those who had made the victory possible: "With malice toward none, with charity for all, with firmness in the right as God gives us to see the right, let us strive on to finish the work we are in, to bind up the nation's wounds, to care for him who shall have borne the battle and for his widow and his orphan, to do all which may achieve and cherish a just and lasting peace among ourselves and with all nations."[70] Many Republicans seconded his call for aid for the Union's veterans.

In the war's immediate aftermath, especially following the dreadful and pointless assassination of President Lincoln in April 1865, public acclaim for the returning soldiers came from all directions and both political parties. The parade of Union troops through the streets of Washington, which lasted two days as nearly 200,000 men received public acclaim, passed a banner reading, "The only national debt we can never pay is the debt we owe the victorious Union soldiers."[71] The *New York Herald* made the praise global: "From one end of the world to the other, the people thank our soldiers for having conquered in the people's cause. . . . Their remaining years may be passed in quiet usefulness at their homes."[72]

Walt Whitman, who had experienced the effects of war firsthand, must have captured the feelings of many soldiers when he wrote, "The real war will never get in the books. The actual soldier of 1862–65, North and South, with all his ways, his incredible dauntlessness, habits, practices, tastes, language, his fierce friendship, his appetite, rankness, his superb strength and animality, lawless gait, and a hundred unnamed lights and shades of camp, I say, will never be written—perhaps must not and should not be."[73] But then, to Whitman the soldiers "were of more significance even than the political interests involved" in the war, which had turned the nation into "one vast central hospital." The soldiers, in their willingness to sacrifice for a higher good, were the spirit of the nation.[74]

Union soldiers certainly had every expectation of generosity from the government they had saved, and at first the nation seemed to deliver: on average they received $250 upon being mustered out of service. It was a notable sum in 1865, but only a down payment on what veterans expected, and as the hundreds of thousands of soldiers north and south returned home, they found limited opportunities. By the end of 1865, one million Union veterans had returned to civilian society, tens of thousands of whom could find no employment, especially those who had been seriously wounded. Within a few months of the war's end, newspapers ran ads by veterans seeking any kind of employment, and editorials reminding the unemployed and homeless veterans that their poverty was their own fault. At a reception honoring returning veterans in Chicago, Illinois governor and former major general Richard J. Oglesby warned that they could not expect charity—"You must not expect to be taken and wrapped up in a gay cloak and put upon beds of down, and soup given to you in a silver spoon"—but needed to go get work. Many Chicago businessmen thought the claims of veterans grossly exaggerated, as they had spent most of the war "loafing" around their camps.[75] New York's governor Reuben E. Fenton was more generous, calling for charities to help the homeless veterans who "are numbered by the thousands, and are altogether beyond the power of Executive and Legislative Relief." But though he said, "Their needs cannot be postponed," he had made clear that the veterans could expect no help from the government.[76]

With government officials insisting they could do nothing, and charities good for little more than a bowl of soup, veterans took action. For the first time since the Society of the Cincinnati after the Civil War, advocates for veterans' rights, primarily veterans themselves, spoke out in favor of more public support. A major issue was the building of a Soldiers' and Sailors' Home in Philadelphia, an effort headed by General George G. Meade, the victor at Gettysburg. The government, as Meade regularly charged, was doing nothing to care for those wounded in the war. He faced vigorous opposition from many public officials, such as Massachusetts Governor Alexander H. Bullock, who echoed sentiments heard after every previous American war: the public opposed "adding another to our large permanent institutions, on the twofold ground that it would tend to pauperize the soldier, and that the money which should be expended for his benefit would be absorbed by the necessary salaries and incidentals of a great establishment." He also insisted that the wounded veterans themselves pre-ferred to be cared for by their families.[77] Opponents of a facility for wounded veterans followed Bullock in arguing that the government did not care for the wounded for their own good, for care would make them dependent. As the president of the Sanitary Commission, the Reverend Henry Bellows proclaimed that caring for wounded veterans would undermine "self-respect, self-support, and the true American pride of personal independence."[78] The Sanitary Com-mission pretended to care for veterans while insisting on three fundamental principles: no "outside interference with natural laws and self-help"; families should care for veterans; and veterans should get jobs.[79]

As in the past, veterans ran up against the twin barriers of parsimony and ideology. The government offered those who lost a leg $75 and $50 for an arm; if he preferred, the veteran could receive an artificial limb instead of money. Most took the money.[80] Despite the unprecedented violence and hardship of the Civil War, the government would not change its basic attitude that veterans were supposed to look after themselves, no matter what price they paid for serv-ing the nation. As the years passed, veterans found themselves persistently ig-nored and often hated. In popular perception, veterans became criminals. It was certainly the case that the growth in the prison population after the war was linked to the great number of homeless veterans. In 1866, 215 of the 327 prisoners in the Charlestown, Massachusetts, prison were Union veterans. The prison's warden was sympathetic to their plight: "they are young men who en-tered the service before they had learned a trade, and before their principles were firmly fixed; and on their discharge they were unable to find employment, or had learned the vices of the camp, and so fell readily into crime." Studies in Michigan, Ohio, and Kansas found that two-thirds to three-quarters of their prison populations were veterans.[81]

Once more, as it had after the Revolution, the public resented their return-ing soldiers.[82] Veterans repeatedly noted a complete vacuum of recognition for their service. One veteran said, "I would have felt better to have met at least one person who would have given me a hearty handshake and said he was glad to see me home, safe from the war. It almost seemed, sometimes, as if I had been away only a day or two, and had just taken up where I had left off."[83] Deemed unstable and prone to violence, veterans faced employer bias. *The Soldier's Friend* advised veterans to not mention their military service when seeking work: "There is no disguising it boys; the people are afraid of us!"[84] George Bliss, a Rhode Island veteran, complained, "When peace came and our services were no longer necessary, we found not only the offices were filled by those who remained at home, but also that an old soldier was looked upon with some suspicion. Many thought that a soldier's life was evil."[85]

Civilian contempt reached its nexus in the tramp scare of 1877, when a hysterical terror of rampaging homeless veterans swept the nation. The Civil War left the country, *Scribner's Monthly* argued, with thousands of veterans cut "loose from remunerative work, and they have become rovers, nominally looking for employment, but really looking for life without it." The experience of war followed by unemployment destroyed their character, as they lost their self-respect and "their sense of manhood and of shame, and have imbibed the incurable disease of mendicancy." Sadly, these veterans were now beyond help, overtaken by "a hopelessly demoralizing mental disease," which led them to threaten the nation's peace and security. Government action was called for, but to suppress, rather than aid, these dangerous veterans.[86]

For the first time, drug addiction emerged as a problem among veterans. Opiates became widely available as painkillers during the Civil War, with the U.S. Army alone issuing nearly ten million opium pills. Army surgeon Joseph J. Woodward estimated in 1879 that 45,000 veterans were addicted to opiates. Though rarely discussed in public, the few references in print indicate that veterans were blamed for contracting "the soldier's disease."[87] Here, as with poverty, the veterans themselves were seen as bearing responsibility for their problems. Just a few months after the war ended, *Leslie's Illustrated Weekly* reported on the inability of returning soldiers to find employment, often as a result of "the hard but truthful fact that there is a prejudice in the minds of employers against the returned soldiers." Nonetheless, all difficulties encountered by the veteran were ultimately his own fault: "He has, as a soldier, been pleased to encourage a belief in his recklessness. He has felt somewhat proud to hear tales of his whisky-drinking abilities and foraging operations, in which the laws . . . are set at utter defiance. They have encouraged in the minds of citizens the belief that the army has acted as a school of demoralization and they are suffering the results."[88] A quarter century later *The Nation* would repeat this logic, arguing that veteran benefits damaged the soldiers' "reputation for self-sacrificing devotion."[89] William M. Sloan dismissed pensions as "socialism," and thought veterans "should be content with the honor, which pales before no other, of having saved their country in the hour of their greatest need." With such "hard-earned laurels" to their benefit, the veteran should give no thought to money or government-funded medical benefits.[90]

Opponents of government aid to veterans may have had cause for concern because, unlike after previous wars, Civil War veterans refused to accept public indifference. The movement for a veteran advocacy group began in New York City in August 1865, with the creation of the United States Soldiers and Sailors Protective Society. Veterans told the press that they just wanted to return to productive civilian lives, but that they found their path blocked by biases. The following year, Dr. Benjamin Stephenson, a veteran from Decatur, Illinois, formed the Grand Army of the Republic (GAR), which would transform the treatment of veterans. Stephenson perceived that the only way to attain adequate care for those who had saved the Union was political activism. America's first truly effective lobbying organization, the GAR aimed to insure that no politician opposed to veterans' benefits could hope to get elected—at least in the North.[91] The GAR tied its fortunes to the Republican Party and quickly spread its influence across the Midwest and Northeast, co-opting local veterans groups, including the Soldiers and Sailors Protective Society. Many people feared the very concept of a "veterans vote," of a single-interest group such as the GAR, and numerous contemporaries advised that a little gratitude on the part of the public toward their returning soldiers would prevent its spread. The Massachusetts Board of State Charities warned that if local communities did not step forward to help the wounded and unemployed veteran, they would soon see the government building expensive structures to serve those needs. But Congress, legislatures, and the general public resisted providing aid to veterans, insuring the rise of the GAR as the most powerful lobbying organization of the nineteenth century. As an indication of the GAR's power, in 1869 they successfully pressured Congress to create a national Memorial Day; but they followed up that victory with much more significant legislation, such as the Arrears Bill of 1879, which gave bounties to those who enlisted before the government had offered these bonuses and granted pensions to disabled veterans. President Rutherford B. Hayes, himself a veteran, signed it as a moral duty on the part of the nation.[92]

The GAR's membership grew from 61,000 out of the 1.5 million Union veterans in 1880 to 270,000 in 1885—though most posts were segregated.[93] A good example of their influence came with the reelection campaign of Democrat William Warner of Ohio in 1884. As chair of the House Committee on Pensions, Bounty, and Back Pay, Warner had resisted a number of proposals by the GAR. The head of the Pension Bureau, Colonel W.W. Dudley, who had lost a leg at Gettysburg, spent two months in Ohio campaigning against Warner. James Tanner, a power in the GAR, stated, "Every old soldier in that Congressional district owes it to the large number of his needy and suffering comrades in the country at large . . . to make an example of Warner and terminate his congressional career now." Warner credited the GAR for his defeat.[94] By the time Democrat Grover Cleveland, who was not a veteran, became president in 1885, the Pension Bureau had expended some $200 million dollars to 520,000 Union veterans, constituting the single largest item in the federal budget. Cleveland initially supported veterans aid, but in 1887 he vetoed the Dependent Pension Bill, which would have extended pensions to veterans disabled after the war's end. The GAR focused their anger on Cleveland, who lost a close election to Republican Benjamin Harrison in 1888. This power of the GAR frightened *The Nation*, which called it a "money-making machine" and charged, "For some years there has been a strong tendency on the part of many old soldiers to convert their supposed patriotism into a club for securing undeserved pensions."[95]

In 1890, Congress passed the most wide-reaching veterans act, the Dependent Pension Act, which granted benefits for all Union veterans and widows who could not earn a living, without regard to the source of injuries or length of service. *The Nation* again expressed the outrage of many who saw Union veterans as standing "in the public mind for a helpless and greedy sort of person, who says that he is not able to support himself, and whines that other people ought to do it for him." In contrast, Confederate veterans survive "by working hard and depending on themselves."[96] What *The Nation* did not mention was that many Confederate veterans had also organized in their interest, but their group, the Ku Klux Klan, largely sought to reverse the war's outcome. Otherwise, it was left to state governments to see to the needs of Confederate veterans, and even the most ardent Democratic white-supremacist states did little for those who had fought. By 1893, one million Union veterans received $150 million in pensions, compared to 26,538 Confederate veterans and widows who received a total of a little over $1million. In addition, there were seven national soldiers' homes with 14,193 inmates and twenty state homes with another 5,325 inmates. The GAR had proven its power and served as the model for future veterans' organizations.[97]

It is often difficult to give a true sense of the losses imposed by the Civil War, as well as the costs that would continue to weigh on the nation for generations to come. Unlike our current professional military, which tends to draw its personnel from the nation's poorer citizens, the soldiers and sailors of the Civil War came from all classes and included more than half of the eligible males on both sides of the Mason-Dixon Line. Soldiers fought in close formation in the face of withering fire, losing great numbers of their comrades and suffering more casualties in a single day than have been lost in several American wars. The technology of war was brutal: lead bullets, which travel at a relatively low velocity and lose their shape on impact, carried in clothing and dirt, causing infections and large wounds that usually resulted in massive bleeding. Bullets struck nearly a quarter of a million men during the Civil War, 14 percent of whom died.[98] Those not killed in battle faced the dangers of disease; in the first eighteen months of war, the Union lost 2 percent of its total force to fatal diseases, while the Confederacy lost 3.8 percent of its men.[99]

The Civil War may be called "America's Iliad," but its "charnel house" appears more accurate. In 1860, the Census Bureau found 31 million people living in the United States; 620,000 died in the Civil War, or 2 percent of the population—the equivalent percentage today would be 6 million deaths. A great number of Americans saw these dead, if not on the battlefield itself, then in the after-action photographs of Mathew Brady. After seeing an exhibit of Brady's photographs, the senior Oliver Wendell Holmes wrote that this new technology confronted even civilians with the nature of war, for viewing them is "like visiting the battle-field":

> Let him who wishes to know what war is look at this series of illustrations. These wrecks of manhood, thrown together in careless heaps or ranged in ghastly rows for burial, were alive but yesterday. How dear to their little circles far away, most of them!—how little cared for here by the tired party whose office it is to consign them to the earth! An officer may here and there be recognized; but for the rest,—if enemies, they will be counted, and that is all. "80 Rebels are buried in this hole" was one of the epitaphs we read and recorded. Many people would not look through this series. Many, having seen it and dreamed of its horrors, would lock it up in some secret drawer, that it might not thrill or revolt those whose soul sickens at such sights. The honest sunshine [of these photographs] gives us . . . some conception of what a repulsive, brutal, sickening, hideous thing it is, this dashing together of two frantic mobs to which we give the name of armies. The end to be attained justifies the means, we are willing to believe; but the sight of these pictures is a commentary on civilization such as a savage might well triumph to show its missionaries.[100]

# 5

# Indian Wars

From the Trail of Tears to Wounded Knee, the U.S. government pursued a policy of clearing the nation of its native inhabitants.[1] Far more brutal than other nineteenth-century wars, America's Indian wars were marked by racism, misunderstandings, and atrocities on both sides. And just as with the Civil War, both sides in these wars were American. Many soldiers who took part in these campaigns came to suspect the morality of their government's policies, though their opposition remained a private matter. And, perhaps because of the ambiguous morality of these wars, U.S. veterans received little public support or sympathy after they left the service—the cult of Custer aside—while Indian veterans were consigned to abysmal lives on reservations, except for the few who found employment with Buffalo Bill's Wild West Show. While warriors on both sides of the conflict felt contempt for their opponents, many came to perceive virtue in the other, especially when they acted contrary to their violent stereotypes.

Throughout the nineteenth century, the United States remained divided over the justice of Indian policy. "Indian fighters" like Andrew Jackson, William Henry Harrison, and Richard M. Johnson were elected to national office, while opponents of the mistreatment of the Native Americans formed the Whig Party and fought to protect Native rights. In the second half of the century, dissent with the wars of attrition against the Plains Indians became most evident with the widespread public interest in and support for the Nez Perce resistance to the theft of their homes, which seriously damaged troop morale and undermined the army's campaign. With the slaughter at Wounded Knee in 1890, the Indian wars came to an end amid sharp divisions within the military and serious questioning of the way in which vested interests had used the army for their own purposes.

## The Elusive Seminole and the Morality of War

The Seminole people fought three wars with the United States between 1817 and 1858, taking advantage of the difficult Florida terrain and environment to exhaust the army in a series of frustrating campaigns. The first war ended with Andrew Jackson declaring victory and leaving the Seminoles in possession of much of Florida. Unlike the other "Civilized Tribes"[2] to the north, the Seminoles would not give in to President Jackson's insistence on their removal to west of the Mississippi River—a policy that resulted in the horrendous Trail of Tears. Led by the brilliant guerrilla warrior Osceola, the Seminoles launched an effective resistance to U.S. authority that climaxed in the total defeat of Major Francis Dade's company in December 1835. In the ensuing seven years, the United States sent nearly every ranking officer in the army—as well as one civilian commander, Governor Richard K. Call—in an effort to find the formula that would defeat the Seminoles: Generals Duncan Clinch, Winfield Scott, Thomas S. Jesup, Zachary Taylor, Walker K. Armistead, and William J. Worth. Jesup resorted to trickery, arresting Osceola when the warrior came to parlay under a flag of truce and promising freedom to the runaway slaves fighting with the Seminoles, while Taylor tried to destroy his enemy in one decisive battle, resulting in the humiliation at Lake Okeechobee in December 1837. Worth turned to small-unit campaigns that targeted the Seminole's food supply—a strategy that had worked exceedingly well for the United States since General John Sullivan's campaign against the Iroquois in the Revolution. In 1842, Worth followed Jackson's example and declared the war over, though several hundred Seminoles remained in Florida.

In 1848, Lieutenant John T. Sprague of the Eighth Infantry Regiment wrote an account of his experiences fighting the Seminoles, in addition to a great many official documents, never intended for publication. Sprague had no affection for the "savages" he was assigned to pursue; yet even while venting his frustration with the elusive Seminoles, he felt equal anger for the white settlers he held responsible for provoking this unnecessary war when they "threatened and maltreated" the Seminoles. Nonetheless, Sprague expressed pride in having followed orders to the best of his abilities and doing his duty as a soldier:

Travellers complained of being intercepted on the highway, maltreated and robbed. Houses were said to have been forcibly opened, in the absence of the occupants, and provisions stolen. To put a stop to these proceedings, a company of mounted militia was ordered out on the 2d of April [1827], to scour the country, and bring the depredators to justice. The chiefs appealed to the agent for protection, denying unequivocally that their warriors had been guilty of overt acts. Those attributed to them they believed, as many respectable persons did, had been committed by vagrant whites, who under the cry of hostilities shielded themselves from punishment. . . .

[Sprague includes a journal by his friend C.R. Gates of the 8th Regiment, at that time commanded by Colonel William J. Worth, to demonstrate a typical campaign.]

Left Camp Simmons on the 3d December [1841], at ten o'clock, and marched eight miles—country very wet. . . .

December 4. Marched sixteen miles to a pine ridge ("Choa-la-p-ul-ka"); wet prairie most of the way; killed several snakes in the road. . . .

December 7. Started at ten o'clock, with five days' provisions. . . . Crossed the Oc-hol-wacoochee at eleven; water knee-deep, and boggy; . . . Captain Scriven's pack thrown into the water, lost his sugar and bread. Waited till one—Big Cypress close by—marched through water all the afternoon, and stopped at the only dry place in sight at half-past four. . . .

December 8. Lieutenant Gore, with sixteen men (two from each company being left), and ten of Captain Thornton's dragoons, to remain to guard the pass; Lieutenants Sheppard and Brown remain sick; we marched with all our packs at seven; waded a mile through cypress islands, . . . at two miles we came to a pine island, where [the Seminole leader] Waxie Hadjo's trail came in from the north—his old village is a mile off. We here took a drink (from a bottle the colonel sent us) to the success of the expedition. . . .

December 11. The guides and two Indians went round the camp this morning, and discovered the track of ten Indians going N. W. some days old. [George A.] McCall[3] with Sampson . . . have gone out to examine the country, and endeavor to find which direction the Indians have taken. . . . The country around has at one time been very dry, as we find huts in the Cypress where the water is now a foot deep. . . .

Captain McCall returned at four, P. M. . . . He went about fifteen miles altogether. . . . He found a trail of seven men and a woman, followed it some time and then they scattered—he followed one for two miles, and then lost it: in hunting for it, he came across a pumpkin field of about two acres, and four huts; he also found one other field—he says the trail was about a week old. . . . This afternoon we destroyed all the fields and huts except those we occupied, as we may want them again—I should judge there were about twenty-five acres destroyed. We killed two snakes, eight feet long—they are very abundant through the country. . . .

December 14. Captain Larned went with his company S. E. on a scout, and found a trail, on which he continued. Captain McKavitt went to Waxie Hadjo's town, and struck N. E. through the Cypress three or four miles, till he came to a prairie two or three miles long; found a large trail five or six days old, going south. . . .

December 20. Started from camp about seven; went westerly . . . till we came to the edge of the cypress; we here were halted by the firing of a musket on the left, shortly after, another, and another; it proved to be a flanker who got lost; he was not paying attention when we took a turn north; after waiting an hour or more, and hunting for him, he came up.

We then entered the swamp westerly, went a mile nearly, and came to a flag-pond, (very bad place to get through,) water waist-deep; after emerging from it a short distance, we came upon an Indian camp, with signs of the day before; rested a short time, and then pursued the trail . . . through swamp another mile and a half; there found evident signs of the Indians. The guides refused to go in front. We went half a mile further, when the cypress was more open on the trail. . . . Here the advance were fired upon by about twenty Indians, who were posted about forty yards in front and to the left, behind the cypress. Sergeant Down of my company was shot dead at the third shot; the ball hit just above his left collar-bone, and cut the artery; he was in the advanced guard. . . . Foster, of D company, 4th infantry, was shot also in the advance; was shot in his right arm, and the ball passed through the left; shot dead. The Indians ran, after the first fire, to the left and right; some companies pursued a short distance, and returned, as the thicket was very dense. I went back, and after finding the dead bodies, brought assistance and carried Down to camp. . . . A sentinel fired at night; the men turned out promptly; no cause of alarm discovered. . . .

February 1. Arrived at Fort Simmons about eleven. . . . The men got pretty blue on wine, porter, &c., (none better entitled to indulgence.) . . .

February 7. Got all aboard [to leave Fort Simmons] by daylight, . . . and reached Fort Harvie about seven. . . . Thus ended the Big Cypress campaign. . . . The only reward we ask is the ending of the Florida war.[4]

But the Seminole wars dragged on, chewing up men and their commanders, embittering many soldiers to what they, like Sprague and Gates, perceived to be a pointless conflict. Though Captain Ethan Allen Hitchcock led the party that discovered the remains of Dade's command, he did not respond as one might expect with calls for revenge. Rather, he condemned the government that had sent U.S. soldiers on such a foolish and unjust mission. Hitchcock's official report to General Edmund P. Gaines follows:

February 22, 1836. . . . [We] came upon the rear of his battle-ground about nine o'clock in the morning. . . . We first saw some broken and scattered boxes; then a cart, the two oxen of which were lying dead, as if they had fallen asleep, their yokes still on them; a little to the right, one or two horses were seen. We then came to a small enclosure, made by felling trees in such a manner as to form a triangular breastwork for defence. Within the triangle, along the north and west faces of it, were about thirty bodies, mostly mere skeletons, although much of the clothing was left upon them. These were lying, almost every one of them, in precisely the position they must have occupied during the fight—their heads next to the logs over which they had delivered their fire, and their bodies stretched with striking regularity parallel to each other. They had evidently been shot dead at their posts, and the Indians had not disturbed them, except by taking the scalps of most of them. Passing this little breastwork we found other bodies along the road, and by the side of the road, generally behind trees which had been resorted to for covers from the enemy's fire. Advancing about 200 yards further we found a cluster of bodies in the middle of the road. These were evidently the advanced guard, in the rear of which was the body of Major Dade, and to the right, that of Captain Fraser.

These were all doubtless shot down on the first fire of the Indians, except, perhaps, Captain Fraser, who must, however, have fallen very early in the fight. Those in the road and by the trees fell during the first attack. It was during a cessation of the fire that the little band still remaining, about thirty in number, threw up the triangular breastwork, which, from the haste with which it was constructed, was necessarily defective, and could not protect the men in the second attack.[5]

Hitchcock continued to serve, as he would later in the Mexican War, and to be troubled by what he saw as an immoral war. As the war persisted, becoming the longest since the Revolution, Hitchcock recorded a crisis of conscience that led him to consider leaving the service:

June 22 [1840]. . . . I saw the beginning of the Florida campaigns in 1836, and may see the end of them unless they see the end of me. The government is in the wrong, and this is the chief cause of the persevering opposition of the Indians, who have nobly defended their country against our attempt to enforce a fraudulent treaty. The natives used every means to avoid a war, but were forced into it by the tyranny of our government. . . .

The treaty of Payne's Landing was a fraud on the Indians: They never approved of it or signed it. They are right in defending their homes and we ought to let them alone. The country southward is poor for our purposes, but magnificent for the Indians—a fishing and hunting country without agricultural inducements. The climate is against us and is a paradise for them. The army has done all that it could. It has marched all over the upper part of Florida. It has burned all the towns and destroyed all the planted fields. Yet, though the Indians are broken up and scattered, they exist in large numbers, separated, but worse than ever. . . . The chief, Coocoochee, is in the vicinity. It is said that he hates the whites so bitterly that "he never hears them mentioned without gnashing his teeth."

. . . Our policy now is to ask the Indians in, assuring them that we are their very good friends (the evidence of which it is difficult to make them see), and finally to buy them, with about ten times the money that would have purchased the whole tribe at the beginning of the intercourse with them, before we had outraged them by injury, fraud, and oppression. We can do more with silver than with lead, and yet save silver in the end.[6]

In January 1843, the Seminoles awarded Hitchcock the name Pa-ga-chu-lee, "the Controlling Spirit," and many agreed to move west. However, in 1855, a third war broke out, as volunteers, rather than the U.S. Army, battled to remove the last Seminoles from Florida. During these years, Hitchcock's personal crisis continued. Through the Mexican War, he confined his deepest doubts to his diary until October 1855, when he finally resigned his commission in protest of his nation's policy of making war on the Indians rather than abiding by their treaty commitments. A few years later he would become friends with a rising Illinois politician, Abraham Lincoln, serving as his personal military advisor during the Civil War. Lincoln gave Hitchcock the opportunity to carry his ideals into practice when he assigned him the task of presiding over the board of officers that worked with Francis Lieber in preparing the military's *Instructions for the Government of Armies of the United States*— also known as General Order No. 100—in 1863. This military code, the first written in the United States, sought to make the soldier a moral agent, establishing standards of conduct that, it was hoped, would render war more humane. In addition to demanding the ethical treatment of civilian populations in time of war, the *Instructions* explicitly forbade the killing of prisoners and the use of torture.[7]

## Forgotten Wars

Though not forgotten by the Seminoles, Shoshones, Santee Sioux, Modocs, and many other Native peoples, numerous nineteenth-century wars have largely fallen out of popular historical consciousness. For instance, even while busily killing one another by the hundreds of thousands in the Civil War, the United States continued its battle against the Native Americans. Chauncey Cooke, whom we met in the previous chapter, enlisted to end slavery, but found himself immediately sent to put down the Santee Sioux uprising in Minnesota. Completely overshadowed by the Civil War, the Santee Sioux War of 1862 remains little known today despite its conclusion in the largest mass hanging in American history.[8]

The Eastern Sioux people, often known as the Dakotas, suffered through a string of treaty violations in the mid-nineteenth century that repeatedly reduced their home territories. By 1862, the Santee Sioux faced starvation and extermination. In August, after a fight with a white hunting party ended in the death of five whites, the Santees determined to drive the settlers from their lands. The ensuing war claimed hundreds of lives—the exact number remains unknown—and ended with the expulsion of the surviving Santees from Minnesota. On the day after Christmas 1862, the government hanged thirty-eight Santees. Chauncey Cooke was one of the thousands of soldiers sent to Minnesota to crush the Santee. Cooke had not signed up to kill Indians, and since he deemed the Santee rebellion justified, he was troubled by his involvement in what he saw as an unjust war:[9]

Sept. 21, 1862. . . . Dear Mother.— . . . We reached St. Paul and everybody was on the shore to greet us. They are mighty glad to have soldiers come as the Indians are gathering in big forces, and there may be bloody times. After waiting for orders we steamed on to Fort Snelling six miles above, and after landing in the bushes at the mouth of the Minnesota River, we climbed the high bluff where the Fort is located. They call this fort the American Gibraltar, if you can guess the meaning, steep wall nearly around it, and some big black cannons pointing in all directions.

I tell you those cannons have a wicked look. They are the first I have ever seen. . . . We . . . expect to start up the Minnesota and Mississippi Rivers to hunt Indians in a day or two. . . . There is a lot of buck Indians in the stone jail of the fort, who are guarded. They are some of the ringleaders, who incited the massacre. One of them looks just like One Eye, who staid around our place so much. Chauncey.

St. Cloud, Minn., Oct. 2, 1862. Co. G. 25th Regt.
Dear Parents: . . . No Indians yet. The old settlers tell us the buffaloes were here but a few years ago. I have seen some of their horns, sharp, black wicked things. Their trails can be seen on the prairies and along the river banks. I remember father saying the buffaloes and Indians would disappear about the same time. . . .

Oct. 20th, 1862. . . . Colonel [Henry H.] Sibley has recovered all the white prisoners and nearly 2,000 Indian prisoners. The question seems to be whether to let the Sioux remain or drive them from the homes of their ancestors into some western reservation. It seems likely that they will be driven away. Mother, this whole Indian question is wrong. . . . I am losing heart in this war against the Indians. When you come to think that all this beautiful country along the Minnesota River was bought for 2 cents an acre and that the government still owes them this pitiful sum for it, I am sorry for them. The boys tell me I am no better than an Indian when I talk about it, but I can't help it. God made this country and gave it to the Indians. After a while along comes Columbus with his three cockleshell boats, takes possession of all the continent in the name of the Almighty, Queen Isabella of Spain, and the Indians are treated as wild beasts. I often think as I have heard father say, "if this is the spirit of the present Christianity, God will damn it."

Your soldier boy, Chauncey

. . . Nov. 22— . . . There are some things in this war that make me feel that I am an infidel. Why does God crush all these poor Indians and give it all to the white because he has wealth? They owned this land from ocean to ocean by the best title on earth given by God himself and yet because we are stronger we drive them away from the homes of their fathers and the graves of their ancestors and claim that Christ is on our side.

I have been studying the *Dacota Friend* the woman left here in the hotel, and I believe there is something terribly wrong in this war. I know the Indians have been wronged and mistreated. But what can a fellow like me do? I could not eat any supper tonight and I dared not tell the boys what I was thinking about. I knew they would joke me and make fun of me. I feel that Obed Hilliard is nearer to me than any of the boys and yet he says the Indians ought to be shot. . . .

What was their crime? The white man had driven them from one reservation to another. They were weary and broken hearted and desperate at the broken promises of the government. And when they took up arms in desperation for their homes and the graves of their sires they are called savages and red devils. When we white people do the same things we are written down in history as heroes and patriots. Why this difference? I can't see into it. I often think of what father said of justice in the world. That . . . it is the winning party the lions of the earth, that write its history.[10]

Chauncey Cooke hit on one of the great truths: that the winners tend to write history. It is relatively easy to understand why so many Indian wars fall through history's cracks, as they appear to so many Americans—then and now—of no real significance. In recent years, historians have paid a lot more attention to these forgotten wars, but their works often attract only local interest. One such obscure conflict was the Modoc war, which straddled the border of Oregon and California in 1872 and 1873. The Modocs had fought white encroachments on their lands from 1852 through 1864 in a series of bloody encounters, before finally signing a treaty under which they joined the Klamath and Snake peoples on a new reservation. But the Modocs and Klamaths were traditional enemies, and the latter, larger group made life on the reservation miserable for the Modocs. In 1870, some three hundred Modocs followed Keintpoos—known as Captain Jack to the whites—in leaving the reservation and returning to their homes in the Lost River region. Oregon's superintendent of Indian affairs, Alfred B. Meacham, supported the Modocs and recommended to Washington that they be established on their own reservation. But local white settlers complained to the government and demanded that the Modocs be returned to the Klamath agency. In November 1872, Meacham's successor as superintendent, Thomas B. Odeneal, instructed Major Thomas Green, commander of forces at Fort Klamath, to move the Modocs back to the Klamath agency. Green did not expect resistance and sent Captain James Jackson with forty soldiers of the First Cavalry to round up the Modocs. Jackson surprised the Modocs where they were camped next to the Lost River on the morning of November 29. When Jackson ordered the Modocs disarmed, the Modocs began firing, inflicting heavy casualties on the cavalry. They then fled to the lava beds on the south shore of Tule Lake.

The Modocs continued their hit-and-run operations until July 1873, when, ground down by the relentless pursuit of Colonel Jefferson C. Davis, a veteran of Sherman's march to the sea, and out of food and ammunition, they finally surrendered. At that point the army discovered that just under sixty warriors had held off one thousand soldiers for more than six months. The Modoc leaders—Captain Jack, Boston Charley, Black Jim, and John Schonchin—were tried by a military court without benefit of legal counsel and executed at Fort Klamath. The government sent the remaining 155 Modocs to Oklahoma. Private Maurice Fitzgerald, a recent immigrant from Ireland, hated the Modocs, yet offered a surprisingly sympathetic summary of the war:

> Taking everything into consideration, it must be admitted that the government dealt harshly with this little band of brave, if treacherous, savages. They were fighting for what they deemed an inalienable right to retain possession of a locality that had belonged to them and their ancestors from time immemorial, and from which it was sought to forcibly eject them for no good cause, as they could see it.[11]

## War on the Plains

The best known of all Indian wars, and the one that forms the template for such conflicts in the public imagination, is the war against the Sioux in the mid-1870s. It was the responsibility of the U.S. Army to establish order in the West and secure the conquered territory for its new settlers. Any Native peoples who got in the way were moved onto Indian agencies—which became known as reservations in 1877—with force if necessary. The Plains Indians handed the army a few humiliating defeats, essentially forcing the United States to abandon much of the Overland Trail for several years during the Civil War. The army's task was often made more difficult by the violence of white civilians and militia units. During the period of greatest violence, the years of the Civil War and Reconstruction, groups of whites slaughtered Indians in great numbers. In 1861, the Colorado militia under Colonel John Chivington committed one of the most notorious atrocities, firing howitzers on the sleeping Cheyenne village at Sand Creek, which was under the protection of the U.S. Army. Chivington's men then went on a rampage, raping, murdering, and sexually mutilating the survivors, mostly women and children. The militia succeeded in killing nearly two hundred people and in starting a war with the Cheyenne; cheering Denver crowds welcomed the militia's display of body parts.[12]

But it was not just civilians and militia units who massacred Indians. In 1868, Colonel George Armstrong Custer led the Seventh Cavalry in a surprise attack on a village under the army's protection at the Washita in Oklahoma, killing Black Kettle, an ally of the whites, and one hundred others before hastily abandoning part of his command as he fled before a counterattack.[13]

The army's two top commanding officers, Generals Philip Sheridan and William Tecumseh Sherman, both explicitly framed their campaigns in terms of "exterminating" the Indians. It is probable that more women, children, and old people died than did Native warriors. Government sources attributed the death of 919 soldiers to the Natives between 1865 and 1898—with more than one-third of this total falling at the Fetterman Massacre in 1866 and Little Bighorn in 1876. It is impossible to know the number of Natives killed in these wars, though it certainly numbered in the thousands. It is important to recall, as many of these memoirs make clear, that many Natives fought with the army in these wars.[14]

The northern plains served as the center of military operations in these years. The Black Hills of the Dakota Territory belonged by treaty to the Sioux and Cheyenne—until rumors of gold began circulating in 1874. That year Custer led an expedition that discovered that there was indeed gold in these mountains. Conveniently, the federal government then determined that the Black Hills were not in fact Indian lands. Outraged at this violation of their sacred lands—and of their treaties with the United States—the Sioux and Cheyenne united under the leadership of the Unkpapa chief Sitting Bull and the Oglala warrior Crazy Horse to resist the whites. The government responded by sending much of the U.S. Army to put down this Indian uprising. One member of this campaign was John G. Bourke. Like many young men during the Civil War, this son of Irish immigrants lied about his age in order to enlist in the Fifteenth Pennsylvania Volunteer Cavalry. Congress awarded Private Bourke the Medal of Honor for his gallantry at the Battle of Stones River, Tennessee. When the war ended, General George H. Thomas nominated Bourke for West Point, an exceptional honor. From 1871 until his retirement from the military as a captain in 1886, Bourke served as aide-de-camp to Colonel and then Brigadier General George Crook, traveling extensively and taking part in most of the Indian wars of the period. Like Ethan Allen Hitchcock, Bourke used his time in the military to become a scholar of note and an expert on several Indian languages, including Apache. After he left the military, Bourke published several books and gained a reputation as a first-rate anthropologist, even earning praise from Sigmund Freud, who wrote the introduction to one of his books. His most popular book was *On the Border with Crook*, which he based on the diaries he kept while serving in the West. Bourke died in 1896 and was buried at Arlington National Cemetery. Below he describes the first stages of the campaign against Crazy Horse and Sitting Bull, which culminated in the Battle of the Rosebud:

The Sioux advanced boldly and in overwhelming force, covering the hills to the north, and seemingly confident that our command would prove an easy prey. In one word, the battle of the Rosebud was a trap. . . . I will restrict my observations to what I saw. . . . The Sioux and Cheyennes, the latter especially, were extremely bold and fierce, and showed a disposition to come up and have it out hand to hand; in all this they were gratified by our troops, both red and white, who were fully as anxious to meet them face to face and see which were the better men. At that part of the line the enemy were disconcerted at a very early hour by the deadly fire of the infantry with their long rifles. As the hostiles advanced at a full run, they saw nothing in their front, and . . . advanced in excellent style, yelling and whooping, and glad of the opportunity of wiping us off the face of the earth. When Cain's men and the detachments of the Second Cavalry which were lying down behind a low range of knolls rose up and delivered a withering fire at less than a hundred and fifty yards, the Sioux turned and fled. . . .

But, in their turn, they re-formed behind a low range not much over three hundred yards distant, and from that position kept up an annoying fire upon our men and horses. Becoming bolder, probably on account of re-enforcements, they again charged, this time upon a weak spot in our lines a little to Cain's left; this second advance was gallantly met by a countercharge of the Shoshones, who, under their chief "Luishaw," took the Sioux and Cheyennes in flank and scattered them before them. I went in with this charge, and was enabled to see how such things were conducted by the American savages, fighting according to their own notions. There was a headlong rush for about two hundred yards, which drove the enemy back in confusion; then was a sudden halt, and very many of the Shoshones jumped down from their ponies and began firing from the ground; the others who remained mounted threw themselves alongside of their horses' necks, so that there would be few good marks presented to the aim of the enemy. Then, in response to some signal or cry which, of course, I did not understand, we were off again . . . right into the midst of the hostiles, who had been halted by a steep hill directly in their front. Why we did not kill more of them than we did was because they were dressed so like our own Crows that even our Shoshones were afraid of mistakes, and in the confusion many of the Sioux and Cheyennes made their way down the face of the bluffs unharmed.

. . . [W]e were at one moment close enough to [the enemy] to hit them with clubs or "coup" sticks, and to inflict considerable damage, but not strong enough to keep them from getting away with their dead and wounded. A number of our own men were also hurt, some of them quite seriously. I may mention a young trumpeter—Elmer A. Snow, of Company M, Third Cavalry—who went in on the charge with the Shoshones, one of the few white men with them; he displayed noticeable gallantry, and was desperately wounded in both arms, which were crippled for life.[15]

The Battle of the Rosebud lasted six hours and, though Crook was left in possession of the field, effectively prevented him from joining up with Custer, thus setting the stage for the Battle of the Little Bighorn.[16] Colonel Custer and General Alfred Terry each led a column of troops converging on the Sioux and Cheyenne. Custer had strict orders to unite his forces with Terry's before moving against the Indians, but hoping for a repeat of his "victory" on the Washita, Custer left his artillery behind and led the Seventh Cavalry on a rapid march to the Little Bighorn River in Montana. On June 25, 1876, Custer stumbled into the largest concentration of native warriors known to have gathered on the plains, 1,500 men under the brilliant leadership of Crazy Horse. With the Washita serving as his model, Custer divided his force into three parts, sending Major Marcus Reno and Captain Frederick Benteen to attack the Indian camp along the river while he swung around the other side. But Crazy Horse outmaneuvered Custer, sweeping down on the Seventh Cavalry from the high ground and inflicting the worst single defeat suffered by the army in the Indian wars. Custer and his 225 men all lost their lives.

Captain Frederick Benteen commanded three companies in the Seventh Cavalry during the Little Bighorn campaign. Though from Virginia and the son of a slave-owning secessionist, Benteen enlisted in the Union army at the start of the Civil War and fought in several battles, including the siege of Vicksburg. Benteen joined the Seventh Cavalry in 1867, commanding Troop H until 1882, when he was promoted to major. After the Washita massacre, Benteen accused Custer of abandoning part of his command, resulting in the death of twenty soldiers. At the Little Bighorn, Benteen rode with Major Reno to attack the Indian village. He wrote his wife on July 4, 1876, with an account of the battle:

> I got my first sight of the Valley and river—and Reno's command in full flight for the bluffs to the side I was then on—Of course I joined them at once. . . . Custer sent him in there and promised to support him—after Reno started in, Custer with his five Co's instead of crossing the ford went to the right—around some high bluffs—with the intention—as is supposed—of striking the rear of the village . . . —and I can tell you 'twas an immense one. . . . After the Indians [attacked Custer] . . . it was a regular buffalo hunt for them and not a man escaped. We buried 203 of the bodies of Custer's command the 2d day after fight.
>
> . . . When I found Reno's command . . . Weir's Company was sent out to communicate with Custer, but it was driven back. We then showed our full force on the hills with Guidons flying, that Custer might see us—but we could see nothing of him, . . . but could see immense body of Indians coming to attack us from both sides of the river. We withdrew to a saucer like hill, putting our horses and packs in the bottom of saucer and threw all of our force dismounted around this corral. . . . The Indians amused themselves by shooting at our stock [and] men. . . . Well they pounded at us all of what was left of the 1st day and the whole of the 2d day—withdrawing their line with the withdrawal of their village, which was at dusk the 2d day.

Benteen concluded that had Custer followed General Terry's orders and waited to effect a juncture of their armies, they would have beaten the Indians, "But Custer disobeyed orders from the fact of not wanting any other command—or body to have a finger in the pie—and thereby lost his life."[17]

Custer's defeat stunned the military. John G. Bourke wrote that for Crook's men "the shock was so great that men and officers could hardly speak when the tale slowly circulated from lip to lip."[18] Many soldiers associated with Custer felt that "he sacrificed the Seventh Cavalry to ambition and wounded vanity." The commander of the Seventh Cavalry, Colonel Samuel Sturgis, whose son died with Custer, castigated his subordinate as "a very selfish man" who "was insanely ambitious for glory," while General Terry left no doubt that he would have court-martialed Custer had he survived.[19] And yet, the public responded very differently to the news of this military disaster, which reached the East Coast on July 4, 1876, just as the nation was celebrating its centennial. The press moved quickly to transform Custer into a martyr, and he received a hero's burial at West Point, where he had finished last in his class.

Since there were no survivors of Custer's immediate command, descriptions of the Battle of the Little Bighorn rely on native sources. Several years later, Hamlin Garland, a well-known novelist at the time, traveled west and interviewed Two Moon, a Cheyenne war chief who had been present at the Little Bighorn:

I went to water my horses at the creek, and washed them off with cool water, then took a swim myself. I came back to the camp afoot. When I got near my lodge, I looked up the Little Horn towards Sitting Bull's camp. I saw a great dust rising. It looked like a whirlwind. Soon Sioux horsemen came rushing into camp shouting, "Soldiers come! Plenty white soldiers."

I ran into my lodge and said to my brother-in-law, "Get your horses; the white man is coming. Everybody run for horses."

Outside, far up the valley, I heard a battle cry, *Hay-ay, hay-ay!* I heard shooting, too, this way [clapping his hands very fast]. . . . After I had caught my horse, a Sioux warrior came again and said, "Many soldiers are coming."

Then he said to the women, "Get out of the way, we are going to have hard fight."

I said, "All right, I am ready."

I got on my horse, and rode out into my camp. I called out to people all running about, "I am Two Moon, your chief. Don't run away. Stay here and fight. You must stay and fight the white soldiers. I shall stay even if I am to be killed."

I rode swiftly toward Sitting Bull's camp. There I saw the white soldiers fighting in a line [these were Major Reno's men]. Indians covered the flat. They began to drive the soldiers all mixed up—Sioux, then soldiers, then more Sioux, and all shooting. The air was full of smoke and dust. I saw the soldiers fall back and drop into the river-bed like buffalo fleeing. They had no time to look for a crossing. The Sioux chased them up the hill, where they met more soldiers in wagons, and then messengers came saying more soldiers were going to kill the women, and the Sioux turned back. Chief Gall was there fighting, Crazy Horse also.

I then rode toward my camp, and stopped squaws from carrying off lodges. While I was sitting on my horse I saw flags come up over the hill to the east like that [he raised his finger-tips]. Then the soldiers rose all at once, all on horses, like this [he put his fingers behind each other to indicate that Custer appeared marching in columns of fours]. They formed into three bunches [squadrons] with a little ways between. Then a bugle sounded, and they all got off [their] horses. . . .

Then the Sioux rode up the ridge on all sides, riding very fast. The Cheyennes went up the left way. Then the shooting was quick, quick. Pop—pop—pop very fast. Some of the soldiers were down on their knees, some standing. Officers all in front. The smoke was like a great cloud, and everywhere the Sioux went the dust rose like smoke. We circled all around him—swirling like water round a stone. We shoot, we ride fast, we shoot again. Soldiers drop, and horses fall on them. Soldiers in line drop, but one man rides up and down the line—all the time shouting. He rode a sorrel horse with white face and white fore-legs. I don't know who he was. He was a brave man.

Indians keep swirling round and round, and the soldiers killed only a few. Many soldiers fell. At last all horses killed but five. Once in a while some man would break out and run for the river, but he would fall. At last about a hundred men and five horsemen stood on the hill all bunched together. All along the bugler kept blowing his commands. He was very brave too. Then a chief was killed. I hear it was Long Hair [Custer], I don't know; and then five horsemen and the bunch of men, may be so forty, started toward the river. The man on the sorrel horse led them, shouting all the time. He wore a buckskin shirt, and had long black hair and mustache. He fought hard with a big knife. His men were all covered with white dust. I couldn't tell whether they were officers or not. One man all alone ran far down toward the river, then round up over the hill. I thought he was going to escape, but a Sioux fired and hit him in the head. He was the last man. He wore braid on his arms [a sergeant].

All the soldiers were now killed, and the bodies were stripped. After that no one could tell which were officers. The bodies were left where they fell. We had no dance that night. We were sorrowful. . . . There were thirty-nine Sioux and seven Cheyennes killed, and about a hundred wounded.[20]

The Sioux followed up Little Bighorn with a series of hit-and-run raids against the army, setting fire to the grass where their herds grazed and sniping at the soldiers. But in the months following the Battle at the Little Bighorn, the army moved relentlessly against the Sioux and Cheyenne, corralling them onto bleak reservations. When Crazy Horse surrendered the exhausted and starving remnants of his band, the Plains Indians had been effectively crushed. His people emaciated and ill from the harsh winter and his warriors nearly out of ammunition, Crazy Horse surrendered on May 6, 1877, and was killed "resisting arrest" four months later. Sitting Bull escaped to Canada, but returned to the United States to star in Buffalo Bill Cody's Wild West Show and live peacefully at the Standing Rock Agency until 1890. In that year the Sioux made one last, tragic effort to escape their confinement.

## The War Against the Nez Perce

One of the most remarkable conflicts in American history, the Nez Perce War of 1877 saw the army chasing a small group of Native peoples over hundreds of miles and losing several battles, while much of the public cheered on the Indians. In contrast to the war against the Plains Indians, who could not be forgiven for totally defeating the golden-locked Custer, the war against the Nez Perce divided the country, even in the West. Newspapers rushed daily reports of the chase on their front pages, and the public grew fascinated by the ability of these "simple" people to constantly elude the army, which had all the advantages of modern technology, including railroads and telegraphs. Along the way the Natives committed acts of surprising civility, rescuing women and children from danger, sharing lunch with tourists in the new national park at Yellowstone, speaking excellent English, and dumbfounding their enemies with brilliant battlefield tactics.[21]

As with so many other wars the United States waged against native peoples, the Nez Perce War began with an obvious injustice. The federal government had long recognized the Nez Perce as friends and allies; after all, these were the people who had famously saved Lewis and Clark's Corps of Discovery from starvation back in 1805 and then taught them how to make canoes. William Clark even reported that they played a ball game together, noting, "Those people has shewn much greater acts of hospitality then we have witnessed from any nation or tribe since we have passed the rocky Mountains," and that their conduct should resound "to their immortal honor."[22] The United States backed up its gratitude with two treaties guaranteeing the Nez Perce possession of their lands in Idaho and Oregon in perpetuity; the Nez Perce responded by assimilating, becoming English-speaking, Christian dairy farmers.

Like the Civilized Tribes of the Southeast who had been forced onto the Trail of Tears in the 1830s, the Nez Perce became the target of white envy. Violating treaties and President Grant's proclamation of protection, white settlers encroached—often violently—on Nez Perce territory in the 1870s. Under pressure from the state of Oregon, which demanded all lands belonging to the Nez Perce within its borders, President Grant revoked his executive order in 1875. White settlers rushed in, killing several Nez Perce in the process of expropriating their lands. No charges were brought against any white for these murders, even when one of them confessed. It was evident to the Nez Perce that white courts did not dispense justice equally.

The Nez Perce leadership acted with restraint, and even found support in the U.S. Army and its commander of the Military Department of the Columbia, General Oliver O. Howard. But the Bureau of Indian Affairs ordered the Nez Perce to give up their Oregon lands and move to the Lapwai agency in Idaho. The federal government refused to negotiate with the Nez Perce and, in January 1877, ordered their removal to Idaho. As the Nez Perce struggled to comply, three young men, goaded by an elder for not avenging the killing of relatives by whites, murdered four white men and raped two women. These crimes destroyed any hopes for peace and turned another Indian tragedy into a great American epic. Two of the primary chiefs, the brothers Joseph and Ollokot, persuaded most of their people to head east to the plains, where they hoped to join their old friends the Crows in living off the buffalo which they thought still plentiful. In June 1877 they set off, pursued by the U.S. Army.

The press picked up on the story immediately, with even hostile papers acknowledging that the Nez Perce had been defrauded by the government and neighboring whites. Many whites came to perceive nobility in the Nez Perce search for safety, and elevated Joseph into a heroic symbol of the Native peoples. A great many of the soldiers chasing the Nez Perce, from privates up to General O.O. Howard, felt real sympathy for these dairy farmers-turned-warriors who kept slipping from their grasp. Lieutenant Charles E.S. Wood was a recent West Point graduate serving under General Howard when the Nez Perce War broke out. As he approached his first battle with the Nez Perce on June 23, 1877, Wood hastily jotted in his journal: "Nearing the field, peculiar nervous feelings of going to death, shrinking from the exposure; about desire to be out of the expedition. Old soldiers [feel] the same way. Each fright more dreaded than the last. The desire to investigate immortality, thoughts on death, inability to change the morals and tenor of life and thought; each one's expectation that *he* will escape."[23] In an account based on his journal, Wood describes the campaign:

[Young Joseph] resisted intrusions into his territory. . . . [A]t the request of the Interior Department, General Howard was directed to occupy the Wallowa Valley with troops, and, if necessary, to drive Joseph upon the reservation. . . .

On June 14, 1877, the non-treaty bands began their horrible murders of men, women, and children. The small band which began the work swept over the Camas Prairie and Salmon River country, falling upon the unsuspicious dwellers in the lonely cabins, firing the houses, and throwing the living into the flames. . . .

Joseph, White Bird, and Too-hul-hul-suit, all seemed to be in command, but—and as one of Joseph's band told the writer—Joseph was after this fight called "the war-chief." He was everywhere along the line; running from point to point, he directed the flanking movements and the charges. It was his long fierce calls which sometimes we heard loudly in front of us, and sometimes faintly resounding from the distant rocks. As darkness covered us, the rifles grew silent, till only an occasional shot indicated each side's watchfulness.

The packers and non-combatants had been set cooking, and during the evening a sort of pancake and plenty of ammunition were distributed to each man. A spring in a ravine was secured, but one man sent to fill canteens never returned, and it was found that the enemy were in possession of it. Next day, however, the spring was retaken. All through the night, from the vast Indian camp in the river-bottom, rose the wail of the death-song and the dull drumming of the *tooats*. The dirge of the widows drifted to us through the summer night—now plaintive and faint, now suddenly bursting into shrieks, as if their very heart-strings had snapped. But mingling with these unpleasant sounds came the rapid movement of the scalp-chant, hum, hum, hum, hurrying to the climax of fierce war-whoops.

With the dawn the stray popping of rifles grew more and more rapid, till as the sun shot up into the sky both sides were hard at work again. Joseph, unlike his men, did not strip off his clothes for battle, as is the Indian custom, but wore his shirt, breech-clout, and moccasins; and though (as I was told by one of his men) he was wholly reckless of himself in directing the various fights, he did not receive a wound.

On this second day, the Indians being more determined, if possible, than on the day before, and our side having received reinforcements, General Howard, at two o'clock in the afternoon, ordered a charge upon their position. Colonel Marcus Miller led the attack, which was desperately resisted. Some of the Indians made no effort to retreat, and were killed in their rifle-pits. But this ended the fight. They fled across the river, hastily gathered the women and children who had not been sent off the night before, and throwing on pack-animals such effects as they could secure in their haste, they were soon seen speckling the distant hills, as they streamed away to Kamiah ferry and the Lo Lo trail. . . .

Joseph had turned north-eastward toward the National Park of the Yellowstone, and his rear-guard had crossed the Corinne stage-road a few hours before General Howard's command reached the same point. This was a great disappointment, as we had every reason to believe that this time we would intercept him. The next night we encamped in a prairie dotted with clumps of cottonwood trees and camas meadows. That night, just before dawn, our sleeping camp was startled into half-bewildered consciousness by a rattling fire of rifles, accompanied with the zee-zip of bullets through the air and through tent canvas, and by unearthly war-whoops. It was a back hit from Joseph.

Our men, still half stupid with sleep, groped about for shoes and cartridge-belts and swore at the mislaid articles; but each one knew his drill, and as fast as he equipped himself he crawled away from the danger-ous white tents, formed on the line, and began replying to the enemy. The mule-herd, successfully stampeded, was flying in a terror momentarily increased by the naked Indians yelling demoniacally at its heels, while Indians in front were shaking the bells stolen from the necks of the lead-animals. These Indians had crawled in among the herd during the night, and cut the hobbles and taken off the bells. Our cavalry were at the picket line trying to saddle, and at the same time to control, their frightened horses, while the Indians who had remained behind were doing their best to stampede and add to the disappearing mule-herd. Our own Indian scouts, naked and lithe and silent, glided through the bushes and from rock to rock.

The dawn showed the mule-herd far away over the prairie, disappearing toward the hills. The cavalry was already in hot pursuit, and overtook and recaptured the herd, but only for a moment; for Joseph had so calculated his plans that at this point our troops ran into an ambush of the whole Indian force, and could not pay any attention to the herd, the most of which Joseph finally secured. The foot troops then moved to the support of the cavalry, and the engagement became general, and was only ended at about two o'clock in the afternoon by the withdrawal of the Indians. We then returned to our camp, and made a reduction and rearrangement of baggage to suit the crippled pack-train. . . .

The loss of pack-animals, and the destitution and sickness among the men, compelled a halt of three days, during which time Joseph reached the Lower Geyser Basin of the National Park, and captured some tourists. . . . A miner named Snively . . . escaped to us from the hostile camp. He said he was well treated, and that Joseph used him as guide, for he was wandering in these mysterious regions without any exact knowledge of the country. The time he thus lost enabled us to take a shorter line and press closely on him. General Sturgis and the Seventh Cavalry, fresh in the field, were ahead of Joseph; and again we confidently expected to hold him in the mountains, from which there was but one pass in the direction Joseph was going, and another toward the Stinking Water. . . . Joseph made a feint toward the Stinking Water pass, and having got General Sturgis moving in that direction, he slipped out under cover of the hills, by way of Clarke's Fork, and crossed the Yellowstone toward the Musselshell basin. He had led his whole people much over a thousand miles through the ruggedest wilderness of the continent, and now he again paused to rest at Rocky Canon. But Sturgis, reinforced by General Howard's freshest cavalry, overtook him here, and again he started the caravan of women, children, and old men, under escort, while he and the warriors held their position and protected the retreat. Thus he made a running fight of two days, extending one hundred and fifty miles to the lakes near the Musselshell. Here he distanced all pursuit, and was never again overtaken until he had crossed the Missouri, nearly completing a retreat of almost two thousand miles, and was within thirty or forty miles of [Canada].

. . . During this march every vicissitude of climate had been felt: the cold, drenching rains of early spring, and the heat of summer, the autumn extremes of temperature, when the midday in the mountains was very hot, and at night water froze an inch thick in the buckets. The men who pursued Joseph through his entire course were mostly foot troops. They were necessarily reduced to the most meager supplies, and found the country ahead of them swept clean by the hostile tribe.

On September 12, General Howard sent word to General [Nelson] Miles that Joseph had foiled all attempts to stop him, and earnestly requested him to make every effort to intercept the Indians. . . . Joseph, who did not know of any other available troops in the field, and was watching only Generals Howard and Sturgis, was encamped along Eagle Creek. . . . A blinding snow-storm shielded General Miles's approach on the morning of September 30, till he was almost upon them. Instantly, on discovering the advance, the Indians seized the crests of the knolls immediately surrounding their camp, and the cavalry charge was successfully repulsed. Every officer or non-commissioned officer who wore a badge of rank was killed or wounded, save one. . . .

The troops held most of the higher crests commanding the camp. The Indians with wonderful labor and ingenuity literally honeycombed a portion of the site of their camp, and other more advantageous transverse gulches, with subterranean dwelling-places, communicating galleries, etc. Their dead horses were utilized as fortifications and as food. Here they held their own, refusing all offers of surrender, and saying in effect: If you want us, come and take us. . . . Had he not lost the herd that moved his motley horde, it is more than probable that Joseph would have made another of his successful fights in retreat.

On October 4 General Howard, with two aides, two friendly Nez-Perces (both of whom had daughters in the hostile camp), and an interpreter, arrived in Miles's camp while the firing was still going on. The two old Nez-Perces, "George" and "Captain John," rode into Joseph's camp next day. They told him General Howard was there, with promises of good treatment; that his whole command was only two or three days behind him. With tears in their eyes they begged Joseph to surrender. Joseph asked if he would be allowed to return to Idaho. He was told that he would, unless higher authority ordered otherwise.

Then old "Captain John" brought this reply (and his lips quivered and his eyes filled with tears as he delivered the words of his chief):

> Tell General Howard I know his heart. . . . I am tired of fighting. Our chiefs are killed. Looking-glass is dead. Too-hul-hulsuit is dead. The old men are all dead. . . . He who led on the young men [Joseph's brother, Ollicut] is dead. It is cold, and we have no blankets. The little children are freezing to death. My people—some of them—have run away to the hills, and have no blankets, no food. No one knows where they are—perhaps freezing to death. I want to have time to look for my children, and to see how many of them I can find; may be I shall find them among the dead. Hear me, my chiefs; my heart is sick and sad. From where the sun now stands, I will fight no more forever!

It was nearly sunset when Joseph came to deliver himself up. He rode from his camp in the little hollow. His hands were clasped over the pommel of his saddle, and his rifle lay across his knees; his head was bowed down. Pressing around him walked five of his warriors; their faces were upturned and earnest as they murmured to him; but he looked neither to the right nor the left, yet seemed to listen intently. So the little group came slowly up the hill to where General Howard, with an aide-de-camp, and General Miles waited to receive the surrender. As he neared them, Joseph sat erect in the saddle, then gracefully and with dignity he swung himself down from his horse, and with an impulsive gesture threw his arm to its full length, and offered his rifle to General Howard. The latter motioned him toward General Miles, who received the token of submission.[24]

The federal government did not respect Howard's agreement with Joseph, ordering the Nez Perce sent to Oklahoma. Many white Americans rushed to the Nez Perce's defense and petitioned for their right to return home; the people of Bismarck even treated the Nez Perce as honored guests, throwing them a lavish banquet that included salmon brought especially from the Northwest. Generals Howard, Miles, and Terry all worked to persuade the Indian Bureau to alter its policy. In 1879, Chief Joseph, known among the Nez Perce as Young Joseph, wrote a remarkably fair account of the causes and course of his war with the United States, ending with a plea for justice for his people, "Whenever the white man treats the Indian as they treat each other, then we will have no more wars."[25] In 1885, after nearly eight years of battling for their rights, the surviving 268 Nez Perce were finally allowed to return home.[26]

Charles Wood did not stay in the military long after the war's end, quitting the service to study law. He settled in Portland, Oregon, and became a prominent pro-union attorney and vocal member of the American Anti-Imperialist League; he considered Chief Joseph a close friend, whom he visited often. Joseph remained an articulate spokesman for the rights and dignity of the Native people until his death at his home at the Colville Reservation in eastern Washington in 1904. Wood died in 1944 at the age of ninety-two.

## Wounded Knee

Originally, it was called the "Battle of Wounded Knee." Soldiers present on that bitterly cold winter day of December 29, 1890, insisted that they acted in self-defense. The government agreed, awarding numerous commendations, including the Congressional Medal of Honor to a private who continued shooting fleeing Indians even after his overheated Hotchkiss gun had burned his hand. Congress ultimately awarded twenty Medals of Honor to those who participated in the Battle of Wounded Knee, which far exceeds the number awarded for any other single military action in American history.[27]

Coincidentally, the Bureau of Ethnology had recently sent their brilliant young scholar James Mooney to observe the Ghost Dance, a religious revival among the Plains Indians that many at the Bureau of Indian Affairs viewed with suspicion and dread. Mooney arrived at the battlefield site shortly after the encounter, while dead bodies still lay upon the ground, frozen in grotesque death poses. This pioneer anthropologist set about interviewing both the soldiers and the survivors, trying to get a sense of what had driven so many Natives to leave the safety of their reservations. The Ghost Dance represented an effort to revive a fading Native culture before it disappeared entirely under the bulk and power of the United States. Its spiritualism convinced many people, especially among the Sioux, to seek salvation in the old ways, which meant leaving the forced-assimilation policies of the reservations behind. Panicking, the Indian agent at the Standing Rock Reservation ordered the arrest of Sitting Bull, whom he feared might become a leader of this Sioux revival. Forty agency policemen showed up to arrest the sixty-year-old chief on the morning of December 15, killing him with shots to the head and chest in the ensuing scuffle. Two weeks later, the efforts of the army to force the Sioux back to their reservation led to the calamity now known as the Wounded Knee Massacre. Mooney returned to the area in 1896 to measure the impact of these events, publishing *The Ghost-Dance Religion and Wounded Knee* that year. Though it did not receive much attention at the time, Mooney's book remains an essential source for scholars of the Native people at the end of the nineteenth century:[28]

On the morning of December 29, 1890, preparations were made to disarm the Indians preparatory to taking them to the agency and thence to the railroad. . . . Shortly after 8 oclock in the morning the warriors were ordered to come out from the tipis and deliver their arms. They came forward and seated themselves on the ground in front of the troops. They were then ordered to go by themselves into their tipis and bring out and surrender their guns. The first twenty went and returned in a short time with only two guns. It seemed evident that they were unwilling to give them up, and after consultation of the officers part of the soldiers were ordered up to within ten yards of the group of warriors, while another detachment of troops was ordered to search the tipis. After a thorough hunt these last returned with about forty rifles, most of which, however, were old and of little value. The search had consumed considerable time and created a good deal of excitement among the women and children, as the soldiers found it necessary in the process to overturn the beds and other furniture of the tipis and in some instances drove out the inmates. All this had its effect on their husbands and brothers, already wrought up to a high nervous tension and not knowing what might come next.

While the soldiers had been looking for the guns Yellow Bird, a medicine-man, had been walking about among the warriors, blowing on an eagle-bone whistle, and urging them to resistance, telling them that the soldiers would become weak and powerless, and that the bullets would be unavailing against the sacred "ghost shirts," which nearly every one of the Indians wore. As he spoke in the Sioux language, the officers did not at once realize the dangerous drift of his talk, and the climax came too quickly for them to interfere. It is said one of the searchers now attempted to raise the blanket of a warrior. Suddenly Yellow Bird stooped down and threw a handful of dust into the air, when, as if this were the signal, a young Indian, said to have been Black Fox from Cheyenne river, drew a rifle from under his blanket and fired at the soldiers, who instantly replied with a volley directly into the crowd of warriors and so near that their guns were almost touching. . . . The survivors sprang to their feet, throwing their blankets from their shoulders as they rose, and for a few minutes there was a terrible hand to hand struggle, where every man's thought was to kill. Although many of the warriors had no guns, nearly all had revolvers and knives in their belts under their blankets, together with some of the murderous warclubs still carried by the Sioux. The very lack of guns made the fight more bloody, as it brought the combatants to closer quarters.

At first the volley of the Hotchkiss guns trained on the camp opened fire and sent a storm of shells and bullets among the women and children, who had gathered in front of the tipis to watch the unusual spectacle of military display. The guns poured in 2-pound explosive shells at the rate of nearly fifty per minute, mowing down everything alive. The terrible effect may be judged from the fact that one woman survivor, Blue Whirlwind, with whom the author conversed, received fourteen wounds, while each of her two little boys was also wounded by her side. In a few minutes 200 Indian men, women, and children, with 60 soldiers, were lying dead and wounded on the ground,[29] the tipis had been torn down by the shells and some of them were burning above the helpless wounded, and the surviving handful of Indians were flying in wild panic to the shelter of the ravine, pursued by hundreds of maddened soldiers and followed up by a raking fire from the Hotchkiss guns, which had been moved into position to sweep the ravine.

There can be no question that the pursuit was simply a massacre, where fleeing women, with infants in their arms, were shot down after resistance had ceased and when almost every warrior was stretched dead or dying on the ground. . . .

TURNING HAWK, Pine Ridge[30] . . . When we were about a day's journey from our agency we heard that a certain party of Indians (Big Foot's band) from the Cheyenne River agency was coming toward Pine Ridge in flight. . . . These people were coming toward Pine Ridge agency and when they were almost on the agency they were met by the soldiers and surrounded and finally taken to the Wounded Knee creek, and there at a given time their guns were demanded. When they had delivered them up, the men were separated from their families, from their tipis, and taken to a certain spot. When the guns were thus taken and the men thus separated, there was a crazy man, a young man of very bad influence and in fact a nobody, among that bunch of Indians fired his gun, and of course the firing of a gun must have been the breaking of a military rule of some sort, because immediately the soldiers returned fire and indiscriminate killing followed. . . .

AMERICAN HORSE.[31] The men were separated, as has already been said, from the women, and they were surrounded by the soldiers. Then came next the village of the Indians and that was entirely surrounded by the soldiers also. When the firing began, of course the people who were standing immediately around the young man who fired the first shot were killed right together, and then they turned their guns, Hotchkiss guns, etc., upon the women who were in the lodges standing there under a flag of truce, and of course as soon as they were fired upon they fled, the men fleeing in one direction and the women running in two different directions. So that there were three general directions in which they took flight.

There was a women with an infant in her arms who was killed as she almost touched the flag of truce, and the women and children of course were strewn all along the circular village until they were dispatched. Right near the flag of truce a mother was shot down with her infant; the child not knowing that its mother was dead was still nursing, and that especially was a very sad sight. The women as they were fleeing with their babes were killed together, shot right through, and the women who were very heavy with child were also killed. All the Indians fled in these three directions, and after most all of them had been killed a cry was made that all those who were not killed or wounded should come forth and they would be safe. Little boys who were not wounded came out of their places of refuge, and as soon as they came in sight a number of soldiers surrounded them and butchered them there.

Of course we all feel very sad about this affair. I stood very loyal to the government all through those troublesome days, and believing so much in the government and being so loyal to it, my disappointment was very strong. . . . Of course it would have been all right if only the men were killed; we would feel almost grateful for it. But the fact of the killing of the women, and more especially the killing of the young boys and girls who are to go to make up the future strength of the Indian people, is the saddest part of the whole affair and we feel it very sorely.[32]

An Irish immigrant who had arrived in the United States just three years earlier, twenty-year-old Private Hugh McGinnis was shot at Wounded Knee. His memory of events leading up to the first shots matches Mooney's account. He takes up the story from when the troops move in to seize the Sioux's guns:

It was as if someone had dropped a match into a powder keg. The whole field exploded into action. Warriors discarded blankets in a flash to reveal hidden weapons and whirled to fight. We were firing at each other at point blank range. With bloodcurdling war whoops, braves without guns rushed us in an attempt to hack their way through our ranks with knives, hatchets and warclubs. They were determined to reach their horses, and our troop taking the brunt of the attack, was simply cut to pieces.

The white hot fury of this mad melee defies my attempts at description. The air was rent with savage cries and the thunder of cannon, and the nostrils were assailed with the stench of burnt powder and blood. In our frantic struggle with the swarming Sioux, we were unaware that our position had become doubly untenable. But fantastic as it sounds, the surrounding troopers were firing into this seething mass of humanity, subjecting us as well as the Indians to a deadly crossfire. . . .

That battlefield was a terrible thing to behold. The memory is still enough to make me shudder. I was lying in a pool of blood, surrounded by the shattered bodies of my comrades. Father Craft, stabbed through the lungs was lying nearby. Jim was in terrible shape, with a gaping wound in his chest. Murphey was dead, Macque had been shot through the heart and our Captain was crumpled on the snow near the center of the ring. The only officer killed in the foray, Captain George Wallace, had sustained four bullet wounds only to die from the skull-crushing blow of a warclub.

Many years later McGinnis wrote that the passage of time had "never completely erased the ghastly horror of that scene and I still awake at night from nightmarish dreams of that massacre."[33]

# 6

# The Wars of Empire

The turn of the twentieth century seemed to welcome war. A new ideology, holding that the world's nations were engaged in a life-and-death struggle in which only the strong would survive, swept Europe, the Americas, and Japan. It was the time of the alpha male, the tough guy taking risks, demonstrating his strength and dominance through competition and conflict. Actual physical strength was not requisite; rather, attitude mattered. In the United States, the younger generation rebelled against the notion of rough sports and occupations as appropriate only for brutes. They wanted to break free of these civilized restraints, especially with civilization so triumphant. As the historian Frederick Jackson Turner proclaimed in 1893, the frontier had ended and America's future lay with urban industrialization. Since Turner insisted that democracy emerged from the frontier, however, the end of the frontier would likely spell the end of democracy—unless, of course, the United States found new frontiers.

America's leading political and intellectual figures perceived character-forming value in violence and war, for the individual and the nation. On Memorial Day 1895, the Civil War veteran Justice Oliver Wendell Holmes Jr. of the Massachusetts Supreme Court addressed Harvard's graduating class on the tragedy that war had fallen "out of fashion, and the man who commands the attention of his fellows is the man of wealth." In a speech which quickly became famous, "The Soldier's Faith," Holmes argued that war and the ideals that drive a man to serve his country give meaning to life:

For my own part, I believe that the struggle for life is the order of the world, at which it is vain to repine. . . . Now, at least, and perhaps as long as man dwells upon the globe, his destiny is battle, and he has to take the chances of war. If it is our business to fight, the book for the army is a war-song, not a hospital-sketch. It is not well for soldiers to think much about wounds. Sooner or later we shall fall; but meantime it is for us to fix our eyes upon the point to be stormed, and to get there if we can. . . .

War, when you are at it, is horrible and dull. It is only when time has passed that you see that its message was divine. I hope it may be long before we are called again to sit at that master's feet. But some teacher of the kind we all need. In this snug, over-safe corner of the world we need it, that we may realize that our comfortable routine is no eternal necessity of things, but merely a little space of calm in the midst of the tempestuous untamed streaming of the world, and in order that we may be ready for danger. We need it in this time of individualist negations, with its literature of French and American humor, revolting at discipline, loving flesh-pots, and denying that anything is worthy of reverence,—in order that we may remember all that buffoons forget. We need it everywhere and at all times. For high and dangerous action teaches us to believe as right beyond dispute things for which our doubting minds are slow to find words of proof. Out of heroism grows faith in the worth of heroism.

. . . It is the more necessary to learn the lesson afresh from perils newly sought, and perhaps it is not vain for us to tell the new generation what we learned in our day, and what we still believe. That the joy of life is living, is to put out all one's powers as far as they will go; that the measure of power is obstacles overcome; to ride boldly at what is in front of you, be it fence or enemy; to pray, not for comfort, but for combat; to keep the sol-dier's faith against the doubts of civil life, more besetting and harder to overcome than all the misgivings of the battle-field, and to remember that duty is not to be proved in the evil day, but then to be obeyed unquestion-ing; to love glory more than the temptations of wallowing ease, but to know that one's final judge and only rival is oneself: with all our failures in act and thought, these things we learned from noble enemies in Virginia or Georgia or on the Mississippi, thirty years ago; these things we believe to be true.[1]

Holmes's message found many disciples among the younger generation. Old liberals like Carl Schurz found this trend appalling. In 1896, when it briefly seemed that the United States might go to war over the Venezuelan border, Schurz noted "the strange teachings put forth among us by some persons, that a war, from time to time, would by no means be a misfortune, but rather a healthy exercise to stir up our patriotism, and to keep us from becoming ef-feminate." As a consequence, young men were "busily looking round for some-body to fight as the crazed Malay runs amuck looking for somebody to kill." Schurz found the idea that Americans needed "foreign wars to preserve their manhood," or that patriotism would "flag unless stimulated by hatred of some-body else . . . as preposterous as it is disgraceful and abominable."[2]

Schurz stood for the old standards of reason, self-restraint, and respectabil-ity; but the new age had its lion in Theodore Roosevelt, the energetic bard of "the strenuous life." Roosevelt dismissed the old liberals as "foolish sentimentalists" and called for a new Manifest Destiny to bring "law, order, and righteousness" to the world as "it is only the warlike power of a civilized people that can give peace to the world." The United States should expand across the globe for the benefit of others, but it *must* do so if it were to survive. History demonstrated to Roosevelt that "it is the great expanding peoples which bequeath to future ages the great memories and material results of their achievements. . . . But the people that do not expand leave, and can leave, nothing behind them."[3] Lest any Christians hesitate before such enthusiasm for war, Roosevelt's ally Senator Albert Beveridge assured them, "God . . . has made us the master organizers of the world to establish system where chaos reigns. . . . He has marked the American people as the chosen nation to finally lead in the regeneration of the world. This is the divine mission of America."[4]

Though it is impossible to know the degree of popular commitment to this aggressive, imperialist Social Darwinism, Congress and the executive branch marched to its beat at the century's turn. In 1898, the United States extended its military reach beyond North America, invading Cuba in order to liberate it from Spanish rule. In the process of that "splendid little war," as Secretary of State John Hay called it, the United States became a colonial power, capturing and claiming Puerto Rico, Guam, and the Philippines.[5] Rather than incorporating these colonies into the United States, as had been done with previous acquisitions, the government treated these "possessions" as conquered lands, refusing for the first time to extend the rights of citizenship to their inhabitants.[6] The people of the Philippines felt particularly betrayed by American conduct, launching the Philippine insurrection in a vain effort to reclaim their independence. In the resulting conflict, which lasted several years and led to the death of an estimated 700,000 Filipinos, American forces responded savagely, slaughtering entire towns in reprisal for attacks on U.S. forces, killing prisoners and civilians indiscriminately, and using "enhanced interrogation methods" such as the notorious "water cure." As a consequence of this new empire, American troops would return repeatedly throughout the twentieth century to various Caribbean nations, including Cuba and Haiti, and intervene to overthrow democratically elected governments in several Central American nations. These campaigns would be conducted in a fashion that Marine Commandant General Smedley Butler thought would shame the Mafia.[7] These largely forgotten wars evoked contrary responses from American soldiers, as many resigned in disgust and others defended their actions with a racist disdain for the native populations.

## The New Empire

The United States did not simply stumble into its overseas empire. In 1893, U.S. Marines aided American sugar planters in overthrowing Hawaii's Queen Liliuokalani. The planters hoped to be annexed to the United States so that they could enjoy the benefits of the McKinley Tariff, which granted a subsidy to sugar growers. But when President Grover Cleveland refused to countenance this plan, the planters created a republic under their control and waited for a sympathetic president, which they found in William McKinley. In 1897, the new president filled important offices with many of the most influential supporters of American imperialism.

Still, advocates of imperialism needed a justification for expansion; the dying Spanish Empire presented that opportunity. Cuban revolutionaries had battled for independence from 1868 to 1878 in the Ten Years' War and had revolted again in 1895. In 1896, the Spanish commander, General Valeriano Weyler, adopted the brutally effective *reconcentración* policy—essentially free-fire zones similar to those used by William T. Sherman in his war against the Plains Indians. The American press, led by William Randolph Hearst and Joseph Pulitzer, expressed outrage over such unconscionable conduct toward civilians. Their reporters graphically described the full horror of counterinsurgency, firing up support for the liberation of Cuba.

Spain's new Liberal government, seeking to appease the Cuban rebels, granted limited autonomy to the island in January 1898. Soon after, the United States sent the battleship *Maine* to Havana Harbor as an indication of support for a free Cuba. On February 15, the *Maine* exploded, claiming the lives of 260 Americans. Though the probable cause of the explosion was a faulty boiler, the press immediately blamed Spain for the disaster, as cries of "Remember the *Maine*" swept the nation. On March 29, President McKinley issued an ultimatum to Spain demanding Cuban independence, which Spain refused. On April 11, McKinley called on Congress for a declaration of war against Spain, which Congress declared on April 25, with the Teller Amendment denying any intention to annex or control Cuba. As the public understood, this war was purely for the liberation of Cuba. It is easy to imagine their surprise, then, when the first action of the war came not in the Caribbean, but on the other side of the planet, when the U.S. Navy sailed into Manila Harbor on May 1 and sank the entire Spanish fleet.

After locating the Philippines on the map, most Americans wondered how it was that the navy had struck so quickly at a target vastly remote from the theater of operations.[8] The answer lay with the assistant secretary of the navy.

Immediately after McKinley's inauguration, the Department of War had begun preparing for a conflict with Spain, with secret plans to take advantage of the situation to seize the Philippines. The assistant secretary of the navy, Theodore Roosevelt, then exceeded his authority in appointing an aggressive commander of the Pacific Fleet, Commodore George Dewey. In the crisis following the explosion that destroyed the *Maine*, while the United States was still pursuing diplomatic negotiations with Spain, Roosevelt bypassed the secretary of the navy and ordered Dewey to Hong Kong with instructions to attack the Spanish fleet in the Philippines in the event of war. Like many other imperialists, Roosevelt saw a war with Spain as an opportunity for the United States to seize territory across the Pacific. On the day Congress declared war, Roosevelt again ignored the official chain of command and gave Dewey the go-ahead to attack the Spanish fleet. He then resigned as assistant secretary of the navy in order to organize a volunteer company that would become known as the Rough Riders.

The United States was primed for war, and its capabilities far exceeded the moribund Spanish Empire's. When the cruiser *Charleston* fired at the Spanish fort in Guam in June, the Spanish commander, unaware of the war, rowed out to apologize for not having cannon to return what he thought was a salute. The United States seized the island. When Dewey moved on the Spanish fleet at Cavite naval base in Manila Bay, he sank every one of Spain's wooden ships, losing a single sailor to heat stroke. With the Philippines and Guam falling like ripe fruit into American hands, Congress annexed Hawaii on July 7; in a matter of weeks, the United States had become a leading Pacific power.

Meanwhile, enthusiasm for the war ran at a fever pitch. One million Americans volunteered for service, an influx of troops for which the army and government were completely unprepared. The ensuing chaos would cost thousands of soldiers their lives.

## Modern Naval Warfare

When the Civil War ended in 1865, the United States had one of the largest navies in the world, though it focused on coastal operations. Congress immediately stopped funding ship construction and decommissioned most ships, so the navy became stagnant and largely useless. But when Alfred T. Mahan, president of the recently created Naval War College in Newport, Rhode Island, published *The Influence of Sea Power upon History*, the navy found itself at the center of American expansionism.

Mahan laid out the imperial plan. First, the United States needed to build a powerful modern navy; then it would extend its power beyond its borders, build a canal across Central America, take control of the Caribbean, seize strategic Pacific islands—especially Hawaii—and establish naval bases. The country had to take these steps, Mahan warned, or witness its slow decline as other nations surged forward. Mahan's congressional supporters effectively increased funding for the navy, overseeing the construction of the first steam-powered, steel, big-gun cruisers, the *Maine* and *Texas*, followed by the first four steel battleships. This small but highly modern fleet would perform brilliantly in the one-sided war with Spain.

The war provided outstanding publicity for the navy. In the weeks after the declaration of war, the country's newspapers followed the U.S. battleship *Oregon* as it sailed from San Francisco around South America on its way to join the Atlantic squadron for an attack on Santiago, Cuba. Daily reports chronicled the ship's journey down the Pacific coast of South America and through the hazardous Straits of Magellan. Once it was in the Atlantic, the papers anxiously reported that four Spanish cruisers and numerous torpedo boats were hunting the *Oregon*. The public thrilled to every new cable describing this epic journey of a single ship whose captain continually outwitted the supposedly superior Spanish force. Along the way, the ship set the record for the journey from one coast to the other, traveling 14,000 miles in 73 days, and arrived in time for the Battle of Santiago on July 3, 1898.

Captain Charles Edgar Clark, a Civil War veteran who had seen service at the Battle of Mobile Bay, assumed command of the *Oregon* on March 17. The ship left San Francisco two days later, more than a month before the declaration of war, accompanied part of the way by the gunboat *Marietta* and the cruiser *Buffalo*—the former *Nictheroy*, recently purchased from Brazil. The *Oregon* had 25 officers and 425 seamen, one of whom kept a journal that he published later that same year, giving a sailor's view of the decisive naval engagement of the war:

June 3. Nothing doing but laying off here [Santiago de Cuba] and watching what looks like to me a big hole in the ground. . . .

June 6. . . . Bombard the forts and water Batteries to day for 4 hours but don't know how much damage we done. . . .

June 14. The New Orleans was ordered to run in close to the shore and do some Bombarding By herself Just to break the Monotony and to let us believe we were at war. We done a good Job all right, she silenced the east Battery and the west one too. . . .

June 16. At 3.30 A.M. this morning all hands was called and the coffee was passed around with some hardtack and canned Beef at 4 A.M. . . . Then we went at it to try and see if we could not knock those Batteries off the earth. Bombarded until 7.15 A.M. . . . we silenced all the Batteries. . . .

June 20. Bully for the Soldiers, they are here at last. . . . Some of the papers say there is 20,000 of them, that is enough to eat the place up for lunch. . . .

June 22. The soldiers are landing all O.K. and doing well. . . .

July 4. The fish has come out to see us. On the 3rd the Spanish fleet came out of the Harbor to fight and get away if possible. . . . Well the Fleet came out and went to Davy Jones's locker. It was just 9.25 A.M., first call had sounded on our ship for Quarters and we all had our best duds on; we were going to listen to the Articles of War this morning and to have church right after, But we never did. All of a sudden the Orderly on watch made a dive for the Cabin head first, and told the old man the Fleet was coming out of the Harbor. The old man jumpt up astanding. As soon as some of the men seen the ships there, they went to their Quarters with out any further delay. I was standing on the Quarter Deck waiting for the last call to go. I heard the news and looking around . . . seen the first one [Spanish ship]. I thought she looked Bigger than a Mountain. . . .

By 9.27 the Oregon fired the first shot of the Battle of July 3rd, 1898 at the first ship that come out of the Harbor. . . . About 7 or 9 minutes after they got started good, one of our 6 inch guns blew up one of the Torpedo Boats [the *Furor*], struck her square amidships, she sunk like a rock with all on board. And right here is where I had to stop for a moment to admire one of their Gunners. I do think he was one of the bravest men I ever had the pleasure to look upon. That man must have known he was going to a sure Death, he stood on Deck and kept firing at us all the time, and the last time I seen him he was Just going up in the air.

As the ships came out of the harbor they circled to the right, or Westward, and Capt Clark knew they were trying to escape. They did not think the old Oregon was such a runner as she was a fighter, so we Just tailed on with them and giving them shot for shot. In about 20 minutes the first ship [the *Teresa*] went on the Beach, plumb knocked out, and 15 minutes later the second one [the *Oquendo*] went on the Beach, a short ways from the first. Then came the tug of war for we had to run to catch the Vizcaya and the Colon, but we catched them both. The Vizcaya was about 4000 yards ahead and the Colon was about 3 miles ahead, and the poor men in the fireroom was working like horses, and to cheer them up we passed the word down the ventilators how things was going on. . . . So we got in range of the Vizcaya and we sent her ashore with the secondary Battery and 6 inch guns, and then we settled down for a good chase for the Colon. I thought she was going to run away from us. But she had to make a curve and we headed for a point that she had to come out at. We all think there is no man in the Navy like Capt Clark, he is a Brave man, he stood on the Forward 13 inch turret through the thickest of this fight and directed his ship to the final results.

> Coming back to Santiago we waited until we got to where the first ship went on the Beach and there fired the national salute. . . . I hear there is over 1800 Prisoners and 650 killed and 800 wounded on the third. . . .
>
> July 5. . . . There is Spanish men of war and Torpedo boats strung all along the Beach for 60 miles.[9]

The war moved quickly. Admiral William Sampson's easy destruction of the Spanish fleet attempting to flee Santiago and the reduction of the harbor's defenses by naval bombardment set up the army's victory over the Spanish forces a few days later and the surrender of Santiago on July 15. The Spanish government requested an armistice on July 18, and a ceasefire was signed August 12. By August 20, the *Oregon* was taking part in the naval parade celebrating victory in New York harbor.

The navy's performance during the Spanish-American War won popular acclaim, while proving Admiral Mahan's point that a modern fleet would provide the United States with global reach. In the ensuing years, Congress passed repeated appropriations to build the U.S. Navy into an international competitor with Britain and Germany.

## The Splendid War

The historian Arthur M. Schlesinger Jr. once wrote, "Most wars are popular for their first thirty days."[10] The Spanish-American War barely lasted long enough to become unpopular. Though there were very few military actions in the four months from the declaration of war to the cease-fire, the press poured forth an astounding number of articles and personal accounts celebrating the heroism and glory of American troops. It seemed as though every shot fired in the war found its Homer.

The rapidity of communication held a rapt public's attention. For the first time, Americans could read of a military action within hours of the engagement as on-site reporters—what we now call "embedded" journalists—wrote hasty accounts of the battle and cabled them immediately to their papers. Reporters brought the war to communities across the country by interviewing soldiers and identifying them by their hometowns, rather than by name. Even personal accounts from soldiers found their way into national publications, as when *The Outlook* invited readers to send in letters they had received from those serving in Cuba (but ignoring the war in the Philippines). In their introduction to these letters, the editors cast a rosy perspective on the military experience, though the letters themselves—without attribution beyond town of origin—often contradicted their happy glow. Thus the editors write, in a complete denial of reality, "An examination of the letters which we have so far received from camp leads to the conclusion that the food and sanitary arrangements are, on the whole, excellent." On the other hand, a corporal in the First Illinois Infantry Volunteers wrote that "the heat and hardships were intense, so that men fell by the way (a company of eighty-four men arriving at one camping place with only twelve left in line)." Just a few months later, *The Outlook* called for an investigation into "mismanagement in the War Department." Now that the war was over, the magazine could admit what the published letters had demonstrated: "Almost all the letters that have come to us from the front contain statements of the shocking condition of things in the commissary and medical branches of the service."

Their initial framing of the letters required a high level of what George Orwell called "cognitive dissonance." The following letter from a Massachusetts volunteer who had worked as a waiter before the war describes getting shot through the lung in battle outside Santiago on July 1. This letter was written from a hospital in Tampa:

At about a quarter of six a shot from the cannon flew over our heads; then we knew the battle had begun. We then went forward on the double-quick, marched through woods and crossed fields. We had to cut barbed-wire fences and cut down wooden ones, till we got to the road; then we were near the town. All at once a volley came over our heads, and we all ducked and got up laughing. . . . We then went out on skirmish line, each man going forward and each about five feet apart. The bullets were flying all around us, but the first volley seemed to have taken all the fright out of us, for no one held back, but seemed to try to get in the fight first. It was not long before a man would fall here and there; but we did not stop. We would run like time, then lie down, get the order "forward," get up and run forward, then drop down in the grass. The bullets would throw the dirt up in our faces and all around us. Zip! Zip! plunk! Zip! zip! Plunk! That was the way, yet all the time and hundreds—just one string of singing bullets.

It was during one of these rushes, while I was getting up, that a bullet hit me. I was on my hands and knees. I fell over and lay there. Then the boys began to fire. I got up on my knees to shoot, but all I could do was to put in the cartridge. I was so weak I fell over. I then called two of the boys to carry me to the rear. They carried me about a hundred yards and laid me down behind a large cactus plant. They tried to tie up the wound, but the bullets were so thick I told them to lie flat. About five minutes later the bullets stopped, and they started to put on some bandages, but a volley came and the boy from E Company was hit in the hip, and C. was hit in the right shoulder. I told them to crawl away if they could, and they did so. I then got out two handkerchiefs and held them on the holes for an hour and a half. Every once in a while pieces of the cactus plant would drop down, cut off by the bullets. It was awful lying there, listening to the cries of the wounded and dying, the singing of the bullets, and the explosion of the shells. But the firing then went to the left, so the boys came back after the killed and wounded, and carried me down in the road. There I lay for another half-hour, till the doctor came around. . . .

The Reverend W.E. Wright, chaplain to the Thirty-fourth Michigan Volunteer Regiment, wrote the following letter from outside Santiago:

Near Santiago, July 31, 1898
It helps like medicine to get letters from home. . . . I would go to see the other half of the regiment but I am not quite strong yet and besides I have had a funeral every day for the last few days and can't get the time. . . . You cannot imagine anything more hideously horrible than our hospital "system;" piles of stores at some places, while here we have no tents, no cots, no food, no medicine, no stimulants, and men fading away all about us.
    . . . What angers me is the *unnecessary* hardship brought about through indifference, incompetency, and senseless adherence to a *theoretical* system that has proved itself unworkable. Men with us who served in the Civil War assert that our troops suffer far more than did those in the war of 1861–65.[11]

The battle that captured the greatest attention and helped make Theodore Roosevelt a national figure was San Juan Hill. Reporters loved Roosevelt, with his clipped, enthusiastic speech and ceaseless energy. He was always good for a quote, if not a spectacle, and the heroism of his First Volunteer Cavalry Regiment, or Rough Riders, at Kettle Hill deserved praise. However, the press suffered from severely limited vision, apparently unable to recognize the other troops also charging bravely under fire up the steep embankments. As the Michigan chaplain Reverend Wright noticed, Roosevelt's troops were accompanied the whole way by the African American soldiers of the Tenth Cavalry.
    In 1866, Congress created the first peacetime black regiments, the Ninth and Tenth U.S. Cavalry Regiments, known as the Buffalo Soldiers. These regiments performed with distinction during the Indian Wars in the last third of the nineteenth century; twenty-three of their members received the Congressional Medal of Honor. A sergeant in the Tenth Cavalry, Horace W. Bivins, was an oft-decorated veteran of the Indian campaigns and one of the most successful marksmen in the army when Congress declared war on Spain. In a memoir

published the following year in a history of the Tenth Cavalry by Herschel V. Cashin, Bivins describes the invasion of Cuba and the dramatic Battle of San Juan Hill—more accurately, San Juan Heights. On July 1, 1898, General William R. Shafter attacked the Spanish fortifications protecting Santiago. On the Spanish left, American forces battled for control of El Caney while the Fifth Corps attacked the San Juan Heights on the right. Employing artillery and Gatling guns to deadly effect, American forces swept the Spanish off the highest hill in the area, San Juan. The battle was a fierce and costly one for the United States, which suffered 205 killed and nearly 1,200 wounded, while the Spanish defenders suffered 215 killed and 376 wounded—but reporters had eyes only for Theodore Roosevelt and his Rough Riders, ignoring the contributions of the regulars, white and black. As Cashin wrote in the preface to *Under Fire in Cuba*, there is a tendency for "the average historian to either entirely ignore or very grudgingly acknowledge the courage, valor, and patriotism of a so-called alien race." That inherent racism became apparent as the Buffalo Soldiers moved south from their bases on the Great Plains:

We left Fort Assinniboine, Montana, April 19th. . . . We received great ovations all along the line. Thousands of people were thronged at the places where we would stop and we were treated royally; at Madison, Wisconsin, we were presented with enough flags to decorate our train and were given cigars and many other pleasantries. Our band would play in response to the ovations that were given us from time to time.

After reaching Illinois we received both flags and flowers from the ladies and schoolgirls. I planted one of the flags given me on the crest of San Juan Hill, July 1, 1898. As we neared the south the great demonstrations became less fervent. There were no places that we entered in which we were courteously treated.

The signs over the waiting room doors at the Southern depots were a revelation to us. Some read thus: "White waiting room." On the door of a lunch room we read: "Niggers are not allowed inside." We were traveling in palace cars and the people were much surprised that we did not occupy the "Jim Crow" cars, the curse of the South. . . .

June 14, 1898, will ever be a memorable day in the history of the American Republic, for on that day the advance guard of the military expedition sailed for Cuba pursuant to the orders of General N. A. Miles, commanding United States army. . . .

June 17th we saw land to the southwest. Several islands could be seen near Point Lookout lighthouse in Bahama Channel. A small sailboat came near us from the lighthouse. From its masthead was flying the American flag and under it the Cuban flag. The crew consisted of three Cubans (two of them very dark and one light). Cheer after cheer went up from our boys. The Cubans seemed to be overwhelmed with joy. . . .

On June 27th a Spanish spy was captured about two and a half miles from our camp near El Caney by a Cuban. This spy was up in a mango tree on a high knoll drawing a map of our camp and pickets. . . . Two Cuban officers, mounted, and two sentinels, dismounted, took the spy and went up the road towards General Shafter's camp. Our gun detachment was in camp at the entrance and to the left of a large gate; as the Cuban officers passed us I brought the men to attention and saluted, they returned with a machete salute. Our spy went the way of all spies in war time.

. . . Orders were issued for an attack to take place July 1st on El Caney, with a view of making a turning movement, swinging well to our right and passing through the village of El Caney, striking the left flank of the enemy, perhaps ultimately reaching to the northern side of Santiago. . . . Each man was given three days' rations—eighteen hard-tacks and nine slices of raw bacon. We marched the early part of the night, bivouacking near the road ready to take up our position in the battle line at earliest dawn. It is worthy of note that the moon favored us during all the latter part of June and the early part of July, enabling us to use many hours of the night that would not have been possible in darkness. . . .

June 30th while lying under a mango tree drawing a map of our camp. . . . I received orders from detachment commander to march our detachment to regimental headquarters for muster. . . .

Grimes' Battery was ordered into position on El Pozo Hill at 6:43 A.M. He opened fire on blockhouses out from the city. After we had fired several shots the enemy replied with shrapnel fire at correct range and with accurately adjusted fuse. When the battery opened fire I was so anxious to get the range that I went upon the hill (one hundred yards away). Just as I reached the battery Captain Grimes gave the command: "With shrapnel at 2,800 yards, load!" Several general officers were at the battery in action. At that moment I heard a deep roar near the city, like distant thunder. In a few seconds a shell came over the battery just a few feet above it and went 100 yards beyond and burst among our men, killing two and wounding several. An officer was near me, mounted; the shell passed so near him that his horse shied and the saddle turned, throwing him to the ground. I went to his assistance, then ran down the hill to my battery. Just as I reached it a shell burst about ten feet directly over me, wounding Private Watson, Troop F, Tenth Cavalry, and a piece of it struck one of our ammunition boxes, exposing the shells. It was lucky that it did not explode, as there were 175 shells in the pile. I reported to our battery

commander: "Sir," I asked, "do you wish to bring the battery into action?"
He directed that the mules should be taken to shelter and ammunition
placed out of range of the Spanish guns. . . .

Our battery kept up the fire on the blockhouse and Entrenchments on
San Juan Hill until the blockhouse to the right was taken by the Rough
Riders and the Tenth Cavalry. . . .

While sighting my gun to fire the eighth shot, a bullet passed through
the thick iron plated hub of the gun carriage wheel and struck me near the
left temple. It stunned me for about two minutes. I recovered, resighted
my gun, pulled the lanyard, then watched with my glasses the result of the
shot. It dropped in the Spanish trenches. Great confusion occurred. I
could see Spanish officers with raised pistols or drawn swords at each end
of the trenches. Some were using their swords on the men to keep them
from retreating. I fired several shots—loading and firing the gun myself.
Every time the gun was fired it would jump back from five to eight feet. I
would load, place it in position, sight it, pull the lanyard, then watch the
result of my shot.

. . . We moved down the road, crossed a small stream, turned to the
right and took position on a ridge between the two blockhouses. We
passed several dead and wounded. I passed my troop commander, First
Lieutenant William H. Smith and First Lieutenant William E. Shipp,
Tenth Cavalry lying dead, but did not know them. We were then ordered
to take position on San Juan Hill.

We reached that point about 1:30 P.M., and then opened fire on the
blockhouse and trenches in the basin in which Santiago lies at six hundred yards range. About fifty sharpshooters were stationed in this house,
which had portholes all around it and even holes cut through the roof
large enough to sight a gun. Our shots were very effective, knocking great
holes in the house rendering it untenable and killing a large number of
men. . . . At 5:15 we withdrew from the field, having used nearly all of our
ammunition in firing from the hill. . . . At the close of the first day's battle
our men were occupying the crest all along San Juan Hill, six hundred
yards from the enemy's entrenchment, and one and a half miles from the
city of Santiago. . . .

During the day there were a great many casualties resulting not entirely
from aimed fire, but from bullets clearing the crest of our entrenchments
and going far beyond, striking men as they were coming up into position,
or as they were going back and forth bringing water and caring for the
wounded. Many casualties also resulted from the fire of sharpshooters
stationed in trees so thick with foliage that they could not be seen. Just as
we were about to break camp a doctor was shot dead within twenty feet of

me, while in the act of mounting his horse to go upon the firing line. Notwithstanding the deadly fire of the sharpshooters men were to remain within our lines and continue firing. How very inhuman was it for the enemy to fire upon our Red Cross—shooting doctors and members of the hospital corps while dressing a wound or carrying a wounded man to the rear! This seems incredible. I know of one wounded man being carried to the hospital by three men; when near the hospital one was shot dead, then the second man fell, while the third man dragged his wounded comrade into the bushes and waited until a squad of men came along and assisted in carrying the wounded man to the desired place. . . .

On the 3d . . . Our men began to get sick. . . . The doctors gave orders that all drinking water should be boiled. This order was not strictly carried out. It was so hot that the men in many cases paid no attention to it. I found two springs near a mango and cocoanut grove and reported it. It was fixed up and a guard from the Ninth Cavalry was stationed to guard these springs day and night. All of our drinking water came from them. I have been there when more than a hundred men would be in line waiting for their turn. . . .

July 17th a telegram of congratulation reached us. At 11:45 we were assembled and heard the reading of it. Then we were drawn up in line to witness the surrender. . . .

On July 26th, as I rode over the battlefield, I could plainly see in many places the earth drenched in human blood. On my return to camp I was taken sick with the fever and had camp dysentery. I was carried to the hospital on a litter and for twelve days lay at the point of death. The doctors gave me up to die. For six days I did not eat anything. Our hospital was situated on the brow of a hill, our only covering was a fly stretched above us. There were fourteen of us under this one fly. We had to lie with our heads uphill and dig holes in the ground with our heels to keep from slipping down on our comrades. It rained daily and as our tent fly did not shed water very well and both ends of course being open, we kept wet day and night. We had to lie on the wet ground. . . . A colored surgeon, Dr. A. M. Brown, United States Volunteers, was assigned to our regiment, but before his arrival, our chaplain, William T. Anderson, who is also an M.D. by profession, had arrived and had given relief to many of the sick men of our regiment. . . .

I returned to duty August 19th . . . but at 9:30 A.M., August 11th, a telegram came ordering our regiment to prepare to return to the United States. . . . We had done our duty as United States soldiers and were now sailing for our home.[12]

Bivins noticed a great deal not often covered in contemporary accounts, including the participation of Cuban rebels.[13] He also accurately recorded the deadly effectiveness of the Spanish soldiers, an effectiveness evident in the number of Americans killed in battle.[14] On the other hand, he modestly downplayed his heroism in continuing to fire his Hotchkiss gun after the other two members of his crew had been wounded. Promoted to squadron sergeant major for his outstanding service in Cuba, Bivins again saw combat on Samar Island in the Philippines in 1901, retiring soon thereafter to Billings, Montana. In World War I, Bivins returned to duty as a captain, a rare promotion for an African American. After the war, he went home to Montana, where he died in 1937.

## Casualties of War

As with most wars, disease claimed more lives than did combat in America's imperial wars. But the troops suffered from an array of tropical diseases for which the United States was completely unprepared. Malaria, dysentery, and yellow fever laid low thousands of soldiers, killing at least 2,500 in the few months of the Spanish-American War alone. On top of that, the United States succeeded in killing a few thousand additional soldiers by utterly failing to insure the healthfulness of the food supplied to its troops. Corrupt to the point of treason, American corporations knowingly supplied the military with tainted food, essentially poisoning soldiers for private gain. Battle proved safer than eating government-issued meat, as 385 Americans died in combat during the Spanish War, while some 2,500 died from the notorious "embalmed beef."

The experience of Roosevelt's Rough Riders provides an excellent example of the gap between national ambitions and the realities of military operations. At the end of the war, Roosevelt reported that 1,500 of his men had malaria, and less than 20 percent of the entire army was ready for active duty. When informed by the War Department that his troops were to remain in Cuba on garrison duty, Roosevelt wrote to General William R. Shafter that leaving these troops on Cuba was akin to a death penalty. Careful to supply a copy of his letter to the Associated Press, Roosevelt wrote: "Hardly a man has yet died from it, but the whole command is so weakened and shattered as to be ripe for dying like rotten sheep, when a real yellow-fever epidemic . . . strikes us, as it is bound to do if we stay here at the height of the sickly season. . . . Quarantine against malarial fever is much like quarantining against the toothache." Roosevelt then painted the War Department into a corner by confidently stating "that as soon as the authorities at Washington fully appreciate the condition of the army, we shall be sent home." In case they hesitated, he added, "If we are kept here it will in all human possibility mean an appalling disaster, for the surgeons here estimate that over half the army, if kept here during the sickly season, will die."[15]

Facing public pressure for immediate action, the War Department saw little alternative to moving these troops out of Cuba, thus creating a disaster unique in America's postwar experience. In some ways, the new chauvinism of the age, which insisted on men toughing it out and on women staying out of their way, bears some responsibility for the ensuing health crisis. The surgeon general, Dr. George M. Sternberg, refused to allow women to serve as nurses in Cuba, even experienced Red Cross volunteers. Sternberg insisted that just a "mild" fever had hit the troops, nothing to worry about. And yet ships arrived in Hampton Roads, Virginia, with as many as 80 percent of the soldiers ill. The rate of sickness had skyrocketed aboard the ships because the men were fed contaminated meat but no fresh water, and there had been no medicines on hand to treat them.[16]

One of these ships, the *Concho*, became a symbol of military incompetence and the mistreatment of soldiers, a hearse sailing along the East Coast. The ship's captain, Samuel Risk, intended to stop in Jamaica to take on fresh water and other essentials, but General Shafter ordered him to head straight to Hampton Roads without stopping. With nearly everyone on board sick, the *Concho* sat for three days in Hampton Roads awaiting orders, during which time more corpses were added to those already lying on the deck. The ship was ordered to sea to bury its dead and then sailed on to New York. When the ship, reeking of death, arrived in New York, the sick were removed to Hoffman's Island, the *Concho* was thoroughly disinfected, and the task of avoiding responsibility began. The city's chief health officer insisted it was not his responsibility, as did the surgeon general, who continued to maintain that there were no major medical issues facing the military; the secretary of war blamed the soldiers for leaving the hospitals in Cuba before they were properly recovered. President McKinley ordered a full investigation—by the War Department. To no one's surprise, the War Department concluded that nothing was wrong, though Captain Risk should have really been more emphatic on the need for water.[17]

But an even worse disaster lay ahead: at Montauk, New York. The army established a medical base there, Camp Wikoff, for troops returning from Cuba, assuring local residents that none of these soldiers would have anything so tawdry as a contagious ailment.[18] In a superb instance of bureaucratic idiocy, the War Department ordered troops to leave Cuba for Montauk before the camp had even been built.

Seriously ill soldiers were crowded aboard over-burdened old transports such as the *Grande Duchesse*, which had a single latrine for nearly one thousand men. The ship, like the *Concho*, became a floating death trap. Private Charles Johnson Post described how his friend Fred Engels "was discovered in his cabin, dead. How long he had been dead no one knew." His bunkmate was found sprawled unconscious on the floor of their room, which "was filthy with dysentery and neglect." Engels's body was thrown overboard. But then, in the "slow, sweet cool of dawn, we saw against the horizon the low purple silhouette of the hill of Montauk Point." The men aboard the *Grande Duchesse* thought they were saved. "We were home. . . . Sick men slapped each other on the back; men clawed up the ship's rail and looked hungrily at the distant shore. Stronger men helped weaker to the rail. There was wine in the very air." They had arrived at Camp Wikoff.[19]

But everything went wrong at Camp Wikoff. The first of the ill soldiers to arrive on August 9, 1898, found no shelter, no food, no water, no hospital, and it was raining. In fact, almost no work had been done on the camp, and more troops were arriving regularly, eventually swelling to thirteen thousand men. The wells they dug quickly dried up or brought forth contaminated water, leading to a ration of just a cup of water a day. The base commander, Brigadier General S.B.M. Young, housed the sick in large tents, but had only planned for 500 beds. Instead of food for soldiers, the army provided massive amounts of food for horses. The War Department also held back on medicine, convinced that the ocean air alone would cure yellow fever and typhus. The latter disease quickly spread through the camp, and many soldiers, fearing for their lives if they stayed in Montauk, fled to New York City, where several died on the city's streets. When food finally arrived, it was hardtack and had been shipped in wooden crates filled with worms. Given War Department accounts showing the shipment of an extensive variety of food, it was quickly evident that someone somewhere was appropriating these supplies meant for the nation's ill soldiers for private use.[20]

Charles Post left a vivid and bitter account of Camp Wikoff, where they were more prisoners than patients, let alone soldiers:

> [Our] only food supply was the volunteer civilian nurse. . . . There were almost twenty tents in our street, and he had about a hundred men to feed. He did all he could, faithfully and steadily. If he had not, we would have had nothing; no man, from the beginning of the war to its end, has my greater respect.
>
> It was on the third day, possibly the second, that a medical student came into the tent and examined us. He was what was known as a "contract surgeon" and he must have had two years in a medical school to qualify for such a job. . . . He gave the delirious soldier a bandage around his head; to me, five two-grain quinine pills and one fuzzy blue-mass pill of about vetinary size. The soldier with broken bones was told to lie quiet and later he would get a change of bandages! Lie quiet! How much sprightliness could you achieve with your right arm and left leg broken,

and maybe a rib or so[?] Also, the 'surgeon' insisted that I must get into hospital pajamas. . . .

The broken-winged soldier and I agreed that I must not get into my pajamas. "You can't get out of this camp if you're in pajamas—you can't run the guard. You've got to get out. There's plenty help outside. Get yourself out!"

. . . I swallowed the quinine pills, but I threw out the blue mass, a sort of compound cathartic made from mercury, I believe, and a very popular remedy nearly a century ago. It was the last medical examination I received in that quarantined hospital, and the last medicine. . . .

I knew that if I could get out I could get word to newspapermen somewhere. Whatever the hospital camp had been intended to be, it was not; it was in utter breakdown. . . . [The] grass between the tented streets was flecked with blood and dysentery. Few could make the latrine at the far end of the camp. Tents were latrines. . . . Then packing cases, sawed in half lengthwise, were brought in—one for about every five tents. They were neither emptied nor treated with chemicals, but they were a luxury measured by the effort that had gone before. One poor devil, weak and emaciated, toppled over and lay until he gathered strength enough to crawl off. Through all this the civilian volunteer nurse kept plugging away. I have often wished I had known his name.

It is difficult to realize the utter emptiness of time in those days. We measured time in food; in the time between chills; and when the fever left us, . . . we measured it in dysentery, and in latrines. . . . Yet, somewhere, Army contracts were flowing in the gentle warmth of political protection.[21]

Post managed to escape with the help of some Red Cross volunteers who had been trying to get in to help. He was stunned to learn that the army had not only been refusing the assistance of the Red Cross, but had refused to allow them into Camp Wikoff. As Post spread the story of conditions at the camp, he learned that several corporations had negotiated considerable contracts with the army for supplying goods and services that had never been delivered. "Every dollar of their profits," Post concluded, "was flecked with the blood of dead and dying men."[22]

Ultimately, more men died at Camp Wikoff than had on the battlefields of Cuba.[23] The public took notice when Rough Rider Lieutenant William Tiffany, a member of the famous jewelry company, died at the camp from "exposure and starvation."[24] The soldiers verged on rebellion, treated so poorly that one asked if they were "prisoners or patients."[25] The local paper, which had tried so hard to put forth the best face on the camp, finally reported, "There must be a screw loose somewhere when Uncle Sam's soldiers, backed by a country of unlimited resources, are allowed to starve on transports and compelled to depend upon charity for food when they land on our shores."[26] As local citizens rushed to fill the void created by the War Department, they questioned how matters had gone so disastrously wrong. As one East Hampton woman wrote, "These starving men whom we are feeding, who are so reduced that they come to me and beg, and who burst out crying when they get more than they can eat, who are they? Paupers reduced to want through their own fault? No! but the members of one of the finest armies the world ever saw . . . the victors of Santiago, come home to die for want of food."[27]

The military produced a number of bizarre explanations for the rapid spread of disease at Camp Wikoff, most memorably that the troops were just suffering from homesickness and nostalgia. The War Department naturally accused the press of exaggerating the troubles at the camp.[28] Meanwhile, similar events occurred at Camp Alger in Virginia—appropriately named for the secretary of war, Russell A. Alger—where the wells were cleverly dug next to the garbage dump, with predictable results. Secretary Alger, the spiritual forebear of Donald Rumsfeld, visited the camp, and, to the shock of reporters accompanying him, reported conditions excellent and that "The sick seem to be very cheerful."[29] The War Department cleverly camouflaged the depth of the crisis by keeping no records of affairs at Camp Wikoff, not even the names of those who were admitted there, making thousands of soldiers disappear as worried families scrambled for news of their whereabouts. Nor did the War Department inform families of the death of their sons. Once more, though, Secretary of War Alger blamed the troops for dying: "The whole trouble has been in the volunteer troops not knowing how to care for themselves and carelessness in warding off disease."[30] Camp Alger was hastily closed in September, the dead thrown in cheap pine coffins, and the whole mess covered over, with the military denying that anything had ever gone wrong. Major General Adna R. Chaffee summarized the official attitude in 1901: "Soldiers do not like sympathy; sympathy is for women and children. Soldiers are men."[31]

Most soldiers expressed relief to just get out of the army alive.[32] Mostly they returned home to public acclaim, if not support. The war, so brief, had remained popular, though its brevity also meant that veterans could not expect to receive any special treatment. In a move that would become familiar to many veterans of America's twenty-first-century wars, a number of banks even foreclosed on soldiers who could not make their mortgage payments while serving their country.[33]

Meanwhile, the war came to its official end. The United States and Spain began peace talks in Paris in October, 1898, failing to invite any representatives from Cuba or the Philippines. When the two nations signed the treaty in December, Cuba gained its independence, though it was pressured to integrate the

Platt Amendment, allowing the United States to intervene in Cuba's internal affairs, into its 1901 constitution. More startling, Spain transferred control of Puerto Rico, the Philippines, and Guam to the United States. For the first time in its history, the United States did not extend citizenship to its new territories and made no promises of future statehood, a position upheld by the Supreme Court in the *Insular Cases* (1901), declaring that residents of these new territories did not have constitutional rights. The American republic had become an imperial power with colonies stretching from the Caribbean across the Pacific to Asia. Colonial power required an expanded military and a new type of warfare, transforming the American military experience.

## The Philippines

Emilio Aguinaldo y Famy thought he had a deal with the Americans. Aguinaldo had emerged as the leader of the Philippine rebellion against Spanish rule in 1896, but agreed to a truce with the Spanish, took a sizable bribe, and settled in Hong Kong the following year. By 1898, it seemed that Philippine independence had been postponed for several years, when suddenly an American fleet appeared in Hong Kong harbor. Aguinaldo met with Commodore Dewey and—in his telling—agreed to aid the U.S. effort in return for Philippine independence. Dewey claimed to have no memory of such an agreement. He did, however, transport Aguinaldo to the Philippines, where the disgraced leader quickly revived his rebel organization and issued a call for a national uprising. This new rebellion gained momentum from the overwhelming success of the U.S. Navy on May 1, 1898.

The American press worked overtime to make the one-sided destruction of the Spanish fleet at Manila more of a challenge than it was, emphasizing the number of Spanish ships and the "formidable guns" of the Spanish shore batteries. In this version of the battle, victory resulted from the heroism, "efficiency," and "accurate marksmanship" of the American seaman, while the Spanish demonstrated an "absolute lack of skill."[34] But the Americans faced more danger from the heat than from the Spanish, as indicated by the narrative of a veteran sailor named Joel Evans, who entered the first battle of his long career in Manila Bay.[35]

For Evans, as for many others, the victory over the Spanish marked the triumph of the racially superior Anglo-Saxon. The Philippine people clearly saw it in a different light. In the month after the U.S. victory at Manila, some thirteen thousand volunteers rushed to lay siege to the capital, while throughout the islands, Philippine forces seized Spanish garrisons and took control of cities, mostly without bloodshed. In June 1898, Aguinaldo declared the Philippines an independent nation and established a government. Meeting with American officers in July, Aguinaldo confidently expected the United States to recognize his new government: "I have studied attentively the Constitution of the United States and in it I find no authority for colonies and I have no fear." He was, of course, correct—in theory.[36]

In August, the American and Philippine forces launched the battle for Manila. As Spanish defenses crumbled, General Wesley Merritt ordered that Philippine troops be kept out of the capital. Meanwhile, the United States was trying to decide what to do with the Philippines. Spain had collapsed everywhere the United States attacked, leaving President McKinley convinced that he had a divinely sanctioned right to determine what he should keep, no matter how little he knew about the territory in question. Meanwhile, the British writer Rudyard Kipling was urging the Americans to join their British cousins in taking up "the White Man's burden":

> Take up the White Man's burden
> Send forth the best ye breed
> Go, bind your sons to exile
> To serve your captives' need;
> To wait, in heavy harness,
> On fluttered folk and wild
> Your new-caught sullen peoples,
> Half devil and half child.[37]

A great many leading Americans were delighted to take Kipling up on his challenge, but few had any idea how best to take advantage of the Philippines; even Admiral Mahan was baffled. McKinley's cabinet favored taking Manila, and the president instructed the peace commission to demand the island of Luzon from the Spanish. But there was widespread public support for much more. *National Geographic* insisted that the United States should "take its rightful position among the nations of the earth. . . . Our policy in the future must be an aggressive one."[38] On October 25, McKinley changed his mind and sent the commissioners a cable instructing them to take all of the Philippines, though insisting that he was just responding to public demands for the islands. McKinley declared his desire to "civilize and Christianize them," ignoring the fact that they were already mostly Catholic.[39]

With the Treaty of Paris in January 1899, the United States paid Spain $20 million for the entire Philippines; no Filipinos participated in the decision. Aguinaldo issued a public statement condemning the avarice of "a nation which has arrogated to itself the title, champion of oppressed nations."[40] His objections fell on deaf ears, as within a matter of weeks the war against Spain had turned into a war against the Philippines, with deep racial animosities underlying the conflict—almost from the start of the Philippine resistance to American occupation, U.S. soldiers began applying familiar racist epithets to the native people.

African American troops found themselves in a particularly bizarre position, battling for white supremacy. When the African American Twenty-fifth Infantry Regiment landed, a nearby white man shouted, "What are you coons doing here?" Several of the soldiers shot back, "We have come to take up the White Man's Burden."[41] One black soldier serving in the Philippines, who preferred to remain anonymous, wrote the following letter home. He warned that applying "home treatment"—by which he meant racial segregation—to the Philippines would arouse animosity and resistance. The African American troops often got on well with the local population, sharing a sense of oppression at the hands of the whites and appreciating living in a society free of Jim Crow laws. One thousand black servicemen chose to stay on in the Philippines, and many of them married local women:[42]

On July 22, after a 22 days' sail, we arrived at Manila. I find the city far exceeding my idea of it as to cleanliness, civilization and general makeup.

I have mingled freely among the natives and have had talks with American colored men here in business, and who have lived here for years, in order to learn of them the cause of the Filipino dissatisfaction and the reason for this insurrection, and I must confess they have a just grievance. All this would never have occurred if the army of occupation had treated them as people. The Spaniards, even if their laws were hard, were polite and treated them with some consideration; but the Americans, so soon as they saw that the native troops were desirous of sharing in the glories as well as the hardships of the hard-won battles with the Americans, they began to apply home treatment for colored peoples: Curse them as damned niggers, steal and ravish them, rob them on the street of their small change, take from the fruit vendors whatever suited their fancy and kick the poor unfortunate if he complained, desecrate their church property, and after fighting began, looted everything in sight, burning, robbing the graves.

This may seem a little tall—but I have seen with my own eyes carcasses lying bare to the broiling sun, the result of raids on the receptacles for the dead in search for diamonds. The troops, thinking we [black troops] would be proud to emulate their conduct, have made bold of telling of their exploits to us. One fellow, a member of the Thirteenth Minnesota, told me how his boys did; another, a Tennessean, told me of how some fellows he knew had cut off a native woman's arm in order to get a fine inlaid bracelet. On upbraiding some fellows one morning, whom I met while out for a walk (I think they belonged to a Nebraska or Minnesota regiment, they were stationed on the Malabon road), for the conduct of the American troops toward the native and especially as to raiding, etc., the reply was:

"Do you think we could afford to stay over here and fight these damned niggers without making it pay all it's worth? The government only pays us $13 per month; that's starvation wages. White men can't stand it."

Meaning they could not live on such small pay. In saying this they never dreamed that colored soldiers would never countenance such conduct. . . .

I want to say right here, if it were not for the sake of the 10,000,000 black people in the United States God alone knows on which side of this subject I would be. And for the sake of the black men who carry arms and pioneer for them as their representatives, ask them to not forget the present administration at the next election. Party be damned! We don't want these islands, not in the way we are to get them, and for heaven's sake put the party in power that pledges itself against this highway robbery—expansion is too clean a name for it. . . .

I am informed that more colored regiments are to be formed. In which case, let us ask you with all good Afro-Americans, to endeavor to secure us officers of our own race. We probably do grand things under white officers, but it is not for them we do it, but for our people. . . . I want it understood that between black troops and white officers there is no affinity.[43]

In the succeeding year, American forces defeated Aguinaldo's forces in a conventional war for control of Luzon. U.S. forces fought brilliantly, adapting to circumstances and taking advantage of their opponents' shortcomings. Once they realized that the untrained Filipinos consistently fired high, the Americans adopted what would have been a suicidal tactic against professional opponents: charging straight at the enemy. Demoralized Filipinos repeatedly fled before the seemingly unstoppable Americans. Colonel Jose Alejandrino reported that, despite heavy fire, "the American lines continued to advance and no men fell. Our men became alarmed at the fact that the American troops seemed to be invincible."[44] With his armies shattered on the battlefield, Aguinaldo decided in November 1899, to abandon conventional warfare for a guerrilla campaign. The ensuing revolution, which is generally called the Philippine insurrection, was nasty, brutish, and long. President Theodore Roosevelt would declare the war officially over in 1902, by which time 4,200 U.S. soldiers had lost their lives. Yet the rebellion would persist on some islands until 1913, killing an estimated seven hundred thousand Filipinos. The United States would again employ free-fire zones, slaughtering civilians out of irritation with their inability to locate and identify the insurgents. More startling, torture became an active part of official military policy. Under orders from superiors, many soldiers took part in extracting information or punishing insurgents with torture; many others refused and eventually made public their disgust with such practices. As Mark Twain said in his powerful essay, "To the Person Sitting in Darkness," "We have invited our clean young men to shoulder a discredited musket and do bandits' work under a flag which bandits have been accustomed to fear, not to follow; we have debauched America's honor and blackened her face before the world."[45]

American troops did not quite understand the type of war they were fighting, putting down a rebellion for national independence in the name of conquest. Their opponents were often teenage boys and girls. The enemy ambushed the Americans, firing a few shots, and then fled. They found the Filipinos, in the words of a Lieutenant Baines, "what I consider savages; they were very low in intelligence, treacherous, cruel."[46] Frustration levels grew; in one of the most notorious incidents of the war, General Jacob H. Smith gave these orders to Marine Major Littleton Waller: "I want no prisoners. I wish you to kill and burn: the more you kill and burn, the better you will please me." He wanted the island of Samar reduced to "a howling wilderness."[47] When Waller asked for clarification of these orders, Smith told Waller to kill everyone over ten years old. Waller did his best to follow orders, even executing the native porters who were carrying his troops' supplies. Secretary of War Elihu Root, unknowingly replicating the language of Lieutenant Baines, held these actions "justified by the history and conditions of the warfare with the cruel and treacherous savages who inhabited the island." The use of past tense is telling.[48] Though a court-martial found that "there was no overwhelming necessity, no impending danger, no imperative interests, and, on the part of the natives, no overt acts to justify the summary course pursued," neither Smith nor Waller was punished for the slaughter of civilians.[49]

Many Americans initially refused to believe the stories coming out of the Philippines. The *New York Times* dismissed them as "forged or distorted documents" crafted by anti-imperialists to turn Americans against the war. After all, the documents relayed details "so grotesque" as to be incapable of being committed by Americans troops. Their very horribleness served as "clear proof of falsity or inaccuracy."[50] But even the *New York Times* had to admit the validity of tales of torture when the government made no effort to deny them, instead defending such actions as justified by the nature of modern warfare. A series of embarrassing courts-martial verified the facts but meted out few punishments.

In several instances, privates were punished for acts of inhumanity, while the officers who gave the orders remained untouched—out of 350 courts-martial reported by Secretary of War Root, just two officers were defendants.[51]

The most notorious practice undertaken by American forces in the Philippines was the "water cure." Testifying before the Senate Committee on the Philippines in 1902, the governor of the Philippines, William Howard Taft, admitted that U.S. troops used the torture known as the "water-cure treatment" against both insurgents and civilians, but he downplayed its brutality, insisting that there were "amusing instances" of Filipinos requesting the torture so that they could claim to have given information under duress.[52] To clarify what was meant by the water cure, the *New York World* offered this description to its readers:

This is used to extort information from Philippine prisoners. The victim is first bound hand and foot and laid on his back on the ground. Great quantities of water are then forced down his throat until he can hold no more. Pressure is then applied to the stomach until some of the water is expelled from the mouth, when more water is forced down. This process is repeated until the victim either gives the information required or dies.[53]

Experts debated whether the use of torture in the Philippines was more dehumanizing to the victims or to the American soldiers. As one editor put it, "officers who become brutalized and hardened by torturing the weak enemy will ere long show the same brutality toward those under them." There was at least one reported instance of a U.S. private who died while being given the water cure as punishment for insubordination.[54]

Stories of torture and the killing of civilians united an array of citizens in opposing this new American empire. The Anti-Imperialist League included leading intellectuals like William Dean Howells, Ambrose Bierce, Edgar Lee Masters, the humorists Mark Twain and Finley Peter Dunne, the ancient political reformer Carl Schurz, former presidents Benjamin Harrison and Grover Cleveland, and the nation's leading industrialist, Andrew Carnegie. American anti-imperialists found allies in other nations, probably none more influential than the Englishman John A. Hobson, whose insightful *Imperialism* appeared in 1902.[55] When the Anti-Imperialist League started collecting personal accounts from returning soldiers, the Republican leadership came under pressure to investigate charges of crimes against humanity. In 1902, the Senate organized a Committee on the Philippines chaired by the pro-war Henry Cabot Lodge of Massachusetts, a friend of President Roosevelt. But the hearings quickly got out of Lodge's control, as even friendly witnesses described outrageous actions with sanguine nonchalance. What had once been unthinkable had become routine, so that officers like General Robert P. Hughes could not understand why anyone would object to his casual racism and descriptions of the killing of women and children. The following is the testimony of Private William Lewis Smith and Corporal Richard T. O'Brien of the Twenty-sixth Infantry.

Q. [Senator Joseph L. Rawlins][56] You may state whether or not you witnessed what is known as the water cure.

A. [Private Smith] I did, sir.

Q. And where did you see it?

A. At the town of Igbaras.

Q. On what day?

A. November 27, 1900.

Q. Upon whom was it inflicted?

A. Upon the *presidente* of the town and two native police. . . . We arrived at the town about daylight in the morning. . . . There was an outpost put all over the town, so that no people could leave town by the gates, and we proceeded to quarters. . . . I was one of a detail that was sent out to ask the *presidente* to come over to the quarters. On the way we met him and proceeded to the house of the padre, the priest of the town, to get him. He was not at home.

The *presidente* went along over to the quarters. When I got back to the quarters, the boys were sitting around, and I went upstairs, and the first that I saw of the *presidente* was that he was stripped. He had nothing on but his pants. His shirt and coat were off, and his hands were tied behind him, and Lieutenant Conger stood over him, and also a contract doctor by the name of Dr. Lyons, and as we stopped there they proceeded to give him what is known as the water cure. It was given from a large tank. I should say the tank held—well—a hundred gallons, anyway. . . . He was thrown on his back, and these four or five men, known as the water detail of these Gordon Scouts, held him down. Water was administered by the opening of the faucet. We could not get close enough to see exactly how it was done, because if we would congregate there at all the officers would tell us to pass on. . . . We would go back and forth and see it at times.

. . . [A]fter he had confessed what they wanted . . . they all stood over him . . . and they asked him if he sent any word out to the insurgents when the troops arrived in town. One of the native police in the meantime disclosed that he had, that he had sent him personally, so in order to get that from him Lieutenant Conger called for the water detail. This time it was given by means of a syringe. Two men went out to their saddlebags and obtained two syringes, large bulbs, a common syringe, about 2 feet of common hose pipe, I should think on either end. One was inserted in his mouth and the other up his nose. We could all stand by there and see that. When this doctor said to get a pail of water, and they started into the building with him, Captain Glenn was there, and he said, "No, this is good enough right on the outside." So we all had a chance to witness it that time; and as the water did not seem to have the desired effect, the doctor stood over him and said to get a cup of salt. One of the men went upstairs and procured a cup of salt and it was thrown into the water and the interpreter stood there all the time, and after he had it some time he did disclose what they wanted, and he said he was willing to guide us out there. We went out and stayed the greater part of the day, but did not see anything of the insurgents. That is what I saw of the water cure.

Q. What became of that town?

A. It was burned about 8 o'clock under orders of Captain Glenn. Lieutenant Conger started out with his men—that is, the Eighteenth Infantry—to burn part of the town. Captain McDonald, of the Twenty-sixth, took his men and went to the lower end of the town. We started burning after they started burning at the other end, in order to give the natives time to get out before their buildings were burned.

Senator Dubois.[57] Did you personally do any of the burnings?

The Witness. Yes; I did set fire to some buildings.

Q. [Rawlins] How were those occupied?

A. By native men, women, and children alike. Nearly all of the buildings were bamboo and nipa,[58] and all you have to do is to light this nipa roof and it is gone in a short time. . . . They only had time to save the clothes that they wore at the time.

Q. Was any discrimination made as to whose buildings should be burned, and whose not?

A. The church was to be saved and the quarters occupied by our men, and five large buildings that were not made of this bamboo construction, but were made of wood—good buildings. They were to be saved for the occupancy of the women and children after the rest of the town was burned.

Q. You have already stated, I think, that this water cure was inflicted by Lieutenant Conger of the regulars, by scouts under his command?

A. Yes, sir. The way he had of ordering it done was "Water detail"; that is all I heard him say. The men went on then and did the rest of it. The men stood over, as did Captain Glenn and Dr. Lyons, and witnessed it both times.

Q. After the town was burned and after you returned the *presidente* what became of him?

A. He was taken to Iloilo for trial; I don't know what his sentence was. . . .

Q. [Senator Dietrich][59] You say that the *presidente*, after having received the water cure the second time, acted as guide to show you where the insurgents were?

A. In the mountains, yes. . . .

Q. He seemed to be in good condition, did he?

A. Yes, sir.

Q. And the water cure did not seem to injure him very much?

A. No; it does not seem to injure anyone very much after forcing the water out of him. They forced it out by placing a foot on the stomach.

Q. [Senator Beveridge][60] The chief effect is fright, is it not?

A. Yes, sir. . . .

Q. Do you know of many outrages by the natives upon the American troops? . . .

The Witness. No, sir; I do not know. . . .

*Testimony of Richard T. O'Brien*

[O'Brien]. There was a price on Captain [Fred] McDonald's head there. That was a generally known fact.

Q. Who put the price on it?

A. The insurgents. . . .

Q. [Senator Patterson][61] Do you know why?

A. For his cruelty and seeming barbarity. . . .

Q. [Senator Carmack][62] There is a statement by you published in a New York paper of an occurrence on the 27th of December. What year was that?

A. 1899. That was in the barrio of La Nog. . . . We entered the town. It was just daybreak. The first thing we saw was a boy coming down on a *carabao*,[63] and the first sergeant, William Stahlburg, shot at the boy. I don't know whether he intended to kill him or not. I know he didn't hit him. They boy jumped off the *carabao* and fled. . . . That was a sort of silent signal for a volley. Everybody fired at him. . . .

Q. [Beveridge] At the boy?

A. Yes, sir.

Q. I don't suppose you fired?

A. Yes, sir; I did. I am supposed to obey.

Q. Were you ordered to fire?

A. No, sir.

Q. What did you fire for, then?

A. I can not tell. A man fires when he is in those places. . . .

Q. You just fired a volley at the boy and quit?

A. Yes, sir. That brought the people in the houses out, . . . and how the order started and who gave it I don't know, but the town was fired on. I saw an old fellow come to the door, and he looked out; he got a shot in the abdomen and fell to his knees and turned around and died.

Q. Were you shooting then, too?

A. Yes, sir.

Q. And had you any orders to shoot?

A. Yes, sir.

Q. Who ordered you to shoot?

A. I don't know, sir. . . . After that two old men came out, hand in hand. I should think they were over 50 years old. . . . They had a white flag. They were shot down. At the other end of the town we heard screams, and there was a woman there; she was burned up, and in her arms was a baby, and on the floor was another child. The baby was at her breast, the one in her arms, and this child on the floor was, I should judge, about 3 years of age. They were burned. Whether she was demoralized or driven insane I don't know. She stayed in the house. . . .[64]

Many military personnel felt a great deal of sympathy for the Philippine people. Ensign John R.M. Taylor (who would rise in rank to rear admiral) interviewed numerous leaders of the rebellion and published translations of these encounters in hopes of persuading his government to treat the Filipinos with greater respect.[65] In 1901, the governor of the Philippine province of Tayabas, Major Cornelius Gardner, warned of the dangers of exporting racism to America's colonies and suggested a counterinsurgency policy based on respect for the native population. His confidential report was roundly ignored by his superiors, but came to light as the result of a Senate inquiry in 1902, effectively ending Gardner's military career:

After a two years' experience in this province I am convinced that the Tulisan [rebel] element can only be successfully operated against by constabulary or native troops, assisted by the native police of the towns, and that whatever insurgents, as such, there still remain in the province, had best now be operated against by natives and not by United States soldiers, and for this reason: In the first place a force of 300 men or more, composed of natives of this province, can easily be recruited here, which, fairly well treated and regularly paid and properly uniformed, could be depended upon to be loyal to its officers and the United States. Since I have been governor I have traveled all over this province with no other escort than natives. Secondly, as civil governor I feel it my duty to say that it is my firm conviction that the United States troops should, at the earliest opportunity, be concentrated in one or two garrisons, if it is thought desirable that the good sentiment and loyalty which formerly existed to the United States Government among the people of this province should be conserved and encouraged.

Being in close touch with the people, having visited all the pueblos one or more times, having lived with them in their homes, I know that such a sentiment once existed. Of late, by reason of the conduct of the troops, such as the extensive burning of barrios in trying to lay waste the country so that the insurgents can not occupy it, the torturing of natives by so-called "water cure" and other methods in order to obtain information, the harsh treatment of natives generally, and the failure of inexperienced, lately appointed lieutenants commanding posts to distinguish between those who are friendly and those unfriendly and treating every native as if he were, whether or no, an *insurrecto* at heart, this favorable sentiment above referred to is being fast destroyed and a deep hatred toward us engendered. . . .

Almost without exception soldiers, and also many officers, refer to the natives in their presence as "niggers," and the natives are beginning to understand what the word "nigger" means.

The course now being pursued in this province, and in the provinces of Batangas, Laguna, and Samar, is in my opinion sowing the seeds for a perpetual revolution, or at least preparing the people of these provinces to rise up in revolution against us hereafter whenever a good opportunity offers.[66]

Not only was the army's morale undermined by the brutality of U.S. policies, but opposition at home also grew, as many anti-imperialists came to blame the army for following inhumane orders. In Meadville, Pennsylvania, a crowd attacked some young men attempting to enlist for service in the Philippines.[67] That was an unusual case; more common was a popular belief that the military posed a threat to American democracy, an attitude which would feed the lack of preparedness for the nation's entry into World War I. For the first time since the Mexican War, a large number of Americans questioned the morality of war in the midst of a major military effort. To quote Twain once more, "We have crushed a deceived and confiding people; we have turned against the weak and friendless who trusted us; we have stamped out a just and intelligent and well-ordered republic; we have stabbed an ally in the back and slapped the face of a guest; we have bought a Shadow from an enemy that hadn't it to sell; we have robbed a trusting friend of his land and his liberty."[68] And in the years ahead, the United States would send its soldiers to support American interests in numerous conflicts that would attract little public attention but undermine the nation's international reputation. As many scholars and soldiers have noted, there is a direct line from the Philippine insurrection to the Vietnam War.[69]

# 7

# World War I

The United States entered the First World War promising to make the world "safe for democracy." Europe had rushed to war in August 1914, in what many Americans saw as little more than a collective suicide that had little to do with them. President Woodrow Wilson struggled to maintain American neutrality, winning reelection over the more bellicose Republicans in November 1916 on the promise, "He kept us out of war." Yet just one month after his second inauguration, Wilson drove up to the Capitol surrounded by cavalry to call on Congress to declare war on Germany and its allies. There were many reasons for the entry of the United States into the war, most notably Germany's use of submarine warfare in an effort to cut off the flow of food and material to Great Britain and France. Cynics also highlighted the superior skill of British propagandists, who painted a horrific portrait of the marauding Huns—as Kaiser Wilhelm II had called his own troops. There was also the none-too-subtle fact that American exports to Britain and France rose from $756 million in 1914 to $2.7 billion in 1916, while trade with Germany diminished to near zero as a consequence of the effective British blockade. And then there were the $2 billion in loans from American banks to the Allies that had to be protected.[1] In this context it is little wonder that Senator George Norris charged, "We are going into war upon the command of gold" to "preserve the commercial right of American citizens to deliver munitions of war to belligerent nations."[2]

The government of the Russian czar had collapsed just one month earlier, allowing Germany and the Austro-Hungarian Empire to begin transferring troops to the western fronts in France and Italy. The strictest calculation indicated that the United States posed little immediate threat to the Central Powers: with just one hundred thousand men, the American military ranked seventeenth in the world. Though first-rate, the fifteen-thousand-strong Marine Corps was scattered through the American Empire, while the U.S. Navy alone seemed to pose a real threat to Germany. But even here, the Germans, with their sizable submarine fleet, felt confident. Admiral Eduard von Capelle, Germany's naval minister, assured the Reichstag that the Americans would never make it to Europe "because our submarines will sink them. Thus America from a military point of view means nothing, and again nothing and for a third time nothing."[3] The admiral would be proven wrong.

## America Comes to Europe

Though the United States declared war in April 1917, its troops did not begin arriving in great numbers in France until 1918, just in time to block the Germans' spring offensive that was decimating the French armies. By August the United States had fielded 1.3 million men, a decisive force that inexorably altered the balance of power in western Europe.

Until the time of America's entry into the war, from fall 1914 through spring 1918, the combatants on the western front were locked in the bloody gridlock of trench warfare.[4] Machine guns and artillery had made every effort by either side to break the stalemate a lethal exercise. On July 1, 1916, Field Marshal Sir Douglas Haig launched yet another effort to crack through the German lines; the resulting Battle of the Somme was the deadliest day in British military history. On that single day, one-fifth of the one hundred thousand men who crossed no-man's-land died, while another 40 percent were wounded. Canada's First Newfoundland Regiment essentially ceased to exist. Haig's response was to order repeated attacks that claimed thousands more lives but failed to shift the front line in any significant fashion. It was slaughter and deserved no other name.[5] It was into this maelstrom that the United States entered in 1918.

The commander of the American Expeditionary Force, General John Pershing, successfully maintained an independent command rather than giving in to Allied demands that American troops be integrated into the weakening French and British armies. He also resisted what he saw as a trench-warfare mentality, one which accepted static positions. Instead he promoted a campaign of mobility, one which many historians feel cost the Americans unnecessarily heavy casualties, while others credit Pershing's open-field tactics with knocking the Germans out of the war.[6]

Trench warfare exceeded the abilities of even the most able commanders to formulate effective actions. Technology had advanced in uneven ways, giving armies the means to inflict horrendous casualties on an opponent, but not the means to adequately control the machines of war. Once a battle was joined, plans collapsed and commanders usually lost contact with their subordinates and could see little through the all-encompassing smoke, while the terrible explosions drowned out any meaningful communication at the front. As John Keegan trenchantly summarized the nature of warfare in 1914 to 1918: "Generals were like men without eyes, without ears and without voices, unable to watch the operations they set in progress, unable to hear reports of their development and unable to speak to those to whom they had originally given orders once action was joined. The war had become bigger than those who fought it."[7] General Pershing hoped to avoid the pitfalls of this new warfare by relying far more on junior officers and sergeants.[8]

Pershing's obstinacy appeared to pay off at Belleau Wood. On May 27, 1918, the Germans unleashed the greatest artillery barrage of the war, as six thousand guns fired two million shells in four hours at Chemin des Dames ridge. The Germans then rolled forward, breaking through to Chateau-Thierry, fifty miles from Paris. The Second and Third American Divisions rushed forth to stop the German advance; at their center stood a brigade of U.S. Marines, responsible for holding the road to Rheims that ran through Belleau Wood. Pummeled by the Germans, the marines held doggedly on. When a French officer suggested to Captain Lloyd Williams that they should retreat, Lloyd responded, "Retreat? Hell, we just got here." The Marine counterattack stopped the Germans in their tracks.[9]

Marine Private E.A. Wahl described the Battle of Belleau Wood in a letter to his girlfriend, dated June 27, 1918:

Just as the day was breaking, about 3 A.M. of the 4th, we drew up in the main street of a little deserted village in the midst of the boom and flash of big guns. We climbed out with our machine guns and equipment and trailed off into a little near-by woods. Excitement began to drive away our weariness then. We were told to rest, and that we wouldn't be going into the lines until evening. Managed to sleep for a couple of hours, but the roar from the artillery and machine guns in front became so heavy as the day advanced that rest was impossible. Stretchers with wounded French Marines began coming up from the lines. Ambulance after ambulance dashed down and dashed back again. We realized that we were at last in the thick of things. About noon a couple of high-explosive shells dropped near us. Then another and another. We were caught in an enemy artillery barrage that lasted about two hours. Our first casualty occurred then, a Corporal Johnson was hit by a piece of shell through the back, and died a few minutes afterwards.

We sought shelter everywhere, falling flat on our faces as we heard shells come screeching down. That was our only protection. We just had to lie flat wondering if the next was going to get us. One shell landed about fifteen feet from me and exploded. I heard a scream at the same time and looked up. It had landed in a hole where two chaps from another company were lying. Several of us rushed over to the spot and pulled them out. They were horribly cut up, but not dead. . . . I can't begin to describe my state of mind—you will just have to imagine it. We were getting our first real taste of the horrors of war.

At dusk we fell into single file and started down a road toward the lines. Dead and wounded were liberally distributed along the road. Shell-shock victims acting like crazy men were being led to the rear by comrades. I will never forget that first trip through the pitch darkness of tangled woods down to our first positions. Bullets whistling around us snipping off tree branches, big shells screaming and crashing in all directions, stumbling into shell-holes and over fallen trees, taking about three hours to reach our positions—it tested one's endurance to the limit. We arrived about midnight to a position on the edge of the woods overlooking a piece of No Man's Land. Threw off my pack and ammunition boxes and fell right to sleep. Didn't even trouble to dig or find a hole. Awoke at daylight amid an awful din. The infantry around us was preparing to make an attack and our artillery was throwing over a barrage. Everybody was awake and on the job. We could see the Boches [Germans] running out of a little patch of woods to our left that our guns were shelling heavily. We opened up on them. We silenced one of their machine guns in the woods that was shooting directly into us. Then our infantry started over after them. Several of the boys dropped on the way, but most of them made it. Only a few of the Boches were left in the woods and most of them called, "Kamerad!"

The whole sixteen days was just a nightmare of this sort of business—attacks and counter-attacks. I cannot describe it. The aggressiveness of the Marines halted this drive of the Germans, I am told. We are the pets of the French people these days. We advanced and held ground which the French troops that we relieved were evacuating. It has been costly, though. Ted Fuller (Captain) an old classmate of mine was killed. Major Cole, of the Machine-Gun Battalion, was wounded badly and died a couple of days afterwards. Our Colonel Catlin was shot through the right lung by a sniper, but is getting along fine, I understand.[10] . . . So, you see, destruction plays no favorites here. It is not only the lowly private that gets picked. We have lost some splendid chaps from our company.

The Germans have suffered terribly, though. Whenever we have made an advance and taken over positions evacuated by them we find their bodies lying about everywhere.[11]

In September, a half million fresh U.S. troops launched their first major offensive, at the St. Mihiel salient, followed two weeks later by the Meuse-Argonne offensive—both significant American victories. German General Erich

Ludendorff attributed the collapse of his army's morale to "the sheer number of Americans arriving daily at the front."[12] German strategy on the western front had been based on a series of calculations that involved exhausting the French and British—an approach that had brought both Allied armies to the point of complete collapse and, in the French case, open mutiny. And now here were these Americans arriving in their fresh millions; perhaps they were not the best-trained troops in the world, but they were enthusiastic and seemingly limitless—it was well known that 24 million men had registered for the draft in the United States. Against such numbers the Germans could not hope to contend, as the September battles made abundantly clear. Both the St. Mihiel and Meuse-Argonne offensives had been well planned and effectively prosecuted, clear indications of what Germany would face if the war continued.

During the brief duration of American participation in the war, most soldiers maintained a conviction that they were doing the right thing. On May 4, 1918, Adrian Edwards, a lawyer from Carrollton, Illinois, who had volunteered to serve in the U.S. Army, expressed his faith in the cause in a letter to his mother:

Somewhere in France
My Dear Mother:

I am about to go into battle and have instructed the company clerk to send you this letter in case I become a casualty, hence the receipt of this letter by you will indicate that I am either with God or a prisoner in the hands of the enemy. . . .

Do not grieve that I am among the missing, but rather rejoice that you have given a son in sacrifice to make the greatest military caste of all time lay down the sword—to save civilization, to prevent future wars, to punish the Germans, who have disregarded every law of God and mankind, whose only god is the god of war and military force—and to make the world safe for democracy. . . .

War was absolutely necessary on the part of my country, and although I was thirty-four years old and nobody expected me to go, yet some one had to go; some one must make the sacrifice, some mother must lose her son.

In the light of these facts, and knowing our country's great need, I volunteered, and have never for one moment regretted my decision, and I will not, although my life and a useful career must end. Life is not the highest boon of existence. There are ideals that are superhuman, interests greater than life itself, for which it is worth while fighting, suffering, and dying. . . .

Good-bye, Mother; I will see you in the next world. You may know I died fighting for you, my country, and all that life holds dear.

Your son Adrian[13]

Edwards died in battle that same day.

## Air Combat

The airplane introduced an entirely new element into warfare. While its utility in World War I was largely limited to reconnaissance and artillery observation, it captured the public imagination and added to the psychological trauma of modern war as attacks could now come from above.[14] The U.S. Army established the Aeronautical Division in 1907 under the Signal Corps but never developed it beyond a tangential effort linked solely to reconnaissance. As a consequence, the United States had to rely almost entirely on French and British planes during the war. General Billy Mitchell, commander of the AEF's Air Service, did an outstanding job organizing air support during the St. Mihiel offensive in September 1918. Mitchell also proposed what could have been one of the most dramatic developments of the war: the massed dropping of paratroopers behind German lines. General Pershing supported the proposal, but the war ended before this innovation could be put into effect.

The first American pilots mostly began as enthusiasts who forced the military to pay attention to aircraft. Many of them joined the Lafayette Escadrille, bringing France a great deal of good publicity, especially after James McConnell wrote an exciting book in the grand tradition of glorious warfare shortly before he was shot down and killed in 1917.[15] Combat in the air appeared to many soldiers and civilians a return to the personal combat missing from trench warfare. The contests in the air often occurred before an audience in the trenches below, lending these dogfights, as they were called, the air of medieval jousting. McConnell's book captured that aspect of the war with gusto.

One of the first professional pilots in the American military was Alfred A. Cunningham. At the age of sixteen he had enlisted with the Georgia Volunteers to serve in the Spanish-American War, spending some time in Cuba on garrison duty. In 1909 he gave up selling real estate in Atlanta and joined the Marine Corps. While stationed at the Philadelphia Navy Yard in 1911, Lieutenant Cunningham used his own money to rent an airplane and taught himself to fly. The following year, Cunningham received official flight training at Annapolis, becoming the Marines' first aviator in March 1913. In February 1917, Cunningham organized the Marine Corps Aeronautic Company, which included seven pilots. With the U.S. declaration of war, the Marines, like every other branch of the service, began a rapid expansion. Cunningham hoped to build up the marine air corps and oversaw the training of more pilots. On orders from the Marine Corps commandant, Major General George Barnett, Cunningham went to France to study French and British aviation training and operations, arriving in Paris in November 1917. His diary records that trip:

> Monday, November 19, 1917. . . . Everyone I talk to is extremely pessimistic about the war. Most of them seem to believe it is hopeless to hope to whip the Germans and they are unanimous in saying that if we don't hurry the Germans will win. The French people, men and women, seem fairly cheerful but if you watch them closely they have a desperate tense look when not on their guard. My opinion from what I see and hear is that if we do not do something big next summer, it is all over. If we do, it will last two years longer and we win.
>
> Thursday, November 22, 1917. . . . Went over to the Invalides and saw all kinds of captured German guns and howitzers. . . . They had on view one Fokker monoplane, an L.V.G. biplane and a Rumpler 2 seater which were captured in excellent condition. They were all interesting, especially the motors, one of which had 5 valves to each cylinder, 3 intake and 2 exhaust. The most interesting thing I saw was Capt. [Georges] Guynemer's little Spad, the "Veaux Charles," which means Charles, old fellow. He downed 19 boches with this machine. The French have it decorated profusely with the tri-color and flowers all over it. . . .
>
> Saturday, November 24, 1917, Army Ecole de Aviation, Tours, France. Got up at 7 a.m. and Maj. Dunsworth had his Hudson at Hotel for me at 8. Rode out to the Ecole de Aviation. . . . It is quite a big place with 10 very large wooden hangars and several Bessioneau canvas hangars. . . . They have about 65 Caudron training planes and 2 Nieuport of chasse model but old. This place can be made into an excellent school but is in bad shape now. . . . Am afraid Dunsworth is not much of a C.O. Most of the men who handle the machines are Algerians. There are a great many women working in the shops. . . .
>
> Monday, November 26, 1917, Ecole de Aviation Francaise, Avord, France. . . . Arrived in Avord at 9:30 a.m. and found that the aviation school was 2 miles from the station and no way to ride. I started out on foot in mud 2 inches deep and my feet were wet and freezing when I arrived. Was introduced to the Commandant, Col. Fabre, and the Chief of Flying, Capt. Levy. Both were extremely nice. The Colonel cannot speak English so I cannot know him well. Capt. Levy was manager of a South American railroad and speaks English very well. He is the real head of the school and has a very fine organization. This school is larger than all the

other schools in France combined. They have 800 airplanes in commission and have 11 flying fields besides the big one at the main station. There are 3000 mechanics here. They have every kind of machine here made in France. . . .

Sunday, December 2, 1917, Hotel de France, Pau, France. . . . Saw the machine in which young Fowler was killed day before yesterday. It was certainly a wreck and had blood all over the cockpit. I saw pieces of Fowler's flesh still hanging on the windshield. They kill here more than 1 pilot every day, which, when one thinks of it, is an enormous percentage. There must be some fault with their training methods. . . .

Monday, December 3, 1917. . . . I went to the acrobacy field and witnessed some of the finest acrobatic flying I ever saw by Sergt. Petib and another flyer. They did everything that can be done with an aeroplane. . . .

Tuesday, December 4, 1917. . . . After visiting the hangar where the Wright Bros. made their first flight in France, I was driven to the acrobacy field and watched the pupils do the reinversements, "barrel" etc. for the first time. You could see from the ground they were nervous about it. Lieut. Simon then went up in "The Black Cat" and did the most wonderful stunts within 500 ft. of the ground. He is the best flyer in France and a very nice fellow. I like the Nieuport very much but it is certainly quick and nervous. There are an unusual number of Americans here learning to fly for the French Flying Corps. The French seem to be giving out of good material for aviators. . . . I like Pau better than any place I have been in France. The scenery is beautiful and the people seem to be human. . . .

Tuesday, December 18, 1917. . . . Got up frozen stiff. The weather fairly clear. Persuaded a French pilot of a biplane fighting Spad to take me over the lines. We went up like an elevator and talk about speed! We were over the lines in no time and I was all eyes. The archies [antiaircraft fire] bursting near us worried me some and made it hard to look all the time for boches. I saw something to one side that looked like a fountain of red ink. Found it was the machine gun tracer bullets from the ground. After a few minutes we sighted a boche 2 seater just below us. We made for him. It was the finest excitement I ever had. I got my machine gun ready. Before we got to him he dived and headed for home. On 1 of our rolls I let loose a couple of strings of 6 at him but it was too far for good shooting. After following him a ways over the lines we turned to look for another. None were out so we came home. Finest trip I ever had. . . .

Thursday, December 20, 1917, French front near La Cheppe. . . . About 9 a boche biplane came over and a Frenchman from 65th tackled him. The fun only lasted a minute and Mr. Boche came spinning down and fell in a field just across the road. We were there in no time. Both were killed, of course. Pilot had a bullet in his head. The observer was killed by the fall. The photographer went over and took a photo which he promised to send me. About an hour later another boche came over and 2 Frenchmen from 15th shot him down but he fell some distance away and I did not go over. Watched the Archies trying to hit our machines the rest of the day.[16]

Cunningham returned to the United States in January 1918, with plans for the joint navy and marines Northern Bombing Group, with the goal of attacking German U-boat bases along the Belgian coast. The plan was approved and in March 1918, Cunningham organized the First Marine Aviation Force, which performed well in the last months of the war. Cunningham was awarded the Navy Cross for his organizational work, retiring from the Marines because of ill health as a major in 1935 and dying four years later.

What the public liked about the war in the air was its single combat between dashing pilots. A few American pilots, such as the ace Edward Rickenbacker, fed that image, but the letters of Hamilton Coolidge provide a more realistic view of flying in wartime. Coolidge, a direct descendent of Thomas Jefferson, attended Groton and Harvard with Theodore Roosevelt's son Quentin. The two friends enlisted in the U.S. Army Air Service, Coolidge joining the Ninety-fourth Aero Squadron in June 1918. He quickly became an ace, shooting down eight enemy aircraft, and was awarded the Distinguished Service Cross. In the letter below to his mother, he describes aerial combat and the death of Quentin Roosevelt:

Sunday, July 21 [1918] Mother Dear, . . . From the air it is often difficult to distinguish where the lines are or to tell just what is going on. What you do see are thousands of shell-holes, the frequent flashing of guns, and a great quantity of smoke; sometimes large heavy columns of it, more often hundreds of little streaks of smoke.

Last night, we flew at a very low altitude, quite peacefully for a while, until suddenly, woof! a fierce shock rocked my little ship, and in a few seconds there were many of those disturbing black puffs all around and among us. We all began to squirm and twist and that throws off their aim, but golly, how a close shot makes one jump when it arrives unexpectedly! A group of six Huns appeared, obviously trying to pick a scrap—because why? We were in their territory and half a gale of wind was endeavoring to push us further in. They knew that all they had to do was to keep us bothered for a short while after which our gasoline supply would be insufficient to carry us home against that heavy wind. Even if they did not shoot a single one of us down, we should be forced to land in their territory and become prisoners. But we saw the situation as clearly as did they (for a wonder) and refused to delay a single minute. You can see that it is important to grasp the situation quickly and not to fight when conditions are strong against you, even though there appears to be a tantalizing prey. I'm afraid that that is how poor Quentin was lost. You knew about his loss surely? I think he forgot about the strong wind against him when he saw the Boches. Undoubtedly he fought splendidly, but when it was over, he had drifted still further into Bocheland and had insufficient fuel to come out. Probably also they kept bothering him every foot of his way.

Really it is almost laughable the way you move and countermove, retreat or advance, in preparing a big combat or "dog-fight." These do not often happen because circumstances usually make it foolhardy for one or the other patrol to fight. The ordinary case is where a whole patrol picks on a few planes over which it has an advantage of position etc. Then frequently another formation comes to the rescue and you have an unpremeditated "dog-fight." . . . War provides *such* a good justification for flying!

Coolidge was killed on October 27, 1918—just two weeks before the war's end—when German antiaircraft fire hit his plane over the Ardennes.[17]

## The Horror of Modern Warfare

World War I marks a dramatic change in military memoirs, not just in the United States but in many other nations, as veterans did not hesitate to describe graphically the horrors of war. Even letters home became far more explicit than in the past, though they often adopted a terse, almost telegraphic style that Ernest Hemingway would soon make his own. As one veteran wrote in the introduction to his book, "There is no plot, no climax, no happy ending to this book."[18] Machine guns, submarines, tanks, airplanes, poison gas, trench warfare—the technology of war overwhelmed the human imagination, as did the random and hideous nature of death. A stray fragment of shell could tear away a soldier's face in an instant, while a single small splinter could enter the wrong organ, killing a person without visible cause.[19] No-man's-land was littered with body parts, and digging new trenches could turn up an arm here or a head there. Military personnel witnessed so many new horrors that it quickly became apparent that humans had made a great leap forward in their ability to kill one another and to wipe out the evidence of their own civilization. The ruins of towns and farms, of humble homes and the soaring spires of cathedrals demonstrated to all who saw them a dark future.[20]

For so many of those who served, World War I negated the very idea of progress that had been at the heart of American identity. The war seemed like a giant leap backward into the horrors of primitive warfare, in which competing peoples hacked away at one another until only a few were left standing. Both romance and reason dissipated with the clouds of poison gas as the war dragged to its exhausted end. All sense of heroism and glory, or human wisdom and compassion, died in the trenches of northern France. "I was always embarrassed by the words sacred, glorious, and sacrifice and the expression in vain," Ernest Hemingway wrote in *A Farewell to Arms*. "I had seen nothing sacred, and the things there were glorious had no glory and the sacrifices were like the stockyards at Chicago. . . . There were many words that you could not stand to hear and finally only the names of places had dignity. . . . Abstract words such as glory, honor, courage, or hallow were obscene beside the concrete names of villages, the numbers of roads, the names of rivers, the numbers of regiments and the date."[21]

Despite censors and orders to write only positive letters, many soldiers wrote home truthful accounts of the everyday nature of trench warfare. The following letters are from Corporal Adel Storey of Wichita, Kansas, to his parents:

At the Front in France, April 10, 1918
My Dear Father And Mother: We are in the trenches now. The weather conditions are fairly good now with the exception of being cloudy, so that the trenches could not dry up. It is so muddy that I think I am getting web-footed. We are sure getting used to the noted mud of this country, for we eat in mud, sleep in mud, and live in mud, and if there is anything else to do, I guess we do it in mud too. We are living in dugouts down in the side of the trench. We don't have very much to do in the daytime, but we have plenty to do at night. Generally, in the evening there is some artillery dueling until dark, and then at various intervals a machine gun somewhere along the trench opens up. Occasionally we get a gas alarm some time during the night and rockets are sent up so we can see what is going on out in No Man's Land. It seems to me about the easiest way to startle a fellow is to have him on post by himself, and then have the sentry next to him shoot at something (or nothing) with his rifle or machine gun.

There are several ruined towns near here. They are nothing but heaps of stone now. All the people have long since left this part of the country, leaving it entirely to military operations. . . .

At the Front, May 12, 1918
My Dear Mother And Father: . . . I do not know of much that is new or startling; it is just the same thing day in and day out. It manages to rain

about every other day or so and keeps the trenches in continual mud. If it were not for the boards that we have in the bottom of the trenches, we would nearly have to swim all the time.

. . . We have to wear our gas respirator and helmet at all times. . . . Our respirator and helmet weigh a little over six pounds, and with one on your head and the other hanging round your neck, you can imagine how it feels. And then, none of the passageways or tunnels and lots of the dugouts are high enough to stand up in. I think, though, that my neck must be a couple of inches shorter than it used to be from bumping my head on the beams. . . .

I don't know very much war "dope," for I haven't seen a paper dated later than the 5th, so you must know more than I do. I wish this war were over, though. Even though I have only been in this country six months to-day, I am getting tired of it already. We nearly always have time to sleep in the daytime, but at night we either have to stay up all the time, or, if we lie down, we have to lie with cartridge belt and gas masks on, and rifle and bayonet by our sides. It is night now, and I am sitting here writing with my belt and mask hanging on the chair, pistol on the table and rifle leaning against the wall, waiting for—I don't know what next. We never know one minute what is going to happen the next.

I don't know whether I have ever mentioned the rats which infest the trenches or not, but I know that you have read of them in different places. Never in my life have I seen rats of such size as these are here. They don't run from us, either, like any ordinary rat does. They will fight like a good fellow when you fool with them. . . . One of the fellows remarked the other night that this is the first time in his life that he had seen cats run away from home by the rats. But it is a fact, when everything is quiet at night around the trenches and in the dugouts the rats are out in force and the cats take refuge in No Man's Land.

Well, I must get ready to go on watch now as it is nearly midnight and my watch is the last half of the night to-night.

I am sorry to tell you, but I must, for if I don't tell you I am afraid no one else will, Fred was injured two or three days ago. I don't know just how nor how seriously, as he was taken to the hospital before I had a chance to see him. . . . Mother, will you write to Mrs. McKaig and tell her? . . .

Lots of love and best wishes to all from Adel[22]

Unlike Adel Storey, Peyton Randolph Campbell was a prosperous young man with a promising career when the United States entered the war. He worked for Pratt & Lambert, an advertising firm in Buffalo, New York, and gained some fame for promoting Liberty Bonds with a phony newspaper front page announcing the German invasion of the United States. Though he probably could have used his influence to get a desk job as an officer, he entered the infantry as a private. From his arrival in France in the spring of 1918, Campbell kept a diary, which he sent to his mother from time to time:

*Wednesday, May 15th* . . . Out here a man is nothing more than what he brings with him inside himself—and that's why the study is so interesting. Some men are found to be all veneer—others—lots of them—find their very best, strongest selves—an ego that in many cases even they themselves have never known before—underneath the shell that has covered them all their lives. . . .

*Thursday, June 13th* . . . When at last we got off the train, we landed in a very prosperous little manufacturing town of three or four thousand— evidently a munitions center, with many new and very beautiful homes, and yet a certain not-quite finished air that was not at all French, and much more American, it seemed to me. However, the greeting we got was truly French—the most enthusiastic we've had anywhere. All the boys were showered with flowers—I'm enclosing a white rose that a little French girl stuck in my hat. One boy—a youngster of about ten—grabbed my hand and trudged along with me for fully two miles, meanwhile giving me all the gossip. . . .

Next morning we started on what was to prove the last lap of our journey, for the present, at least. The sun was scorching and although until now I've experienced no foot trouble worth mentioning, that baking road had me almost ready to cry "Nuff!" . . . [W]e arrived at what one of the boys, in a letter home, has described perfectly as a "poverty-stricken, God-forsaken, one-horse French village." We have pitched our tents in a field on a hillside overlooking the little place, and feel quite settled now, though it's just twenty-seven hours since we got here. The town is so primitive that the natives wear wooden shoes, live in the house with the cattle, and listen to a town-crier at sundown. . . .

[Campbell's outfit moves up to the front.]

*Tuesday, July 2nd* . . . We're holding what is known as the "second line." Nothing much happens here except when the enemy attacks and licks the first line, which is quite a distance away. As it's a very quiet sector, it's hardly like real war, but the scenery is genuine enough to suit anyone! Our trench is situated on the side of a hill, overlooking a valley and another hill beyond. Behind us are other trenches which seem to be held by some infantry reserves. The old ditch is about thirty yards long, and at each end is a dugout—one or two-room affair, with a little area at the rear, and a place for a kitchen beyond that. The dugout is lined with wood, and has a ceiling of corrugated iron. Above this there is a solid layer of sandbags and stone perhaps four feet thick. . . .

[By August the Americans are in pursuit of the retreating Germans.]

*Saturday, August 10th* . . . As we lumbered on, we entered a section of country that has recently been evacuated by the enemy. This made the scenes remarkably different from those of the stagnant, crystallized front we left. Everywhere were signs of the struggle—the roads alone, as always, have been rebuilt and were nearly perfect. As for the rest—chaos! Piles of rubbish hurriedly thrown together—houses a mass of stone, slate, tile and freshly-splintered timber. Here a bridge blown up—there a huge shell-hole on the railroad, the bent and twisted ends of the rails vividly illustrating the force of the explosion. On every side, shell-holes—shell-holes— shell-holes. The roadsides, the houses, the broad grainfields are all dotted with them. One wonders how life could have existed in the midst of all that—but it did—and for many it must have been a triumphant crisis of life, too! The enemy's need of certain materials is shown by the fact that every telegraph and telephone pole in this section had been carefully stripped of its wires, and also by the great junk-piles where other metals had been assembled, preparatory to being loaded and shipped back to Germany.

Some of the towns we drove through were quite wealthy, with fine homes and public buildings, costly villas and beautifully-planned streets—but such wreckage you never saw! Gaping holes in the stone and brick walls, giving glimpses into the looted remains of these once palatial rooms. Whenever he had time the Hun tarried to destroy! It was only when he was too sorely pressed for time that he left things of value unharmed.

*Sunday, August 11th* . . . But to come back to the sights of today. A mere chronicle couldn't cover them all—the wrecked planes, the German rifles and other equipment, including much that was brand new—helmets, belts, ammunition-boxes and other things—a whole building full of huge beer-kegs (unfortunately empty!), a dump perhaps fifty yards square, full of new boxes of hand-grenades, of the "potato-masher" type; the graves of Willy Schneider and another "Heinie" whose name I forget, who died on my birthday—I could keep it up for pages!

. . . As I write, every once in a while there's a heavy explosion. That's from the mines which the Germans sowed all through this region, but had no time to explode. The Pioneers are ferreting them out and making them harmless—a job I wouldn't relish a great deal. . . .

*Thursday, August 15th* Our morning greeting was another gentle rain of shells, many of which were falling right in our tiny wood. We were driven from our half-finished trenches, and took shelter in some old funk-holes at the rear of the wood. The shells seemed to follow us there, too, so back we raced to our former shelter. Soon the din subsided, and we were able to lift up our heads and look about us. . . . Once again, not a scratch to show!

. . . [B]etween nine and one "Con" and I sat at our posts, listening to the night sounds of the front. Behind us, and a bit to our left, was a busy battery of 75's. I think "Jerry" hates the 75 as much for its triumphant sound as he does for its marvellous rapidity of fire. The shell leaves the gun with a musical hum that rises in sharp crescendo almost to a shriek. Then as the shell passes the sound dies away, then presently, far off, you hear the dull crash as the shell performs its mission somewhere behind the *Boche* lines. . . .

As we sat there at the gun, "Fritz" launched a gas attack on a neighboring town. The shells passed directly in front of our position, and . . . I'll never forget the sound of them. There must have been literally thousands of them, each one singing its own little chromatic song, the ensemble like the sound of a thousand violins, each humming its own ascending and descending scale—you cannot imagine the weird effect they create, as their voices cross and criss-cross, giving the queerest discords, with an occasional note of perfect harmony. When we were relieved, "Con" and I went in and slept like dead men—our first sleep in two full days.

*Friday, August 16th* . . . We got fire orders today; at last, after six months of preparation, we're going to shoot—real bullets at real Huns. It's only harassing fire, and there may be no Huns near where we're aiming, but at any rate, it's a start!

Our little wood is hardly more than an acre of underbrush, but it's seen busy times in this old war. There are bits of German, French and American equipment scattered everywhere in it—clothing, mess-kits, helmets, old letters and newspapers—one can almost read the history of its skirmishes by the scattered debris. . . .

*Wednesday, August 21st* Once more we're on light rations. It's no easy job bringing up supplies over roads subjected to constant shelling, but that doesn't make it any easier for us up here. I guess it's worse on an open front like this than on one where the front line can be reached through sheltered trenches. But no trench systems for mine! They spell stagnation. . . .

*Thursday, August 22nd* . . . The *Boche* have picked this morning to make a little attack in our sector, and we've spent the whole day firing, until our ammunition was nearly used up. We can't see the *Boche*—that's the tantalizing part of it. "Hig" and I did snipe two this afternoon, though, and great was the rejoicing. . . . This afternoon a lieutenant and what was left of his platoon took refuge in our woods. They were pretty much shot up, hungry and almost crazy with thirst. They drank up all our water before we knew it, and before dark I was so thirsty myself from the heat of our gun that I drank ravenously out of a canvas bucket of soapy water in which at least two of us had washed! And do you know, it wasn't so bad, at that. . . .

*Monday, August 26th* . . . At about twenty minutes' notice I and three of my squad up-staked and hiked off to man one of the anti-aircraft guns hereabouts. To our surprise and pleasure, we found ourselves located in the grounds of a ruined *chateau!* . . .

*Wednesday, August 28th* Our off-duty hours were spent in exploring the endless nooks and corners of the *chateau.* . . . And now it's nearly dark— I'll have to quit and go back to our little camp. . . . Leaving this place is quite a wrench—it's a friendly old garden, with its paternal trees and quaint, rambling outbuildings. I have a queer feeling that I'll come back some day. The day ended with no further event than our return to camp and a cold dinner.[23]

This is the last diary entry. Campbell was promoted to sergeant in the last days of August and killed by German artillery fire on September 4, 1918, near Fismes, France. He was twenty-four years old.

Lieutenant S. Calvin Cumming of the Fifth Marine Regiment was luckier than Campbell. Wounded at Belleau Wood, Cumming was evacuated to a hospital far from the front and given a chance to recuperate. As he notes in the following letter to a friend back home, the marines took heavy casualties at Belleau Wood: 5,200 casualties, half their strength—the bloodiest battle in Marine history to that date. Promoted to captain, he led a company in the final offensive from Sommerance in the Ardennes in the first days of November 1918:

I will tell you a few instances and take a chance on the censor letting them get by. This fighting was all in open country, through woods, wheatfields, and towns—the country being hilly. . . . Four-thirty A.M. June 11, 1918, a whistle blew and the arm motion "Forward" was given, and line after line moved off toward a wood six hundred metres away, across an open and level field covered with grass about six inches high. The ground became covered with a sheet of machine-gun bullets from a Prussian Guard machine-gun battalion and their supporting infantry which was placed to hold the wood, as it was an important position.

We moved forward at a slow pace, keeping perfect lines. Men were being mowed down like wheat. A "whizz-bang" (high-explosive shell) hit on my right, and an automatic team which was there a moment ago disappeared, while men on the right and left were armless, legless, or tearing at their faces. We continued to advance until about fifty yards from the woods, when something hit me and I spun around and hit flat. I didn't know where I was hit, so jumped up to go forward again, but fell. I crawled to a shell-hole nearby. I don't see how I ever got there, as the ground was being plowed by machine guns. I heard later that my company had one officer and twenty-nine men left when we reached the objective. We had gone to this sector with eight officers and two hundred and fifty men.

The Hun machine gunners fire low, as after you are hit in the leg you fall and then they fill your body with bullets, so there is little chance. . . . Also they are wonderful fighters. One instance is that of a Hun who fell shot through both legs and a corporal ran up to him and holding his bayonet at him said, "Kamerad." The Hun raised up on his arm to get his pistol, and seeing it was out of reach yelled back, "No Kamerad." . . .

But going back to the shell-hole; it happened to be one made by a trench mortar and was about six feet deep and ten feet across. I put on a first-aid dressing and started figuring on how to get back to a first-aid station. Shells were still lighting around, shrapnel bursting, machine-gun bullets passing overhead; mingled with the cries and groans of the wounded and dying made it still an unpleasant place to be in.

On cleaning out the woods, a sniper, who was undoubtedly up a tree at the time, had been left behind. From the sound of his rifle I figured he was about fifty yards away, and was picking out any wounded who were moving and had not reached cover. I had lost the rifle that I was carrying, so decided to try my Colt forty-five on him. I crawled up to the edge of the shell-hole and heard a "ping." Deciding that discretion was the better part of valor, I got back down again and looked at my pistol to find it minus a front sight. A few minutes later I heard some one running and another crack from the Hun, and a Marine came rolling in. However, he kindly brought his Springfield rifle with him. After this rifle had spoken three times the way was clear, and I started crawling to a first-aid station. . . . I got picked up later by stretcher-bearers and went through a battalion and regimental dressing-station and in an ambulance where we were taken to an evacuation hospital, which I reached at 1 P.M. Was operated on, stayed three days, put on a hospital train and came straight to this hospital.

Calvin[24]

Cumming respected the fighting ability of his enemy. As in other wars, many American soldiers came to the conclusion that they shared more in common with their opponents than with their officers and leaders. As William Campbell wrote, "But we had all learned one thing: If the common soldiers of each army could just get together by a river bank and talk things over calmly, no war could possibly last as long as a week."[25] Thomas Paine had once suggested that wars were started by the vanity of kings; the twentieth-century American soldier often thought them the result of the vanity of politicians.

Poison gas proved to be a lesser killer than artillery or machine guns, yet it seemed so much worse to the people of the time. Even Adolf Hitler, a victim of poison gas yet a lover of methods of mass murder, refrained from its use in World War II. The great military historian B.H. Liddell Hart wrote of poison gas: "both experience and statistics proved it the least inhumane of modern weapons. But it was novel and therefore labeled an atrocity by a world which condones abuses but detests innovations."[26] What made poison gas so devastating was its long-term effects; those gassed often suffered through years of ill health before being felled by its effects. One of the most famous American victims of poison gas was the great New York Giants pitcher Christy Mathewson. Accidentally gassed during a training exercise in France, Mathewson developed tuberculosis. His career as a player over, Mathewson attempted to move on to coaching, but had to spend much of the next several years in a sanatorium until his death in 1925.

Gustave J. Dill of Buffalo, New York, was drafted into the newly formed Seventy-seventh Division, which consisted entirely of draftees, many of them, like Dill, the children of German immigrants. Dill, an aspiring artist who had won a prize from the National Academy of Design in 1913, created the stencil of the Statue of Liberty that went on the helmets of the Seventy-seventh and gave it the name of the Liberty Division.[27] After seeing action at the Battle of Château-Thierry in July 1918, Dill, serving with the division's artillery, settled into trench warfare for the next several months. Then in October came the big push, and the Seventy-seventh began forcing the retreating Germans back toward the Ardennes forest. In the last days of the war, the Germans launched a gas attack against Dill's unit, which he describes in his diary:

Monday [September] 28th—I slept well on the floor of this R.R. [railroad] section building. The officers took the cellar. . . . Safety first for me is the only phrase for our commanders, who think highly of a whole skin, you men shift for your own. It is this policy which we must endure and trust to luck we will emerge unscathed.

With two other men I sought a garden which the Germans had planted with vegetables. . . . Going over a height I found the panorama most excellent, pictures to paint all about me with long distant irregular hills. About a mile we walked, across shell pitted field, [to] where the Boche lived at ease for a considerable time in a substantial concrete house. A little below in a hollow the dump was situated and a good prize it was. It contained piles of planed lumber, as well as the planer and saw, screws, bolts, . . . in fact most everything to fix up a house, even bath tubs and bowls. . . .

The Boche sent us a high explosive shell while we were rummaging but we lingered a little longer, I picking up [a book of] some small German stories and a cigarette lighter. The vegetable garden I could not discover.

After dinner I took my materials for a sketch on the hill. Undisturbed I worked for about two hours, being able from my position to see how the Boche was shelling the highway. This day he was active with his artillery. Without warning a shell broke about 200 ft. from me, followed very shortly by another. I threw myself on my back as the ground had a good slope hoping to have any stray pieces pass over me. The shells came so frequently that I immediately shifted my position behind a little ridge in the ground where I lay full length on my stomach for ten minutes until it was safe to move. Then I gathered my things and scooted for the building.

Many planes were sailing about taking observations. After mealtime our peace was again disturbed. Shells fell closely around us, showing something or other had brought his attention toward us. We did not have much rest all night long. Intermittent and harassing fire rained upon us. I and another fellow went out to observe how close they were coming. A brief interval ensued when I walked a short distance to answer the call of nature. A sudden onrushing sound made me think quickly, to move for safety as it appeared to be headed directly for us. I dove for the side of the building where I was showered with dirt. In the morning, I saw this shell landed only 30 feet from me.

Sunday Nov. 3rd—Aroused for an early breakfast we started early. . . . There were many dead horses all along the road. The first captured long distance gun I ever saw was mired in a gutter, with the breech removed. It showed the haste in which they retreated. They traveled so fast, we simply kept on marching without knowing where to or an objective. A few prisoners marched by, one was being carried on a stretcher by his comrades, having been wounded in the neck or head as his face was blood and clotted. . . .

Monday 4th—It soon began to rain. How happy I was to think I was under a good roof and marching by day. The rumors had it that the Germans were going Eastward rapidly, so much that contact was barely possible. There was no doubt of the success of our offensive, they were only fighting a rear guard action while the main army was going homeward.

Tuesday 5th . . . Mud, mud, and mud was what we encountered today. . . . This was a long march on poor roads. Much Boche ammunition was every where. . . . Their loss in material must have been great. Up and down long hills, some spots were charming in picture. It rained a little. On the top of a long ascend we broke off to the left into a few wood shacks covered with tar paper formerly occupied by the Germans. Here we selected bunks to rest for the night and batteries took position near the site, where an electric plant was situated but burnt on the Boche retreat.

While waiting for the supper, about 20 men were congregated within, conversing. Several shells fell in the immediate neighborhood, one quite close. I decided after this one fell it was dangerous, so I thought to move away from my allotted corner to the middle of the room, fortunately that I decided so. About 10 minutes after my decision, without warning a high explosive shell struck the shack exploding inside, spreading confusion. I felt a heavy shock strike my right side. Bluish smoke filled the room. I ran toward the door calling gas; everyone seemed to ignore the training they received regarding an exploding shell containing gas. The door was closed and in their haste the men fumbled before an exit was possible.

On getting out I made an effort to adjust my mask, getting the mouthpiece on only. One man was in advance of me turned about and yelled, "look at this," holding his wrist with the other hand and the blood dripping freely. Another yelled behind me. I turned and saw him holding his hand over his eye and bloody. With my mask partly on I assisted in calling for first aid and moved out of the gas area. More men than I expected had been injured; some severely.

Going out on the road where we emigrated I found two of my comrades lying on stretchers badly hurt. My hand was bloody. I felt my person for any sores or wounds but only found small bits of [blood] still clinging to my clothes. . . . Opening my clothes I could discover nothing but a bruise one inch long that I had dressed but did not mind. My throat had been burned by gas, so the medical man said it was compulsory for me to get treatment. I returned for my overcoat and personal things at the same time. Walking down to the foot of the hill where the major now decided was the better P.C. and the other wounded had assembled, I gave to those some hot coffee from my canteen and saw that one fellow was very low and about to die. No ambulance was on hand so we dispatched a man on horseback for a conveyance. At 8 P.M. an ambulance took away all but 3 or 4 of us.

It rained very hard. I saw the sky was illuminated, an indication that the Germans were burning and retreating again, but shells continued to drop. Assuring myself that no transportation would be available before the next day, I lay on the cold floor for some sleep.

Wednesday 6th—Without breakfast, we boarded a truck, which had brought up supplies. Capt. Roosevelt, a relative of the Col., was on the seat so we were sure of getting somewhere. It was a long round-about way, consuming the entire morning (7:45–1:45) ere [we] reached the first station. . . . The same all over, mud, and congested traffic with troops going forward.

. . . Briceaux— . . . at 10:30 P.M. we arrived. Some more recording, then to the X-ray room for examination where upon the table I sat, with no result, other than to see the coins in my pockets. It looked cheerful and good to see the nurses and clean rooms. In another few minutes I was in the ward assigned to me. They brought in a stretcher case under ether. A similar case below proved a very noisy one. A delirious patient was swearing and talking loudly. I thought I would not sleep, but the inviting sheet and white pillows soon lulled me into a sound sleep. It was midnight. While undressing I discovered a sore spot in my right side of my ribs; evidently something hit me there.

Thursday 7th—I awakened at 7 A.M. and so comfortable, just as it had been in months past, and breakfast was served to me in bed, the only time in my adult life. . . .

Wednesday 13th & Thursday 14th— . . . In the afternoon I was transferred to another ward. . . . I found several German wounded prisoners in my ward, one of whom was a lieutenant of infantry whom I engaged in conversation. Later I volunteered to write for him a few lines if he wished; he was profuse in his thanks for my offer, which I performed later; also for several others. Among them was a youthful looking lad, to whom a medical captain wished me to confer. I accordingly spoke to him, learning he had been severely wounded in the stomach and belonged to the same kind of unit as I did. He was very cheerful and pleasant. To consider him an enemy never came into my mind. After helping the Lieut. and watching the doctor dress his two wounds, the wound in the wrist being very bad, I expressed a desire to be with our troops to reach the Rhine, whereupon he requested I call upon his home, giving me his address as W. Herbeke, Reinscheid bei Coln.[28]

Dill never got to visit Germany, being kept under medical care for the next several months as complications from the poison gas arose. He did, however, take the opportunity to learn French and woo a number of young French women, whose names and addresses fill the last pages in his diary. He returned to New York—and to obscurity—in 1919.

## Repercussions

The war to make the world safe for democracy emboldened many activists at home. Labor unions enjoyed a brief summer of positive gains, only to be mercilessly crushed at war's end during the Red Scare.[29] Many African Americans found the presence of segregation in the military and throughout the South vastly hypocritical and intolerable, intensifying their efforts to fight back against the violence of white terrorists.[30] And suffragists redoubled their battle for the right to vote, employing imaginative new tactics of civil disobedience—such as reading the high rhetoric of Woodrow Wilson's speeches in front of the White House, and then burning them as so many empty promises. With the passage of the Nineteenth Amendment in 1920, women won the franchise just 133 years after the Constitution promised a free government in the name of "We the people."[31]

Wars often exert pressure on cultural norms. The American Revolution had tested the bonds of deference and political allegiance, the War of 1812 tested American self-confidence, the Mexican War valorized violence over gentility, the Civil War shook America's racial attitudes, the Indian Wars shattered standards of humanity, and the Spanish-American War undermined republican values. With the First World War, women's role in wartime wavered for the first time. In the nineteenth century, women had been kept as far from the military as possible. Even the camp followers who had undertaken so much of the domestic labor in the eighteenth century had diminished in number, soldiers being expected to do their own cooking and cleaning by the time of the Mexican War. The U.S. military, unlike its European counterparts, worked to keep female nurses away from the troops, seeing women in general as an inept and disruptive influence. The combination of a vibrant women's movement and military necessity began the century-long process of the military's acceptance of women in their ranks.

More women served in the military in World War I than in any previous war: 22,000 nurses in the army and 1,400 in the navy. The navy also had 12,000 clumsily named Yeomanettes, performing mostly clerical duties, and the Marines had 305 Marinettes. This war, like future wars, demonstrated the near impossibility of keeping women away from the ill effects of warfare, as several hundred died of disease and from poison gas, and a few were held as prisoners of war by the Germans. Incredibly, the government determined that women prisoners were not eligible for their pay during their time in captivity since they were not soldiers. That traditional bastion of masculinity, the U.S. Marine Corps, showed more class by paying their women well and giving them the same medical benefits as men, though women marines would only be allowed to perform clerical work.[32] One of the first women to enlist in 1918 was

Martha L. Wilchinski, whose boyfriend was already serving in France with the Marines. She wrote him a jolly letter informing him of her enlistment:

> Dear Bill: I've got the greatest news! No, I haven't thrown you over; I'm still strong for you, Bill. No, it's no use; don't try to guess. You're not used to that much mental effort, and you might get brain-fag. . . . I know it'll be hard at first, but it'll grow on you after a while . . . —I'm a lady leatherneck; I'm the last word in Hun hunters; I'm a real, live, honest-to-goodness Marine! . . .
>
> You know I always had a kind of a hunch that the Marines would realize the necessity of women some day. . . . [W]hen I heard they had at last hung out a sign at the recruiting station—"Women wanted for the United States Marine Corps"—I was ready. . . . I was there when the doors opened in the morning. I was one of the first all right—the first six hundred! You'd think they were selling sugar or something. Well, when the crowd heard that you had to be willing to go anywhere as ordered and you had to be a cracker-jack stenog [stenographer], they thinned out some. And from what was left the lieutenant picked out twelve to go over to the colonel and have him give us the double O [a close examination]. I was one of them, of course. . . . You're only a corporal, Bill, so you may not know what a colonel is. A colonel is a man who talks to you over the top of his glasses and looks through you as if you were a piece of smoked glass. You know me, I'm not afraid of anything this side of sudden death, but during the three seconds he looked at me I had everything from nervous prostration to paralysis agitans.[33] That's called psychological effect. I wouldn't admit it to a soul but you because it's scientific and will probably go over your head, anyway. . . .
>
> Well, only three of us came out alive. The others had fallen by the wayside. Then the colonel came in and told us to come over and be sworn in. . . . It was terribly impressive. Something kept sticking in my throat all the time. I don't know whether it was my heart or my liver. I had to swallow it several times before I could say, "I do." . . .
>
> And then I got my orders. Travel orders they call them. . . . The only traveling I have to do is to come down from the Bronx in the new subway, and that's not traveling, that's just plain suffering. . . .
>
> I hear some people are giving us nicknames. Isn't it funny the minute a girl becomes a regular fellow somebody always tries to queer it by calling her something else? There are a lot of people, Bill, that just go around taking the joy out of life. Well, anybody that calls me anything but "Marine" is going to hear from me. "Marine" is good enough for me. . . .

I can't sign myself as affectionately as I used to, Bill. You understand, I'm a soldier now and you wouldn't want me doing anything that wasn't in the Manual.

Yours till the cows come home, Pvt. Martha L. Wilchinski[34]

When Wilchinski was promoted to corporal in September 1918, she wrote Bill of her pride and sense of accomplishment, signing herself "Your comrade in arms."[35] Promoted again to sergeant, Wilchinski was assigned with several other women to the Marine Corps Publicity Bureau. She and Sergeant Lela Leibrand wrote numerous magazine articles during the war; Leibrand also made the first military training film, *All in a Day's Work.* Few professional soldiers embraced the presence of female military personnel, and after the war all service branches did their best to encourage women to resign, as did Wilchinski and Leibrand—the former becoming editor of *Variety* magazine and a poet of some note, while the latter became a filmmaker with Fox Studios (her daughter was the actress Ginger Rogers).

The war's impact on race relations was similarly complicated and disruptive. Reflecting the high-water mark of the racism that gripped the nation in the early decades of the twentieth century, the U.S. military sought to limit the participation of African Americans. Racism started at the top with President Woodrow Wilson, who had ordered the segregation of Washington, D.C., and the post office. His secretary of the navy, Josephus Daniels, reversed traditional practices by segregating the navy in order to "avoid friction between the two races,"[36] while the officer corps held firm to a debilitating racism.[37] The Marine Corps remained an all-white institution, while the navy accepted just over five thousand African Americans, most of whom held the most menial jobs. With ill grace, the army, which had a tradition of black troops in segregated units, allowed for a few black lieutenants and captains, but with the understanding— on the secretary of war's personal instructions—that they would never command white troops.[38] But even that limited authority was repeatedly undermined. Colonel Herschel Tupes, the white commander of the all-black 372nd Infantry, sought to completely eliminate his black officers out of respect for the racism of white troops. In an official request to General Pershing dated August 24, 1918, Tupes explained his logic:

1. Request that colored officers of this regiment be replaced by white officers for the following reasons:

First: The racial distinctions which are recognized in civilian life naturally continue to be recognized in the military life and present a formidable barrier to the existence of that feeling of comradeship which is essential to mutual confidence and *esprit de corp.*

Second: With a few exceptions there is a characteristic tendency among the colored officers to neglect the welfare of their men and to perform their duties in a perfunctory manner. They are lacking in initiative.

Pershing approved the gradual replacement of the black officers.[39] In such circumstances, it is understandable that the Germans circulated a flier asking black troops why they were fighting for a racist country.[40]

Nonetheless, a total of 404,000 African Americans served during World War I, 42,000 of whom saw combat.[41] Some of these troops attained notable distinction: the French government cited the 369th Infantry eleven times, awarding it the Croix de Guerre—despite efforts by the Americans to prevent the French from issuing such commendations. Evidence aside, the army's senior officers remained convinced that black troops would perform badly under any circumstances, ignoring the lessons of the Civil War and the outstanding service of the Buffalo Soldiers; the War Department refused to make use of its regular black units, assigning the Twenty-fourth and Twenty-fifth Infantry and the Ninth and Tenth Cavalry to garrison duty. They also seemed to pay no attention to the colonial regiments of black troops used to good effect on the western front by both Britain and France—the latter's known collectively as the *Tirailleurs sénégalais*. Repeatedly, the high command attempted to confine black troops to the most menial tasks, which they thought more "suitable" to their race.[42] The army worried that using blacks in combat might lead to the promotion of some of these soldiers, resulting in an excess of black noncoms and officers. To insure failure, black artillery officers were *not* trained in the use of artillery.[43] It is little wonder that most blacks who served in the U.S. military felt betrayed by their country. The Chicago blues singer Big Bill Broonzy put his frustration to music:

> When Uncle Sam called me, I knew I would be called the real McCoy.
> But when I got in the army, they called me soldier boy.
> I wonder when will I be called a man?[44]

Many black troops changed their attitudes toward the United States as a consequence of their service in France. For instance, a young lieutenant in the 368th named Charles Houston was stunned by the friendliness and appreciation of the French people—and the absence of segregated accommodations. He was then disgusted when the army intervened and made the local restaurants and hotels where he was stationed establish segregated facilities. After the war, he went to Harvard Law School, becoming the first African American to edit its law review; headed the NAACP legal office that battled segregation; became a law professor at Howard University; and recruited a number of brilliant young attorneys, most importantly Thurgood Marshall. World War I led Houston to devote his life to ending Jim Crow in the United States: "The hate and scorn showered on us Negro officers by our fellow Americans convinced me that there was no sense in my dying for a world ruled by them. I made up my mind that if I got through this war I would study law and use my time fighting for men who could not strike back."[45]

For such reasons, the war worried many racists. From President Wilson on down, there was concern that the participation of African Americans in the military endeavor in Europe would, by introducing them to different cultures and the use of firearms, make blacks less willing to accept segregation back home in the United States. Frustrated with the respect the French showed brave soldiers regardless of skin color, and concerned that the *Tirailleurs sénégalais* might serve as a positive role model for black Americans, the U.S. high command demanded that their French liaison officer, Colonel Jean L.A. Linard, prepare instructions for French officers to pay greater regard to the racist ways of their American counterparts. The headquarters staff assured Linard that Americans were "unanimous" in their racism, and that therefore any questioning of these cultural norms would constitute a grave insult to the United States. When the French Ministry of War learned of this document, they ordered it destroyed, but W.E.B. DuBois, editor of *The Crisis*, received a copy and published it in its original French with an English translation. As DuBois noted, it offers insight to the thinking of the American command as they faced the dangers of fighting a "war to make the world safe for democracy." The army awarded Linard the Distinguished Service Medal for rendering "invaluable service to the American Expeditionary Forces and to the cause in which the United States has been engaged".[46]

French Military Mission Stationed with the American Army, August 7, 1918

SECRET INFORMATION CONCERNING BLACK AMERICAN TROOPS

1. It is important for French officers who have been called upon to exercise command over black American troops, or to live in close contact with them, to have an exact idea of the position occupied by Negroes in the United States. The information set forth in the following communication ought to be given to these officers and it is to their interest to have these matters known and widely disseminated. It will devolve likewise on the French Military Authorities, through the medium of the Civil Authorities, to give information on this subject to the French population residing in the cantonments occupied by American colored troops.

2. The American attitude upon the Negro question may seem a matter for discussion to many French minds. But we French are not in our province if we undertake to discuss what some call "prejudice." American opinion is unanimous on the "color question" and does not admit of any discussion.

The increasing number of Negroes in the United States (about 15,000,000) would create for the white race in the Republic a menace of degeneracy were it not that an impassable gulf has been made between them.

As this danger does not exist for the French race, the French public has become accustomed to treating the Negro with familiarity and indulgence.

This indulgence and this familiarity are matters of grievous concern to the Americans. They consider them an affront to their national policy. They are afraid that contact with the French will inspire in black Americans aspirations which to them [the whites] appear intolerable. It is of the utmost importance that every effort be made to avoid profoundly estranging American opinion.

Although a citizen of the United States, the black man is regarded by the white American as an inferior being with whom relations of business or service only are possible. The black is constantly being censured for his want of intelligence and discretion, his lack of civic and professional conscience and for his tendency toward undue familiarity.

The vices of the Negro are a constant menace to the American who has to repress them sternly. For instance, the black American troops in France have, by themselves, given rise to as many complaints for attempted rape as all the rest of the army. And yet the [black American] soldiers sent us have been the choicest with respect to physique and morals, for the number disqualified at the time of mobilization was enormous.

CONCLUSION

1. We must prevent the rise of any pronounced degree of intimacy between French officers and black officers. We may be courteous and amiable with these last, but we cannot deal with them on the same plane as with the white American officers without deeply wounding the latter. We must not eat with them, must not shake hands or seek to talk or meet with them outside of the requirements of military service.

2. We must not commend too highly the black American troops, particularly in the presence of [white] Americans. It is all right to recognize their good qualities and their services, but only in moderate terms, strictly in keeping with the truth.

3. Make a point of keeping the native cantonment population from "spoiling" the Negroes. [White] Americans become greatly incensed at any public expression of intimacy between white women with black men. They have recently uttered violent protests against a picture in the "Vie Parisi-enne" entitled "The Child of the Desert" which shows a [white] woman in a "cabinet particulier"[47] with a Negro.[48]

African Americans came home to discover a revived and powerful Ku Klux Klan determined to keep blacks in their place and to end the influence of the Catholic Church. In 1918 seventy-eight Americans were lynched while the country fought to make the world safe for democracy; the following year race riots erupted in Chicago and Omaha, and ten veterans were among the seventy-nine African Americans lynched that year.[49] Paul Filton spoke for many of his fellow African American veterans:

We are not asking favors. We are demanding our rights. If the bigots are counting upon still relegating us to the back door of public hostelries, hat in hand, they are reckoning without their host. If that modern "Ku Klux Klan" thinks that these hard fighting, straight-shooting veterans of the World War are the same timid fieldhands, crouching in terror, they have another "think" coming. We are going to demand, not social equality—no Negro wants that, but an equal chance in this fair land that they have helped to make safe. An equal chance with the Chinaman, Indian, Italian, Jew, Irishman, Yankee, or any one of the numerous races that go to make up this nation. We are full fledged citizens. . . . We are component parts of this body politic. We have helped to gain the Victory for Democracy and we must share in the fruits.[50]

While many African American veterans returned determined to fight for their civil rights, others gave way to disillusionment and despair, some staying on in Europe rather than having to put up with their nation's virulent racism. Those who chose to "return fighting" found growing black communities in northern cities, the product of the great migration of African Americans out of the South. Meanwhile the War Department did its best to purge itself of black soldiers and sailors, creating a nearly all-white military in the 1920s. The only questioning of this policy within the military establishment came from a few army officers who worried that in case of war "the white population upon which the future of this country depends would suffer the brunt of loss, the Negro population none." When it came to combat, black troops made excellent cannon fodder.[51]

## "Normalcy"[52]

World War I famously ended on the eleventh hour of the eleventh day of the eleventh month in 1918. Such peculiar desire for symmetry aside, the war did not end for all of America's military personnel. For several thousand soldiers, the war continued for an additional year or two as President Wilson's willingness to intervene in European affairs led to another one of America's forgotten wars: the invasion of Russia. Seeking to overthrow the new Soviet government, U.S. troops occupied the area around Murmansk until June 1919, and parts of Siberia until April 1920. For the first time in its history, American soldiers organized in opposition to their military operations, demanding to be returned home.

In August 1918, the 339th Infantry Regiment, drawn mostly from Wisconsin and Michigan, joined Allied troops in Archangel, while contingents from several regiments operated in Siberia. With the armistice, morale plummeted as a great many soldiers began to ask why they continued to fight. A document titled "Facts and Questions Concerning the N.R.E.F. [North Russia Expeditionary Force]" circulated among the American troops in Archangel, demanding to know why they were still fighting when Germany had been defeated. The U.S. government had failed to explain why they were "meddling with a Russian revolution and counterrevolution" with military force, an action "we have been unable to reconcile . . . with American ideals and principles."[53] A regular flow of press releases assured the public of Allied victories, the approaching collapse of the Bolshevik forces, and the joy American troops took in fighting for the greater—though unexplained—good. The War Department also censored their troops' letters in order to prevent accurate reports of this brutal war finding their way into the public press.

In response to this blanket of lies, soldiers began smuggling letters home with wounded comrades. A great many of these letters were published in local newspapers and reprinted in the *Congressional Record* by opponents of America's intervention. One soldier wrote, "No one had been able to tell the men why they were fighting in Russia, and naturally their morale was not what it should have been." Another soldier observed, "We are one outfit that hasn't had to worry about finding jobs after the war. We keep right on with what we are doing." A Milwaukee doctor serving with the 339th noticed that they "were fighting a people against whom war had never been declared and we didn't know why we were fighting them." In what would become a common plaint by American soldiers risking their lives in undeclared wars, one soldier questioned why they were dying for people "either incapable or unwilling to help themselves."[54] Members of Congress from states supplying these troops began demanding their return. The War Department responded by ordering greater censorship and by issuing a new batch of prevarications about Allied successes.

While a few thousand American troops shivered through the harsh Russian winter of 1918–19, the War Department set about dismantling its vast war-making machine. The U.S. military demobilized four million soldiers in the eighteen months following the armistice, overwhelming an economy that was in the process of shifting from war production. These soldiers returned home to find the cost of living a full 100 percent higher than it had been in 1914, keen competition for jobs, and a labor force on the verge of rebellion. Providing management with a potent counterweight to the unions, the soldiers were not simply hired to replace unionized workers, but also used to bash a few of the more radical heads.[55] Most significant to the latter development was the founding of the American Legion in 1919. One of the founders, Brigadier General William G. Price, bluntly stated the legion's attitude: "it will uphold what is right so firmly and forcefully that whatever party is wrong will learn to fear it."[56] White veterans rushed into the organization, 650,000 joining the first year; but black veterans did not find themselves welcome. The legion proved a very useful tool for America's corporations, as the veterans' group drove political radicals and labor organizers out of towns across the nation.

While some veterans proved their patriotism by siding with management against labor, others posed a threat to the social fiber. After World War I, as after the Civil War, the public became convinced that it was in the grip of a crime wave driven by veterans. It was certainly the case that a great number of veterans, especially African American, found their way into the nation's expanded prison systems, but there were few efforts at either statistical analysis or preventative measures.[57] Nonetheless, states and municipalities acted on the perception, some cracking down on homeless veterans, while others urged Congress to step into the breach and provide some form of assistance to those who had served in the Great War.

Congress responded to this pressure, and, unlike after previous wars, actually attempted to do something to care for the nation's veterans, though their efforts tended to prove counterproductive. Congress appropriated $9 million for the creation of hospitals and rehabilitation centers for the 200,000 seriously handicapped veterans, and created the Veterans' Bureau to oversee the many efforts to aid the returning soldiers, with newly elected President Warren Harding appointing Colonel Charles R. Forbes the bureau's first director in 1921. Forbes struck many as an odd choice, since he had once deserted from the U.S. Army.[58]

While prosperity spread through the upper and middle classes during the halcyon days of the 1920s, veterans faced near epic levels of parsimony. Those who served during the war had been promised a bonus for their service. The perennial secretary of the treasury, Andrew Mellon, who just happened to also be one of the richest men in the United States, opposed the granting of any bonus as likely to lead to inflation and persuaded President Harding to veto the bill that would have delivered the promised reward for services.[59] Many wealthy people selflessly opposed the bonus for the good of the veterans, in order to keep their heroic sacrifices from being tainted by the tawdry aura of filthy lucre. As George Eastman put it, a bonus would make "mercenaries out of our patriotic boys." Pierre S. du Pont, who had added to his considerable fortune through military contracts during the war, was a bit more abrasive in characterizing the veterans as already "the most favored class in the United States," who clearly had no need for a bonus. That servant of the rich and powerful, the *Wall Street Journal*, dismissed veterans seeking government aid as "panhandlers."[60]

The Republican administrations of 1921 to 1933 did their best to make the veterans feel guilty for asking for help. President Calvin Coolidge offered up one of his bromides in rejecting a bonus bill in 1924: "Patriotism which is bought and paid for is not patriotism."[61] Congress passed a bill over his veto, though only by establishing that the veterans would have to wait until 1945 to collect their $1,000. With the advent of the Great Depression in 1929, many veterans began calling for at least some part of their promised bonuses to be delivered early. When Congress passed a compromise bill that would allow veterans to borrow money on half the value of their bonuses—at 4.5 percent interest—President Herbert Hoover vetoed it with the assurance that local communities offered all the assistance anyone needed. The government seemed intent to make every veteran regret his service.

Sergeant Walter W. Waters of Portland, Oregon, was one of the many destitute veterans driven over the edge into dire poverty in the first years of the Depression. He and his wife frantically searched for work to support their two children. Pulling newspapers out of trash cans, Waters read of "loans to railroads and to large corporations," and unsurprisingly felt that he also deserved some form of assistance.[62] In May 1932, he attended a protest meeting in Portland and heard talk of veterans going to Washington to make their case before Congress. Waters joined many other veterans who spontaneously began hopping trains headed east. The employees of many railroads let the veterans alone, while the management of other railroads ordered a crackdown and threw the riders off their trains—only to find that local supporters, including members of the National Guard, would give them rides in the back of trucks and in fleets of beat-up cars. When Waters arrived in the capital, he found one thousand veterans already there, with thousands more pouring in over the ensuing weeks. The estimated twenty-five to forty thousand veterans formed themselves into the

Bonus Expeditionary Force or BEF—with a few thousand black veterans in their midst, the BEF was far more integrated than the AEF had ever been. Through the intervention of the capital's chief of police, Pelham Glassford, himself a veteran, the Bonus Army was allowed to camp out on the Anacostia flats in southeast Washington. When Glassford could not persuade the secretary of war to make surplus military equipment available to the veterans, he organized a fund-raising effort on their behalf. Glassford assigned police officers who were veterans to work with the Bonus Army; relations between the protesters and police were so positive that the BEF named Anacostia Camp Marks after police Captain S.J. Marks.

The Bonus Army marched, held rallies, met with members of Congress, picketed the Capitol, and watched their hopes evaporate as Congress defeated the latest bonus bill. Political leaders, newspapers, and army intelligence warned that the BEF was the vanguard of revolution, a front for communism or fascism, subversives endangering democracy. On July 28, the peaceful relations between veterans and police ended with the eviction of a group of protesters from the old National Guard Armory on the corner of Third and Pennsylvania. Police clubbed those who did not move fast enough, and in an ensuing scuffle the police shot and killed two veterans. Tear-gas shells were fired into the crowd; one killed a baby.[63]

At this point, Herbert Hoover turned to General Douglas MacArthur, who sincerely believed that the Bonus Army intended to overthrow the government. Aided by Major Dwight D. Eisenhower and a contingent of cavalry under Major George S. Patton, MacArthur moved on the Anacostia encampment on the evening of July 28. After deploying tear gas, MacArthur ordered his infantry to move in with bayonets fixed. Most of the engagement consisted of jostling, pushing, and setting fire to the veterans' huts and tents. The veterans were evicted, MacArthur declared victory and announced that only one-tenth of the Bonus Army marchers were actually veterans. Later a Veterans Administration survey would find that 94 percent of the Bonus Army were veterans, 20 percent suffering from disability.[64]

The treatment of the veterans in Washington, D.C., was a public relations disaster for Herbert Hoover, and certainly did his reelection campaign little good. Not that veterans benefited from the change of administrations, as Franklin Roosevelt also opposed a bonus bill, vetoing one in 1934 and another in 1936; but in the latter year Congress passed the bill over the president's veto, finally offering some relief to those who had fought to make the world "safe for democracy."

Writing in 1926, the veteran pilot Elliott White Springs prophetically spoke for those who questioned the ideals they fought for:

War is a horrible thing, a grotesque comedy. And it is so useless. This war won't prove anything. All we'll do when we win is to substitute one sort of Dictator for another. In the meantime we have destroyed our best resources. Human life, the most precious thing in the world, has become the cheapest. After we've won this war by drowning the Hun in our own blood, in five years' time the sentimental fools at home will be taking up a collection for those same Huns that are killing us now and our fool politicians will be cooking up another good war.[65]

# 8

# World War II

In the summer of 1940, as Britain fought alone against the might of Adolf Hitler's mechanized forces, U.S. President Franklin Delano Roosevelt convinced a reluctant Congress to prepare for war. America's expanding military production brought an end to the Great Depression, while the nation's first peacetime draft began the process of building up the country's armed forces. When Japan launched its surprise attacks on American and British bases throughout Asia and across the Pacific to Hawaii on December 7, 1941, the United States was, though still unprepared in many ways, in a position to put up a credible resistance. In the years ahead it would accomplish much more than that, surpassing the production levels of all the fascist governments combined and creating the most powerful, far-reaching, and effective military the world had ever known. The war ended with the United States demonstrating its power in the starkest and deadliest possible form, dropping atomic bombs that obliterated two Japanese cities.

Like all wars, World War II was a waste of human life, but on a scale never before attained. Those who witnessed the slaughter often suffered various forms of emotional trauma, or constructed complex rationales to explain what they had seen. The primary gloss has been that World War II was "the Good War," sidestepping entirely the widespread suffering on all sides. As Paul Fussell wrote, "For the past fifty years the Allied war has been sanitized and romanticized almost beyond recognition by the sentimental, the loony patriotic, the ignorant, and the bloodthirsty."[1] The best reporters covering the war found no end of bravery, but it was never of the romantic kind preferred by their editors and the American public; rather, it was the effort to keep alive and do one's job in the face of unremitting horror that drove the GI to ultimate victory.[2] As Ernie Pyle wrote, "just toiling from day to day in a world full of insecurity, discomfort, homesickness, and a dulled sense of danger" required a sort of courage unappreciated by those at home.[3] The GIs fought not for high ideals but for the guys around them; Baron von Steuben's "community of the line" kept the democratic army of the United States to its dangerous task in the face of the far better trained German and Japanese armies. Yet there remained a deep division within American military forces. Even while fighting an ideology of tyranny and murderous racism, the United States remained a segregated land, and its military forces continued to separate black and white troops right through the war, even denying the most courageous black soldiers the recognition they deserved. That racism spilled over into the campaign against the Japanese, who were identified as an inferior and savage people deserving death. Lieutenant John F. Kennedy, preparing to leave Purvis Bay in the Solomon Islands, saw a huge billboard on the hillside bearing the message, over the signature of Admiral William F. Halsey, "Kill Japs! Kill more Japs! If you do your job well, you will help to kill the little yellow bastards."[4] Halsey, who referred to the Japanese as "bestial apes," swore that by the time the war ended that Japanese would only be spoken in hell.[5]

Despite their divisions, the goal of nearly every American engaged in World War II remained the desire to return home. The war was a job that had to be done so that someday they could once more walk through their own front doors. American soldiers witnessed levels of violence never before seen, including the Holocaust and the first use of atomic bombs. But perhaps the most exceptional quality of the average soldier's experience came with the war's end and the passage of the GI Bill. Never in American history were veterans treated with such lavish respect. An entire generation of men found themselves propelled into the middle class as the federal government funded their college education, paid for their medical care, gave them priority in employment, and helped them buy homes. Any trace of anger or bitterness the returning soldiers may have felt toward their government evaporated in the nation's warm embrace and assurance that they had done no less than save the world from tyranny.

## Going to War

Lenore Terrell Rickert was a U.S. Navy nurse stationed at Pearl Harbor in 1941. She was making her rounds in the hospital when she heard a plane overhead: "Because of the patients, our aircraft never flew over the hospital." She ran to the window and saw a plane "coming in between the two wards." She knew immediately that something was wrong and ran to give the alert. Those patients who could walk rushed to return to their ships. "One patient, whose eyes were both bandaged, got out of bed, crawled underneath, and pulled a blanket down to lie on, so we could use the bed for the wounded. Everybody was worrying about the others and not themselves." Staff and patients worked together, helping out as they could. "Everybody wants to know if we were afraid. Fear never entered into it."[6]

Mildred Woodman was also in Hawaii, serving as a nurse with the U.S. Army at Schofield Field. She was awakened by the sound of explosions. She ran outside and saw planes flying through the mountain pass toward the airbase. "The large bright insignia of the rising sun was boldly on the side of each plane. They flew so close I could hear the radio communications between the pilots." She took off for the hospital, which had been hit by the Japanese despite the red cross painted on its roof. The nine operating rooms quickly filled and then overflowed with the wounded. "I kept hearing planes overhead, but we were too busy to be afraid or to ask what was happening." She took part in amputations and operating on serious chest wounds. Woodman thought these "the bravest of men. . . . Many wanted to go out and fight back."[7]

Second Lieutenant Robert T. Smith of Hooper, Nebraska, was serving in the U.S. Army Air Corps when he resigned his commission in July 1941 to join Colonel Claire Lee Chennault's American Volunteers Group, also known as the Flying Tigers. The Flying Tigers fought with the Chinese against the Japanese invaders. Britain and the United States supported Chennault's efforts, as indicated by the fact that Smith's squadron was stationed at Toungoo, an RAF base in Burma. Though war raged in Europe and China, the United States was officially still at peace, and the Flying Tigers limited their activities to training Chinese pilots. Smith led a fairly leisurely life, though the rain depressed him; typical diary entries read: "Did absolutely nothing . . . just lay around sleeping and reading. . . . Spent the P.M. trimming my nails, shaving, bathing, etc. Really exciting!" But things started to heat up on October 20: "Col. Chennault lectured to us this morning, and said we were in a precarious situation here, due to the tension between the U.S. and Japan, and their interests in the far East. Said Japan was massing troops on the Thailand border. Sooo—it looks very much as if we might be attacked any day. . . . If the Japs do come, we probably won't know of it until about the time they get here."

In late October the base went on alert twice as strange aircraft, suspected to be Japanese, were seen flying over the airstrip. The base commander started giving lectures on Japanese tactics, the Chinese ace Major Wong came to talk of his experiences of air combat with the Japanese, and Colonel Chennault returned to lecture on night fighter tactics. For the first time the colonel scheduled gunnery practice on November 11: "It was the first gunnery mission on the range. We all did lousy." A week later the pilots decided to paint shark heads on the front of their planes: "Looks mean as hell." By the end of November there were one hundred P-40s at the base. Smith started to expect war with Japan any day:

Dec. 7 Nothing new to report and no prospects even.

Dec. 8, 1941 Boy did all hell break loose today?! We all went over to the line after breakfast, and about 7 o'clock somebody ran in to the ready-room and said the U.S. was now at war with Japan. We could hardly believe it even tho it was confirmed on the radio. Everybody stood around laughing and kidding about it, altho it was easy to see there was really plenty of tension. Here we are in the middle of the works now—with the Japs pounding Hawaii, Manila, Singapore and Thailand—60 miles away. . . . Plans were made for our Sqdn. to go to Rangoon, as they need more support for the R.A.F. there. . . . If they don't bomb our field here before we get away, we'll be lucky.

Dec. 9 We started patrol over the mountain toward the Thailand border today.

Dec. 11 Word comes up that the Japs have bombed an airdrome within 200 miles of Rangoon. We are slated to leave at 9:00 in the morning [for Rangoon]. . . .

Dec. 15 [Rangoon] I wish somebody would make up their mind what the hell they want to do with us and then do it. This is the dumbest war I ever saw. . . .

Dec. 18 Wish they'd [the Japanese] come and give us some action. . . .

Dec. 21 Damn! We got a telegram last nite from Kunming which said the first pursuit Squadron had intercepted 10 Jap bombers and shot down three for sure, and 2 or 3 more thought to have gone down. That was damn good work, but we're all mad because they got into action before we did. . . .

Dec. 23 Rangoon, Burma. Boy, it all came today! We got a report at 10:00 a.m. that large numbers of bombers were on the way. 14 ships from the Sqdn. and 10 Buffaloes from RAF took off. We intercepted them at 12,000 ft. 15 mi. east of Rangoon. Two waves of bombers, 27 in each wave, and about 40 fighter escorts. We started making runs on them and shooting like hell. After bit I couldn't see any of our fellows up there. Found a bomber away from the formation, made about 3 passes, and on the last one went in to about 50 yds., firing all 6 guns, and he blew up right in front of me and down in flames. Went after another, and McMillan and I together put out his right engine and smoke trailed out. He was losing alt. last time I looked, but about that time I was jumped by 3 Jap fighters. Shot at one and dove away. Went back up and fired at more bombers till ammo out. Greene was shot down by fighters, bailed out, and they strafed him going down. Wasn't hit, landed OK. Martin and Gilbert both shot down and killed. My ship had a few holes in it. Several killed at the field here, and about 1,000 in Rangoon. Fires all over and smoke very thick. After the raid, refueled and went on patrol. A busy day. Let em come. We got about 15 ships to their 3.

Dec. 24 12:00 p.m. Two of our ships put out of commission on ground by fighters strafing field yesterday during raid. Reed hit a hole in runway and nosed up. Leaves us with 12 ships able to fly. Mine OK. . . . Bangkok radio broadcast by Japs says they're coming over to give us some Xmas presents tomorrow. So we'll have to be ready for them. Five of the RAF Brewsters destroyed on that ground yest. That leaves them about 15 ships. Shell holes all over the runways and field. All buildings riddled by m.g. bullets by the fighters that strafed the field.

Went into town tonite and it is like a ghost town. Everybody has evacuated and only 2 or 3 joints open. Some of us ganged up with a bunch of seamen from the freighter Tulsa, in port here. They took us aboard and fed us and gave us Amer. cigarettes etc. A swell bunch. Now for some sleep—I may need it.

Dec. 25 About 11:00 a.m. we got word the Japs were on the way in again, so both flights took off, 6 in one and 7 in Mac's. I was on Mac's wing. Went to 16,000 ft. and patrolled near Rangoon. They came in from N.W. at 19,000 ft. Three waves of bombers, 27 in each, and about 30 fighters. Mac took our flight into one bomber formation and we started making passes at the left flank. On the third pass I got the last man, he started smoking badly and dove out heading for the ground. Turned around and saw a fighter coming towards me. Turned at him and opened fire at about 400 yds. head on and held it. They poured into him and he passed about 10 ft. below me. Turned again and he was in flames and went down in the gulf. Went back and shot more bombers. Several fell out of formation and crashed all over. . . . Mac and Overend both shot down and made belly landings, but we didn't know it till they finally got home late. Had given them up for dead. . . . All told we got about 14 bombers and 12 fighters. My ship shot full of holes—34 in all—five by cockpit. Rangoon had a number of fires from bombs, and the field hit on runways but not much damage. A strange Xmas.

Dec. 26 Cruickshank got my ship patched up and I was all set to test it when we got a raid warning at 10:00 a.m. We could only get 7 tommies in the air and the R.A.F. had about 7 Brewsters. They lost about 5 out of 12 yest. 3 killed. We went to 22,000 ft. and patrolled for 2 hrs. but never saw a sign of any enemy ships. They didn't come in at all, which was OK with us. We have a lot of work to do to get more ships in shape. Got 2 more down from Toungoo yest. after the raid. . . . It's getting hot as hell around here. The way the enemy has been coming, we're outnumbered about 7 or 8 to one. . . . God how we need more ships and men. . . . Food situation is bad and our ammunition low. Some fun.

Dec. 27 . . . Still no definite word as to reinforcements.[8]

The remaining planes in Smith's command left Burma on December 31 for China, where Smith became a squadron leader, shooting down nine Japanese planes. In July 1942, the Flying Tigers disbanded and Smith joined the First Air Commando Group, flying fifty-five combat missions and earning the Silver Star and Distinguished Flying Cross. Promoted to lieutenant colonel, Smith returned to civilian life as a television scriptwriter in Los Angeles.[9]

President Roosevelt declared it a "day of infamy," but December 7, 1941, was also a day that unified America. The country had been attacked and Congress moved quickly to meet the crisis, declaring war on Japan the following day with only a single dissenting vote.[10] Germany and Italy fulfilled their pact with Japan by declaring war on the United States, pulling America once more into a European conflict. Congress granted the president authority to send U.S. troops anywhere in the world to battle fascism. In an instant, the United States was not only engaged in the largest and deadliest war in history, but was also an ally of the Soviet Union.

Most Americans had little idea what kind of war they were entering, and the sort of demands it would place on its military personnel, both physically and mentally. For instance, the army's Quartermaster Corps completely missed the mark on the number of grave registration units they would require.[11] In May 1942, Dwight Eisenhower wrote, "The actual fact is that not one man in twenty in the Govt . . . realizes what a grisly, dirty, tough business we are in."[12] The story of the "Honey" is a good indicator of the unrealistic attitude of the U.S. Army. At the war's start the army was convinced that the light tank was all they would need, giving preference to the ten-ton Stuart tank, also known as the "Honey." With one-inch armor plates and a 37mm gun, the Honey was favored even by George Patton, who did not yet appreciate how pathetic it would prove against the German Panzer with its 75mm gun. The Germans and Japanese approached war far more seriously, and it took a year for the United States to catch up with their opponents in terms of equipment. However, from the end of 1942 on, there was no stopping the U.S. military machine.

The industrial might of the United States proved decisive in World War II. Most common soldiers reached the same conclusion as scholars and artists, that modern warfare has little of romance about it, with victory belonging, in Geoffrey Perrett's words, "to the side with the biggest factories."[13] Louis Simpson, a Jamaican-born private in the 101st Airborne, brilliantly summarized the nature of the war in a poem on a battle near Dusseldorf:

> Now and then a shell flew over.
> For every shell Krupp fired,
> General Motors sent back four.[14]

American factories ran around the clock as government regulators monitored every aspect of the workplace, from safety standards to wages. Women entered the workforce in record numbers, taking jobs that had traditionally been seen as a male preserve, with Rosie the Riveter becoming a national symbol of patriotic dedication and female competence. American production figures were staggering, well beyond what the supposedly more efficient fascists accomplished: 300,000 planes, 88,000 tanks, and 86,000 warships poured forth from factories and shipyards. These record levels of production were attained by unionized workers, as the federal government now required management to accept collective bargaining as the legitimate right of workers. Most of the 16.4 million Americans who served during the war also came from working-class families. In many ways, World War II witnessed the triumph of the common man over the self-proclaimed superman.

The greatly expanded American military consisted primarily of young men and women, mostly born in the 1920s, who had come of age during the Great Depression. They knew hardship and privation, remembered parents losing their jobs, had had to move when banks foreclosed on homes or landlords kicked them out of the house, had stood with anxious parents in breadlines, or, like my father, dug through trash cans behind markets and restaurants. For some of these young people, the beginning of the war seemed exciting and full of potential. Robert Kotlowitz, calling on Wordsworth, described it as "bliss" to be nineteen and sailing off to great adventures in France in 1944: "We would sail across the Atlantic, unthinking and blind, in the self-absorbed way of all traveling armies through history, and learn by doing, by being there. Nevertheless, it was still a kind of bliss."[15] For many others, those first days of war simply meant freedom from want, the military representing their first steady job.[16] World War II changed everything. The war took tens of thousands of American lives, but saved many others; and the United States remained untouched by war, while all the other world powers were devastated.

## The Slog

Veterans of World War II often say that the war consisted of long periods of boredom punctuated by brief bursts of pure terror. Boot camp tended to be followed by sitting in some disbursement center waiting for transport, followed by tedious boat trips, more sitting in camps, lots of marching, digging in, the dull daily routines of being on guard—mostly the war consisted of "the slog." But then, suddenly, and often without any warning, would come a day or more of death and destruction. For many combat veterans, the experience is one that will never leave them. "I was only in combat for six weeks," Robert Rasmus said, but he remembered "every hour, every minute of the whole forty-two days."[17] Given what happened in the Second World War, it is surprising that anyone could forget the details. As the Homer of GIs, Ernie Pyle, wrote during the war, the "run-of-the-mass soldiers . . . see from the worm's eye view, and our segment of the picture consists only of tired and dirty soldiers who are alive and don't want to die . . . of shocked silent men wandering back down the hill from battle; . . . of jeeps and petrol dumps and smelly bedding rolls and C rations and cactus patches and blown bridges and dead mules and hospital tents . . . and of graves and graves and graves. That is our war, and we will carry it with us as we go from one battleground to another."[18]

In December 1941, Don Moss was a promising young artist who had just gotten a job with the Boston printing firm Spaulding-Moss and was planning to propose to his beautiful girlfriend, Jane Dale. His future seemed assured and comfortable, until December 7. Like so many of his generation, Moss went off to war from a sense of duty, full of the certainty of youth, and having no idea what he was getting into:

> Right after the Japanese bombed Pearl Harbor, my buddy [Harry Briggs] and I headed down to the post office to enlist [in] the Army Air Corps. . . . We were both rejected; I didn't have 30/30 vision and Harry had a bad back from a hockey accident. Back to work in Boston, I asked Mom to let me know when my draft notice came. February 2, 1942, she called and I walked over to the Marine Corps Recruitment office and signed up. . . .
>
> My decision was firm but met tearfully by both Mom and Dad. With all kinds of advice, they told me to take care of myself, be brave and hang in there and we all *knew* that I would return. . . . I wanted to be a part of the best [and] felt the Marine training would be tougher, enabling me to fight better and protect myself. (I was a brave but naïve young man.) . . .
>
> Parting was terribly painful with Jane. My family saw me off on a dreary uncomfortable troop train in South Station, Boston, crowded with other young Marine recruits, all nervously awaiting what lay ahead. . . . I kissed my family goodbye and boarded the train bound for Parris Island, South Carolina. . . .
>
> Looking around, we were as rag-tag a group as I had ever seen. More recruits were picked up. . . . Some were obviously from college while others looked like tough Bronx street kids. Despite the total mix of ethnic backgrounds from Brooklyn to Ivy League colleges, we had one common bond, to kill the whole Japanese army. We knew we were joining the finest fighting force in the world.
>
> . . . We were given the worst of thin turkey sandwiches as the train ride got rougher, passing through small towns and bleak Southern landscapes,

bells ringing at the darkened remote railroad crossings. The seat hadn't been cleaned since the Civil War. Our cattle car clacked on through the night past Southern slave shacks, bleak silhouettes on the edges of tobacco fields. It was eerie with the engineer tooting through all the lonely crossings. This trip was a first for all of us crossing bridges above brown swamps and rivers with millions of tall Southern pines. . . . When no one was watching, I took out the eight by ten glossy photo of Jane's beautiful face, my thoughts completely of my love. . . .

[At Parris Island] A tall grim D.I. [drill instructor] screamed orders at the seediest looking examples of male humanity ever assembled. Very quickly we fell out of the cars in a long line. Frankly, we were scared shitless of these supermen Marine D.I.s, their World War I Smokey the Bear hats at an angle. They all looked wildly angry. And why shouldn't they? It was their awesome responsibility to make Marines from this incredible flock of misfits in six weeks. . . .

After six weeks of the most intense training without let-up, we graduated with the highest platoon grade ever made from Parris Island. From early morning until late at night, we were transformed into Marines. . . . We were given a day off to clean up and prepare for the trip to Camp LeJeune, North Carolina. We weren't aware of the toughest part to come.

"You shitheads are here to learn to fight!" Captain Martin Rockmore[19] swaggered before us, glowering at his new E Company. . . . We marched for miles in the hot dusty red clay through stands of Southern pines, trudging under the weight of heavy combat packs. No one flinched. Now we knew what was expected of us and Rocky did everything we did and more. He set a blistering pace but my old credo, "If you can do it, I can," made me try harder. He seemed merciless, but we respected him as our leader. As days turned into weeks, we became stronger and mentally tough as nails. It dawned on us now that this great feeling of physical well being, of being the best, was what *esprit de corps* was all about. We'd follow this captain anywhere, and we did. We followed Rocky through the hell of Guadalcanal.[20]

Moss's E Company crossed the country to San Francisco and then took the navy transport ship *George F. Elliott*,[21] first to New Zealand and then to Guadalcanal. The Japanese seized the Solomon Islands in the spring of 1942, as part of their effort to isolate Australia. Naval intelligence, which had broken the Japanese secret code, learned that the Japanese were preparing an airfield on Guadalcanal from which to attack shipping bound for Australia. Admiral Ernest J. King, chief of U.S. naval operations, determined to take the island in what would be the first American amphibious attack of the war. The ensuing contest for the ninety-mile-long island would last six months.

Japanese planes sank the *George F. Elliott* shortly after the Marines had disembarked and after the Japanese naval victory at Savo Island, the Marines were left isolated on Guadalcanal. The U.S. Navy kept the pressure on the Japanese in a series of air and naval battles over the next months that amounted to a war of attrition. The island finally fell to the Americans in February 1943. In combination with the Battle of Midway in June 1942, Guadalcanal halted the Japanese advance and began the slow turning of the tide back toward the Japanese homeland.[22]

After Guadalcanal, Moss became a corporal and in Melbourne, Australia, fell in love with an Australian woman. With her, he met Eleanor Roosevelt, "a very warm and cordial lady." He transferred to Intelligence, where his artistic skills led him to become a mapmaker, and took part in operations around New Guinea and New Britain Island: "Because air-ground communication was unsophisticated then, we were sometimes strafed by our own aircraft." On occasion it seemed to Moss that the commanding officers had little regard for the enlisted men, seeing them as expendable. He was outraged that a friend of his "died in the next horror, an unnecessary crime perpetrated by MacArthur, the bloody Peleliu. Years later I read that Admiral Halsey didn't want us to take that island. . . . Peleliu was never used for anything. Good Marines died needlessly."[23] After the war, Moss made a career from his artistic skills, settling in New York and working for *Sports Illustrated*.[24]

The battles, of course, occupied Moss's memory most, but accounted for only a small part of his total time in service. Like many Americans, Moss found that serving presented opportunities for travel previously unknown—and constituted a vital form of education. "I had this great sense of adventure," Robert Rasmus recalled. "My gosh, going across the ocean, seeing the armies, the excitement of it. I was there." For basic training he was sent south to Fort Benning, Georgia. "I'd never been outside the states of Wisconsin, Indiana, and Michigan. So when I woke up the first morning on the troop train in Fulton, Kentucky, I thought I was in Timbuktu." He heard a New England accent for the first time in his life at Fort Benning, and "the southerner was an exotic creature to me." He was young and thrilled by all these changes, at that age when one's "need for friendship is greatest. I still see a number of these people. There's sort of a special sense of kinship."

But then Rasmus got very sick at Fort Benning and most of his division went off to Europe: "I remember letters I sent my buddies that came back: Missing in action. Killed in action. These were the eighteen-year-olds. It was only because I got the flu that I wasn't among them." Suddenly the reality of war hit him, and he went off to Europe knowing that he truly faced death. Yet, "I was absolutely bowled over by Europe, the castles, the cathedrals, the Alps. It was wonderment. I was preoccupied with staying alive and doing my job, but it seemed, out of the corner of my eye, I was constantly fascinated with the beauty of the German forests and medieval bell towers. At nineteen, you're seeing life with fresh eyes."[25]

Many others found service an opportunity to educate themselves, with reading at the center of whatever free time they had. Robert Kotlowitz recalled that "none of us would be without something to read. We were stocked for the future, books packed into each fatigue pocket. A book marked the shortest, straightest, and most invigorating lifeline to the real world—the world outside that would continue on its way, in its own orbit, no matter what might happen to us. That's what I believed. That's what most of the readers in the Yankee Division believed."[26] Forty years after the war's end Paul Liley still had a collection of GI paperbacks specially printed to fit inside fatigue pockets. He recalled his time in the military giving him the chance to read his way to "the high school education I never had." The enthusiasm for books he picked up during the war would lead him into college and a career as a teacher. But the books were only part of his education, he added: "my buddies taught me everything else I needed to know."[27]

Repeatedly, veterans offer the same explanation for their adherence to duty, even under the most disorienting and dreadful circumstances: concern for their fellow soldiers. After World War II, General S.L.A. Marshall concluded that what sustained soldiers in combat was their relationship with their fellow soldiers.[28] Stephen Ambrose made this small-unit cohesion the centerpiece of his justly celebrated *Band of Brothers*.[29] Nothing in my years of working with and listening to veterans undermines this simple truth: American soldiers stay in line under fire out of concern for their comrades. Many veterans expressed these feelings in simple terms. Robert Rasmus insisted, "The reason you storm the beaches is not patriotism or bravery. It's that sense of not wanting to fail your buddies."[30] Forty years later he ran into Richard "Red" Prendergast on the street in Chicago. The two men had not seen each other since Prendergast had been taken prisoner during the war, but they recognized one another immediately.[31]

World War II veterans are a famously laconic lot, making it difficult to capture their emotional life. Fortunately, some left diaries that expressed their inner voices. Timothy L. Curran was thirty years old when he left his wife Mary to serve as an army flight surgeon. He poured out his longing for home and for his wife in his diary:

March 17 [1943] Arose at 5:45 A.M. This is probably the last time I shall see Mary for a long while. Even though I have been expecting this moment for a long while I wonder now whether I can endure a long separation. It was only a few months ago that we were apart for only a month and I thought that it would never end. Yet even though she feels as I must at this moment, she refuses to give way to her emotions. It makes it so much easier for me that way. I left the house at 6:30 and joined the group. . . . It's impossible to describe one's thoughts at a time like this. Everything is so uncertain as to when I'm going, when I'll return, whether I'll return intact, crippled, or not at all. When I do come back, Mary thinks that possibly I may be having another mouth to feed. In a way it would be so wonderful, but I don't like to think of her going through all that alone. I want to be by her side, just as we have been together all these months that we have been married. . . .

April 8 [in the Atlantic] . . . Eight months married today. It has all gone by so quickly and happily. I only hope that this damned war gets over very soon so I can get back to Mary without ever having to worry again about going away. . . .

April 10 . . . The moon . . . looks exceptionally beautiful as it shines on the water. It sure is a romantic setting, but that doesn't do me much good when Mary is thousands of miles away and can't be by my side to enjoy it with me. I guess that would be asking too much, for here I am only 3 weeks away from her and already wishing I could have her with me again. There are too many months ahead to be thinking of such things now.

In December 1944, after serving in Africa, Sicily, and France, Curran still longs to go home, writing that he is not sure how much longer he can hold up—and then the journal ends mid-sentence. He was finally sent home one year later, in December 1945.[32]

In the Saar region of Germany, in March 1945, a Lieutenant Wilson led his company through fierce house-to-house fighting in a ruined village. Just as he was directing his men up a street, he was shot. "My God, I'm hit!" he cried out. He ordered one of his men to slap him, as though the shock would hold off death. He died seconds later. One of his men collected Wilson's identity card and was stunned to see that his lieutenant was just twenty-one years old. This information depressed his men, for they had looked up to Wilson as a reliable authority figure.[33] So many Americans were so very young, as soldiers often are, but for some reason that youth appeared more out of place in the ruthless slaughter of World War II. "Maybe it was the naïve optimism of youth," wrote Marine E.B. Sledge, "but the awesome reality that we were training to be cannon fodder in a global war that had already snuffed out millions of lives never seemed to occur to us." Death and maiming did not seem possibilities; what concerned them "was that we might be too afraid to do our jobs under fire."[34]

## The Persistence of Racism

From the Revolution through the First World War, African Americans had been certain that their willingness to fight for their country would prove their worth to white America. But they had been consistently disappointed; for the majority of whites, racism trumped patriotism. World War II should have been the great breakthrough, for the United States had committed to total war—the complete commitment of all its national resources—in a battle against racist fascism. Yet, once more, the need to maintain white supremacy at home trumped military necessity. In the warped perspective of racism, it was somehow better for white men to risk their lives in battle than to employ willing black troops— for the danger of blacks proving their equality under fire posed too great a threat to cherished ideas of racial character. The Selective Service and Training Acts of 1940, codifying the first peacetime draft in American history, included section 4(a) which clearly stated, "There shall be no discrimination against any person on account of race or color." Yet somehow all branches of the U.S. military saw nothing discriminatory about retaining segregated units.[35] During World War II nearly eight thousand black men rose to officer ranks, but all served in all-black regiments, most of which were assigned the most menial duty.[36]

Even when kept from combat, African Americans proved their heroism from the first day of war to its last, slowly winning a small degree of respect. Dorie Miller offered a graphic illustration of this courage and of the grudging and generally retarded acceptance the military came to grant its black personnel. On December 7, 1941, Miller was serving in the kitchen aboard the *West Virginia* at Pearl Harbor. Amid the disorienting and terrifying Japanese surprise attack, Miller ran to the bridge and pulled the ship's wounded captain to safety. He then seized a machine gun and blew four Japanese planes out of the sky. It took a year for the navy to acknowledge Miller's "distinguished devotion to duty, extraordinary courage and disregard for his own personal safety" in awarding him the Navy Cross. But they kept Miller in the kitchen, where he was killed aboard the *Liscombe Bay* in 1945.[37] When the Japanese launched their surprise attack on American bases in the Philippines, the first casualty was Robert Brooks of Kentucky, who had half his head taken off. After his death, his unit discovered that he had "passed" as white in order to serve in an armored battalion. Their commander, Major General Jacob L. Devers, recommended that the airfield be renamed Brooks Field. "For the preservation of

America, the soldiers and sailors guarding our outposts are giving their lives," Devers wrote. "In death, there is no grade or rank. And in this, the greatest democracy the world has known, neither riches nor poverty, neither creed nor race draws a line of demarcation in this hour of national crisis."[38] But of course it did, otherwise Brooks would not have had to pretend to be white in order to serve his country the way he thought most fit.

Through the war, the military held back on recognizing distinguished service by black troops, being more afraid of antagonizing southern politicians than of the Nazis and Japanese. More than one million African Americans served in World War II, yet only nine received the Distinguished Service Cross and no Medal of Honor recipient was black.[39] The army at least recognized their hypocrisy, preparing a training manual for white officers of black troops which bore a restricted classification. *Army Service Forces Manual M5: Leadership and the Negro Soldier* advised, "The officer will not be able to answer adequately all questions which Negro troops may ask concerning their relation to a democratic Army. But he can make certain that, within his own unit, the democratic principles which the Negro soldier has come to accept as an American ideal will operate." The next sentence then expects a major leap of cognitive dissonance, calling on the officers to "assure his troops that Army *standards* of training, performance, and leadership of Negro and white troops are identical." That said, the manual insisted, "While the Army takes no position on the role of the Negro in American life, it does take a stand on his use in the Army. The Army's policy is to use its manpower, Negro and white, at the maximum level of efficiency . . . possible."[40] But what was possible was limited by the perceived need to maintain racist structures and myths.

It took little reflection to perceive the irony of a deeply racist and segregated United States proclaiming its moral superiority over its fascist enemies. Langston Hughes spoke to the obvious contradictions in a poem/letter to President Roosevelt:

> I am a soldier
> Down in Alabam
> Wearing the uniform
> Of Uncle Sam.
> But when I get on the bus
> I have to ride in the back
> Rear seats only
> For a man who's black. . . .
> I ask why YOUR soldiers
> Must ride in the back,
> Segregated—

Because we are black?
I train to fight,
Perhaps to die.
Urgently, sir,
I await your reply.[41]

Each individual African American who served his or her country in World War II had to ask the same question that Hughes raised: were they fighting for democracy only to preserve segregation? Edgar A. Huff of Alabama joined the Marines in 1942 because he wanted to be part of "the toughest outfit in the world." The Marines had just given in to pressure from the Roosevelt administration and started accepting black recruits; Huff was one of the first fifty African Americans to join up. He was put into a segregated Negro Marine Corps under white officers and trained at Montford Point next to the all-white Camp Lejeune. A short time later he was at the Atlanta bus station wearing his uniform and was arrested by two marine MPs for "impersonating a marine," since, as one of the MPs said, "There ain't no damn nigger marines." A captain who arrived at the jail to bail out some drunk marines told Huff the same thing. Huff was still in jail on Christmas; the visiting navy chaplain would not even talk to him. Finally, he was able to get a message through to Colonel Samuel Woods, the commander at Montford Point, who ordered his immediate release. Huff eventually fought in the Pacific theater, Korea, and Vietnam, retiring in 1972 with the rank of sergeant major and a chest full of decorations.[42]

The only black combat unit deployed on the European front in the Second World War was the Ninety-second Infantry Division, and the army appeared determined to see it fail, appointing a known racist, General Edward M. Almond, as its commander. Even fifteen years after the war's end, Almond continued to insist that the use of black troops would disrupt and diminish military performance: "It is absurd to contend that . . . the characteristics demonstrated by Negroes . . . will not undermine and deteriorate the white army unit into which the Negro is integrated. . . . [I]t is very questionable whether people of the traits exhibited by Negroes should be entrusted in key combat units in any degree."[43] Given such an attitude, it is not surprising that Almond recommended just four enlisted men in the Ninety-second Infantry for the Distinguished Service Cross—all of whom were denied. More decorations were awarded to African Americans who served in World War II after the war than during it, as the children of veterans and historians fought to gain the recognition heroism deserved. In 1997, President Bill Clinton sought to correct this unjustified act of exclusion by ordering a study of the historical record. The study found that just eight of the 4,750 Distinguished Service Crosses awarded in World War II went to African Americans, 0.2 percent of the total, and not a single black soldier was recommended for the Medal of Honor—unlike every other war this country has fought. Based on this report, Clinton awarded seven Medals of Honor, all but one posthumously.[44]

In 1943 Willie James Macon of Alabama was drafted into America's segregated army to fight for freedom. Macon's regiment in the Quartermaster Corps was entirely black, except for the officers, who were mostly white. But, unusually, Macon's white commander earned their trust: "We liked the guy. We soldiered for him. Everybody tried to stand on their hands and toes for him. He was really a nice guy." Macon insists that shared respect paid off for his commander, who rose from lieutenant to colonel during the war. Macon was sent to the Philippines, which the United States had recently recaptured, though Japanese resistance on the islands persisted until the surrender. Being black, Macon was assigned to drive a truck, though that hardly removed him from danger, since mines remained a constant concern. The members of Macon's unit saw themselves as responsible for their trucks; "this is your baby," he said, "you got to take care of it." One of Macon's closest friends was Jesse, who often rode shotgun with him. On one mission Japanese planes bombed their convoy: "I felt something was happening, so I told [Jesse] to jump out. He jumped because I was driving. When I got to the next curve, I jumped. They bombed the truck. But when he jumped out, he landed on a mine. It blowed him all to pieces. That's what hurt me so bad."

When the war ended, Macon and many other members of his unit wanted to remain in the Philippines, which lacked the racism they knew at home. Macon, again like some others, even thought in terms of marrying a Filipina. "We tried to stay another twenty years, but [the Army] wouldn't let us," and shipped them all home. Arriving back in the United States in February 1946, "I felt like a stranger." Macon found that nothing had changed in terms of race, despite everything black Americans had done for their country during the war. On the other hand, many blacks felt very differently as a consequence of their experience, demanding the equality for which they had fought. The ambiguous nature of the feeling of so many African American veterans of World War II is evident in the pride Macon felt in his wartime service, and the sense of betrayal that his country failed to honor its ideals. Fifty-seven years after the war, the army awarded Macon a service medal, which he refused to accept, yet in 2005 he was buried with full military honors, as he had requested.[45]

One significant and often overlooked aspect of the experience of African Americans in World War II is that many veterans returned home to a segregated and hostile South and resolved to fight for democracy in their own country. One such veteran was Robert F. Williams of Monroe, North Carolina, often credited with being the most influential early voice in black militancy. In 1947, when the Ku Klux Klan threatened to desecrate the body of a dead veteran, Williams joined other African Americans to defend the remains of Benny Montgomery. As Williams wrote, military service had taught them "what a virtue it was to fight for democracy." It had also taught them not to be afraid of other men with guns. When the Klan showed up and found the funeral home surrounded by a platoon of armed men, they turned around and left. At that moment Williams understood "that we had to resist, and that resistance could be effective if we resisted in groups, and if we resisted with guns."[46] Williams would go on to lead Monroe's successful chapter of the NAACP, which consisted primarily of working-class blacks, and, as he wrote: "Most important, we had a strong representation of returned veterans who were very militant and didn't scare easy."[47] These returning veterans deserve recognition for helping to start the civil rights movement that would transform America.

Racism did not target African Americans alone. Japanese Americans—unlike those of Italian and German heritage—were subject to widespread public suspicion and legal limitations. The internment of over one hundred thousand Japanese Americans during the war—and the concomitant appropriation of their property—is one of the darker pages in the history of the United States, as was realized at the time.[48] Within a few months of the establishment of the camps, the *New Republic* referred to them as "concentration camps."[49] In an extensive article on the camps, *Fortune* magazine pointed out the un-American nature of the internment: "By continuing to keep American citizens in 'protective custody,' the U.S. is holding to a policy as ominous as it is new. The American custom in the past has been to lock up the citizen who commits violence, not the victim of his threats and blows." The editors asked the obvious question: what is to prevent this logic of detention from being extended to other groups? "The possibilities of 'protective custody' are endless, as the Nazis have amply proved."[50]

As both these magazines pointed out, Americans of Japanese descent served in the U.S. military during the war, many with distinction. Peter Ota found it "ironic" that he served in the army while his family sat "in a concentration camp waiting for the war to end." The military "didn't know what to do with us Japanese Americans," and put them in segregated units. "Should they send us to the Pacific side? They might not be able to tell who was the enemy and who was not." Ota knew one thing for certain: "I had to prove myself. . . . We all had this feeling."[51] And they proved themselves according to the highest military standards. The 442nd Regiment, which saw action in Italy, France, and Germany, became the most decorated regiment in the history of the U.S. military, its Japanese American personnel receiving twenty-one Congressional Medals of Honor—among them future senator Daniel Inouye.[52] Henry Kondo, a Nisei—or second-generation Japanese American—from Pasadena, California, volunteered to serve in the army, despite the internment of members of his family. "Even unto death," he declared, "we'll show we're Americans in every way." He paid for his patriotism with his life, being killed in action in Italy. A ceremony was held for Kondo in his hometown. Present were several African Americans and Hispanics, demonstrating their solidarity with other Americans denied their full rights and respect. The salute to the flag was led by Lieutenant Jack Robinson, who had been a star football player at UCLA. After the war he became known as Jackie Robinson, breaking the color barrier in professional baseball. Wartime courage often translated into postwar heroism.[53]

## Industrial Death

An estimated twenty millions soldiers died in World War II, but that number is likely only one-third of the total, for the belligerents in the Second World War targeted civilians, and succeeded in killing some forty million of them. This was truly a war without mercy. The bodies were everywhere: on battlefields and in cities, frozen in ice and strewn across sun-speckled fields—and soldiers got used to them. "As far as I could see, an area that previously had been a low grassy valley with a picturesque stream meandering through it was a muddy, repulsive, open sore on the land," Marine Eugene Sledge wrote of the once-beautiful area below Okinawa's Shuri Castle. "The whole area was pocked with shell craters and churned up by explosions. Every crater was half full of water, and many of them held a Marine corpse. The bodies lay pathetically just as they had been killed, half submerged in muck and water, rusting weapons still in hand. Swarms of flies hovered about them."[54]

The portrayal of war is often romantic, films and newspapers presenting scenes of glory and little that is gory. Alternatively, Americans often perceive war as a precision enterprise, in which technology insures victory while minimizing loss of life for our side. In World War II, many military leaders confidently predicted that the air war could bring the enemy to its knees. This faith in "shock and awe" originated with Giulio Douhet, an Italian fascist advocate of airpower in the 1930s. Douhet predicted that within two days of an air attack against urban centers, a "panic-stricken people" would flee the cities "to escape this terror from the air." Any society would experience "a complete breakdown," as civilians, seeking to end their "horror and suffering" and "driven by the instinct of self-preservation, would rise up and demand an end to the war."[55] In 1942, Air Marshal Arthur "Bomber" Harris told Winston Churchill that his massive bombing campaign would "knock Germany out of the War in a matter of months." Though the Americans often disagreed with Harris's deliberate targeting of civilian centers, they accepted his general premise.[56]

Before the war the United States denounced the bombing of civilian centers. In 1937 Franklin Roosevelt denied the legitimacy of Japan's bombing of Chinese cities: "[W]ithout warning or justification of any kind, civilians, including vast numbers of women and children, are being ruthlessly murdered with bombs from the air."[57] When the Germans did the same in Spain in 1938, the State Department condemned this "inhuman bombing of civilian populations," and when Germany invaded Poland in September 1939, Roosevelt once more spoke out against the "barbarous" air war against cities: "The ruthless bombing from the air of civilians in unfortified centers of population during the course of the hostilities which have raged in various quarters of the earth during the past few years, which has resulted in the maiming and in the death of thousands of defenseless men, women and children has sickened the hearts of every civilized man and woman, and has profoundly shocked the conscience of humanity."[58] Yet Roosevelt's conscience was not so shocked as to prevent his approval of a devastating air war against Japan and Germany that claimed an estimated 400,000 Japanese and 500,000 German lives.[59]

However, as the United States Strategic Bombing Survey, which included such brilliant young men as George Ball and John Kenneth Galbraith, verified after the war, Allied bombing had stiffened the resolve of the German people to carry on the war while failing to cripple industrial production—in fact, German production increased during the war as it went underground. Despite the horrendous firestorms created in Dresden, Lübeck, and Hamburg by British and American bombers, airpower did not defeat Germany; massive ground forces did.[60] Similarly, in the Pacific theater, the Allies expected that their air and naval power would crush the Japanese before troops had to go ashore. Massive bombardments from the air and sea would decimate Japanese defenses, while the air war against Japan would destroy civilian support for the Imperial war effort. None of these expectations were fulfilled.[61]

Robert Sherrod, a journalist who went ashore at Tarawa with the Marines in 1943, experienced "the hard facts of war," which are carnage and slaughter. "The facts were cruel, but inescapable," he wrote. "Probably no amount of shelling and bombing could obviate the necessity of sending in foot soldiers to finish the job. The corollary was this: there is no easy way to win the war; there is no panacea which will prevent men from getting killed." The American people could not understand why airpower alone was not enough to defeat the enemy, and were disturbed and often outraged by the casualties suffered. Sherrod blamed the very language of reporting. Journalists "gave the impression that we were bowling over the enemy every time our handful of bombers dropped a few pitiful tons from 30,000 feet. The stories . . . gave the impression that any American could lick any twenty Japs." Instead of describing Japanese resistance and American deaths, the dispatches "came out liberally sprinkled with 'smash' and 'pound' and other 'vivid' verbs." These victorious verbs might impress the readers, but they failed to "impress the miserable, bloody soldiers in the front lines where the action had taken place." He quotes one sergeant as saying, "The war that is being written in the newspapers must be a different war from the one we see."[62]

In an age of industrial war machines, the statistics pile up until they can appear meaningless. How does the human mind grapple with nineteen thousand people killed in a single day on the beaches of Normandy, or over one hundred thousand in an instant at Hiroshima? How do we conceptualize the death of some sixty million people in a six-year period? The individual death can lose all meaning, except for those most intimately engaged. That connection ran in both directions, toward one's comrades, and to those one was trying to kill. Even though the United States engaged in a war with two of the worst enemies it had ever faced—as wartime propaganda repeatedly reminded the troops— soldiers often expressed surprising sympathy for the opposing troops. Robert Rasmus served with the 106th Division at the Battle of the Bulge. After a particularly bloody engagement, he crossed through the field past the dead German bodies: "Looking at the individual German dead, each took on a personality. These were no longer an abstraction. They were no longer the Germans of the brutish faces and the helmets we saw in the newsreels. They were exactly our age. There were boys like us. . . . Once the helmet is off, you're looking at a teen-ager, another kid."[63] Similarly, Robert Lekachman, a member of the same Seventy-seventh Division on whose helmets Gustav Dill had stenciled the Statue of Liberty in the First World War, first saw a Japanese person on Guam. This Japanese soldier was dead: "He looked pitiful, with his thick glasses" and "a sheaf of letters in his pocket." Lekachman felt sorry for the young man, who "looked like an awkward kid who'd been taken right out of his home to this miserable place."[64]

American combat forces were built upon intimate connections, upon the close comradeship of brothers-in-arms. The death of one of their number could energize or demoralize a unit; soldiers could risk their lives heroically—or foolishly—for comrades, or lose all sense of mission. It was a delicate balance that depended so much on the character of the individuals involved, and on the level of training they had received. That training paid off at Normandy on June 6, 1944. The Allies threw everything they had at Germany's coastal defenses in the largest amphibious landing in history: 150,000 men on 7,000 ships, supported by 18,000 airborne troops, 15,000 planes, and 50,000 vehicles. But the mass of numbers did not matter in this instance, as D-Day all came down to the soldiers and their persistence. In the most adverse conditions imaginable, American units held together and kept advancing in the face of hostile fire and heavy casualties. "We fought as a team without standout stars," recalled Sergeant Carwood Lipton. "We were like a machine. We didn't have anyone who leaped up and charged a machine-gun. We knocked it out or made it withdraw by maneuver and teamwork or mortar fire. We were smart; there weren't many flashy heroics. We had learned that heroics was the way to get killed without getting the job done, and getting the job done was more important."[65]

## Prisoners of War

Never had so many Americans been taken prisoner of war as in World War II. Some 150,000 Americans spent time as prisoners of their nation's enemy, many of them never to return home. In 1929 the Third Geneva Convention laid down the standards by which prisoners of war should be treated. The Germans mostly adhered to these accords, though they did occasionally mow down groups of prisoners, as at the notorious Malmédy massacre during the Ardennes campaign of December 1944, in which an SS unit killed eighty-six U.S. soldiers. Following the collapse of their offensive, the Germans marched thousands of American prisoners across Germany through freezing winter snows. While such treatment led to the deaths of hundreds of POWs, Japan's conduct exemplified cruelty and inhumanity. Not a signatory of the Third Geneva Convention, Japan's government rejected any notion of treating their prisoners humanely, encouraging their soldiers to act brutally to all those taken captive. The Japanese starved and tortured their prisoners, using thousands of POWs as slave labor, beheading those who resisted.[66] The Bataan Death March of April 1942 exemplified Japanese maltreatment of prisoners, as 78,000 U.S. and Filipino POWs ran a sixty-five-mile gauntlet of privation and beatings to their prison camp, losing an estimated 10,000 soldiers on the way. After the war the Americans discovered that one-third of the POWs held by the Japanese had died in captivity, compared to 1 percent of the Americans in German captivity. The Allies sought not just justice at the postwar Nuremberg and Tokyo War Crimes Trials, but also to assert the necessity of respecting the Geneva Conventions.[67]

Leon Peragallo was a high school student hanging out with his friends in a grocery store when they heard that the Japanese had bombed Pearl Harbor. They all promised one another to do what they could to beat the Japanese. Rather than wait to be drafted, Peragallo enlisted in the air force as soon as he turned eighteen. He wanted to be a pilot or navigator, but "washed out along with 60% of my classmates. I was shocked and depressed, but I was O.K. when we were told that we would be trained for positions on combat flight crews." He trained as a gunner, was sent to join the massive air fleets assembling in Britain, and was assigned to a B-17 bomber, the "Angel in Di-Skies." Peragallo flew numerous missions, as many as seven in nine days, bombing German cities and frontline troops—including "a sad and sobering situation" of dropping bombs on American troops by mistake.[68] On August 2, 1944, they set off on "a milk-run" to bomb a railroad bridge outside Saint-Quentin, France. As they approached the target, they took a direct hit to one of their engines. After successfully hitting the bridge, they turned for home. Hit again by antiaircraft fire, the B-17 kept losing altitude until it was skimming over the treetops approaching the North Sea. Hoping to avoid capture, the pilot guided them over the icy waters and ditched the plane. The crew got quickly into a lifeboat and then watched as their plane "turned up-right, nose down, and slowly sank into the North Sea":

> About 24 hours after we had ditched, we saw a boat on the horizon coming toward us from the east. There were two Dutch fishing boats, which came up to our rafts. A couple of their crew members pulled us into their boat. They were Dutch fishermen, wearing wooden shoes and all. They quickly helped us to go below deck to a small cabin to hide us. In a very short time another boat, of the German Navy, came along side. There was a shouting match between the fishermen and the Germans, who were angry that the Dutch picked us up. Our entire crew back on deck, with the Jerrys pointing their guns at us, wanting us to get in their boat. We hesitated, then one Jerry shot a machine gun burst over our head. We all moved fast to their boat, which was lower than the fishing boat. I landed on deck on my side, it hurt.
>
> The Germans then took us to Zeebrugen, Belgium. . . . We were all now Prisoners of War of Germany.
>
> Two guards transported us to a hospital to get us medical attention. At this time I was in bad shape and could not walk without help, nor stand up. One of the guards went into the hospital to get us medical help. After a while the guard came out with a doctor. The doctor was over six-feet tall, bald head, wearing a monocle in a dirty white coat that reached his ankles. He came out yelling and arguing with the guards. Campbell, our radio operator could speak a little German. The doctor was yelling at the guards for bringing us there and he would not give us medical attention because a few days before Hitler had given an edict to kill all captured American Airmen. (We had heard about this order back at the base and this order was carried out by many civilians and military.)
>
> However, one of the guards went back to see if he could get someone else to help. . . . [He] finally got a medical soldier to help. He proceeded to take the metal out of my ankle with his jackknife, also cleaned out some wires from my heated suit that were imbedded in my thighs from flack. Two large pieces of metal had gone deeply into the calf and thigh, which I still have today. . . .
>
> Still lying on the floor, down this long stairs comes the same doctor who didn't want to give us medical attention and he had a needle as big as

a nail. I was lying on my back and he motioned to pull down my pants and gave me a shot in the groin. He then stomped off cursing and yelling. I guess it was a tetanus shot; it must have worked because I didn't get an infection. My wounds never healed (lack of nourishment) until I got home to the good old U.S.A. Praise the Lord for the tetanus shot. . . .

[In Brussels] I had my first interrogation by an S.S. Captain. As trained, we gave only name, rank and serial number. They put on a big show, yelling, threatening, etc. . . .

On the fourth day, they rushed us out of our cells. There were about six Americans, one was an American "Hot Shot" fighter pilot.

As we approached the elevator, an English speaking guard was yelling that we had better give all the information they wanted. Then the fighter pilot started arguing with the guards. The guards then started to hit us with their rifle butts. The fighter pilot starts pushing the guards, then all hell breaks loose. A German officer comes to the scene, tells everyone to get into the elevator. We reached the ground floor, then a courtyard. There were soldiers in black uniforms [SS troops]. There was another big argument, the fighter pilot was going berserk. Suddenly the officer yells, take them all out and shoot them. They made us line up against a wall in the courtyard. I thought, "Here we go again, I'm dead."

As we faced the firing squad, an airman next to me said, "What are we going to do now?" I said, "Pray!" And we did. The firing squad aimed at us, guns cocked, an officer giving the command to shoot; then suddenly an officer running out of the building yelling, "Halt! Halt!"

They then hurried us into a truck and off we go. . . . I believe it was all a hoax; the fighter pilot was probably a German, a good actor, but his uniform did not look authentic to me. However, the firing squad sure looked real to me.

. . . [On a train to Frankfurt] The train had stopped in a railroad station of a city at night. We could hear aircraft overhead. The British bombed at night, the Americans bombed during daytime. Bombs were dropping close by, anti-aircraft guns were shooting. Then what sounded like hail falling, . . . shrapnel coming back down from German anti-aircraft bursts at the R.A.F. planes overhead. The bombs were getting closer to our train; everyone scurrying to the bomb shelter along with German civilians giving us the "evil eye," gesturing and yelling at us.

As we left the bomb shelter in a mob scene, we got separated from the guards and thought, "Escape." One of the guards was yelling in broken English: "Vhere ist mein boys? Boys! Boys, komst du here, mein boys." So we went back to the railroad car and stayed there until morning because part of the track and station took severe hits from the bombing and had to be repaired. We then proceeded to Frankfurt, observing the results of bombings along the way, unbelievable destruction.

We arrived in the main railroad station in Frankfurt in early afternoon. . . . As we were standing in the station waiting for the next move, a crowd of German civilians encircled us yelling, screaming, running toward us trying to hit us with umbrellas. I figured we were in big trouble, but the guards cocked their rifles and yelled at the people and dispersed them. Welcome to Germany. We could see they hated us, and I understood why. . . . I really respected those guards after that. They were old but disciplined soldiers doing their job. . . .

We then proceeded by foot to . . . a Luftwaffe interrogation prison. Our guards turned us over to black uniformed S.S. soldiers who immediately started to push us around, yelling "Schnell!" "Rause!" German "normal talk" was yelling and orders. . . . Each of us was put into solitary confinement cells. . . .

On the second day, two guards with rifles came and brought me to be interrogated. . . . It was a big office with [a captain] sitting behind a desk. He was very cordial, speaking perfect English. . . . I decided to go with name, rank and serial number only, as per orders. Back to the cell I went. The captain and the guards saw I was really hurting. Knowing this, they figured I would break down and tell them everything I knew.

The next day I was questioned by the same officer who said he had relatives in Chicago, trying to put me at ease. He asked me questions, I answered "I don't know." . . . He then got angry, said in English to the guard, "Take him back to his cell and let him rot." So rot I did for about six days. Several times I was awakened by guards coming into the cell at night, knocking me off my cot with rifle butts yelling, "Tell the Captain what he wants to know!" They scared the living daylight out of me. But it was normal procedure as I could hear the same goings on in cells around me that sounded more violent. . . .

Later, one afternoon I was taken in to see the captain again; more questions, more threats. Then he explained I had two choices: answer the questions and then go to a P.O.W. camp . . . or "to a concentration camp where you will stay until you die"—yelling at the top of his lungs. At that point I was so angry at the intimidation I didn't care what happened. I stood up on my feet and yelled back at him. . . . He then called the guards, who roughed me up a bit, and back to the cell I went.

Peragallo and the rest of his crew were transferred to a POW camp in Poland, Stalag Luft 4, where he reunited with one of those other young men with whom he had heard the news of Pearl Harbor, George Bertuzzi. The camp was abandoned in February 1945 before the advancing Soviet troops, and the prisoners marched west in freezing weather. They often slept outside in the snow, and many prisoners died along the way. By March they had reached Germany, and kept on marching, until finally they reached Lübeck. At the beginning of May, British tanks entered the city and the Germans surrendered shortly thereafter. Many of the POWs were grabbing souvenirs from the German soldiers who were now their prisoners, with Lugers being especially popular. Peragallo turned down the opportunity: "As for a gun, I could not stomach them any more." Peragallo was promoted to sergeant and awarded two Air Medals. It took a while to return to the United States, but finally he made it back to Glastonbury, Connecticut: "This had to be the happiest moment of my life. The first food I had to eat was Mom's apple pie. I had been dreaming of this moment. I ate the whole pie." Back home, Peragallo learned that the War Department had informed his parents in August 1944 that he was missing in action. They had assumed he was dead until learning near the war's end that he was a prisoner of war. Peragallo realized that apple pie meant a lot to his mother as well.[69]

Drafted at the age of eighteen in 1942, Joseph B. Lichtenbaum was sent to Europe the following year, writing his family regularly. His twelve-year-old brother Harry was present in December 1943 when his mother received a telegram from the government informing her that Private Lichtenbaum was missing in action. Families receiving the news that soldiers listed as missing in action had in fact been taken prisoner were not always reassured by this news as knowledge of Japanese and German atrocities spread. "There was another woman who lived nearby . . . whose son was also missing-in-action," Harry Lichtenbaum recalled. "By sharing their anguish, they seemed to draw strength from each other as the months crept by." In June 1944, another telegram arrived announcing that Joseph was a prisoner of war in Stalag 344 in Germany. "He's alive, he's alive," Mrs. Lichtenbaum told Harry.

"I watched as my mother put together 'survival packages' for Bud," Harry continued, "which were given to the Red Cross to deliver. She would pack the boxes with warm gloves, mufflers, underwear, shirts, pants, socks, soap, toothpaste and brushes, paperback books and playing cards. She always included writing paper and pencils, even though he was not allowed to write to us." He only received a few of the boxes his mother had sent. "Nevertheless, he said he was only living because of the Red Cross packages" she had sent. He had even been able to use the paper and a pencil she sent "to keep a diary that he kept hidden from the enemy." As the Allies approached Stalag 344, Joseph was moved to a POW camp in Bavaria and his family lost track of him, his mother worrying for his safety. But then another telegram came in April 1945. His camp had just been liberated by American troops and he was on his way home:

"My mother held that telegram in her hands for a very long time. It was the first time I had seen her cry."[70]

A member of the 106th Infantry Division, Richard "Red" Prendergast found himself in the Ardennes forest in December 1944, where he was taken prisoner in the sudden German advance. Prendergast and the other Americans taken prisoner when the Germans overran their position were put on a troop train headed east. The Germans tended not to mark trains as carrying POWs, so it came under RAF attack. It was night, and the RAF dropped flares, "and they see this big beautiful train, a very lovely target. They just pasted us something terrible." The prisoners, packed into the cars, could not escape. Prendergast estimated that some five hundred Allied prisoners died that night: "Just one of those goof-ups that happened so often in war." Sent to Stalag 4-B, Prendergast worked in a chemical plant outside of Dresden, where he was the night the city was firebombed—an event famously described by another American POW, Kurt Vonnegut.[71] Prendergast proved luckier than the thousands of civilians who died in the flames of Dresden.

## The War's End

The winter of 1944 to 1945 witnessed Hitler's last great gamble with the Ardennes campaign, and some of the most bitter fighting experienced by American troops in the European theater. Less well known than the Battle of the Bulge, but just as nasty, was the struggle in the Huertgen forest on the western edge of Germany near the Belgium border, where Americans suffered 28,000 casualties in "one of the worst US reverses in north-west Europe."[72] Lieutenant Arthur C. Neriani of the Eighth Infantry Division, who had seen a great deal of action, found the battle over these densely forested hills the most horrific he encountered, as Americans fought hand to hand with well-entrenched German forces. Neriani refused to accept a Bronze Star for his action in the Huertgen forest, "because I felt that I had not done enough to earn that decoration when others had done more, or were killed, and received no recognition." Neriani and his men just wanted to end the war and go home, which required battling across Germany:

> Fighting in Huertgen Forest was a terrible scene and a terrible experience. The Germans had all the advantages. They were familiar with every tree and rock and path in the forest. They were experts with camouflage, mines, wire and machine guns, and their plus was in their pillboxes. All the forest fire-lanes, each about twenty years wide, were equipped with concrete pillboxes arranged so that when we advanced we had to pass them, and

each was protected by a neighboring one. It took many pounds of explosives to blow up a pillbox, and this could be done only at close range at the cost of many lives. The most successful way to destroy a pillbox was by surrounding it if possible. When we were able to do this, any Germans still alive inside would surrender.

The battle of Huertgen Forest was, in my opinion, a terrible waste of soldiers' lives. There was no need to go through the forest. Of 120,000 GIs who took part in the action, 30,000 became casualties. . . . The Germans boasted that American losses in Huertgen Forest were four times the number of German casualties. During the winter our M-1 rifles would not operate properly until someone devised a powder lubricant that kept the guns from jamming. The former lubricants had simply frozen and rendered the guns useless. For the Americans, Huertgen was so disastrous that many soldiers reached the point of despair and jumped out of their foxholes or slit trenches, hoping to be shot and receive minor wounds that would remove them from being all-day, every-day targets of the German guns. . . . I saw the ambulances steadily bringing up replacements and taking away the dead bodies. . . . It had no military significance to either side. . . .

After the 28th Division was decimated, then replaced, our target was the town of Huertgen at the northern edge of the forest. It was captured by Company E of the 121st Infantry, commanded by 1st Lieutenant Boesch.[73] He said they had been fortunate because the Germans had dug a trench from the house they were staying in to the forest. Boesch and his troops crawled up the trench at night and were first to reach Huertgen [on November 29, 1944]. With the help of the 121st they routed the Germans out of the houses and cellars and captured more than 200 prisoners. . . .

The cold weather brought temperatures of ten below zero and a foot-and-a-half of snow. . . . It was so cold we had two of everything we wore. [We] never changed the pants or got a shower until something like the end of March. The only things you took off were your shoes [to change socks]. . . . The ground was frozen solid. . . . Some of the fellows in the rifle platoon would take the M-1 and shoot a clip in a round hole, then with a bayonet they would dig out the hole. When they got it deep enough, they would put in a concussion grenade and the . . . grenade would open up the soil. . . .

After the capture of Huertgen, we were gaining little ground because of the pillboxes north of the town. I was asked to fire my anti-tank gun into the slits of the pillboxes at about 300 yards. It almost turned into a disaster for my one gun. I saw that mortar fire would be coming, and after five rounds I took my gun out of action immediately. Mortar fire was raining down on the attic from where I was directing our fire. . . . As mortar and artillery fire began to hit the roof . . . I dove down the stairway.

We followed a firebreak that led to the road to Huertgen, which was about 400 yards away. The Germans fired upon everything that moved through the break. . . . After all the damage we sustained, we sent a patrol into the woods. Sure enough, there was a Nazi soldier up in a tree with a phone. He was directing their mortar and artillery fire, and it was accurate. He called the mortars on my squad, but he was quickly disposed of. . . .

On the morning of December 16, 1944, when the Battle of the Bulge [began], we observed some parachutists in our area. Word quickly spread that they had to be Germans. To aid their attack, the Germans dropped about two hundred men in our rear areas, hoping to mislead our reinforcements and find gasoline supplies for their vehicles. . . . The parachutists were wearing American uniforms, and one even had an M.P. sleeve. Our unit saw five of them marching in step toward our rear area. They were stopped and asked questions such as "What's a jellybean? Pronounce it. Who is Joe Di Maggio?" Obviously, they did not pronounce "jellybean" as we do, since there is no "j" sound in German. [They were executed as spies.] Our general had the German parachutes sent to Belgium, where they were made into silk scarves to be distributed to all officers of the 8th Division as required articles of dress. I still have mine. . . .

Among the saddest sights of the Huertgen action was the scene exposed as the snow melted. Frozen for some time, arms were sticking up through the snow. They were men of the 28th Division who we had relieved early in November. The Germans had cut off the swollen fingers that wore gold wedding bands in order to remove the rings. Gold teeth had been knocked loose and removed. As the landscape cleared of melting snow, more and more bodies were revealed with arms reaching toward the heavens. While on patrol we captured a German who had been living on the food retrieved from dead Americans.[74]

Nerian had engaged in some of the bloodiest battles in western Europe and then encountered the Holocaust face-to-face. They were images that would remain with him. Discharged in 1946, he returned home and met his son for the first time.

As the German army collapsed on both the eastern and western fronts, Allied troops pushed into Germany from both directions. On March 7, 1945, units of the Twenty-seventh Armored Infantry Battalion took the Ludendorff Bridge over the Rhine River at Remagen. More significantly, General George C. Patton's Third Army crossed the Rhine farther to the south two weeks later and raced across Germany. American, British, Canadian, and French forces spread through western Germany, taking hundreds of thousands of German prisoners and discovering the horrific nature of Hitler's Nazi regime. Soviet and American forces met at Torgau on the Elbe on April 25. Five days later Hitler committed suicide as Berlin fell to the Soviet army. Germany surrendered unconditionally to the Allies on May 7, 1945.

A draftee, William M. Blair graduated from officer candidate school in 1944 at the age of twenty and was sent to France on the *Queen Mary* as a second lieutenant. There he joined the Eighty-fourth Infantry Division just in time for the Battle of the Bulge. By February they were marching toward the Rhine. The following month, Blair was wounded in the leg by German artillery. After a brief stay in a hospital, he rejoined his division in April, just in time to arrive at the eastern side of the Elbe. His colonel selected Blair to lead a patrol to learn if the Russians were in the area. Blair led eight men across the Elbe in a small boat, receiving German fire on the way, but without effect:

I took the cook, who could speak Russian, [and] a radioman, . . . and the three of us started to advance through a field toward the town of Balov. Balov was a small community, which we could see from our side of the Elbe River. I left the rest of the patrol spread out on the banks of the Elbe in case we should run into trouble. They would be able to provide us with protective fire or they would be in the position to get back to the American side if necessary.

It was an extremely foggy morning, and as we were advancing through the field, the town of Balov was probably 300 yards away. Through the fog . . . we could hear mechanical sounds. . . . Shortly thereafter, we could see, overlooking a bank, a barrel of a gun traversing the area back and forth. We didn't know if it was a piece of German artillery that was tracking our area or not.

We continued to advance and shortly I could see three people come down across the bank and start moving in our direction. I used my binoculars and said to the radio man and the cook, our interpreter, "They are not wearing German uniforms."

As we came really close to them I realized they had to be Russian. . . . I put my right hand out and I struck my breast like a "Me Tarzan" approach and said, "Me American." The fellow grasped my hand and smiled, and said, "Goddamn am I glad to see you." [It was] one of the most amazing things that I ever had happen. He was a graduate of City College of New York and of the Sorbonne in Paris. He was an intelligence officer assigned by the Russians to join the tank force coming toward the Elbe from the Russian side to effect a link up with the Americans.

We went into a restaurant [where] tables were set up. Our entire patrol sat around this assembly of tables with a Russian between each American. There the leader of the tank task force proposed a toast to President Roosevelt [who had died two weeks earlier] and I in turn proposed a toast to Stalin. . . . I had with me a 45 pistol with our division insignia on the grip which I presented to the Russian leader. . . . The Russian commander in turn gave me his 45 pistol which obviously, by a look at the pistol, had been used to a considerable degree over a considerable period of time. That pistol I have in my possession today.

Blair returned to the east side of the Elbe with a number of Russians. The next morning one of his men came to him:

"Lieutenant, you got to come up and see this."

When I went upstairs and looked around, we were completely surrounded by Germans,—all of who had pistols, rifles, etc. Our personnel rolled a farm wagon out of the barn; the Germans all put their pistols, their binoculars, their rifles on the wagon. They wanted to leave all of their armament with the Americans and surrender to the Americans. Their goal: don't surrender to the Russians. . . . The Russians experienced tremendous losses to the Germans, much more so than the Americans did. So they [the Germans] did not want to be a prisoner of war to the Russians. They were delighted to be a prisoner of war to the Americans.

On May 26 Russian General Pavel Belov awarded Blair the Order of the Red Star. Shortly thereafter the U.S. Army awarded him the Bronze Star for his courage in leading the patrol across the Elbe to "complete the first juncture effected between the Allied troops." Blair remained in Germany for another year before being discharged and returning to the United States, where he became a bank teller.[75]

The end of the war with Japan proved more ambiguous, victory leaving a taste of ashes in the mouths of many Americans. Through 1943 and 1944, General Douglas MacArthur's "island-hopping" campaign proved extremely effective in pushing the Allies closer to Japan, though at a terrible cost in lives. The coordination of air, sea, and land forces overwhelmed the Japanese, culminating in the Battle of Leyte Gulf, the largest naval battle in history, in October 1944, and the liberation of the Philippines the following year. The United States brought the war to Japan's cities in a devastating air campaign that included the firebombing of Tokyo on the night of March 9, 1945, the deadliest air raid in history, claiming the lives of one hundred thousand civilians.[76] The Japanese responded to these American successes with suicidal fury, literally hurling themselves at their enemy in the kamikaze attacks.[77] What neither they nor the American forces battling toward the Japanese homeland knew was that the United States had launched the vast and highly secretive Manhattan Project back in 1942 with the single goal of developing atomic weapons.[78]

Hundreds of thousands of American soldiers were in training for the invasion of Japan when the atomic bombs were dropped on Hiroshima and Nagasaki on August 6 and 9, 1945. They had heard the stories of the final resistance on Okinawa in May and June of that year, which claimed the lives of 12,000 Americans soldiers and 110,000 Japanese soldiers, as well as some 160,000 civilian lives, many of whom committed suicide or were forced to do so by their own soldiers.[79] The troops preparing for the invasion knew that one-third of the landing force on Iwo Jima had been killed by the Japanese. This knowledge did not lend itself to much concern for the Japanese people. Most soldiers asked the same question, "How many of us would have been killed on the mainland [of Japan] if there were no bomb?" Another records sitting on a pier with some friends, "sharpening our bayonets, when Harry [Truman] dropped that beautiful bomb. The greatest thing [that] ever happened. Anybody sitting at the pier at that time would have to agree."[80]

William L. Laurence, the *New York Times* science reporter, joined the mission that dropped the atomic bomb on Nagasaki. His observation plane, commanded by Captain Frederick C. Brock, followed the *Great Artiste,* the B-29 carrying the atomic bomb under the command of twenty-five-year-old Major Charles W. Sweeney:[81]

Does one feel any pity or compassion for the poor devils about to die? Not when one thinks of Pearl Harbor and of the Death march on Bataan. . . .

We flew southward . . . and at 11:33 crossed the coastline and headed straight for Nagasaki about 100 miles to the west. Here again we circled until we found an opening in the clouds. It was 10:01 and the goal of our mission had arrived.

We heard the prearranged signal on our radio, put on our arc welder's glasses and watched tensely the maneuverings of the strike ship about half a mile in front of us.

"There she goes!" someone said.

Out of the belly of The Great Artiste what looked like a black object went downward.

Captain Brock swung around to get out of range; but even though we were turning away in the opposite direction, and despite the fact that it was broad daylight in our cabin, all of us became aware of a giant flash that broke through the dark barrier of our arc-welder's lenses and flooded our cabin with intense light.

We removed our glasses after the first flash, but the light still lingered on, a bluish-green light that illuminated the entire sky all around. A tremendous blast wave struck our ship and made it tremble from nose to tail. This was followed by four more blasts in rapid succession, each resounding like the boom of cannon fire hitting our plane from all directions.

Observers in the tail of our ship saw a giant ball of fire rise as though from the bowels of the earth, belching forth enormous white smoke rings. Next they saw a giant pillar of purple fire, 10,000 feet high, shooting skyward with enormous speed.

By the time our ship had made another turn in the direction of the atomic explosion the pillar of purple fire had reached the level of our altitude. Only about forty-five seconds had passed. Awe-struck, we watched it shoot upward like a meteor coming from the earth instead of from outer space, becoming ever more alive as it climbed skyward through the white clouds. It was no longer smoke, or dust, or even a cloud of fire. It was a living thing, a new species of being, born right before our incredulous eyes. . . .

Then, just when it appeared as though the thing has settled down into a state of permanence, there came shooting out of the top a giant mushroom that increased the height of the pillar to a total of 45,000 feet. The mushroom top was even more alive than the pillar, seething and boiling in a white fury of creamy foam, sizzling upward and then descending earthward.[82]

Japan's government agreed to surrender on August 14, signing the terms of surrender on September 2, 1945, aboard the battleship *Missouri* in Tokyo Bay. World War II was over, at a cost of some sixty-five million lives, more than half of them civilian.

Few American soldiers witnessed the bomb's immediate effects; one who did was Robert B. August. August had initially put in for flight training in the navy, but discovered he got airsick, so he enlisted in midshipman school, emerging as a lieutenant JG, a "90-day wonder":

Yesterday some of us had the opportunity to go down to Nagasaki, to view the results of the atomic bomb. Of course the astounding thing is to realize that a single bomb did as much damage. And in such a short time. . . . [T]here just isn't much left there to clean up—only debris in such small pieces, Mom, that you would be able to easily pick up most of them. Why, I saw in one section where there was so little debris that a bulldozer had leveled off an area, right in the center of the worst havoc, and the GIs were using it for a baseball field. It looks as though a great hurricane had struck the place, an area possibly one mile wide and two or three miles long, but taken most of the larger pieces of rubbish with it as it passed. With the exception of the steel frameworks of factories stripped clean of all but the girders and an occasional chimney, there is very little left standing. The gases and heat must certainly have been terrible for even those huge round factory chimneys that resisted the pressures and the steel frameworks of buildings, if they were distinguishable at all, seemed to lean in the same approximate direction from which the greatest pressure of gases had come.[83]

As Tolstoy noted in *War and Peace*, the history of any war is but the weak effort of the scholar to impose reason upon chaos, to craft a narrative structure that will somehow make sense of human slaughter. World War II is no different, though we are aided by a moral clarity rarely allowed the historian. While there is no doubt that the United States acted correctly in battling fascism, the details remain subject to debate, disagreement, and doubt. After his unit was slaughtered along the German border, Robert Kotlowitz met with the division historian who twice attempted to get him to change the story of what happened. The historian wanted Kotlowitz to construct a more heroic narrative than what the private had insisted was the truth, that the "battle" was the affair of an instant, as all his comrades were slaughtered by machine-gun fire in a matter of seconds and then left on the field for the next ten hours, several bleeding to death in the process. Kotlowitz would not change his story. "His poor history," he said, in sympathy for the historian who wanted a heroic epic to match his vision. "The poor story he wanted me to tell that would heighten the self-importance of the Yankee Division, the one he knew before he even met me. And then the real one, the one I was trying to tell him, which he had been forced to listen to so many times today. It had to be bitter for him." The historian left in disgust, intent on making history conform to his desires. Like many veterans, Kotlowitz felt sorry for those who could not face the reality of World War II.[84]

## The Good Veterans

Sixteen million Americans served in World War II, 43 percent of all adult males and some 2 percent of the adult women.[85] Unlike the spreading cynicism and depression that followed World War I, there was little sense that the United States had behaved hypocritically. Rather, as revelations of the Holocaust entered the press, most Americans felt certain that they had done exactly the right thing in taking down the fascists. As one veteran asked, "could Truman have unilaterally committed American troops to Korea unless there had been the lingering romance of the Second World War? I rather doubt it." Americans still trusted their president and their own virtue. "I think things began to sour and innocence end in, say, 1952 and 1953, as the Korean War dragged on."[86] But that war would not affect public perceptions of the Second World War.

Returning veterans found numerous opportunities upon their return, benefiting from a booming economy. There was a slight easing of military manufacturing as the war ended, but it took off again with the new Cold War, and the federal government poured money into the economy, adhering to the Keynesian economics of the New Deal. As a consequence, unemployment rarely rose above 4 percent in the decade after the war. Equally significant, veterans had a friend in President Franklin Roosevelt, who had prepared for peace even before the United States entered the war, considering even the treatment of veterans after the war ended. For instance, the Selective Service Act of 1940 guaranteed that the jobs of those drafted would be held until they returned. General George Marshall began demobilization plans in 1942, so that the transition would be as smooth as possible for veterans and civilians. In a July 1943 fireside chat, Roosevelt addressed veteran affairs: "While concentrating on military victory, we are not neglecting the planning of things to come. . . . Among many other things we are, today, laying plans for the return to civilian life of our gallant men and women of the armed services. They must not be demobilized into an environment of inflation and unemployment. . . . We must, this time, have plans ready—instead of waiting to do a hasty, inefficient, and ill-considered job at the last moment."[87] On November 1944, Roosevelt presented his veteran benefits plan to Congress, the Serviceman's Readjustment Act of 1944, aka the GI Bill of Rights.

The GI Bill would prove one of the most significant pieces of legislation in American history. The bill offered veterans up to 52 weeks unemployment compensation, loans of $2,000 at 4 percent interest to buy homes or establish businesses, and training and education allowances of $500 a year with living subsidies of $50 to $75 a month. Roosevelt's plans for veteran benefits did confront opposition, representing, as they did, a promise of enormous government spending, an expansion of federal authority, and opportunities for social mobility never before realized in American history. Not surprisingly, the *Wall Street Journal* labeled such government support "a halfway house to socialism."[88] Some academics failed to appreciate the opportunities the GI Bill presented to the nation's colleges. In fact, the University of Chicago's president Robert M. Hutchins warned that the GI Bill would have a negative effect on higher education, as the nation's "colleges and universities will find themselves converted into educational hobo jungles. And veterans unable to get work and equally unable to resist putting pressure on the colleges and universities, will find themselves educational hoboes."[89] Columbia's Willard Waller shared

Hutchins's contempt for the unwashed, declaring veterans "Our Gravest Social Problem." Unless carefully controlled, "the veteran is a threat to society."[90] Some, such as the Reverend Bernard I. Bell, feared that the GI Bill would hand over political power to the veterans. After all, he reasoned, "It was veterans who put over every political and economic revolution in Europe between 1919 and 1939; in Russia first, then in Italy, in Germany, in Spain. These countries all went totalitarian during those post-war years because the democratic leaders were not revolutionary enough, daring enough, to satisfy the veteran type of mind."[91] Since it was obvious that veterans learned loose morals while serving their country, the United States could also expect a collapse of morality, according to J. Gordon Chamberlin: "The grass may cover war's scars on earth; but the spirits of men, once blighted by war, will pass on that blight."[92]

In Congress, opposition to the GI Bill was led by the racist and anti-Semitic Representative John E. Rankin of Mississippi, ironically a founder of the American Legion and the chair of the House Committee on Veterans' Affairs, who correctly feared that offering college education to veterans would lead to the social transformation of the United States. However, those who feared and distrusted the nation's soldiers represented a small minority of public opinion, which overwhelmingly found gratitude and reward the proper response for those who had risked everything to save Western civilization. In Congress, Rankin was ably countered by Massachusetts Representative Edith N. Rogers, who guided the GI Bill around every barrier thrown up by the fearful southerner. When President Roosevelt signed the GI Bill into law on June 22, 1944, he presented the first pen to Rogers.

What made the GI Bill work so well was the widely held belief that America's veterans deserved its benefits. When General Omar Bradley was named head of the Veteran's Administration in 1945, he told his staff, "We've got to look on veterans as individual problems, not as numbers in a file. Our job is to give the veterans service. And we must not forget that the service we give them they have earned by sweat and blood. It is a service they have paid for."[93] It is hardly surprising then that veterans speak warmly of the GI Bill. "The GI Bill made all the difference in the world to me," said Richard Prendergast. "I could never have afforded college" without it.[94] But there is often a reflective melancholia to this sense of gratitude. On the day after the invasion of Normandy, Brigadier General Norman "Dutch" Cota had asked a young private named George Roach what he would like to do when the war was over. Roach hoped someday to go to college, preferably Fordham. Five years later, thanks to the GI Bill, Roach graduated from Fordham. In 1990 Roach stated, "I don't think there has been a day that has gone by that I haven't thought of those men who didn't make it" on Omaha Beach, the men who died so that he might someday go to college.[95]

Women veterans also had mixed feelings about their service, some sharing the disillusionment of African Americans who found that the democracy for which they fought did not fully include them. Founded in 1942, the Women's Auxiliary Army Corps changed to the Women's Army Corps (WAC) in 1943 after Representative Edith Rogers pushed for it to become a regular part of the army. The Women Airforce Service Pilots (WASP) went through a similar process, though they saw much more action as they flew sixty million miles during the war with an outstanding safety record. The navy created the WAVEs and the coast guard the SPARs. Yet, though the women in both groups were under the impression that they had served their country in the military, they were informed after the war that they were not in fact veterans, an outrageous injustice not corrected until 1977. As a consequence, these veterans were denied the benefits of the GI Bill. Yet studies of women veterans from World War II routinely find that they held their service to have been an extremely positive experience, 27 percent of them making the military a career. The independence they discovered and treasured is indicated by the results of one study that found that 45 percent of these women never married, compared to 5 percent of American women at that time.[96]

Making sense of their experience in this bloodiest of wars was often a complicated matter for veterans. Some bluntly declared it the peak of their long lives: "At that young age, we hit the climax. Everything after that is anticlimactic."[97] Another veteran recalled, "I had the most tremendous experiences of all [my] life: of fear, of jubilation, of misery, of hope, of comradeship, and of the endless excitement, the theatrics of it. I honestly feel grateful for having been a witness to an event as monumental as anything in history and, in a very small way, a participant."[98] While there were those who carried serious mental scars from the war and wanted nothing further to do with it or its memories, most felt pride in their participation in "the Good War."

# 9

# Cold Wars: Korea and Vietnam

The Cold War started almost as soon as World War II ended. Between 1945 and 1990, local struggles throughout the world were understood by Americans in the context of a global battle against communist aggression; civil wars, from Greece in 1946 through Angola in the 1980s, were framed by the bipolar Cold War vision. American troops played varying roles in many of these conflicts, but two "hot" wars came to define the postwar American military experience: Korea and Vietnam. Both raised serious constitutional and moral questions, though only with the Vietnam War did these debates spread into the public sphere. Despite tens of thousands of casualties and a great deal of outstanding scholarship, the Korean War remains largely unknown to the American people, while the Vietnam War dominated public consciousness for at least three decades and is only now fading in perceived significance. While the two wars are rarely discussed together, they were both products of a Cold War mind-set that perceived a monolithic communist threat and demanded its deterrence in any and all "hot spots."

For those who served in Korea and Vietnam, the centrality of these wars has never been in doubt. These veterans share knowledge of the power of Cold War ideology and the limits of American strength. A conviction that technological superiority guaranteed victory guided the nation's military and political leadership through both wars; its soldiers paid the price for this misplaced faith. Veterans often tell of witnessing massive American bombardments that convinced them that no one could live through such a pounding, only to quickly discover otherwise as communist troops rose up seemingly from the earth itself. The repeated failure of intelligence agencies marked both wars, and the Pentagon leadership consistently misunderstood the nature of the wars they were fighting. Korea and Vietnam rapidly devolved into stalemates, lacking clear strategic goals and dragging on for no apparent reason as part of larger geopolitical strategies, leading the public to lose interest, often to the point of behaving as though they did not even know that the United States was engaged in a war. Returning veterans met with indifference at best, and too often with contempt, as they were blamed for failing to triumph in unwinnable wars and held to account for policies that produced high levels of civilian casualties. While troops fighting under the banner of the United Nations in Korea faced enemies on all sides for nearly a year before the establishment of a clearly articulated front line, American forces in Vietnam never had the luxury of a front line—the war was everywhere. The Vietnam War also differed from Korea in the breakdown of unit cohesion. But both wars left heavy burdens on their veterans, who took part in bitter hand-to-hand battles, suffered at the hands of unseen enemies, and witnessed atrocities that haunted many for years to come. These soldiers lived in the shadow of World War II, the supposed "Good War." Theirs would not be good wars.

## A Nasty Little War

When North Korea invaded South Korea in June 1950, the Cold War turned hot. What President Harry Truman insisted on calling "a police action"—so as to avoid the need to ask for a declaration of war from Congress—became, in the words of S.L.A. Marshall, "the century's nastiest little war."[1] It was in Korea that the United States first placed its faith in airpower to attain military victory. But airpower proved of limited utility on the Korean peninsula as for three years the military forces of several nations battled through horridly hot summers and even worse winters. As the war ground on, many soldiers became embittered by the perceived pointlessness of their sacrifices and returned home feeling that they had been betrayed by their government. On the other hand, the Korean War demonstrated the success of America's newly integrated military, proving that all branches of service would continue to function efficiently despite the mandated end to racism.

Initially, the Soviets and Americans had agreed to reunify Korea by 1950, but in 1948 the United States established a repressive government in the South led by Syngman Rhee, with the Soviets following shortly thereafter with an even more oppressive regime under the strangely communist-monarchical family of Kim Il Sung. Almost immediately serious uprisings disrupted the South, the majority of whose population made clear their preference for a democracy. Rhee used the army and police to crush any displays of dissent, which included the mutiny of an entire regiment that refused to fire on civilians. Thousands died in the next two years, as South Korea's prisons swelled with political prisoners. The United States poured money and matériel into South Korea, doing its best to shore up the government while trying to rein in Rhee's enthusiasm for invading the North. As late as June 19, 1950, Rhee attempted to persuade the United States to support his army of just under 100,000 men in crossing the border to end the communist government to the north. Six days later, on June 25, North Korean forces poured across the border into South Korea.

The United States was caught completely off guard. Harry Truman and his military commanders had placed far too much faith in their monopoly on the atomic bomb. The Pentagon had no plans for fighting in Korea, the Joint Chiefs of Staff having declared in 1949 that Korea did not represent any strategic interest for the United States, withdrawing most of its occupation forces. The week prior to the invasion, the military mission in Seoul confidently reported that "the South Korean forces could handle any possible invasion by North Korean forces."[2] As a consequence, Douglas MacArthur, commander of U.S. forces in Asia, initially had few concerns, declaring the invasion "probably only a reconnaissance in force"—an attitude quickly altered after he flew from his headquarters in Japan to Korea.[3]

"We were as surprised as Stalin and Kim Il Sung at Truman's orders to go into action," wrote Corporal Harry G. Summers of the Twenty-fourth Infantry Division.[4] Stationed in Japan, the Twenty-fourth, which Summers called a "hollow" force, was the first ordered into action. Flown to Korea, the advance units, numbering some five hundred men, dug in on a ridge just south of Seoul with responsibility for stopping the communist advance. Brigadier General George Barth of the Twenty-fourth thought his troops displayed an unfounded "overconfidence bordering on arrogance," an attitude replicated by a headquarters which ordered the officers to pack their summer dress uniforms in anticipation of a victory parade through Seoul.[5] Lieutenant Colonel Harold Ayres proclaimed, "Those Commie bastards will turn and run when they find they're up against our boys."[6] As the most powerful nation in the world, the United States suffered from, in Clay Blair's cutting label, a "military superiority complex."[7]

The South Korean army—generally called ROK for Republic of Korea—crumbled before the communist onslaught. Seoul fell on the third day of the war, June 28, and thousands of Koreans streamed south. The first confrontation between North Koreans and American forces came on the morning of July 5, when thirty Soviet-made T-34 tanks bore down on the advance positions of the Twenty-fourth Infantry. American bazookas and artillery opened up on the tanks, but they had not been issued armor-piercing shells, allowing the T-34s to fire away with their 85mm cannon and machine guns. The American retreat lacked all cohesion, as the GIs divested themselves of extra weight, including their rifles, and ran for their lives. Within a few days the entire division was "bugging out"—to use the newly coined phrase—before the communists; the Seventh Cavalry bugged out even before their first encounter with the enemy, throwing aside their weapons in panic. The South Korean landscape was littered with American weapons and equipment as the bugging-out fever spread. In that first week the United States suffered 3,000 casualties, while the ROK lost 44,000 of its 98,000 men. South Korea was crumbling and striking out at all its perceived enemies; despite the protests of Major General William F. Dean, South Korean forces continued to slaughter hundreds of political prisoners, throwing their bodies into mass graves.[8] Only after these initial encounters did army intelligence figure out that they faced a formidable force of 135,000 North Koreans, a great many of whom had fought against the Japanese or with Mao in the Chinese civil war, armed with Soviet-made weapons and led by at least 150 Soviet tanks.

In the ensuing chaos, UN air attacks became indiscriminate. American and Australian planes bombed and strafed ROK forces and civilians, unintentionally killing hundreds of South Koreans. MacArthur escalated the confusion—and civilian casualties—by ordering the bombing of targets controlled by the North Koreans, including civilian areas inhabited by the very people the United Nations claimed to be protecting. In July American pilots received orders to strafe civilians in an effort to keep them away from UN lines. As fleeing refugees swarmed around retreating American and ROK troops, rumors of infiltrators disguised as civilians swept through the U.S. forces, stories lent credence by officers warning their men to be on the lookout for North Koreans in civilian dress. After-mission reports recorded attacks on civilians by U.S. forces, as when pilots from the aircraft carrier *Valley Forge* received instructions that "groups of more than eight to ten people were to be considered troops, and were to be attacked."[9] General Hobart Gay, commander of the First Cavalry Division, ordered that civilians be warned to stay away from UN lines and thereafter considered to be harboring hostile forces and shot on sight.[10] General John H. Church of the Twenty-fourth Infantry Division ordered that no civilians approach within five miles of his lines or be shot on sight, while Major General William B. Kean of the Twenty-fifth Infantry Division declared that all civilians had been successfully cleared from before their lines so that "all civilians moving around in combat zone will be considered as unfriendly and shot." Some leeway was granted to the Eighth Cavalry, which received orders: "No refugees to cross frontline. Fire [on] everyone trying to cross the lines. Use discretion in case of women and children."[11] In essence, the military hastily imposed free-fire zones on the territory of their ally, South Korea. As the Associated Press reported, "In an area once cleared of civilians, anyone in civilian clothing may be shot." Such action was particularly necessary as "All Koreans, North and South, look alike to the Americans."[12]

Not all Americans felt comfortable following these orders to kill civilians. Major General William F. Dean, commander of the Twenty-fourth Infantry, rejected suggestions that artillery open up on the refugees, insisting that wars were not won by killing civilians. Lieutenant William C. Kaluf of the Seventh Cavalry received orders to shoot civilians approaching the American lines, but he refused to do so and let them pass through: "We had enough enemy to shoot at in uniform without shooting civilians."[13] On July 25, Colonel Turner C. Rogers, operations chief of the Fifth Air Force, sent a secret memo to Brigadier General Edward L. Timberlake, the acting commander of the Fifth. The memo was clearly headed, "Policy on Strafing Civilian Refugees," and began by observing that "The Army has requested that we strafe all civilian refugee parties that are noted approaching our position. To date we have complied with the Army request." But Rogers recommended against continuing the policy, as it "may cause embarrassment to the U.S. Air Force and to the U.S. government." It seemed to Rogers that the army should be checking the refugees for arms rather than shooting them immediately.[14] These doubts were overridden by Eighth Army headquarters on July 26, which explicitly ordered, "No repeat no refugees will be permitted to cross battle lines at any time."[15]

It is in this context that a number of atrocities occurred, such as when the aforementioned Major General Gay ordered the Tuksong-dong bridge blown up despite the steady flow of refugees, leading to the death of hundreds of civilians. Corporal Rudy Giannelli watched as explosions cascaded along the bridge: "It lifted up and turned sideways and it was full of refugees end to end. . . . You saw the spans of steel flying and you knew they were killed."[16] Convinced that most refugees were North Koreans in disguise, Gay felt no remorse for these deaths. One of the regiments under his command was the Seventh Cavalry, George Custer's old outfit, which had been responsible for massacres at the Washita and Wounded Knee, and during the anti-insurgency operations in the Philippines. Over three days in late July 1950, the Seventh Cavalry once more lost its moral compass, slaughtering between one and three hundred civilians under the bridge at No Gun Ri—an event the U.S. government consistently denied until the Associated Press broke the story in 1998.

In 2001 the Pentagon released a report that finally acknowledged that the atrocity at No Gun Ri occurred, but framed it as "an unfortunate tragedy inherent to war and not a deliberate killing"—despite the fact that the killings occurred over three days. In its three hundred pages, the report managed to sidestep a number of significant questions while avoiding a large body of evidence, such as the mission reports of the Thirty-fifth Fighter-Bomber Squadron, internal memos, and numerous interviews by Korean investigators with army and air force veterans. The Pentagon wanted above all else to avoid admitting that officers had ordered the killing of civilians. Two members of the advisory committee criticized the final report: Representative Paul McCloskey condemned this "clear failure to report the truth," while Lieutenant General Bernard E. Trainor placed the blame for No Gun Ri "on some level of leadership."[17]

Attacks on civilians did not aid the Americans, who had spread their limited forces over too large an area. Repeatedly, North Koreans outflanked the Americans, taking hundreds of prisoners, including General Dean. Within two weeks the United States lost half its effective strength of sixteen thousand men. As Clay Blair concluded, the initial U.S. intervention in Korea "was one of the most ill-conceived decisions in the history of the American military establishment."[18] In the midst of this chaos and collapse, Douglas MacArthur took decisive action, dividing his command in order to marginalize General Walton Walker and exert greater personal control. He split American forces in half, placing his chief of staff, General Edward Almond, in charge of the Inchon landing on the northwest coast of South Korea on September 10, 1950. Inchon proved a brilliant success, thanks in large part to the matching ego of Kim Il Sung, who had rejected Soviet suggestions that he mine the harbor. But then MacArthur's ego got the better of him. Rather than focusing on trapping the bulk of the North Korean army, MacArthur, who looked forward to the publicity of retaking the South Korean capital, ordered Almond to focus on Seoul. The several days it took to retake that city allowed the majority of North Korean forces to cross back over the 38th parallel. It was at this point that Truman made the pivotal military and political decision of the war, supporting MacArthur's call to cross the border into North Korea. However, contrary to Truman's orders, MacArthur ordered Walker and Almond to press on to the Yalu River—the North Korean border with China.

Numerous officers, such as Colonel Paul Freeman, tried to draw MacArthur's attention to the 300,000 Chinese troops hovering in the north, but MacArthur dismissed such concerns with contempt and was completely unprepared when they poured across the border in November 1950. MacArthur behaved with the same mindless arrogance displayed by Custer as he rode in pursuit of the Sioux, a comparison made by General Matthew Ridgway: "MacArthur, like Custer at the Little Big Horn, had neither eyes nor ears for information that might deter him from the swift attainment of his objective."[19] As UN forces retreated south in "the Big Bigout," MacArthur sought to deflect responsibility by blaming the U.S. government for the defeat.[20]

The UN troops paid the price for MacArthur's arrogance. The battle at Chosin Reservoir remains a testament to the military professionalism of the marines who fought there. As temperatures dropped well below zero, the First Marine Division battled to hold their position as the Eight Army collapsed around them. Surrounded, General Oliver P. Smith pulled his Marines back to Hagaru-ri, from which position he launched a breakout effort that brought them through the Chinese positions six days later to Hungnam. Nearly every one of the 15,000 marines suffered frostbite, taking 4,400 casualties in their fight with the Chinese, who after this fierce contest did not resist the UN retreat from Hungnam. Donald Dugay, a nineteen-year-old marine, just missed taking part in the landing at Inchon as the result of an unusual injury, but recovered in time for the battle at Chosin:

*10-13-50* Got on LST and headed for Won Son where we were supposed to make a landing. The harbor was mined so we sailed north in the morning and south at night. . . . When we did land at Won Son, Bob Hope greeted us; we were the butt of his jokes.

Went north to Hagaru where the temperature was from 20° to 40° below zero. My best buddy [Melton Brock] and I had to start all the vehicles every hour . . . and let them run for about 15 minutes to keep from freezing. At about 3 hours and 45 minutes I told Brock I couldn't take any more, my feet were frozen and painful. He told me to go to our pup tent, that he would finish the watch. He came in about 10 minutes later crying from the pain. I took off his boots for him. It was really cold. . . .

*11-26-50* Capt. Turner had Brock and me inspect a bridge on way to Yalu River, to see if capable of holding trucks and tanks. On the way back we heard an incoming shell. We both dived into a hole made by another shell. Brock tried to climb out of the hole when another shell came in. The concussion knocked him back in. It was funny because he was all arms and legs. That's when we found out the Chinese had us surrounded. On the way back to our CP [command post], Brock was in front on my left about twenty yards. I saw an Army guy I thought was dead. I thought I heard a cough and went back to him to find he was alive but exhausted and freezing. I pulled him up and half carried him for about 2 miles to our CP. I brought him to sick-bay but he was in pretty good shape by that time. He was disoriented and would have frozen or been killed by the Chinese if I didn't hear him. Capt. Turner said seeing as I found him I was to spend the night with him in my foxhole. That's when he [the rescued soldier] told me he wanted to stay with us Marines. He was pissed at the Army for running and leaving him. . . .

During the day we worked on building an airfield to evacuate wounded. Sometimes we carried ammo up for the infantry. On one occasion I saw a radio man about half way up. He said he couldn't go any further. I offered to carry his radio, about 60 or 70 lbs. When we got on top of the hill, I was talking to 2 guys when what I thought was a dead Chinese, fired his burp gun at us. Hit the two on either side of me but not, I thought, me. I carried one of the guys down. . . . I noticed my mitten had blood on it, but I thought it was blood from the guy I brought down. I took care of my wound myself. . . .

*12-5-50* One morning an old Papa-san came out of his house to urinate. A guy in the next hole from me fired his M1 at [the old man's] penis and was laughing. I aimed my rifle at him and said his next shot would be his last. . . . I went to the old man's house, a couple of hundred yards away, and gave him and his family "C" rations. . . . The old man gave me a pipe, which I still have. I had to take it, although I didn't want to. They didn't have many possessions. . . .

*12-13-50* Field with hundreds of dead enemy. . . . Enemy dead were searched for information—such as what outfit he was in. I found a picture of the dead Chinese with his wife and two little kids—something to think about. That's when I realized they were human, like us.

Saw the remains of about thirty that were hit by Napalm. Hope they were enemy. . . .

Dugay made it out of the Chosin perimeter and joined the general retreat south. The following year he took part in another UN offensive.

*June, 1951* We probed a road for mines. Stopped at night and returned to CP. Next morning we loaded up with C3 and blasting caps. Two satchels each. Capt. Turner called for me to go inspect bridges. I asked the guys if they wanted my C3. They said to throw it in back of Jeep. Off they went, five sitting and one on hood of jeep. Before they got to where we left off clearing, the jeep hit a mine and exploded all the C3 the guys were carrying. My good friend Pete Schiro and all the rest killed. I dream of that—a guilty feeling.

One day while probing for a tank that was behind me I came across a dead enemy. I dragged the body to the side of road. The tank came and ran over and crushed him. I tried to stop it but couldn't. Dreams—only it's me being about to be run over.

Another day while probing—I stuck my bayonet into the road just as the tank fired its 90MM. My left ear is still no good. I turned around and fired my M1 at the tank. Then I saw the 90MM cannon lower and aim right at me. I surrendered. They must have had quite a laugh.

I was relieved of probing for mines, after I broke someone in to take my place—a new replacement named Nunes. He seemed too clumsy and I told my Sgt. They kept him on probing duty. I got a Christmas card from my buddy Jacques saying Nunes lost both legs.

As a consequence of his many wounds, Dugay returned to the United States in October 1951.[21]

As American soldiers fell back before the Chinese troops, General MacArthur began calling for a full-scale war against China, perhaps including the use of atomic bombs. MacArthur went further, questioning Truman's policies and challenging his authority as commander in chief. The president lost both his confidence in and his patience with the arrogant and often deadly wrong General MacArthur, and removed him from his command on April 11, 1951.[22]

Fortunately for the United States, the new commander in Korea, General Matthew Ridgway, possessed rare ability to rally and organize his shattered forces. Ridgway placed his reliance on artillery and intelligence, seeking to create a "meat grinder" that would inflict such heavy losses on the Chinese that they would accept a stalemate on the peninsula.[23] Korea thus ended up being America's first "limited war." As Max Hastings has written, "The Western Powers were unhappily reconciled to the concept of Korea as a limited war, in which their highest aspiration was to demonstrate that their own will to defend the *status quo ante* would remain unbroken."[24] This failure to seek total victory would raise a great deal of bitterness domestically and hand the American right wing a bat with which to beat what they perceived as a cowardly liberal establishment—whether the president was Democratic or Republican—for the next twenty years at least. However, it is highly unusual to find anyone who actually served in Korea who feels the same way; generally they welcomed any policy that would bring them home.

Members of the distinct service branches had different experiences of war. Initially the air campaign was conducted from bases near the front lines. But as the war became more uncertain, the air forces pulled back to the safety and comfort of Japan. Arpad J. Ostheimer joined the air force in 1947 in order to learn a trade, becoming an aircraft mechanic. In 1949, he was stationed with the Eighth Fighter Bomber Wing at Itazuke Air Force Base in Kyushu, Japan:

In the fall of 1949, at an Air Base in northern Japan, Misawa, the USAF had a major aircraft accident which caused the destruction of at least twenty F-80 jet aircraft, that would greatly influence our status at the start of the Korean War. . . .

On June 25th I was with some buddies celebrating our troop ship port call, which would take us back to the United States in about twenty days. About 3 P.M., sirens sounded as a call to immediate duty. Our Fighter Bomber Wing was flying F-80s for about 45 days before combat started. This situation caused the accident rates to be very high with significant combat losses. The accident in Misawa delayed the deployment of these aircraft. . . .

In early August 1950, I was shipped to Taegu, Korea, for combat operations during the Pusan perimeter phase of the Korean conflict. The operation became very dicey, so we fled back to Itazuke, Japan. We were then organized to form a new outfit with F-51Ds called the 36th Fighter Bomber Squadron. We then went to Korea shortly after the Inchon landing to an airbase next to the town of Yong Dong Po. We operated there for a short time and then flew into an Air Strip (K-23) located in Pyongyang, Korea [the capital of North Korea]. We flew maximum operations at all times at that strip. In late November the Chinese entered the conflict and our operation became a real problem when the Chinese broke through our lines. We burned eight to ten F-51D aircraft, which could not be flown out of the strip, and bugged out to the previous air strip near Yong Dong Po. In December or early January we were chased out by the Chinese and we flew back to Itazuke, Japan.

Throughout the war the wing principally conducted air-to-ground operations, providing close air support to United Nations ground forces and attacking targets such as supply centers and transportation assets. During the next three years the 8th Fighter Wing flew more than 60,000 sorties while operating from bases in Korea and Japan. The wing participated in ten campaigns and earned three unit citations. The wing finished the war flying the F-86 Sabre beginning in 1953 and became responsible for air defense over South Korea until relocated to Itazuke Air Base, Japan, in October 1954. Its wartime participation in Korea earned the wing two Republic of Korea Presidential Unit Citations and ten campaign streamers, while the 8th Fighter-Bomber Group separately earned a Distinguished Unit Citation. During the war the 8th shot down 18 enemy aircraft, most in the earliest days of the war before the wing's mission changed to air-to-ground operations.

I re-enlisted for three more years as Truman added a year to our current enlistments. . . . [On a troopship in October 1951, he heard] Bobby Thomson [of the New York Giants] hit his pennant-winning home run against the Brooklyn Dodgers. I felt so bad, that I felt like jumping overboard.[25]

Most of what modern Americans know about the Korean War comes from a popular television show that ran from 1972 through 1983, *M*A*S*H*. The series, a comedy with a biting political message, focuses on the staff of a mobile army surgical hospital in Korea—though at times the show seemed to be more about the Vietnam War than Korea. In the early years of the show, the writers interviewed veterans in an attempt to make the show realistic, an effort abandoned over time. Donald G. Martin of Pittsburgh was a member of a Marine mobile medical unit. Having served as a Marine corpsman in World War II when just eighteen years old, he returned home and was accepted at Penn State to study industrial engineering thanks to the GI Bill. As he says, "That was a big thing, a very big thing," to have access to a college education. While at Penn State he joined a reserve unit—an extremely inactive unit, he said, which he thought would never see any sort of action. After graduation he was working in Detroit at the Ingersoll Rand Company, when he was called to report for duty in September 1950. To his surprise, he was immediately inducted into the Marine Corps as a staff sergeant and sent to field medical service school at

Camp Lejeune for eight weeks of training. By December 1950, Martin was in Korea, assigned to the Charlie medical unit of the First Marine Division, which was in the process of retreating before the Chinese onslaught:

[December 1950] We were getting all of our gear together to get the hospital going. . . . It was all put on trucks and we drove north to Taegu. There was a staff of fifty. . . . It was totally Marine, even the doctors were in the . . . First Marine Division. . . . There were over a thousand corpsmen in a Marine division.

In January of '51, winter was setting in there. It was cold; we had all the winter gear on. And we had big squad tents with an oil heater in it. I worked nights so I could sleep during the day when it was warmer. That was the time the Chinese came in and threw us all back. [The Chinese had just pushed south of the 38th parallel.] After we set up this hospital . . . the Chinese broke through our lines and we had to evacuate and go back down south. We were there a while and then we went back to Taegu [after the UN counteroffensive].

. . . Every day the helicopters were bringing in the wounded. I didn't have to exercise a lot of medical expertise. I basically had guys going here and here, and there were people there to take care of them. . . . Some of the people that came in where pretty badly hurt. Guys were blinded, grenade wounds, artillery, and small arms fire.

I was one of the corpsmen in charge of receiving. And that's where I got in trouble. Because one day we had a lot of casualties. And there were bandages all over the floor and everything. And the chief says to me, "Clean up these things. Why didn't you clean them up?"

I said, "Chief, we are engulfed by patients. We don't have time to clean them up." He didn't like that answer. He should have known what was going on, but maybe he thought I was a smartass. About two or three days later, I was in a line company . . . in the Third Battalion. The first day out I was with three or four others marching to join our unit. I was getting kind of tired and my head fell over to the side and my helmet fell off. It was so steep, it [the helmet] rolled completely out of sight. So I had to go without a helmet for a while.

Then we joined the company and were walking north. A couple of short rounds from our own artillery hit our line. We made a camp and a couple of North Korean mortar shells fell in our group and wounded a couple of guys and I helped [with the wounds]. . . . They call me Doc. The Marines really love the corpsmen. They were dependent on the corpsmen. . . .

One day they brought a whole truckload of dead Marines in. And the officer in charge says, "OK, you unload those guys, lay them out." So I had to drag these kids that were just killed and lay them up on the bank where the graves registration could look at them, get their dog tags and all that kind of stuff. And that was kind of sad, because they were young. I was 25 at the time. These guys looked like 17 or 18. They looked like babies. There were 12 or 13 of them. They were just killed. The wounds were just so fresh. They were all dead. They were big guys. You try to handle a guy that weighs 180 pounds dead weight. I had no help. I got them all laid out. I never forgot that.

[We] then moved to the Punchbowl, a natural formation maybe of an extinct volcano [north of the 38th parallel]. It was a big beautiful place. And we could see the Army jets going over and dropping napalm on these hills.

There was a battle for the mountains. Our group was last because the company had been so shot up before. They take turns, the ones that were badly hurt are sort of put to the rear until they can get their strength back, and then they get moved up to where they have to take the point. And that was the day that this company that I was working with had to take the Punchbowl. And they didn't have any opposition.

After being in Korea long enough, I was eligible to be sent to the rear. I went and talked to the division surgeon, who was the guy in charge of all the corpsmen. And I said, "If we can be sent to the rear, how about sending us to the armored amphibious battalion in Japan?" And by God, he did.

. . . The only thing negative about the service is that you're often working for some guy that you don't feel is very swift, you known, a dumb ass. You just sort of resent taking orders from somebody that doesn't know beans. I could have gone into Naval Intelligence, but then I'd have to sign on for six years. And I said, "I don't want to do that."

Discharged from the Marine Corps in January 1952, Martin returned to being an industrial engineer until his retirement thirty-five years later. In looking back on the Korean War, he insists that he best remembers the close friends he made there; the rest he has tried not to think about.[26]

Martin cared for only a small number of the war's wounded, but the mobile units and increased number of corpsmen and medics used by the military in Korea saved thousands of lives. Of the 1,319,000 Americans who served in Korea between 1950 and 1953, 33,629 were killed and 105,785 wounded. The Republic of Korea lost 415,000 killed and 429,000 wounded, while 3,400 other UN troops died in action as did an estimated million North Koreans and Chinese.[27] For a police action, Korea was a very bloody affair.

## Integrating the Military

In social terms, the Korean War bears special significance as the first conflict in which the United States fought with a fully integrated military. Despite persistent racism in the ranks and among members of Congress, the military high command at least had learned the value of black troops during World War II, as evidenced by the 1946 *War Department Circular No. 124: Utilization of Negro Manpower in Postwar Army Policy*. While not calling for integration, this policy statement did call for white and black units to work together in the future. Encouraged by these recommendations, President Harry Truman ordered the integration of the armed forces with Executive Order 9981 on July 26, 1948. While ending military segregation was neither smooth nor uncontested, the Korean War accelerated the process, and the military integrated before any other major social institution in the United States except for some labor unions. With whites and blacks entering combat together, the barriers to integration collapsed, and 90 percent of the military was integrated by the war's end; the army disbanded the last all-black unit on September 30, 1954.

At the beginning of the Korean War, several senior officers disparaged the abilities of African American soldiers. Generals Ned Almond—MacArthur's chief of staff—Walton Walker—commander of the Eighth Army—and William B. Kean all spoke out against the use of black troops and doubted their reliability in combat—a view supported by many American journalists.[28] But the realities of war quickly changed attitudes and personnel as the desperate need for manpower and the loss of officers broke down traditional barriers, leading even to the promotion of black officers to positions commanding white troops.[29] When Lt. Colonel Cesidio Barberis, commanding a battalion in the all-white Ninth Regiment, was offered two hundred black replacements, he did not hesitate to accept these volunteers: "I had previously commanded a battalion of black troops," and here were two hundred men from his former battalion volunteering to transfer from the safety of their labor unit "to the infantry if they could serve with me. I agreed. In fact, I was proud to have them. [General Laurence] Kesier asked me if I realized what a can of worms I was opening up, to which I said, 'So what? They are good fighting men. I need men.'"[30]

The first significant U.S. victory in the war came when the all-black Twenty-fourth Regiment halted the North Korean advance at Yechon in July 1950. Captain Charles M. Bussey described this encounter against North Korean troops dressed as civilians:

Hell was breaking loose in the town. . . . The village of Yechon was cradled deep in a buttonhook mountain, which nearly ringed it and loomed above it. The enemy had fallen back, climbed part way up the mountain, and was raining fire down into the town. . . .

About a kilometer to the north I noticed a large body of men coming out of a defile and heading toward the rear of our vehicle column, which was at my position. I scuffled down the hill, commandeered a dozen of the lollygagging infantry soldiers, and had them carry a .50 caliber machine gun and ground mount, plus one of their water-cooled .30 caliber machine guns, and all the ammo we could carry in two trips, up the hill. I set the guns up about 100 feet apart and watched the group of white-clad men moving purposefully toward my position.

I watched the group of farmer-soldiers coming ever closer and reckoned that farmers scatter and run if you send a long burst of machine-gun fire over their heads, but soldiers flatten out like quail and await orders from their leader. . . .

I sent a burst from the .50 caliber machine gun dangerously close above the heads of the approaching group, which was moving in a loose, hustling, route-step doubletime column astride the levees in the gigantic mire of the rice paddies. True to the form of soldiers, they flattened into the paddy as the bullets flew past them. A whistle was sounded and an arm raised to signal a movement to the west side [of the paddies]. . . . My next burst was not just dangerously close. The signalman and those close to him were broken up like rag dolls in the mouths of bulldogs. The .30 caliber machine gun joined in. Bullets raked and chewed them up mercilessly.

The advancing column was under tight observation from somewhere on the mountain because large motar rounds started barking at us like a giant dog—long, then short, then overhead. I was knicked by a fragment. The gunner on the .30 caliber machine [gun] was hit badly, and his assistant was killed. The enemy mortar was accurate. The shells were bursting about twenty to forty feet overhead, showering us with shell fragments. And we were now drawing small-arms fire from the rice paddies below.

I was locked in and totally committed, but at intervals I wished I was almost anyplace else. I was hunkered over the gun. My assistant gunner was damned good, and I chopped the North Korean troops to pieces. . . . I was ashamed of the slaughter before me, but this was my job, my duty, and my responsibility. I stayed with it until not one white rag was left intact.

Bussey succeeded in holding up the North Korean advance, for which he was awarded the Silver Star.[31]

Beverly Scott from North Carolina hoped to make the army his career. It offered him what he wanted, order, structure, purpose: "And it was honorable.

There was no better institution in American life" for a black man than the army. "Things weren't perfect, but they were better than any civilian institution." He enlisted in 1945 and applied for Officer Candidate School (OCS), from which he graduated in July 1946, at the age of nineteen. "OCS was my first experience with living in an integrated society." The army did not have a separate OCS for blacks, so even though the military was still segregated, Scott found himself bunking with whites, "and that was my first experience with meeting white people on a person-to-person basis." Coming from the South, all his encounters with whites up to OCS had been "adversarial." Whites had insulted him, beat him, treated him with contempt. Now he was working with graduates of Harvard and Yale: "it set the tone for the rest of my life, because OCS taught me that I could successfully compete with these people."

Once he graduated, though, Scott found himself training other blacks in segregated units. When the Korean War broke out, the army needed communications officers, so Scott went to Fort Benning, Georgia, to learn those skills. In January 1951 he landed in Korea as a communications officer with the Twenty-fifth Infantry Division. By that time it was not communications officers the army required, but infantry officers—Scott's original area of training. He was given a rifle platoon, making him the first black platoon leader in the Fourteenth Regiment, and the only black officer in the battalion: "I never had any problems with my men; they were mostly Hispanics, and when they saw that I knew what I was doing, and wasn't going to get them killed or shot up unnecessarily, they relaxed and accepted me." The same could not be said of his relations with his fellow officers. Though he was the senior lieutenant and should have therefore served as the company's executive officer, he was passed over for a junior officer who had the qualification of being white. "I saw right away it was going to be pretty tough for me."

In the fall of 1951, the Fourteenth Regiment moved into the Iron Triangle, three heavily contested towns surrounded by rugged hills. The truce talks had just started, but the war continued. The Americans could see evidence of the Chinese digging in on the ridges to the north: "You never saw the Chinese, but you saw the dirt." Suddenly the war came to resemble World War I, in Scott's view, as the two armies dug complexes of trenches facing one another across five hundred yards of no-man's-land. "It was a miserable time," Scott remembered. "Just a miserable, miserable time. We lost men almost every day, killed or wounded, and it was hard to see the point." Scott nonetheless stayed in the army, rising to serve on the inspector general's staff.[32]

Many white soldiers found the experience of war shifting their racial attitudes, especially after MacArthur's successor, General Ridgway, ordered the immediate integration of all units serving in Korea. The Marine Corps, which had a heritage of racism, changed dramatically during the war. At the war's start there were 1,500 blacks serving in the corps, one-third of them as stewards. By the war's end there were nearly 15,000 African American marines. Repeatedly, white marines would state that the only color that mattered was the uniform's green. "After you've been here a while," one marine stationed in Korea said, "you'll see that color doesn't make any difference." General Oliver P. Smith, commander of the tough First Marine Division, said, "I had a thousand Negroes, and we had no racial troubles. . . . And I had no complaint on their performance of duty." One white marine insisted, "The only discrimination that I can recall was Marine versus those that were not Marines. . . . A Marine Corps trained individual was a Marine, not a white, black or brown Marine, just a Marine and somebody you could rely on."[33] Thanks to the leadership of Generals Ridgway, Smith, and James Van Fleet of the Eighth Army, the military did not embargo medals for heroic African Americans, as they had done in World War II. Marine A.C. Clark won both the Bronze and Silver Stars for separate acts of bravery, and Congress awarded posthumous Medals of Honor to Army Private William Henry Thompson and Sergeant Cornelius H. Charlton.[34]

Many African Americans share the perception that the Korean War broke down racial barriers. Bradley Briggs of the Sixty-fourth Heavy Tank Battalion reported, "All of the platoon leaders under me were white but we had no racial problems." Briggs, like many African American soldiers, won promotion for his duty in Korea, as did Benjamin O. Davis Jr., who became the first black air force general at the war's end. The 187th Airborne also had black officers in command positions with no reported incidences of racial conflict. The air force pilot Captain Daniel "Chappie" James told of his white sergeant being approached by a reporter looking for a story:

"How do you feel about flying with Captain James?"

"What do you mean?"

The reporter said, "I would just like to know how do you feel about flying with him. You know what I mean."

The sergeant said, "No I don't know what you mean. He is a good pilot. He is fine."

"Yes, but I mean, he's uh colored."

And the kid just said, "Is he?"

But for many black veterans, a bitter irony confronted them on their return home, especially those from the South, where Jim Crow signs still proclaimed second-class citizenship for African Americans. Back in the United States, Captain James had the humiliating experience of being called "boy" by a white soldier he had once helped carry off the battlefield. James would later become the first African American four-star general.[35]

## Blaming the Prisoners of War

More than seven thousand American soldiers were held as prisoners of war by the North Koreans and Chinese under horrendous conditions that included deliberate policies of starvation, torture, and efforts at brainwashing. Violating numerous international laws and committing extreme acts of brutality that are best called war crimes, the Chinese hoped to mistreat the POWs into embracing communism. As the POWs came back, they told stories of beatings, water boarding, forced marches, starvation, executions, and a variety of cruel treatments that sought to strip away any vestige of human dignity. Prisoners were kept in their own filth, denied medical care and heat, punched and kicked, mocked, and subjected to endless hours of propaganda. In at least one instance, a group of marines taken prisoner was killed with grenades. One POW described a particularly unpleasant torture: "They would bend my head back, put a towel over my face and pour water over the towel. I could not breathe. This went on hour after hour, day by day. It was freezing cold. When I would pass out they would shake me and begin again. They would leave me tied to the chair with the water freezing on and around me."[36] More than 40 percent of the UN POWs died in captivity, a higher rate than at the Confederacy's notorious Andersonville prison. Anyone who saw the returning POWs— emaciated, bruised, limping wrecks of their former selves—could not doubt for a moment that they had been through a traumatic and harrowing experience. The commander of UN forces, General Mark Clark, spoke eloquently at the return of one of the first groups of POWs: "Because of the heavy personal sacrifices you have made in our great cause, we are humble in your presence." He referred to their mistreatment at the hands of the Chinese: "I am confident you will never have reason to doubt that those sacrifices have our respect and gratitude."[37]

But in sharp contrast to the experience of World War II POWs, Korean War veterans met denunciation rather than a hero's welcome. Many critics, in and out of the military, shamefully followed the lead of Wisconsin Senator Joe McCarthy in demonizing the American soldiers and airmen who had fallen into enemy hands, some of whom returned as "communists in olive drab," in McCarthy's words.[38] The Defense Department made little effort to assist the returning POWs. The army's chief psychiatrist, Brigadier General Rawley Chambers, insisted that the best approach was to "treat them naturally," as though they had "just been around the corner to the drugstore."[39] After quoting the general, *Life* magazine described the experience of Corporal Donald

Legay, who had "spent 29 gray months in a brown mud hut near the Yalu River. The bones of his left arm had been smashed by two slugs, but there were no doctors to take care of him," and he had developed an infection. "We had no feeling we'd ever get out of there," Corporal Legay said. What he most wanted, the magazine reported, was a beer. *Life* also reported that "one planeload of returned servicemen, their names withheld, was taken directly to the Army hospital at Valley Forge, Pa., for 'de-indoctrination' from the Communist brain-washing."[40]

There was a striking lack of compassion from the public, which seemingly did not want to know or talk about the war. *Newsweek* described the American people as "numbed" to stories of the war's horrors and responding with "a muttered curse, a shrug, and the helpless question, 'Well, what could you expect?'" as though the veterans bore responsibility for what they encountered.[41] Neither did the Pentagon have any sympathy for POWs who had weakened under torture and signed communist propaganda statements, such as those accusing the United States of using germ warfare in Korea, investigating 565 of the 4,500 returning POWs, though just six were eventually brought before a court-martial and convicted of military misconduct. Nonetheless, the military lashed out at many of those they investigated, denying them pay and benefits, despite finding no evidence of misconduct.[42]

Korean veterans were quickly consigned to a lesser status than those who had served in World War II. The *New York Times* declared them "a different breed from his older brother who came back from World War II," even though 300,000 World War II veterans served in Korea: "The new veterans are disquieting machine-like products of their special times. . . . There seems to be an almost robot-like disinterest about him that is in disturbing contrast to the assertive individualism of the World War II soldier."[43] The Pentagon joined in this assault on its own troops. In one of the most bizarre actions of its long history, the army sent Major William Erwin Mayer on a nationwide speaking tour to attack the integrity and masculinity of the American soldier.[44] Even though the Defense Department investigation of POWs had found that only a half dozen of these unfortunate men had behaved contrary to military discipline, Mayer declared, without a hint of evidence, that one-third of the POWs had given in to communist brainwashing. He even asserted that they had crumbled without being tortured or physically abused. In an incredible tour de force of illogic, Mayer shifted the blame from the communists to the soft liberalism of the United States, charging that the permissive society had raised a generation of weaklings and men prone to communism. Those who had died in communist captivity had not been the victims of cruelty and starvation, but of their own weakness and lack of spirit. The nation's schools had produced "passive, dependent individuals who died early, and often, apparently, needlessly."[45] One would have thought that an anticommunist would have emphasized the inhumanity of the Chinese and North Koreans, but the real target of America's conservatives remained the New Deal and its legacy, not the distant Asian communist governments.

These ludicrous and inaccurate attacks on the United States and its military forces by an official spokesman of the U.S. Army became popular among conservatives. An evangelical college in Arkansas made kits for use by interested parties, complete with a recording of Mayer's speech delivered by the actor Ronald Reagan.[46] *The Nation* pointed out that Mayer and his adherents had fallen into the trap of blaming the victims for their suffering, but few others questioned Mayer's mythology, and the attacks on those who had fought for their country continued through the 1960s.[47] As with the tramp scare after the Civil War, repeated fictions take on the aura of fact, and the failure of the American military in Korea became an accepted starting place for debate.[48] In 1959 Senator Hugh Scott used the "facts" that one-third of U.S. POWs collaborated and that there were no efforts to escape as evidence of "a flaw in our national character."[49] T.R. Fehrenbach, who had served as an officer in Korea, accepted Mayer's version of reality and castigated America's soldiers for being soft: "They had grown fat. . . . [T]hey represented exactly the kind of pampered, undisciplined, egalitarian army their society had long desired and had at last achieved." The modern soldier lacked the toughness of his predecessors, who held "firm convictions on the superiority of Anglo-Saxon institutions."[50] Even as skeptical a cultural critic as Betty Friedan agreed with the portrayal of the Korean veterans as "apathetic, dependent, infantile, purposeless," and "shockingly non-human." *The Feminine Mystique* dismisses these men as displaying "feminine" personalities.[51]

This tendency to blame the common soldier for the failure of American policy persisted into the country's next "police action," in Vietnam. Looked at another way, the Korean War did not really make sense until the Vietnam War showed the degree to which the government of the United States was capable of making egregious mistakes. Until then, veterans of the Korean conflict were perfectly justified in referring to themselves as the forgotten soldiers.

## The Vietnam War

To a generation of American soldiers, Vietnam was a war without meaning that brought a peace without contentment. No war in American history evoked so much opposition so publically expressed—even among the troops. Mutiny and fragging (killing one's own officers) disrupted military operations, and disobeying orders became routine. American morale was wrecked not just by the lack of a clear sense of mission, but also by the absence of unit cohesion as soldiers rotated out on one-year tours of duty. In a repetition of the Philippine insurrection, American forces again found it impossible to differentiate civilians from enemy combatants, leading to the killing of hundreds of thousands of Vietnamese.

Unlike the Philippine insurrection, the majority of troops serving in Vietnam were not volunteers, but had been drafted into service. When the soldiers came home from Vietnam, they did not find a warm welcome, but generally encountered a willed indifference if not open hostility, as most Americans did not want to hear about what was clearly a defeat for the United States. The psychological impact of the Vietnam War on those who served exceeded that of any previous American war, as thousands of veterans suffered from what was slowly being diagnosed as post-traumatic stress disorder. These veterans did not find the same government support that had been granted the GIs after World War II. Not only did they not receive the full benefits of the GI Bill, they also found the Veterans Administration hospitals suffering from budget cuts and poor management. Those who served in Vietnam would continue to pay the price for many years to come.

President Truman had set the standard for going to war without adhering to the Constitution. A few presidents had acted arbitrarily in the past to commit U.S. troops—McKinley in the Boxer rebellion, Theodore Roosevelt in the Caribbean, Wilson in Mexico, and Coolidge in Central America—but President Lyndon Johnson intended to act on a much larger scale. John F. Kennedy had sent thousands of military "advisors" to South Vietnam, but was just starting to scale back those operations when he was assassinated. Johnson, who did not want to be accused of "losing Vietnam" to the communists as Truman had supposedly lost China, wanted to commit combat forces to shore up the failing Saigon government. In the spring of 1964 his staff, led by William P. Bundy and Walt W. Rostow, prepared a congressional resolution allowing the president to act militarily in Southeast Asia as he saw fit. They then waited for the excuse to present it to Congress. That opportunity came in August 1964, in the Gulf of Tonkin off the coast of North Vietnam, when U.S. naval vessels scrambled to meet a purported communist attack which turned out to be, in Johnson's words, some "dumb, stupid sailors . . . just shooting at flying fish."[52] Of course, Johnson kept that judgment private as he allowed Congress to pass the Gulf of Tonkin Resolution granting him near unlimited authority to commit U.S. troops to battle the communist menace. In short, the president lied about a non-incident that led Congress to abdicate its authority and give Johnson a blank check, which would cost the lives of tens of thousands of Americans.[53]

Ignoring the counsel of George Ball and many other knowledgeable people, the Pentagon pushed ahead with the escalation of the war. By mid-1965 there were 100,000 U.S. troops in South Vietnam; in 1966 U.S. ground forces reached 385,000; and by the end of 1967 there were half a million American troops in South Vietnam. In March 1965, the U.S. launched Operation Rolling Thunder, the longest air campaign in American history, with two million sorties by November 1968, that dropped one million tons of bombs on North Vietnam. The United States lost more than nine hundred aircraft during Rolling Thunder, most brought down by antiaircraft fire. At the same time, the United States bombed the hell out of its ally, dropping four million tons of explosives on South Vietnam by 1973. The air war proved a complete failure both in driving North Vietnam from the war and in halting the flow of support to communist troops in the South.[54]

As in Korea, the United States placed its faith in superior technology, especially its airpower, and, as in Korea, even air supremacy was not enough to win a war against a committed opponent. But it is easy to understand the government's conviction that no enemy could stand before U.S. power. For instance, the antipersonnel cluster bomb released up to six hundred smaller explosive devices in midair, each one of which exploded into thousands of pieces of shrapnel on hitting the ground. And then there was napalm, first used in Korea but "improved" in Vietnam through the addition of polystyrene, which caused the burning jelly to adhere to the human skin with impressive tenacity, and white phosphorous, which made it water resistant.[55] Since the United States quickly destroyed all obvious military targets in North Vietnam, the military went after any and all large buildings, including schools, hospitals, churches, and pagodas, including the Thanh Hoa convent, the Thinh Gia seminary, and the leper colony at Quynh Lap, which was attacked thirty-six times. Any building that could possibly serve a military purpose, real or imagined, was flattened by the American military.[56] Given such overwhelming airpower, it seemed unimaginable that the Vietnamese would be so foolish as to put up with such a ceaseless pounding. As Walt Rostow imagined it, by continuing to inflict more pain, a "crossover" point would be reached at which the communists would lose their will to fight. Any rational person would conclude that no one would want to battle a nation that possessed such weaponry. Yet the Vietnamese communists did so.

The air war proved extremely dangerous, with the United States losing 3,719 planes and 4,869 helicopters.[57] But the loss of men and matériel did not matter greatly in McNamara's war; what mattered was that the machine continued to function, the great conveyor belt of war continuing to spit forth a productive body count. Many soldiers saw themselves caught within an inhuman machine of war. "As the value of Vietnamese life went down in your estimation," Michael Clodfelter wrote, "so too did the realization start to sink in that your body and your life was really of very little importance to the men and the machines who ran the war." All that mattered was winning victories, and human lives only mattered insofar as they aided those victories. The soldier, then, is just "another piece of equipment, like a tank or the M-16 you carry, and your loss would be counted and calculated in those terms. The machine would not care that a man had died, only that another part of its inventory had been lost and would require replacement, like the destroyed tank. And like the totaled tank, the Army would simply put in another order at another factory—a boot camp, where your replacement was being tooled and trained on a different kind of assembly line. It was just exactly as hard and as heartless as that and it was a heavy thing to accept—though accept it we all inevitably did."[58]

The statistics on Vietnam, which Robert McNamara and his Pentagon so adored, are staggering. No one knows how many Vietnamese died during that long conflict that started shortly after the end of World War II and ran to 1975, though estimates usually run toward two million—a number that enters the territory of the incomprehensible. The United States dropped more than eight million tons of explosives on Vietnam, Laos, and Cambodia, which is three times the amount dropped in World War II by all sides. American aircraft sprayed eighteen million gallons of poisonous herbicides over South Vietnam, and left 21 million bomb craters. It is worth emphasizing that this damage was inflicted on the country we were ostensibly protecting.[59]

## A World of Hurt

War was everywhere in Vietnam; there was no such thing as a front line. A desk jockey in Saigon could just as easily be a target as a grunt in the bush. The latter fought the war nearly every day of his yearlong tour of duty; the war was all around him at all times. The mines, booby traps, mortar attacks, and snipers were always present, always ready to catch the American soldier by surprise. As Philip Caputo observed, a marine in the Pacific theater faced combat for six to eight weeks during the entirety of World War II, while the grunt in Vietnam found no safety in country.[60] They felt themselves separated from the reality they had known, subjected to a world of hurt.

The Vietnam War inflicted heavy damage on the military's morale. During the war, the ideal of a democratic army took a battering as there was a clear class structure to combat in Vietnam. One study found that 80 percent of combat troops came from working-class families, and even most of the rest came from the lower end of the middle class. Few frontline soldiers had a parent who was a lawyer or doctor or executive. Just one-fifth of those who served in Vietnam had attended college (compared to half of all Americans in their age cohort), and just 7.2 percent had graduated, most of these men serving as officers.[61]

The draft was supposed to equalize service, especially once deferments were tightened. But conscripting middle-class boys increased opposition to the war, and resistance to the draft increased from 1967 on. According to the Justice Department, 206,000 men refused to participate in the draft, while 93,000 deserted between 1968 and the war's end—three times the Korean War desertion rate.[62] There was, in the estimation of many officers, a complete breakdown of military discipline in Vietnam. Soldiers in the field, who called themselves grunts, complained about the officers' tendency to command from a helicopter high above the field. Most grunts saw few officers other than lieutenants and captains; the battalion commanders were overhead, circling in helicopters, getting a false sense of the situation.[63] Marine Colonel Robert Heinl, writing in the *Armed Forces Journal* in 1971, declared, "The morale, discipline and battle-worthiness of the U.S. Armed Forces are, with a few salient exceptions, lower and worse than at any time in this century and possibly in the history of the United States. By every conceivable indicator, our Army that now remains in Vietnam is in a state approaching collapse."[64] It was not just the ground forces in Vietnam; opposition to the war within the military extended to naval vessels, which were plagued by sabotage, and to air bases, which were hit by protests.[65] One of the clearest testaments to the collapse of traditional standards of military service was the very existence of the Vietnam Veterans Against the War (VVAW). In no other previous American war had military personnel returned home to lead opposition to the conflict.[66] It was a unique and deeply troubling development in American military history, and offered what was probably the most effective and dramatic opposition to U.S. involvement in Vietnam.

The VVAW began in 1967 and included thousands of members by 1971. In the early part of that year, the VVAW held the Winter Soldier Investigation, with former American soldiers describing atrocities they had committed in Vietnam. The April antiwar march on Washington, D.C., climaxed by two thousand veterans throwing their medals onto the Capitol steps, stunned America. John Kerry, spokesman for the VVAW, appeared before Senator William Fulbright's Committee on Foreign Relations on April 22, 1971, and delivered a powerful summation of the veterans' experiences and hopes. Kerry was later elected to the U.S. Senate from Massachusetts:

Each day to facilitate the process by which the United States washes her hands of Vietnam someone has to give up his life so that the United States doesn't have to admit something that the entire world already knows, so that we can't say that we have made a mistake. Someone has to die so that President Nixon won't be, and these are his words, "the first President to lose a war."

We are asking Americans to think about that because how do you ask a man to be the last man to die in Vietnam? How do you ask a man to be the last man to die for a mistake? . . .

We wish that a merciful God could wipe away our own memories of that service as easily as this administration has wiped their memories of us. But all that they have done and all that they can do by this denial is to make more clear than ever our own determination to undertake one last mission, to search out and destroy the last vestige of this barbaric war, to pacify our own hearts, to conquer the hate and the fear that have driven this country these last 10 years and more, and so when, in 30 years from now, our brothers go down the street without a leg, without an arm, or a face, and small boys ask why, we will be able to say "Vietnam" and not mean a desert, not a filthy obscene memory but mean instead the place where America finally turned and where soldiers like us helped it in the turning.[67]

The Winter Soldier hearings shocked America. Here were Vietnam vets telling stories of unnecessary violence that they had committed. Few people knew that the same thing had happened seventy years earlier during the Philippine insurrection, so that the stories seemed unique, unfathomable coming from Americans. Some six hundred veterans told stories of crimes against civilians, petty and serious, from cutting off the whiskers of old men to turning a dog on a passing Vietnamese for no apparent reason to wiping out an entire village. The minor acts of aggression can be mystifying. Sergeant Jack Smith described how his unit threw C-rations cans to kids as they passed by as a friendly gesture: "Then it changed. We'd toss them into barbed wire and watch the kids go tearing after them, cutting themselves up." Marine Sergeant Michael Mc-Cusker of Portland, Oregon, told how a member of his platoon had been killed by a sniper hiding in a village they had just passed:

I turned around and saw this old priest standing there. Somebody shot a gun right behind me and shoved that little priest right into his altar. Then we wiped out that village and another one, I mean with everything—we shot people, pigs, dogs, geese, we burned every hut, it was just madness. All I can remember is shooting and torching and then, later, looking back and seeing all this smoke, two big clouds of smoke with paddies in between.

As Marine Private Thomas Heidtman said, "They were gooks and slant-eyes and we hated them. It's like anybody can be the enemy, so everybody is."[68] A member of Michael Clodfelter's squad leveled an M79 grenade launcher at an old man in a village: "I arose from my morass of sweat and dread to scream out words of protest . . . words that I should have loosened at the first insane moments of this horror." But he was too late, and the old man died slowly before his eyes: "I would, in effect, still be shouting those unheeded words of protest in dozens of anti-war marches for years after I left Nam. I am still screaming them out today . . . too late, far too late. That unheard scream will echo through my soul forever."[69]

Equally troubling were the public comments of Lieutenant Colonel Anthony Herbert, the most highly decorated enlisted man in the Korean War. Herbert, who commanded a battalion in Vietnam, charged his superior officers with covering up reports of atrocities committed by U.S. troops. He was immediately transferred to Fort McPherson, Georgia—about as out of the way as the high command could put him. Herbert then went public with his charges, including his assertion that one major cause of the mistreatment of civilians in Vietnam was the army's commitment to portraying the Vietcong "as some kind of superman when he's a stumblebum just like us." Atrocities resulted when commanders abdicated their responsibility in their search for promotion. "The commanders are out to get a war record. It's called 'getting your ticket punched.' "[70]

Many men serving in Vietnam questioned the reason for the war. Marine Lieutenant Rodney Chastant of Mobile wrote his brother David in September 1967:

Most men here believe we will *not* win the war. And yet they stick their necks out every day. . . . The Marines are taking a fierce beating over here. They don't have enough men. We must have more men, at least twice as many, or we are going to get the piss kicked out of us this winter when the rains come. The Marines have been assigned a task too big for so few. . . . One of the basic problems is that [President] Johnson is trying to fight this war the way he fights his domestic wars—he chooses an almost unattainable goal with a scope so large it is virtually undefinable, and he attacks this goal with poorly allocated funds, minimum manpower, limited time, and few new ideas. . . . We should never have committed ourselves to this goal, but now that we have, what should we do? [Chastant thought the only hope was to elect a new president, one] who will end this ill-thought-out approach to world peace; a man who . . . has the long view of history and nation-making, who does not overreact to the label communism, . . . who can understand that a Ho Chi Minh Vietnam is better than a Vietnam of old men and women without the dedication and vision of its young men, and finally a man who will be content to influence history rather than make it.

Chastant was promoted to captain the following month and killed in action in October 1968 at the age of twenty-five.[71]

## The Experience of Combat

Entering Vietnam was coming into an alien and hostile world. "When we landed in Cam Ranh Bay," Sergeant Robert L. Daniels recalled, "it was like I had never seen anything like it before. . . . I was in a strange land. I was scared to death."[72] Sometimes it seemed like the only way to describe what they experienced was to let loose into a free-form stream of consciousness. Lieutenant Marion Lee Kempner of Galveston wrote his family in 1966:

> Sorry to be so long in writing, but I have just come back from an abortion called Operation Jackson. I spent a three-day "walk in the sun" (and paddies and fields and mountains and impenetrable jungle and saw grass and ants and screwed-up radios and no word, and deaf radio operators, and no chow, and too many C-rations, and blisters and torn trousers and jungle rot, and wet socks and sprained ankles and no heels, and, and, and) for a battalion that walked on roads and dikes the whole way and a regiment that didn't even know where the battalion was, finished off by a 14,000-meter forced march on a hard road.

Kempner was killed by a mine five weeks later.[73]

The biggest problem facing American troops in Vietnam was identifying the enemy. Michael Clodfelter, an artilleryman with the 101st Airborne Division, found himself in 1965, "thanks to the Domino Theory and LBJ," in "the middle of a Southeast Asian jungle." He did not want to be there, but he wanted to do his duty: "The enemy and the war he brought us was a phantom and a fantasy. . . . That was a big part of the problem—just trying to figure out exactly who the hell was the enemy." There had been guerrilla wars before, but "this was guerilla war on a grand scale, a dozen dirty little wars merged into one, one of the great wars of the century but fought on the level of Geronimo's Apache campaigns." Clodfelter traces the process by which American combat troops came to appreciate that it "was much easier to do the killing first and the identifying afterwards":

> Sometimes the enemy seemed so much made of the monsoon mist that we even doubted that he really existed. We arrived in the country expecting

to encounter uniformed communist hordes, but found instead this strange small people wearing peasant garb and those inscrutable smiles. We . . . found it hard to believe that these weak, undernourished-looking peasants could really present a threat and a danger to all our battalions of big, husky, heavily armed G.I.s. It seemed a laughable country and a laughable war—until we started running into the explosive evidence of the enemy's existence, until we started seeing and becoming a part of the red results of their cunning and courage. And then, slowly, as fear mounted frustration and rode down a crippled confidence, as callousness started taking over from condescension in our attitude toward the Vietnamese, our vision blurred, clouded over, and refocused. Where before we had found it difficult to see the enemy anywhere, now we saw him everywhere. It was simple now; the Vietnamese were the Viet Cong, the Viet Cong were the Vietnamese. The killing became so much easier now.[74]

Killing was easy—at first. The price would be paid later, in trying to justify to themselves what they had done and why. George Olsen, a ranger with the Americal Division, wrote a friend in 1969: "The frightening thing about it all is that it is so very easy to kill in war. There's no remorse, no theatrical 'washing of the hands' to get rid of nonexistent blood, not even regrets." Still, he had to admit that when he killed someone, he was more afraid than he had ever been before: "my hands shook so much I had trouble reloading." He was scared, but he killed "that little SOB," who was hoping to kill him, simply because he wanted to live, "to go home, to get drunk or walk down the street on a date again." In an instant "it's all over and you're alive because someone else is dead." Olsen did not live long enough to discover if that absence of remorse would continue in civilian life, as he was killed in action in 1970.[75] Others lived long enough to consider the meaning of their actions. Marine Private Reginald Edwards of Louisiana was on a routine patrol in Cam Ne. With VC suspected in the village, they had a tendency to just shoot first: "Like you didn't go into a room to see who was in there first. You fire and go in." They came to this one bamboo hut "and we was just gonna run in, shoot through the walls." Tracer bullets tended to set the huts on fire. "That used to be a fun thing to do. Set hootches on fire with tracers." In this instance a Vietnamese came running toward them shouting not to shoot. "I almost killed him." But Edwards decided to investigate and went into the hut, which was full of "women and children huddled together. I was getting ready to wipe them off the planet." His knees got weak at the thought: "I dropped down, and that's when I cried. First time I cried in the 'Nam. I realized what I would have done. I almost killed all them people."[76]

Arthur Wiknik's outstanding account of his service in Vietnam, *Nam Sense*, expresses well the veteran's desire to honestly confront the meaning of his experience. Wiknik was drafted in 1968, and, stalling for time, signed up to train as a noncommissioned officer. But in 1969 he was sent to Vietnam: "The military expected me to drop into the middle of the war and, without any experience whatsoever, lead men in combat. I was barely twenty years old." It seemed to him an utterly mad idea, but he hoped "to finish my tour of duty and go home in one piece—and take as many of my men with me as possible." This attitude would "put me at odds with gung-ho superiors who habitually put the mission ahead of the men." Arriving at Cam Ranh Bay, Wiknik was assigned to the 101st Airborne Division, despite a complete lack of training in that area:

> [T]he clerk specialist reviewing my file asked a few questions.
> "Is there anything in your records you think should be removed?"
> "Sure," I answered eagerly. "I've got an Article 15 for being AWOL (Absent Without Leave) from Fort Benning for two days. I was on a three-day pass, but I traveled too far and didn't get back in time."
> He flipped through the pages searching for the document.
> "Here it is," he said, as he tore it out and crumbled it into a ball. "Is there anything else you don't want in there?"
> "How can you do that?" I asked, somewhat surprised.
> "We live to give new guys a clean record so they will have no problems when they reach their units."
> "How come I'm being placed in an airborne division? I'm infantry!"
> "The NCO squad leaders in the 101st have a rather high casualty rate," he said seriously, "so they need you guys pretty bad."
> That was comforting.

Wiknik was sent up to Camp Evans by the DMZ (demilitarized zone at the 17th parallel), home to the Third Brigade of the 101st:

> Lieutenant Colonel Brookes was a tall, imposing figure who demanded to be addressed by his radio call-name—Ajax. From inside his huge operations bunker, Ajax stood at a podium reading from notes to me, his audience of one. He gave the customary pep talk I'd heard a dozen times already since I'd been drafted.
> "We have accepted the challenge of a very important mission in South Vietnam. Freedom will come at a high cost, sometimes at the supreme sacrifice, but we are willing to fight for justice and humanity. We will win this war. The tide is turning. There is light at the end of the tunnel . . ."
> The colonel rambled on, waving his arms but never making eye contact. I felt as if he was talking to the wall. I started to daydream. Perhaps Ajax fancied himself to be like the Greek warrior of the same name or like the

popular laundry detergent so he could clean up Vietnam. Either way, when he finally finished speaking, Ajax shook my hand and directed me to the site that would be my home base for the next year, provided I lived that long.

[Settling in with his platoon, Wiknik went on several patrols over his first few weeks.] Specialist Harrison [was] the platoon's longevity man with more than ten months in the field. Eager to return home, he was always pulling some goofy stunt, trying without success to get sent to the rear. His nasal Kentucky twang and permanent grin sometimes made us think his antics were a sure sign he was a burned-out GI. Standing a scant five and one-half feet tall, three inches shorter than me, he was someone we all looked up to. . . .

"Tell me something," I said curiously, "I've been in the field for two weeks now and still don't know what the hell we're doing patrolling this village."

"Well, it's like this," said Harrison, "the VC are out here every night trying to get stuff from the villagers like food, clothes, money, recruits, even information. But most of the villagers are friendly toward us and don't want anything to do with the Gooks. So, our job is to ambush the VC and let 'em die for their cause."

[The following morning they discover that they had killed a VC in a nighttime firefight.] I couldn't resist the temptation to check out our kill. Death must have been instantaneous. The body lay face down with arms and legs frozen in a running position. Near the right shoulder blade, the shirt had a tiny bloodstained bullet hole. One of the men prodded the corpse several times before rolling it over. Each person stepped back with the same astonished look on his face. I felt nausea. There was a gaping hole in the shoulder big enough to put a softball in. The mutilated tangle of splintered bones and flesh seemed unreal. The face was contorted with teeth gritted and eyes closed. I squirmed inside as the lifeless form became recognizable. The physique was that of a young woman, maybe in her late teens, about my age. We had killed a girl. . . . It was sickening. . . .

"She didn't even have a weapon," I said faintly.

"The Gooks know the rules. Don't get caught after dark."

"Holy fuck!" shouted Stan Alcon as he wandered over. "That's the boom-boom girl I screwed the other day!"

"Are you sure?" asked Lieutenant Bruckner.

"I'm positive. . . . See if she's got my five bucks."[77]

"In Vietnam," Philip Caputo wrote, "the only measure of victory was one of the most hideous, morally corrupting ideas ever conceived by the military mind—the body count."[78] Such a policy encouraged killing Vietnamese with the assumption that they were enemies, for the purpose of the body count. Marine William D. Ehrhart saw the effect of the resulting attitude in the nonchalant way in which he killed a Vietnamese woman because she ran away from him:

> Whenever you turned around, you'd be taking it in the solar plexus. Then the enemy would disappear, and you'd end up taking out your frustrations on the civilians. The way we operated, any Vietnamese seen running away from Americans was a Vietcong suspect, and we could shoot. It was standard operating procedure. One day I shot a woman in a rice field because she was running—just running away from the Americans. And I killed her. Fifty-five or sixty years old, unarmed, and at the time I didn't even think twice about it.[79]

With time, many American soldiers came to a reluctant admiration of the Vietcong. As a young lieutenant wrote after one of his men was killed by a mine: "I am now filled with both respect and hate for the VC and the Vietnamese. Respect because the enemy knows that he can't stand up to us in a fire fight due to our superior training, equipment and our vast arsenal of weapons. Yet he is able. Via his mines and booby traps, he can whittle our ranks down piecemeal until we cannot muster an effective fighting force." His own unit had four killed and thirty wounded in a single month.[80] Similarly, Thomas Giltner found much to admire in the dedication of the Vietcong: "We respected them from day one. . . . They did an awful lot with very little."[81]

A great many grunts thought the United States was fighting the war all wrong. As Private Reginald Edwards said, "we would have done a lot better by getting them hooked on our lifestyle [rather] than by trying to do it with guns. Give them credit cards. Make them dependent on television and sugar. Blue jeans work better than bombs."[82] Others came to feel guilty over their assignments. For instance, Staff Sergeant Don F. Browne took part in the notorious Phoenix Program: "We would get the word that certain people were no longer necessary or needed to be removed." Browne doubted that they ever grabbed a high-ranking VC, being convinced that they tended to take out "a local person in the village who was coerced by the VC into being a leader." The Americans in the program were forbidden from torturing; they left that task to ARVN (Army of the Republic of Vietnam). On one occasion an ARVN sergeant took a suspect into a hut "and strung him up from his ankles." The sergeant then built a fire underneath the suspect: "When his hair caught on fire, he started talking." Browne doubted that such methods worked in the long run.[83] William Ehrhart described how "we would go through a village before dawn, rousting everybody out of bed and kicking down doors and dragging them out if they didn't move fast enough." They would destroy rice, burn huts, kill animals, herd the people into fenced enclosures, interrogate villagers, hand some over to ARVN, and then leave them to their ruined village: "If they weren't pro-Vietcong before we got there," he concludes, "they sure as hell were by the time we left."[84]

On November 12, 1969, journalist Seymour Hersh published a story of American soldiers killing at least 109 civilians in a village called My Lai in March 1968. As the details emerged, events in My Lai turned out to have been far worse than Hersh had initially reported, with many more civilians killed, the army working to cover up the story, and the soldiers having attacked the wrong village. My Lai seared most American consciences, unfairly tarnishing the reputation of American troops who served in Vietnam. Captain Ernest Medina's Charlie Company, First Battalion, Americal Division, moved through My Lai, ruthlessly raping and killing and burning, without regard to age or gender, violating all the rules and norms they had ever learned. An army photographer, Sergeant Ronald Haeberle, was present to photograph the horror, as American soldiers killed an estimated four to five hundred unarmed civilians. It was probably the single worst moment of the most awful war in America's long military history.

Vernado Simpson watched three members of his company rape a young girl and then shoot her in the face. He then shot a woman; turning her over he saw that he had also killed a baby she had been holding: "My mind just went. The training came to me and I just started killing. Old men, women, children, water buffaloes, everything. We were told to leave nothing standing. We did what we were told, regardless of whether they were civilians. They [were] the enemy. Period. Kill." But he went beyond just killing, he began mutilating bodies, cutting out tongues, scalping the victims: "I just lost all sense of direction." He was not alone. He saw other members of his company killing in odd ways: "any type of way you could kill someone that's what they did." Simpson calculated that he personally killed twenty-five people in My Lai while Lieutenant William Calley, commanding the First Platoon, wandered the area ordering his men to eliminate the villagers in response to Captain Medina's orders.[85] When Calley came across two of his men standing over a group of fifteen villagers that included several children, he demanded to know why they had not yet followed his orders "to take care of them." Paul Meadlo responded that they were doing so by "watching over them." Calley became angry: "No. I want them killed." Meadlo hesitated and Calley ordered, "Fire when I say 'Fire.'" He then joined Meadlo in opening up with their M16s. Meadlo began crying and stopped firing as he saw mothers throwing themselves on their children to try and protect them. But Calley kept blasting, finishing off the last of the children. He turned to Meadlo, pleased with his work, and said, "OK, let's go." At that moment there were shouts that a group of women and children were trying to get away. "Get them!" Calley shouted. "Kill them!"

For the next few hours, Calley continued through the village, urging his men to continue killing everyone they could find. He gathered forty or fifty villagers in a ditch and opened fire, ordering his men to kill them all. When Robert Maples tried to help a wounded woman, Calley ordered him, "Load your machine gun and shoot these people." When Maples refused, Calley turned his rifle on him, but was prevented from shooting one of his own men by the intervention of some of the other soldiers. Calley and a few others then killed everyone in the ditch.[86]

There were a few men present who never lost their humanity or their courage. Several members of Charlie Company refused to take part in these violations of military law, and a few did their best to rescue civilians. Most heroic was a helicopter pilot, Hugh Thompson of Decatur, Georgia. The twenty-five-year-old already had five years of experience in the military when he flew over My Lai accompanied by two Huey gunships to provide tactical support. Thompson could see some sort of combat operation below, but he was receiving no enemy fire. He marked some wounded civilians on the ground with green smoke, indicating that they needed medical care. But when he flew back over, they were dead. Thompson swept in to hover just five feet off the ground; the civilians were definitely dead. He watched as an officer walked up to a wounded woman and shot her.

Thompson landed and argued with Lieutenant Calley over what was clearly the massacre of civilians: "I couldn't believe what I was seeing, these men were behaving like Nazis, and we're not supposed to be Nazis."[87] Feeling he had to do something, he saw a group of ten civilians being chased by American soldiers. Thompson landed his helicopter between the civilians and the soldiers, radioed the Hueys for support, and ordered his door gunner to open fire on the Americans if they began shooting the civilians. Thompson leapt out of his helicopter and confronted Lieutenant Stephen Brooks of the Second Platoon, asking his help to save the civilians. Brooks recommended a hand grenade. With the help of the Hueys, Thompson rescued these civilians. He then flew over the village, landing near a ditch where some one hundred corpses lay. Thompson's crew chief, Glenn Andreotta, went into the ditch and emerged with a child about three years old, who was covered in gore, but still alive. Nearly thirty years later, Thompson still choked up as he concluded, "I wish I could have saved more."[88]

Back at their base, the crews of the gunships joined Thompson in telling their base commander, Major Fred Watke, what they had seen. Watke went up the chain of command with his report, and orders were sent back to Medina to stop killing civilians. Thanks to Thompson's vivid outrage over the radio, lots of people knew that something outrageous had gone down in the village of My Lai. But the U.S. Army did its best to cover up the events until Seymour Hersh broke the story. Ultimately, only Lieutenant Calley was tried and convicted of misconduct at My Lai, and the army paroled him in 1974. Hugh Thompson received hate mail, death threats, and mutilated animals on his porch, as well as a commendation from the army thirty years after the massacre for rescuing civilians from an unspecified enemy.[89]

The vast majority of American soldiers realized that orders to destroy villages were wrong, if not downright evil, and a number of songs circulated among the troops, the dark humor covering an abiding bitterness. For instance, "Strafe the Town and Kill the People," which was sung to the tune of a 1950s song, "Wake the Town and Tell the People," did little to disguise the sense that the United States was often in the wrong in Vietnam.

> Strafe the town and kill the people,
> Drop your napalm in the square;
> Do it early Sunday morning,
> Catch them while they're still at prayer.
>
> Drop some candy to the orphans,
> Watch them as they gather 'round:
> Use your twenty millimeter,
> Mow those little bastards down. . . .
>
> See the sweet old pregnant lady
> Running cross the field in fear;
> Run your twenty mike-mike through her,
> Hope the film comes out real clear.[90]

As morale crumbled, conduct became less disciplined and often just plain strange. Robert E. Holcomb, serving with the Fourth Infantry Division in 1970, observed some of the other soldiers "messin' with the people." Holcomb was part of a detail responsible for disposing of spoiled milk from Fire Base Oasis. They drove along a road busy with lots of Vietnamese on motorbikes: "And these two GIs began throwing quarts of milk at the people on the bikes." A number of the civilians were knocked of their bikes, some seemed to be seriously injured. "My friend and I, supposedly in charge of the detail, went over and told them, 'What the fuck's a matter with you? You're doing this today. Do you realize what's gonna happen tonight? Fuck with the people in the daytime, and you can expect mortars at night.' That night, we got mortars."[91]

The Pentagon was justly concerned with one of the clearest signs of sagging morale in Vietnam, the practice of fragging. The killing of officers by their own men gets its name from fragmentation grenades, which were tossed into an officer's tent as an effectively anonymous way of eliminating a hated commander. The worst transgression an officer could commit was to put his men's lives in danger in order to enhance his own reputation or seek a promotion. One lieutenant "made a lot of enemies because he was really tough on some of his people in the field even though the pullout had started. Someone wired a claymore mine to the door of his hootch."[92] It was easy to get away with fragging, since all one had to do was blame the enemy. As another veteran reported of the aftermath of a squad acting together to kill their commander: "Someone called on the radio and told them the captain had been shot by the gooks."[93]

James D. Nell, who was in Vietnam in 1968, reported seeing several instances of fragging: "Grunt will put a price on his head, one hundred, two hundred dollars on his head." When asked where the money came from, he responded, "From the troopers. Guys that pitch in and pay for it."[94] In a letter to his congressman, "One Mad G.I.," as he signed himself, complained that his M16 "failed to function at a critical moment endangering my life and the lives of other men in this company." The cause of the danger was a misfire at a critical moment: "Last night, at 0300 hours I had a clear, unobstructed shot at the captain." With the captain still alive, the soldiers under his command were put at risk. The letter was most probably not intended to be completely serious, as it ended by noting that it could "be weeks before I get another crack at the bastard and in the meantime I am subjected to the ridicule of my associates."[95] Soldiers often offered rewards for the murder of hated officers, with a record $10,000 put up for the killing of Major General Melvin Zais, commander of the 101st Airborne, for ordering the attack on Hill 937. Fortunately for Zais, his tour of duty ended almost immediately after the pointless assault on Hamburger Hill, and he departed with, in his words, "A handful of ashes."[96] A 1971 Pentagon study confirmed 305 cases of fragging in 1969 and 1970, resulting in the death of 73 officers.[97]

The structure of service in Vietnam created a keen sense of isolation. A tour of duty was one year; the individual soldier rotated in and then one year later, if fortunate, left on his own. Short-timers, those with less than a month left in their service, tended toward superstition and terror, convinced that a bullet or booby trap would find them just when the end was in sight. One night in his last month in Vietnam, Arthur Wiknik pulled guard duty:

To keep track of guard time, Grunts passed around a wristwatch with a luminous face. However, on this night one of the Cherries [a new arrival] handed me a large pocket watch that glowed with the Walt Disney cartoon character Mickey Mouse. The mere sight of the smiling Mickey Mouse in a war zone stunned me. With all the chaos and loneliness of Vietnam, here in my hand was a tiny piece of my childhood. It painfully reminded me of how much I hate the war and of how bad I wanted to go home.[98]

Just seeing the watch sparked short-timer's syndrome (STS) in Wiknik. His subconscious was already on its way home, but the reality around him was Vietnam. Those with STS tended to take out their anxieties on the recent arrivals, issuing dire warnings of doom and constantly checking the newcomer for fatal errors. As Wiknik wrote:

> The commonly accepted cause of STS, other than having a lifetime of ordeals crammed into a relatively short period of time, was that GIs arrived and left Vietnam alone. If solders came in as a unit, they would be counting the days together like a class of high school seniors waiting for graduation. The way a GI's tour was arranged, there was no one who shared the same feelings about being close to going home.

The return and its aftermath remained an entirely individual experience. When Wiknik left Vietnam, the only official acknowledgment came with a formal handshake from his sergeant, "Thanks for coming."[99]

Despite the alienation of the individual one-year rotation, the platoon became the center of life for the common soldier; these were the only people they could trust and rely on. As Michael Clodfelter said: "So what it all came down to was that my world became the war, that my extended family became Charlie Company of the Second Battalion of the 502nd Airborne Infantry of the First Brigade of the 101st Airborne Division, and that my immediate family became the men of the Second 'Hard Core' Squad of the First Platoon."[100] Survival, making it home, became the prime mission; as one private told his sergeant, "That's all the guys want you to do, keep them alive."[101] The loss of a member of the platoon became a death in the family. Lieutenant Robert Ransom, a platoon commander, wrote his parents in 1968 shortly before his own death: "I lost my first man last week. He was killed by accident by another man in the platoon." They had been on a night ambush when "the flank man crawled away to take a leak," and on crawling back "another man mistook him for a dink and shot him." Ransom added, "The concern among the team (for that is what we are) is how it will affect the man who shot him. Will he fall to pieces over this and be unable to perform his function? This is what we're worried about first and foremost. War is Hell!"[102] Every generation, it seems, needs to rediscover Sherman's verity.

## The War Comes Home

Many soldiers in Vietnam suffered from a confused patriotism, a credibility gap between what they had been raised to believe and what they actually experienced. Navy Corpsman Luther C. Benton thought "that if we were there, then it must be right. We have to stop communism before it gets to America. I was just like all the other dummies."[103] It is surprising how often one hears references to John Wayne, that image of American heroism.[104] Marine Ron Kovic, shot and paralyzed in Vietnam, wrote movingly of growing up on John Wayne movies, "watching Sergeant Stryker, played by John Wayne, charge up the hill and get killed just before he reached the top." *Sands of Iwo Jima* then cut to a shot of the men raising the flag while the battle hymn of the Marine Corps played, and Kovic and his best friend "cried in our seats." Kovic grew up wanting to be like "John Wayne and the brave men who raised the flag on Iwo Jima." But in the end, "I gave my dead dick for John Wayne."[105] Others with less traumatic injuries suffered similar conflicted feelings, often leading to a sense of betrayal. Reflecting on the pointlessness of the war and of a close friend who never returned from Vietnam, Richard J. Ford carries a persistent burden: "I really feel used. I feel manipulated. I feel violated."[106] Stephen A. Howard thought "we were the last generation to believe . . . in the honor of war. There is no honor in war." His mother raised him to think of military service as what he owed his country: "My mama still thinks that I did my part for my country. . . . I don't."[107]

Many veterans thought they could forget Vietnam, come home, pop a beer, watch a football game on TV, and the jungle would just fade away. But it did not work that way. "I used to think that I wasn't affected by Vietnam," one veteran said. "But I have been living with Vietnam ever since I left." It stuck with him, clinging to his memory: "I remember most how hard it was to just shoot people." During one patrol three members of his unit had been killed by a sniper hiding in a village: "We went over to burn the village down. I was afraid that there was going to be shooting people that day, so I just kind of dealt with the animals." He turned his back on the rest of his platoon and shot a bunch of chickens. He could not shake that memory.[108] Many others have dreams or flashbacks, and very commonly they just feel uneasy being in an unknown environment: "I'm constantly thinking about the war. I walk down streets different. I look at places where individuals could hide. . . . I dream of helicopters coming over my house, coming to pick me up to take me to a fire fight."[109] An entire generation of veterans remain haunted by their experiences.

Veterans' memories are filled with visions of horror; what had been routine in Vietnam became a recurring nightmare back home. Though the name "post-traumatic stress disorder" (PTSD) had not yet been coined, many veterans returned home and knew something was seriously wrong. Robert Holcomb returned to his parents' home in Gary, Indiana, but found he could not sleep in his old room: "I didn't really feel comfortable sleeping aboveground in a bed. So I moved down into a corner of the basement and put everything around my bed. Gun here. Stereo here. All your pot right here. Just like in the war. Then I could go to sleep." But it was not restful sleep, as he woke up with scratches on his hands from hitting the wall during the night. He had dreams that he had "run out of ammunition and we were getting overrun."[110] John Hendricks could not get the image of dead bodies out of his head: "Back then we didn't give a shit about the dead Vietnamese. It was like, 'Hey, they're just gooks, don't mean nothin'.' You got so cold you didn't even blink. You could even joke about it, mess around with the bodies like they were rag dolls. . . . It's not like that now. You can't just put it out of your mind. Now I carry those bodies around every fucking day. It's a heavy load, man, a heavy fucking load."[111]

The surreal qualities of the Vietnam War—a subject Francis Ford Coppola tackled in his 1979 film *Apocalypse Now*—appeared at every turn, as cold beer was airlifted to soldiers in the jungle, in the consumerist nightmare of Saigon's streets, in the R & R trips to the brothels of Bangkok, and most of all in the sudden return home to the United States. John Kerry remembered his flight home:

> There I was, a week out of the jungle, flying from San Francisco to New York. I fell asleep and woke up yelling, probably a nightmare. The other passengers moved away from me—a reaction I noticed more and more in the months ahead. The country didn't give a shit about the guys coming back, or what they'd gone through. The feeling toward them was "Stay away—don't contaminate us with whatever you've brought back from Vietnam."[112]

The American military had no clue how to deal with what they tended to call "shell shock" or "battle fatigue." After the Korean War, *Army Magazine* stated, "It takes five to twelve days for a soldier to recover from combat strains." It thought it possible that a pill could be developed to address this temporary problem.[113] In 1980 the American Psychiatric Association defined PTSD as the response to traumatic events that can alter the brain's chemical composition and can lead to psychotic flashbacks, withdrawal from intimacy, and hyperarousal—which is to say, anger and paranoia. Research in 1990 indicated that half a million Vietnam vets were suffering from PTSD, which should have been treated as a medical emergency—but was not. Instead, many Vietnam veterans found the Veterans Administration to be their worst enemy. Thousands had been poisoned by Agent Orange, a chemical herbicide used without caution to defoliate much of Vietnam and inflict cancer and other medical problems on those in its proximity. The VA attempted for years to deny that Agent Orange caused cancer, leaving a large number of veterans without adequate medical care. Similarly, a 1988 VA study estimated that one-sixth of the three million Americans who served in Vietnam—half a million soldiers—suffered from some degree of what they were just beginning to identify as PTSD. Nonetheless, the VA would ignore its own findings and continue to avoid responding to the psychological consequences of war into the twenty-first century.[114]

Though many Americans desperately wanted to forget the Vietnam War, a flood of outstanding and compelling literature poured forth to confront the country with the realities of war.[115] Arguably, the best novelist to emerge from the war was Tim O'Brien, who served in the Americal Division in 1969 and 1970, and whose edgy *Going After Cacciato* won the 1979 National Book Award. But for many of his fellow veterans, O'Brien's *The Things They Carried* best expressed the feel of Vietnam. Even while telling powerful stories, O'Brien denied the ability of anyone to tell the complete truth about war: "In many cases a true war story cannot be believed. If you believe it, be skeptical," for war stretches our ability to both tell a story, and to believe it. "Often the crazy stuff is true and the normal stuff isn't, because the normal stuff is necessary to make you believe the truly incredible craziness." Of one thing at least O'Brien was certain, "A true war story is never moral." It offers no guides, no models, no sense of virtue. "If a story seems moral, do not believe it. If at the end of a war story you feel uplifted, or if you feel that some bit of rectitude has been salvaged from the larger waste, then you have been made the victim of a very old and terrible lie."[116]

The war in Vietnam did not lend itself to clarity of purpose, especially as far too many soldiers entered the service with a normative standard set by World War II and reproduced repeatedly in combat films. O'Brien caught this sense of distance perfectly in *Going After Cacciato*:

> They did not know even the simple things: a sense of victory, or satisfaction, or necessary sacrifice. They did not know the feeling of taking a place and keeping it, securing a village and then raising the flag and calling it a victory. No sense of order or momentum. No front, no rear, no trenches laid out in neat parallels. No Patton rushing for the Rhine, no beachheads to storm and win and hold for the duration. They did not have targets. They did not have a cause. . . . They did not know good from evil.[117]

Veteran Steve Hassett, in his poem "Christmas," expressed the uncertainty of many who served in Vietnam as to whether they were on the right side of history. Hassett speaks through a letter from a Hessian fighting against the rebels in America, "who will not stand to fight / but each time fade before us / as water into sand." The comparison of American revolutionaries with the Vietcong is troubling as "the women stare with hate" while the men run to prepare ambushes. "There is no glory here," but the troops march to Trenton, to celebrate the New Year.[118] Vietnam was far from "the Good War" on which they had been raised. It is not surprising that veterans felt alienated from both the war and from civilian society, feeling with Kenneth Ruth of the First Air Cavalry that he could not talk about Vietnam with anyone except his fellow vets, because "people can't understand" unless they've been there.[119] The poet Bruce Weigl, a First Air Cavalry veteran, thought those who had fought in Vietnam would have to pass through "a thousand years of grief" before they could return fully to life.[120]

The import of the Vietnam War cannot be easily pinned down, and the debate over its significance persists to this day. From the 1960s into the twenty-first century, critics have blamed the press, the military, the executive branch, bureaucrats, and the general public for America's defeat in Vietnam. Perhaps the best summary, though, came in a postwar conversation between the veteran and scholar Colonel Harry G. Summers Jr. and a North Vietnamese colonel: "You know," Summers boasted, "you never defeated us on the battlefield." His counterpart calmly replied, "That may be so, but it is also irrelevant."[121] The communists had never aimed for battlefield victories. As North Vietnam's military commander, General Vo Nguyen Giap, told Stanley Karnow, "We were not strong enough to drive half a million American troops out of Vietnam, but that wasn't our aim." Their aim was to outlast the Americans, to "break the will of the American government to continue the conflict." Westmoreland's policy of attrition had no bearing on the communists' goals, since "We were waging a people's war," one that relied on wide popular support and mobilization. Americans should have recognized such an approach to warfare, but they put their faith in technology rather than people.[122]

In November 1982, the Vietnam Veterans Memorial, designed by Maya Lin, opened on the National Mall in Washington, D.C. The Wall, as it is generally known, is, in many ways, the exactly correct memorial to the tradition of democratic warfare that started with the Revolution, as it lists the names of the more than 58,000 Americans who died in the Vietnam War. The names of the military personnel are listed in chronological order, starting in 1959 and running through 1975. It is difficult to do justice to the profound impact the Wall has on those who visit it, especially for the families and friends of those engraved. But it is a testament for all Americans of the cost of war.

# 10

# Iraq and Afghanistan

The Vietnam War weakened the U.S. military and left a distaste for foreign military adventures, a feeling generally known as the Vietnam syndrome. For political reasons, Richard Nixon had ended the draft, launching the experiment of an all-volunteer army. At first, most military professionals deeply regretted this transition, which meant that more of their budgets had to go to salaries to lure volunteers, who were often not as well educated as had been the case during the Vietnam-era draft. In 1980, the army chief of staff, General Edward C. Meyer, told Congress that he led a "hollow" force, one denuded of experience, equipment, and morale by the Vietnam War.[1]

Through the 1980s, the government poured money into rebuilding the military, but it was becoming clear that the American public had no interest in protracted wars of any kind. In 1983, President Ronald Reagan sent marines into Beirut in an effort to restore order in Lebanon. When more than two hundred marines were killed by a truck bomb that October, he immediately withdrew American forces. Within a matter of days, though, Reagan rushed to display American strength with Operation Urgent Fury, the invasion of the island of Grenada. This odd little military adventure was in response to the overthrow of the island's Marxist government by other Marxists and ended very successfully for the United States, with medals for all involved. While the American public would support a brief military operation against a small Caribbean island, Reagan's efforts to persuade the country to commit itself to battling communist aggression in Central America fell on deaf ears, as the public voiced a lack of interest in "another Vietnam." Reagan's inability to arouse public enthusiasm for military operations in Nicaragua led to the complicated and bizarre conspiracy known as the Iran-Contra Affair, which further undermined public confidence in the government's foreign policy.[2] At the same time, the massive infusion of funds to the military led not just to the modernization of weaponry, but also to a rapid improvement in the quality of its volunteers. By 1990 the United States could lay claim to the premier professional military force in the world.[3]

Colin Powell, chairman of the Joint Chiefs of Staff in 1990 and a Vietnam veteran, made the most significant attempt to extract intelligent lessons from the Vietnam War with his framework for future American military operations, labeled "the Powell Doctrine."[4] Powell advised that the United States should not commit military forces without public support, clear goals consonant with national security interests, and only after peaceful approaches to a solution had been exhausted. Once force is decided upon, the government should have precise and attainable objectives, international support, and an exit strategy. The United States should go in, do the job, and get out; no more Vietnams. The Powell Doctrine was applied with striking efficiency in the first Gulf War, and completely ignored in the second.[5]

The first Persian Gulf War had a clear objective: the liberation of Kuwait following its invasion by Iraqi troops in August 1990. President George H.W. Bush put together an international coalition, backed by the United Nations and led by the United States, to attain this goal. The coalition forces moved methodically, not beginning their military response until January 17, 1991. After forty days of air strikes, coalition forces under the command of General Norman Schwarzkopf launched the ground attack from Saudi Arabia on February 23. The Iraqi army was largely destroyed within four days, with President Bush calling an end to ground operations after one hundred hours, on February 28. The Persian Gulf War clearly demonstrated that airpower cannot conquer a country, but it sure can do a number on massed forces retreating in terror. On the "Highway of Death," thousands of Iraqi forces fleeing Kuwait were killed by coalition planes bombing and strafing anything that moved. Though Saddam Hussein remained in power in Iraq at war's end, the United States had achieved its goal in an efficient and impressive campaign, watched worldwide on television.[6]

America's political leadership and general public had also apparently learned something from Vietnam. Congress carefully monitored the buildup to war, openly debated the use of military power, and granted President Bush the necessary war powers in a close vote. The public also debated the war with vigor. A great number of Americans questioned what appeared to them an amorphous justification for the war and wondered if Bush aimed to liberate Kuwait more for its oil than for some abstraction of national sovereignty. The president's use of Vietnam-era tropes like "appeasement" and the equation of Hussein with Hitler did not satisfy many Americans who feared "mission creep," the possibility of Iraq becoming another quagmire like Vietnam. For many critics, that aspect of the Powell Doctrine which called for a clear explanation of how national interests were best served by military action had fallen flat. President Bush appeared to have understood that the American public would not support an extended military effort in the absence of a clearer sense of purpose. That awareness may explain his enthusiastic proclamation that the Vietnam syndrome had been overcome in the Gulf War, and his cautious insistence that the

United States had no intention of overthrowing Saddam Hussein because of the lessons of the Vietnam War.[7]

Through the 1990s the American military establishment appeared to be contracting, with a more limited global mission and significant structural changes. As the United States closed military bases at home and around the world, peacekeeping operations, rather than wars, became the Pentagon's primary focus. Some of these peacekeeping missions ended disastrously, as was the case with the United Nations' mandated operation in Somalia in 1992–93. In contrast, NATO's 1996 and 1999 interventions in the Bosnian and Kosovo wars, which included U.S. forces, successfully ended those conflicts, though leaving a backwash of controversy in their wake. As the government shifted its emphasis toward technology, with the expectation that the United States did not need a large standing army in a world without a competing superpower, many commentators expected the role of the military in American life to diminish in the early twenty-first century. But the terrorist attack on September 11, 2001, dramatically altered perceptions and practices.[8]

Even though President Bush's son, President George W. Bush, appointed Colin Powell his secretary of state, he completely ignored the Powell Doctrine in launching his "war on terror." Further, the second Bush administration lied to the American people about the causes and conduct of war, which undermined public confidence and support. The attack on Al-Qaeda, which bore direct responsibility for the September 11 attacks on the World Trade Center and the Pentagon, and their Taliban supporters in Afghanistan, appeared justified to the world at large. However, the Bush administration desperately wanted to launch a war against Iraq, which had nothing to do with the September 11 attacks, and resorted to an intricate web of fabrications to justify America's first preemptive war.

America's current wars raise an array of issues, not all of which can be addressed in this chapter, that have been the subject of numerous books. One of these wars, in Afghanistan, began in deep tragedy and trauma on September 11, 2001;[9] the other, in Iraq, was borne of egregious lies.[10] In May 2003, President Bush claimed, "We found the weapons of mass destruction. We found biological laboratories."[11] No such laboratories had been, in fact, found. Secretary of Defense Donald Rumsfeld insisted of the weapons of mass destruction (WMD), "We know where they are," though he apparently failed to tell his troops.[12] Vice President Dick Cheney would continue to make that claim for several years, until he began denying that he ever made it.[13] Meanwhile, questions of torture that challenged the very standards of military conduct the United States had established at Nuremberg divided the public, as the nation's highest officials sought to rationalize the need for "enhanced interrogation" techniques.[14] The treatment of prisoners at Abu Ghraib and Guantánamo undermined America's international image, while the lack of planning for post-war Iraq damaged the U.S. military's reputation for efficiency.[15]

It also quickly became evident that, despite forests of yellow ribbons on trees and the backs of SUVs, the United States was not fulfilling its commitment to aid returning troops, as scandals swept through the Veterans Administration and examples of the mistreatment of veterans mounted.[16] As the Pentagon sent its troops on multiple tours of duty, some of the nation's major banks violated federal law by foreclosing on the homes of active-duty soldiers, the suicide rate among veterans rose to historically high levels, and the government passed on billions of dollars to private contractors, patriotism appears to have been rede-fined to mean the sacrifice by the very few for the benefit of the rich and powerful.[17]

## Technology, Ideology, and Modern Wars

The U.S.-led overthrow of Afghanistan's Taliban government was a military masterpiece. The first CIA operatives landed in the country on September 26, 2001; Kabul fell to U.S. and Afghan forces on November 13. Unfortunately, the Bush administration almost immediately turned its attention to Iraq, di-verting resources away from its victorious campaign to one that would bog down American military capacity for the next eight years. With Osama Bin Laden cornered in the Tora Bora Mountains on the Pakistan border in early December, the CIA requested an additional battalion of Army Rangers to block the terrorist leader's escape. But the administration insisted that Afghan forces handle the operation; it is almost certain that some of these Afghans aided Bin Laden's escape into Pakistan, where he found a home until his death in 2011.[18] Throughout these operations, Secretary of Defense Donald Rumsfeld clearly exerted greater influence than did the former chairman of the Joint Chiefs of Staff, Colin Powell, and adamantly insisted on a "light footprint" in Afghanistan in order to concentrate on what he perceived as the greater threat in Iraq.[19] General Tommy Franks clarified the lightness of that footprint with just ten thousand total American service personnel.[20]

The Bush administration attempted to fight the wars in Afghanistan and Iraq according to a new set of rules, with the emphasis on few troops and the privatization of tasks traditionally assigned to the military. As Seth Jones has observed, "In terms of historical troop levels, the Afghan mission ranks with some of the international community's most notable failures." When World War II ended, Jones writes, the United States committed 89.3 troops for every one thousand inhabitants of its sector of Germany. Under Bill Clinton, the United States had 35.3 military personnel per thousand inhabitants in East Slavonia, 17.5 in Bosnia, and 19.3 in Kosovo. In Iraq, which most military experts except Donald Rumsfeld thought had too few boots on the ground, the United States committed just 6.1 military personnel per thousand inhabitants in 2003—in Afghanistan the ratio was a bare 0.5 per thousand. Nor did the Bush administration send any civilian police to Afghanistan, as had been done in Bosnia and Kosovo, "where international paramilitary police had been used effectively to help establish law and order."[21] The cornerstone of any counterinsurgency effort is establishing social order, a goal of little interest to the U.S. government until late 2005. The low priority given to public safety is evident in the administration's reliance on DynCorps and other private corporations for police training programs. Turning to contractors may have been in keeping with the administration's ideologically driven privatization of the war effort, but that approach backfired terribly as these companies proved corrupt and alienated the Afghans and Iraqis—earning condemnation from Ambassador Ronald Neumann and Deputy Secretary of State Richard Armitage.

Initially, the United States made little effort to rebuild Afghanistan and Iraq. In April 2002, Bush promised Afghanistan the equivalent of the Marshall Plan, which had done so much to help rebuild Europe after World War II.[22] Yet that promise turned out to be just so much rhetoric. Incredibly, the Bush administration's 2003 budget proposal did not contain a single dollar for humanitarian or reconstruction aid for Afghanistan, nor did the administration order an evaluation of the amount of money needed to effect such a Marshall Plan. Congress appropriated $300 million on its own, less than one-tenth of one percent of the $396 billion appropriated to the military and far short of the billions of dollars the United Nations declared necessary to rebuild the country.[23] Meanwhile, the United States was pouring billions of dollars into Iraq, much of which was never accounted for. Afghan Minister of the Interior Ali Jalali unsuccessfully pleaded with Condoleezza Rice to follow the model of policing pursued in the Balkans in the late 1990s. By summer 2008, not only were the streets of Baghdad still unsafe, but the city's inhabitants received less water and electricity than they had under Saddam, and the United States had still not repaired the sewage treatment plants destroyed in 2003. It is little wonder that many soldiers serving in Iraq and Afghanistan concluded that their government was determined to lose the counterinsurgency after winning the war.[24]

As in the cold wars, Americans brought their cultural biases and expectations to these Mideast conflicts, and once more made little effort to understand the local populations. Just as Ho Chi Minh had said that the Vietnamese people would fight for a century to win their independence and unity, so the insurgents in Iraq and the Taliban in Afghanistan thought in longer terms than Americans, who expected quick victories. The civilian and military advisors to four presidents assumed that the primitive people of Vietnam could not hope to stand up to the technological superiority and sophisticated intelligence of the United States. In the same way, President Bush's aides confidently predicted their wars would be a "cakewalk," exercises in "shock and awe."[25] Once more, the allure of impressive air superiority deceived otherwise intelligent people, and once more, reality demonstrated the limitations of any strategy that did not include boots on the ground.[26] The Afghans have a saying: "You Americans may have all the watches, but we Afghans have all the time."[27]

The current wars began as a response to an attack on American civilians, and yet the government made little effort to meaningfully engage that population in the war effort. The president called upon the American people to shop while the wars raged, passing all the sacrifices on to those who served. These twenty-first-century wars embrace retribution, global reach, and nation building, and nearly every aspect of these conflicts, from causes to consequences, remains contested.

Those engaged in the wars in Iraq and Afghanistan have been given several reasons why they fight, from protecting their homes from nuclear attack to overthrowing an evil dictator; most end up deciding to just do their duty. They find themselves in the midst of complex and disturbing conflicts, in which an abandoned car by the side of the road or a woman in a burqa might suddenly explode. While many of the problems of Vietnam have been corrected—racism, drug use, and a lack of unit cohesion have all been reduced—and few American soldiers speak out against the war while serving overseas, the fundamental question of why they are engaged in combat operations remains.

The wars in Iraq and Afghanistan are unique not because of either public indifference or opposition, but for the reach of technology into the everyday experience of those serving. A century ago, Robert Graves wrote of the perplexing and somehow inappropriate ease with which a soldier could leave the trenches on the western front and be in the midst of Piccadilly Circus within a few hours. Today I can speak via Skype with one of my students serving in Afghanistan while typing these words. Cell phones, Facebook, and blogs all bring the frontline soldier into immediate contact with friends and family on the opposite side of the world. The word most often used by older veterans in discussing these instantaneous forms of communication is "surreal." But to the young men and women currently serving, such developments appear routine.

If Vietnam was the first television war, then Iraq and Afghanistan are the first internet wars. Soldiers keep in touch with family and friends through cell phones and email, while some bold military personnel have launched blogs chronicling daily life in a war zone. Colby Buzzell, a member of the Stryker Brigade, appears to have put up the first war-zone blog. According to Buzzell, he had never heard of blogs at the time of his deployment to Iraq in November 2003. The following June he read a *Time* magazine article on the subject and thought it sounded like a good idea. Thus was born *CBFTW*, an initially anonymous blog whose handle secretly stood for "Colby Buzzell Fuck the War."

Writing his blog became almost a necessity for keeping his sanity, as Buzzell told the stories of his daily experiences in rapid-fire postings: "There were times when I couldn't type fast enough."[28] It took only a few weeks for news of his blog to spread; the number of hits reached into the thousands, and his postings were praised as more informative than much that was published in the American newspapers.

Buzzell's blog remained anonymous, even to his wife, until August 4, 2004, when insurgents ambushed his platoon in Mosul:

> I observed a man, dressed all in black with a terrorist beard, jump out all of a sudden from the side of a building. He pointed his AK-47 right at my fucking pupils, I froze and then a split second later, I saw the fire from his muzzle flash leaving the end of his barrel and brass shell casings exiting the side of his AK as he was shooting directly at me. I heard and felt the bullets whiz literally inches from my head.

Buzzell's graphic description led officers to determine that he was behind the blog and they ordered him confined to base. At first they just monitored his blog, but when Buzzell posted a personal message from Jello Biafra, singer for the Dead Kennedys, opposing the war in Iraq, the military ordered the blog taken down. Buzzell left Iraq shortly thereafter and gathered his blog entries into the book *My War*, a practice that would be followed by several other talented military bloggers. Buzzell stayed in the military, but was not sent back to Iraq because of his PTSD, which he feels also cost him his marriage. He now writes regularly for *Esquire* magazine and remains opposed to the continuing war.

The navy welcomed these blogs, feeling that they helped to build morale by maintaining positive connections with home.[29] The air force and army felt very differently. In spring 2007, the army attempted to control internet communication by requiring that soldiers "consult with their immediate supervisor . . . prior to publishing or posting information in a public forum." Indeed, blogs like Matt Gallagher's present intimate portraits of military service as it is happening, offering the public a perspective on war never before available. Observing his platoon joking and talking over dinner, Gallagher thought of their relationship to the society they served:

> I couldn't help but think about the country that had produced them. These were the men in the flesh that society only celebrates in the abstract. The NCOs had served in the army long enough to stop caring about the whims of the American culture they protected so effectively; the Joes were

just removed enough to not fully recognize how the same society that reared us had detached itself from us the day we signed our enlistment papers. In a volunteer military, we fought for the nation, not with it.[30]

It is inherent in the very notion of warfare that those on the front line will believe they have a firmer grasp of reality, while those in the rear think they are smarter. Lieutenant Gallagher knew several intelligent and competent field-grade officers, but he thought the other kind were "everywhere in Iraq, intent on riding the bureaucratic beast in all its protectionist glory." Gallagher had been trained "to respect the rank, if not the person," but unlike in any other professional organization, "the army mandated that I carry out these men's orders successfully and without complaint, even when they directly assaulted all known logic and experience." He certainly did so, and kept his doubts to himself, but he often questioned the intelligence and sanity of these officers: "Major Moe wasn't so much a person as he was a trend. . . . If a field grade officer didn't grasp the nuances of counter-insurgency doctrine, didn't subscribe to the application of decentralized warfare, believed that all of the war's issues could be quantified into a PowerPoint presentation, . . . and consistently displayed a clueless obtuseness about day-to-day operations, he qualified as a Major Moe." This type of officer made life consistently more difficult and dangerous for those he commanded "by focusing on irrelevant regulations and out-of-date procedures."[31]

Despite all the changes introduced by modern technology, some aspects of war remain unchanged. For instance, Gallagher highlighted the persistence of "Dear John" messages. Whether via email, a MySpace posting, or "in a care package in the form of divorce papers, tucked carefully between a jumbo can of Slim Jim beef snacks and ten logs of smokeless tobacco," rejection takes on a timeless character. As Gallagher notes, "Dear Johns were as old as war itself. . . . Some were filled with excuses, others with guilt, but all conveyed the message plain as day that their sender wasn't willing to wait." The internet, while it facilitates communication, cannot replace the actual physical presence required in maintaining many relationships. Soldiers had already discovered "that when we departed the civilized world to fight a war no one cared about, let alone understood, emotional vacuums ripped open" and crushed the strongest soldier. Being dumped often cut off connections with home, producing a sense of loneliness and isolation that could not be publicly expressed: "Not that anyone cared. After all, these things happened. It was the military. It was war. It was life."

In Afghanistan and Iraq, the routine became subject for insightful internet traffic, and the exceptional became routine: "A burst of automatic weapons fire rippled through the night in the distance, toward the northeast, somewhere in the Sunni sector." The soldiers in their base turned their attention in that direction, but no other shots were fired. "Private Van Wilder called across the update on the radio, boredom saturating every word of the report. This was Iraq. Gunfire happened at night. Gunfire happened every night."[32] Gallagher offers a narrative of a typical Iraq patrol. While protecting a road crew repairing a main highway one night, Gallagher receives a radio call from Staff Sergeant Boondock (Gallagher uses nicknames throughout):

> "We got some real shady mother fuckers low-crawling onto the road, coming down the canal. It looks like two . . . yeah, two personnel."
>
> I had been lying down in the back of my vehicle, reading T. E. Lawrence's war memoir. I bolted straight up when I heard Staff Sergeant Boondock's report. . . .
>
> "Keep watching them," I said, stating the obvious while I sorted through my conflicting thoughts. . . . A few units in the brigade had been shot at, ourselves included, but no one had shot back yet. There was a reason for that. After all the briefings and lectures about previous units' war crimes, cover-ups, scandals, and prison sentences, everyone was trigger shy.
>
> . . . "Any heat signatures?" I sputtered out.
>
> Five or so seconds passed before Staff Sergeant Boondock responded. "Roger! Roger! My golf [gunner] reports that they have set down a boxlike object 250 meters from our position."
>
> Three simple words hung on my tongue like a swing: Light them up. A quick burst or two of 50-caliber machine gun rounds would suffice. . . . Never had this war been so clear, so pure, so obvious, so clean. Light. Them. Up.
>
> But I didn't give that order. I couldn't. . . . Not yet. . . . Everything was too grey, and we currently lived in a black-and-white world and served in a black-and-white army. It was still just too damn grey.
>
> . . . I told Sergeant Axel, the 3 vehicle's gunner, to beam the targets with a bright naked-eye laser in order to let them know we were watching. Then I told him, "If they start digging, or don't stop whatever it is they're doing, or do anything other than totally freeze, open fire and engage the targets." . . .
>
> I had given the order to kill. Haughty enough to condemn two individuals to The End because they had been dumb enough to be seen in a war of shadows.

Gallagher radioed in a situation report to his captain, who, to his frustration, ordered him not to engage. The two shapes left their box and fled. The box turned out to be a bomb with a pressure plate, designed to penetrate an armored vehicle, and was destroyed by explosive ordnance disposal. A few days later, a different unit picked up a teenager who admitted he had been paid $20 to place that roadside bomb; the kid's partner blew himself up a few months later.[33]

In an insurgency, it becomes far too easy to hate all of the native people as enemies. Abbie Pickett was surprised by her own anger after an attack: "I wanted to go out there and hurt somebody as bad as they'd hurt" her fellow soldiers, but she felt guilty over her desire to commit violence. "It took me a long time to shut off my feelings for the Iraqis, because people are people to me."[34] The insurgents' willingness to attack civilians, schools and hospitals, markets and small businesses complicated the matter. On October 27, 2003, Sunni insurgents hit four Baghdad police stations, the Palestine Hotel, and the International Red Cross, killing at least thirty-five people—most of whom were Iraqi civilians. In 2007, Laura Naylor rushed to the wreckage of a police station that she had helped to establish just three months before. Civilians often hung around the police station, thinking of it as a safe place. "I saw the little girls I knew getting dragged out completely charred and burned and dead," Naylor recalled. "I saw a hand sitting in front of the police station. Just a hand. . . . We would get chai—tea—from there every day—that place was gone. I would watch the kids play—gone. The people who would sleep outside every night to stay cool—all gone."[35]

Modern technology brought the war home in other ways, as well. American journalists were "embedded" in units serving in Iraq and Afghanistan, and National Public Radio also welcomed firsthand commentaries. One of the most famous pieces was recorded by Captain Benjamin Tupper in Sharana, Afghanistan, in 2007. In a calm voice broadcast to millions, Tupper described walking down the village street after a light snow and finding "a mysteriously vibrant pink and red object." It took him a moment to realize that it was "the neck stem of a human spine, blasted 150 meters in the air from the site of a suicide bombing":

A lone suicide bomber had walked up to a group of ANA [Afghan National Army] soldiers who had congregated at a street intersection outside of our base. He detonated his explosive vest, which instantly scattered his mortal remains in a truly random pattern. Ground zero was a large blackened circle where he had stood. The blast instantly evaporated the snow and burned the ground below it. His head flew straight up, landing about twenty meters away on the hood of a white Toyota station wagon. It rolled off onto the ground, leaving a red smudge and streak across the hood.

His heart landed about fifty meters in the opposite direction. It sat there, in perfect condition, as if carefully removed from the chest by a surgeon's delicate cuts. An ANA soldier walked by and kicked it down the road like a small soccer ball, a gesture of disgust at this suicide attack.

Tupper, of the Army National Guard serving in an Embedded Training Team (ETT) in Afghanistan, expanded on his NPR commentaries to become a notable frontline blogger. He recorded the extreme hardships of serving in desert regions, survived only by embracing "the suck." To embrace the suck is to take an almost Zen approach to hardship, using it to strengthen the individual soldier and unit cohesion; Tupper called it a "brotherhood of suffering and misery."[36] Stress puts enormous strain on the human body and shuts down the desire to eat, leading most soldiers to lose significant weight in their first month in the field. The same stress minimizes sleep, which rarely settles into a regular cycle as operations occur around the clock. The extreme heat aggravates all other discomforts. And, as is always the case in combat, any notions of privacy vanish once one is in the field, as all bodily functions must, for safety's sake, occur within sight of one's comrades. Thus the absolute need to embrace the suck, as failure to do so would crush morale and undermine the mission.

There is more to military service in modern wars than combat and garrison duties; there are also "hearts and minds" operations (often known as SASO, stability and support operations) aimed at winning over the local population. Soldiers often take pride in these missions, though, as in Vietnam, they may lose their significance in the smoke of battle. In Iraq and Afghanistan, the U.S. military brought medical clinics to communities that had never known a doctor or nurse, offering the free medical aid for which many Americans long.

There are always cultural differences to be overcome, and those around issues of gender proved to be particularly challenging. Benjamin Tupper, like many of those serving in Afghanistan, became unnerved by this "world without women," describing traveling through Afghanistan yet "only meeting half the people." The other half, the women, are invisible, confined to their homes, and on those rare occasions in public, appearing as "blue ghosts," covered in movable tents called burqas. The consequences are so strange as to defy the understanding of many American soldiers. Take, for instance, the Afghan tradition of *bachabas*, boys who impersonate women to arouse male passions. Tupper recounted leaving an internet café in Kabul and walking behind the cubicle of a prominent local mullah who was watching hard-core porn on his computer.[37] While these *bachabas* appear on Afghan pornography videos, the Afghan men watching indignantly deny any homosexual leanings. It was difficult for many Americans to understand this particular mix of misogyny and homophobia—as one vet said, "If they don't like women, and they don't like men [as sexual partners], what's left?"[38]

But there are also moments of human decency that transcend culture. Tupper describes the efforts of one of his men, Corporal Radoslaw Polanski, to save the life of a wounded Taliban, risking his own life in an effort to staunch the bleeding from a femoral artery: "This guy was looking at me with fear in his eyes, expecting me to finish him off. When he realized I was trying to stop his bleeding, he relaxed and put his hand over his heart"—the Afghan gesture of respect and gratitude. As the man died, Polanski held him in his arms.[39]

Despite the opportunity to learn more from the soldiers' blogs, it appears that the majority of American civilians preferred ignorance. Letters arrived from strangers in the United States wanting to show their support for the troops. Gallagher dismissed them on his website as "empty words from an empty people." Sergeant Joseph O'Keefe wrote of the "care packages" they received from the United States: "you cannot imagine all the stupid stuff people sent. We got ninja turtle swords with sound effects, plastic miniature golf sets, sombreros, and all sorts of whacky stuff."[40] Schoolchildren wrote cheerful messages like, "I'm going to study real hard so I don't have to go to Iraq. Do you wish you had done better at school?"[41]

Popular culture may denigrate soldiers as high school washouts, but the majority of those who serve suffer from economic, rather than educational, handicaps. Put bluntly: America's soldiers tend to be poor. But they are far from stupid. In fact, some would argue that they are a hell of a lot smarter than the Yale and Harvard graduates who sent them off to war. Unlike their political leaders, most common soldiers do not underestimate their enemy. As Tupper wrote, "The Taliban insurgency, despite their dirty clothes and rusted weapons, are a bold, creative, and thriving movement that spends more time studying our habits and tactics than fighting us. The result is that when they hit, they have a high rate of success. My experience was that we rarely found them and they always found us."[42]

Also unlike the wise men who planned these wars, a great many veterans of the Iraq and Afghanistan conflicts understand that "this war will not be won militarily." The only victory the United States can realistically hope for "will come when the Afghan government is capable of providing security and some semblance of prosperity and welfare for the people, not because we have killed all the Taliban."[43] Tupper quickly noticed that his base, with its medical clinic, was not subject to attack, while the Taliban routinely fired upon the U.S. military base just two kilometers away. No wonder: "Even the Taliban's children get sick and need care, and they recognize this."[44] While lacking the drama of military action, medical clinics, schools, and effective police forces are the key to success in countries that have enjoyed little social order. Yet, while the Iraqi and Afghan people want a great deal of what the United States has to offer, from its music to democracy, the "collateral damage" of military operations alienates them more effectively than any insurgent propaganda.

For Tupper and other soldiers, blogging became a form of therapy, an attempt to both process and escape their harsh reality: "Knowing that real people, friends and strangers alike, are out there in a safe part of the world, sharing in these experiences, provides me with a sense of calm and release that is profound. It's like a small part of me is temporarily evacuated to your safe and calm corner of the world."[45] From time to time, the military high command experimented with cutting off these uncontrolled blogs, but ultimately they realized that it was not worth the effort, especially as several commanders came to perceive their therapeutic aspects.

Military blogs also give people back home a chance to express their concern and support. It is very rare to find anything but positive comments on these blogs; opposition to the war is a world apart from criticizing the men and women who are working for their country. For those interested, it is easy to recognize the common humanity of these military bloggers. These are our young men and women, doing the best they can on our behalf, even if their government has placed them in harm's way for flawed reasons. As in Vietnam, so many soldiers come to the point of asking, "Why are we still here?" Unlike in Vietnam, most soldiers know that they have the support of the broad American public—though they have come to question the support they receive after they have returned home.

## Instant Replays of War

Technology has had wide impact beyond its use for instant communication. For instance, many more of those injured in combat survive their wounds than at any time in the past. Body armor and superior medical care save thousands of lives that would have been lost in any previous war, but there is nothing that can be done to replace a limb blown off by a roadside bomb. As a result, a higher percentage of severely wounded soldiers return from these wars, veterans who will require medical aid for the remainder of their lives. Others, as in previous wars, suffer psychological damage, often aggravated by their ability to see the war replayed over and over. Digital photography allows anyone—journalists, soldiers, insurgents, civilians—to capture the world of war. It is possible to view the same moment repeatedly, and if it is unavailable on the computer screen, it may be reviewed in one's mind.

Arriving in Iraq could be incredibly disorienting. The sand was extremely fine and got everywhere, like sandpaper on the skin; the sky was almost always blue; and everything else was the same tan color, except for women's black burqas. Stress marked almost every minute off base as potential dangers lay at every turn. On Tyler Boudreau's first day in Iraq, a truck came speeding the wrong way down the highway toward his military vehicle, and his mind raced as he tried to decide whether to shoot or not: "There was no one to ask. There was no manual to reference. There was no time to think it over." The marines readied their weapons but held their fire. "The truck floated quietly past us without exploding into a million bits of fragmentation in our faces. We stared, agog, at the passengers, a family of four or maybe five crammed into the cab staring back at us, all agog as well." As the marines quickly learned, everyone drove on the wrong side of the road, and often on sidewalks, where they existed. "To shoot or not to shoot. . . . That was always the question in Iraq." In Iraq and Afghanistan, war is round-the-clock and 360 degrees, and that is the norm. There were no set front lines; each soldier became the front line: "Every approaching car was like the war on wheels. Every time we fired on them was like an invasion. The entire war was fought from beginning to end every day, again and again."[46]

Yet for many soldiers, the return to the United States marked the beginning of their descent. Boudreau, like most soldiers, was delighted to return home at the end of his tour in Iraq, but, like many others, he was completely unprepared for the transition: "Our bodies had been delivered from war, but our minds lingered on the battlefield. The intensity, the quick-release of our adrenaline, was hidden behind dull eyes and broad smiles. . . . The civilians were the same as they always were, but the Marines they hugged and kissed were not the men they had once known. The consciousness of every man in that unit had been reconfigured. Our identities were altered." The marines had learned a new form of normal in Iraq: "Normal is war, and war ain't hell. War is the foyer to hell."[47]

Like many soldiers home from the front, Boudreau felt that something was wrong, that he was not adjusting well. When he told the doctor of his horrendous nightmares, the doctor responded as did far too many VA (Veterans Affairs) doctors to hundreds of veterans: "That's normal. It'll pass." Rather than labeling it PTSD and offering treatment, the military's doctors prescribed acceptance: "When I told him I was just about jumping out of my skin every time I heard a loud noise, he said that was normal, too. . . . It's what they expected from me. They figured I was in good working order."[48] As it would turn out, the Pentagon had issued orders to avoid a diagnosis of PTSD, to assure veterans and active service personnel that there was nothing wrong with them, to ignore the problem and hope it would go away. But it would not go away. Three years after leaving Iraq, Boudreau wrote, "my heart was still pounding, I was still raging, and I still wasn't sleeping. The Marine Corps made a schizophrenic out of me."[49]

Most people associate PTSD with returned veterans, but the first indicators can appear while still in the field. The foreignness of the opponent and the uncertainty of warfare aggravates the situation. Benjamin Tupper first experienced PTSD one night while serving in Afghanistan. "Even during periods of relative peace and quiet," he recorded, "the war finds ways to creep into your personal space and violate your growing false sense of security." One night, while taking a Gatorade from the refrigerator, Tupper heard the voices of a unit in the midst of a firefight over the radio:

> The urgency, the terror, the frantic tones of their voices had a paralyzing effect on me. The bottle of Gatorade became heavy, and it fell from my hands onto the floor. I immediately had a sense of being alone, vulnerable, helpless.
>
> Flashbacks to moments when I've found myself outflanked, outmaneuvered, outnumbered and under fire. The hot summer night instantly felt cold, and I literally shook. As difficult as it was to stay and listen to desperate calls and orders on the radio, especially alone, I couldn't move. I had become part of their world.

Tupper is certain that his experience of PTSD is fairly typical: "I went to war a married man of fifteen years, and a father of four. My wife and I had just purchased our dream house, which I referred to as our 'forever house.' I came home from the war and never once slept in this house." He frightened his children, alienated his wife, got divorced, drank too much, "fought a myriad of personal demons," and found it difficult to fit back into "normal" civilian life.[50]

The Pentagon did not want to acknowledge or treat these deep, invisible wounds. The very name, post-traumatic stress disorder, removes the condition from the battlefield, transforming this combat-related injury into a disorder. Those with PTSD were made to feel as though they had brought these problems upon themselves. Tyler Boudreau points out that "never once has a veteran been awarded the Purple Heart for combat stress. . . . Perhaps that small token of recognition might have prevented a few of them from taking their own lives."[51]

At times it even seemed that the government perceived their soldiers as entirely expendable. The Defense Department's policy of repeated tours of duty has had a terrible effect on its troops, many of whom are serving despite a sort of psychological protest, taking various antidepressants to keep them on the line. Even suicide threats have often been ignored, resulting in violence to soldiers and others. Sergeant Eli PaintedCrow, who entered the army in 1981, bluntly summarized Iraq and Afghanistan: "This war is full of crazy people."[52]

## Women in the Military

Women have long served in the American military, but in the twenty-first century the nature and extent of their service shifted dramatically. There have been many struggles for equality in the military in recent decades, to force a culture of machismo to accept everyone who is willing to put his or her life on the line for the country. There are those who argue that any nation that accepts women into the military is risking its very survival, as its military culture will surely collapse as a consequence.[53] While the United States has not yet fallen to foreign aggressors as a result of welcoming women into military service, the number of rapes reported within the military would seemingly support those who argue that military discipline collapses as a consequence of integration. Such an argument not only blames the victim for the outrage, but also allows criminals to set policy.

Of course, similar arguments were made back in the 1940s, when calls for the integration of African Americans into the military met caustic resistance. A key counterargument also applies to both situations: refusing to integrate the military denies major opportunities, first to blacks and now to women. It is important to remember that the U.S. military has long doubled as an avenue for social mobility. Those who question the utility of allowing women to serve their country would be well advised to watch the superb documentary *Lioness* or read Helen Benedict's excellent *The Lonely Soldier* or Kayla Williams's powerful and witty *Love My Rifle More Than You*.[54]

Yet Congress has repeatedly acted to prevent women from serving in combat. As D'Ann Campbell wrote in 1993, "The restrictions against women in combat that persisted for decades in the United States were not based on experimental research or from a consideration of the effectiveness of women in combat in other armies. The restrictions were primarily political decisions made in response to the public opinion of the day, and the climate of opinion in Congress."[55] However, it hardly matters what Congress orders, as the nature of modern warfare tends to obscure the battle front. Women cannot officially serve in combat, but they do provide combat support, which often amounts to the same thing since one may now come under attack at any time and place. Women first served in great numbers, with 41,000 deployed, in the first Gulf War, and saw action in Haiti, Bosnia, Kosovo, and Somalia. By the turn of the twenty-first century, women made up 14 percent of active-duty forces and 17 percent of the National Guard and reserves.

Women have paid the price for their service: fifteen women soldiers were killed in the first Gulf War and dozens wounded. In April 2004, twenty-year-old Michelle Witmer of New Berlin, Wisconsin, became the first woman in the National Guard ever to be killed in combat, during a firefight on the streets of

Baghdad, and was awarded a Bronze Star.[56] More than two hundred thousand American women have served in the Iraq and Afghanistan campaigns, some six hundred of whom have been wounded and more than one hundred killed.

MP Jennifer Spranger was among the first troops to enter Iraq in March 2003. She had heard the same lies as the general public, being told the Americans would be greeted as liberators. But she found little more than open hostility; even the children acted with hatred, banging on her vehicle, pretending to shoot her with their hands, trying to grab the soldiers' weapons: "There were no smiles and waves, it was nothing like they told us it would be," she recalled. But then "we went in right after the air war. If it was me, I don't think I'd be greeting us too happily either."[57]

Echoing the sentiments of many Vietnam vets, Spranger saw herself fighting a highly politicized war for false reasons against an elusive enemy. Sergeant Miriam Barton of Oregon also arrived with the first troops in Iraq that March of 2003. She was uncertain of what she would encounter, especially as the president was warning everyone that Saddam had and would use weapons of mass destruction: "We didn't know if we were going to get hit with chemical weapons or WMDs. For all we knew we were going to get hit with a frigging nuke at any moment, because all we'd heard were these stories about how Saddam would sacrifice his own people to kill us." What she found was a very different kind of war: "We would go into Saddam's bases and the Republican Guard would be running out the back. There would be food still cooking and uniforms everywhere, because they'd be stripping their clothes off as they ran and just melting into the population. That's what makes this war so hard; you never know who's the enemy. Everybody's the enemy. And they all want to kill you."[58]

The American military is based on a system of camaraderie, a conviction that one's fellow soldiers have one's back; yet women are often terribly isolated, and subject to male suspicion, confusion, and hostility. Male soldiers are constantly surrounded by other men, reinforcing their masculine identity; women have often needed to behave much the same if they wanted to find acceptance. On many occasions, women gave and received the care that any soldier expects from a comrade. In the midst of a mortar attack on an army base in Baquba, medic Abbie Pickett rushed to help the wounded: "Blood was all over the place. This female was lying on the ground covered in it and a guy called Sergeant Hill was helping her. I said, 'Is this blood all hers, is it an artery hit?' and he said, 'No, I think some of it's mine. I got hit too, but she's worse.'" Pickett persuaded Hill to allow her to help him, possibly saving his life.[59]

But many male soldiers are not certain whether to adhere to traditional protective attitudes or to treat the woman soldier as just one of the guys. A few men become predators, making life hell for a woman trying to serve her country. In Iraq, Chantelle Henneberry of the 172nd Stryker Brigade found herself in a company of fifteen hundred men and eighteen women: "I was fresh meat to hungry men. The mortar rounds that came in daily did less damage to me than the men with whom I shared my food."[60]

This open hostility is indicated by the disturbing number of rape cases among military personnel in recent years, some of which led to the murder of the victim. In July 2005, the body of Private LaVena Johnson was found at her Iraq base. She had been raped, terribly beaten, and shot in the head. The army labeled her death a suicide.[61] In 2007, Marine Corporal Maria Lauterbach, who was pregnant, charged Corporal Cesar Laurean with raping her. Shortly thereafter her burned body was discovered in a fire pit in Laurean's backyard.[62] At least fifteen women soldiers have died under mysterious circumstances during the Iraq War, leading retired Colonel Ann Wright and Congressman Ike Skelton to demand full investigations.[63] Surveys of female veterans find between one-third and two-thirds reporting sexual assault during their time of service, and 90 percent reporting sexual harassment.[64] In Iraq, many officers ordered their women soldiers not to walk alone at night—on their own bases. Staff Sergeant Liz O'Herrin of the Wisconsin Air National Guard received such instructions in 2006: "They tell us (after we hit the deck from an incoming mortar shell) that we shouldn't walk alone at night on base. . . . How am I supposed to track down another female to go eat when I want to? Shower when I want? Females aren't exactly crawling around this joint. Screw you, you deploy me here and tell me it's not safe for me to walk alone to get a bite to eat because I'll probably get raped by one of our own?"[65]

When their superiors would not respond to charges of sexual harassment, some women soldiers decided to deal with the problem themselves. Sergeant Miriam Barton and two buddies "duct-taped one guy to his rack [bed]. Another guy we tied up with dental floss when he was passed out, called everybody around, and then fired a shot and yelled 'Attack!' Public humiliation is a great way of getting your point across." But as Barton's experience demonstrates, it is important to have other women present for backup and support. As Helen Benedict wrote, women soldiers are "less vulnerable to sexist discrimination" when in the company of other female personnel.[66]

The Department of Defense's policy of issuing "moral waivers" to allow those with criminal records to enlist has aggravated the misogynist climate in many units. From 2004 through 2007, the military accepted 125,000 recruits with criminal records, including many who had committed violent crimes.[67] One of the latter was Steven Green, who enlisted despite convictions for assault and a history of mental instability. Green was identified as the "ringleader" of four soldiers who raped and killed a fourteen-year-old Iraqi girl in 2006 and killed the rest of her family, setting fire to their home in an effort to cover up their crime.[68]

Despite opposition, many military personnel support the full integration of women into the military. On June 4, 2011, twenty-year-old Specialist Devin Snyder became the 139th female American soldier to die in the current wars, as the result of a roadside bomb. Those serving with Snyder did not think about how her death in combat violated the law—what they saw was the loss of a colleague, another American, in combat. "Out here, there is no male gender and no female gender," said Staff Sergeant Vincent Vetterkind. "Our gender is soldier."[69]

Few individuals better reflect the dramatic change in the role of women in the U.S. military than Nora Tyson. After joining the navy in 1979, Tyson rose slowly through the ranks until 1993, when Congress voted to allow women to serve on naval combat missions. Shortly thereafter, she became the navigator of the carrier *Enterprise*, eventually becoming commander of an assault vessel. With 44,000 women (13.5 percent of its service personnel), the U.S. Navy has changed considerably since Tyson enlisted. In 2011, Rear Admiral Nora Tyson was awarded command of a strike group, which she commands from the aircraft carrier *George H.W. Bush*, one of the largest warships in the world. "I hope I'm the first of many," Tyson states, as will doubtless be the case.[70]

## Gays in the Military

In 1993, the presence of gays in the military became a hot political issue. The new president, Bill Clinton, had promised to overturn the long-standing policy forbidding homosexuals from serving in the military. Even members of his own party, led by Georgia's Senator Sam Nunn, opposed him, while former Senator Barry Goldwater spoke for a number of libertarian conservatives who felt that the ban should be ended. In the ensuing debates, which saw opponents predicting an army of sodomists and the probable end of western civilization, President Clinton proposed a compromise which became law as part of the National Defense Authorization Act in December 1993. Popularly known as "Don't Ask, Don't Tell" (DADT), the new policy forbade the harassment of homosexual service personnel, while also barring the latter from publicly revealing their sexual orientation while serving. This seemingly contradictory policy was based on the logic that the presence of homosexuals "would create an unacceptable risk to the armed forces' high standards of morale, good order and discipline, and unit cohesion that are the essence of military capability."[71] Over the next eighteen years, DADT would lead to the discharge of more than thirteen thousand military personnel.

There have certainly been homosexuals in the military in the past, but now their presence became highly politicized.[72] Many gay service personnel feel that DADT actually made it more difficult for them to serve by drawing greater attention to their presence and making people more anxious about their status. Nonetheless, it is definitely the case that homosexuals had been subject to harassment and sexual blackmail prior to DADT, with many veterans reporting that lesbians were targeted more often than were gay men. Raymond "Houston" Bridges is one of those gay men who served his country—reluctantly—during the period when the military code called for the dishonorable discharge of homosexuals regardless of any other aspect of their service record. As the U.S. Navy defined the issue, homosexual conduct is "one of the very bad things in life. . . . Homosexuality is wrong, it is evil, and it is to be branded as such."[73]

Bridges was in college in Texas when he was drafted in 1968. After trying to evade the draft, he was "dragged kicking and screaming into the Army." Given his homosexuality, however, Bridges was certain that the army would never take him:

I went to the induction center with a letter from my psychiatrist detailing my emerging sexual identification issues. The Army had their psychiatrist interview me and I'm not sure if he didn't believe me or didn't care, but I was certified as being okay for service, and I was immediately sent to basic training. I was so sure that I would be rejected that I left my dog in my apartment thinking I would be back home immediately. . . . I protested, saying I was homosexual and they didn't accept homosexuals. He told me that they didn't care, but that it was still against military law to do anything homosexual, and now that they knew I was inclined in that direction, they'd watch me closely, and I'd end up doing hard time at Leavenworth if I did anything queer while in the Army.

. . . I was terrified, at first. I wasn't out of the closet enough not to fear the consequences, especially now that they knew I was Gay. Truth is, it was never an issue over the next two years.

. . . The psychiatrist who did my assessment prior to my induction said that he thought all of my issues were the result of my status with the draft, and that if I were in the Army, I wouldn't have to worry about the draft anymore. You know what? He was right. I had a great time. It was like living in a college dorm, only with better drugs. I had no problems and lived a fairly carefree existence. The other guys in the unit figured out I was Gay fairly quickly and a lot of them shunned me, but for the most part, it was a nonissue.

. . . I cannot recall an instance where I was personally harassed. . . . Lesbians, on the other hand, were the target of all sorts of sexual harassment. I had a good friend who had senior NCOs constantly trying to corner her into having sex with them with the threat of outing her if she refused. . . . Men always get the headlines, but there are proportionately more Lesbians serving in the armed services than Gay men.

Charlie Morgan is currently deployed in the Middle East, serving as a brigade equal opportunity advisor and deployed sexual assault response and prevention coordinator. Morgan left the military in 1992 to teach at a rural Kentucky high school. She met Karen Morgan in 1997, and they traveled to Vermont in December 2000 to enter into a civil union. In 2007, they had a child, Casey Elena:

> After 9–11, I felt the need to serve again. . . . I contacted a local recruiter and explained my prior service and would like to reenlist. . . . The following Monday, I arrived at the MEP [Mission Entrance Processing] station in Louisville. I was sworn in at 1600 that afternoon. . . .
>
> Karen and I discussed my service at length and understood the challenges of being in the closet while in drill status. . . . As a high school teacher, however, I was out. My students and faculty knew about my wonderful family. They showed nothing but acceptance; and this is rural Kentucky!
>
> In 2007, I was accepted into Warrant Officer Candidate School. While in school, Casey Elena was born. I was able to list her as a dependent, but not Karen. Casey Elena received a military ID card. That was when we really started to feel the inequities of the military. We had a civil union and a child together; however, only Casey Elena was recognized by the military.

Writing while DADT was still enforced by the Pentagon, Morgan stated that she was constantly bothered that her spouse, Karen, had none of the benefits even though she "has endured all the worry and anxiety as the other spouses." Returning from an earlier tour of duty, Morgan found that Karen could not attend Yellow Ribbon events for family: "That is so unfair since she made the sacrifice as a spouse." While serving in Iraq, Morgan learned that the Department of Defense intended to end DADT. Part of her job as equal opportunity officer now became to prepare the soldiers for the transition:

> Serving as the Equal Opportunity Advisor for the brigade during the repeal of DADT has been an amazing experience. It allowed me to openly discuss the issues concerning DADT freely. When I came out to my brigade commander two weeks ago, he provided insight to not only the restrictions placed upon me and my family, but on him as well . . . that DADT inhibited him from really getting to know me and my family. I never thought about it from that perspective.

I recently gave a "sensitivity training" to a unit which focused on identi-fying the similarities of straight and gay Soldiers, appreciating the differ-ences. . . . On the slide titled "Soldiers" I inserted a picture of a heterosexual Master Sergeant and a picture of myself in full battle rattle. The visual is two soldiers serving their country. The only visible difference is that the Master Sergeant is male and I am female.

The next slide featured the Master Sergeant with his family, which in-cluded his wife and two children. Next to his family picture was a photo of me with my partner and daughter taken during Christmas. I was wear-ing my dress blues in this photo as I am very proud of my service and my family. The mostly male audience immediately focused on the Master Sergeant's picture as if they were afraid of mine. After some prodding, the soldiers started to compare the two photographs. When asked what they saw, one soldier responded, "I see two happy families." I smiled. . . . One Soldier asked if it was okay for me to "come out" like that in this training. I responded, "Yes, I've already told the brigade commander."

Suddenly, the Soldiers started talking about their friend, sibling, cousin, etc., who was gay. It was like the room opened up.

Charlie Morgan's spouse, Karen, offered a perspective rarely heard in the debates over DADT:

I love my country, and I love Charlie and my family. How is that any dif-ferent from the perspective of a straight spouse? Why is my support less valuable than anyone else's? I teach our daughter to be honest, to be proud of who she is, and to love and support her family; and yet it feels contra-dictory and a little hypocritical because I cannot be honest due to the policies of our government. I think this is the psychologically damaging effect of DADT. It teaches that lying or looking the other way is accept-able. . . . I don't think that other families think of the nuts and bolts practi-cal issues such as health insurance, survivors' benefits and issues that we run into. . . .

. . . I wish my support and contributions were viewed as as valuable as those of my straight counterparts and that we could just be who we are, just another family supporting their country and trying to raise a child the right way.[74]

On September 20, 2011, "Don't Ask, Don't Tell" came to an end. That same day, J.D. Smith, the founder of OutServe, an undercover group of some four thousand gay and lesbian service personnel, revealed his identity, as did many others. "That saved my career," said Air Force Lieutenant Josh Seefried, who had become an activist after being outed by a hostile third party. A Pentagon spokesman, Doug Wilson, summarized the military's new attitude: "The key point is that it no longer matters. Our feeling is that the day will proceed like any other day."[75]

This is how the world changes: one courageous act at a time. Through its 235-year history, the U.S. military has evolved in significant ways, occasionally in advance of the society it protects. It has offered opportunities for social mobility to millions of Americans, and citizenship to numerous immigrants. It integrated before any other major public institution and, for its many flaws, has proven in recent years to be more of a meritocracy than American society. Currently, it is reluctantly but slowly moving to break down the last social barriers, acceding to the demands of homosexuals and women to be accepted into its ranks. In these ways, the military is fulfilling the promise of a democratic military, one that truly represents the people of the United States.

## Completing the Mission

Those who have served and are currently serving in Iraq and Afghanistan are notably reflective of their service. To a degree, the web feeds this introspection by providing constant information and an outlet for thoughts and emotions. They know about a government that lied to the public and its soldiers. They can follow the latest scandal as it breaks. But these twenty-first-century soldiers tend to think a lot more about war as war, as a total environment, rather than just as an ideological or patriotic event. They regularly question the nature of their experiences, breaking the isolation that typically surrounds military personnel, and they often engage in nonpolitical but highly professional questioning of their leadership.

As Thomas Ricks pointed out in his important book *Fiasco*, the Bush administration's belief that the war would be swiftly won by airpower led to decisions that adversely affected America's troops. Ignoring the advice of several generals, including Army Chief of Staff General Eric Shinseki, Donald Rumsfeld sent too few troops, with inadequate training and equipment, into Iraq while scaling back the mission in Afghanistan. The Defense Department faced a shortage of troops as the wars persisted and turned increasingly to the reserves and National Guard for repeated tours of duty.[76] Having created a crisis, Rumsfeld dodged all responsibility, which was again obvious to those serving in the Middle East. In December 2004, Specialist Thomas Wilson of the Tennessee National Guard continued the American tradition of common soldiers challenging their superiors when he confronted the secretary of defense on the lack of armor: "We're digging pieces of rusted scrap metal and compromised ballistic glass" out of the trash "to put on our vehicles. . . . We do not have proper armament." Wilson wanted to know what the secretary was going to do about it. Rumsfeld responded, "As you know, you go to war with the army you have, not the army you might want or wish to have at a later time." Denying any responsibility for creating the army we have, Rumsfeld offered an insensitive follow-up: "If you think about it, you can have all the armor in the world on a tank and a tank can be blown up. And you can have an up-armored Humvee and it can be blown up." Even the conservative commentator William Kristol thought America's soldiers "deserve a better defense secretary than the one we have."[77] The same could be said of a president who invited attacks on American troops with a flippant, "Bring 'em on."[78]

In examining their own motivations, many soldiers came to realize that they embraced war as an adventure and a chance to do something of value. Tyler E. Boudreau had been a marine for ten years when the terrorists brought down the Twin Towers. He had been training for years for combat, and he admits that there was a part of him that welcomed the war: "How many times can you run the rounded edge of a bayonet across a man's throat before you crave the sound of a desperate gasp that comes only from the other side of the that blade. How many shots down range can you send into dummies before you find yourself wishing the dummies would bleed?"[79] This generation of soldiers had heard the tragic tales of Vietnam, but they still longed for glory, and were certain that their experience would be different. Boudreau was tired of hearing about Nam: "I prayed for my own war."[80]

Boudreau found his identity and his home in the Marines. He "fell in love with the Corps" once he learned their motto, *Semper Fidelis* (Always Faithful): "For a kid coming from a broken home, that meant a hell of a lot." They could have gone with so many other values—strength, courage, stamina, "something bad-ass," but instead they chose loyalty. "They said, above all, we're never, never going to leave your ass behind. I was hooked. . . . That's what I wanted. I wanted to be among those who said, 'My loyalty dies only when I die.'" It was what he wanted above all else, and it all turned to ash, as Boudreau became convinced that there was no way that the Americans could ever win this war militarily: "The more we asserted ourselves, the stronger we made our FOBs (forward operating bases), the tighter the grip we put on Iraq, the greater the contrast we drew between their religion and ours, the more we lost the very hearts and minds of the people we said we came to win." Neither the Marine Corps nor his fellow marines broke trust, but his government did, sending him to fight a pointless war and then treating the returning soldiers like malcontents looking for a handout.[81]

If there is one particularly enraging aspect of America's twenty-first-century wars, it is the government's reliance on private contractors. Kellogg Brown & Root, or KBR, a subsidiary of Dick Cheney's Halliburton, received $10 billion in noncompetitive bids in the first year of the war alone. KBR took numerous shortcuts to maximize profits, such as fixing up broken trucks for use by American troops, delivering supposedly armored vehicles without armor, supplying contaminated drinking water that caused widespread illness, and even recycling wastewater for use by military personnel. President Bush's decision to privatize warfare came at enormous expense to the American public, which was footing the exaggerated bills, but, as Dina Rasor and Robert Bauman demonstrate in *Betraying Our Troops*, American soldiers paid the highest price.[82] It was bad enough that KBR's drivers made $80,000 a year compared to the soldiers' $30,000, or that the contractors charged exorbitant rates for everything, such as $45 for six-packs of beer—but that the contractors' greed also cost soldiers their lives evokes more than resentment. Many veterans feel that the contractors should have been charged with treason.[83]

To fill perceived gaps, the government also turned to the men and women of the National Guard and the reserves, most of whom expected that the only action they would ever see would be battling natural disasters. Jennifer Spranger could not imagine "anybody who could have been less prepared" for service in Iraq than her Army Reserve unit: "These people are civilians in main lives, bankers and things like that, and they only train one weekend a month. . . . Nobody was a career soldier." Staff Sergeant Tom Dati agreed with this prognosis, pointing out that one reserve "commander was the manager of a Bed Bath & Beyond" before being deployed to Iraq.[84]

And yet they serve. Despite the illogic, the numerous errors, the questionable justifications, the lack of support—despite the many reasons for not serving, they continue to do their duty as they understand it, and hope that it will prove to have been the right action in the long run. They join for many reasons, some economic, many patriotic, a great number for highly personal causes. Joseph O'Keefe enlisted in the Marine Corps because he saw himself having few options. He wanted a college education but could not afford it on his own: "I went down to the recruiting office, bit the bait, and on Friday, September 7, 2001, I signed on the dotted line. My reasoning seemed sound. It was a time of peace, the Corps would help me with college, and I'll be traveling around the world having a blast while trying to figure out what to do with my future. What could go wrong?" Four days later he found out, as the terrorist attacks of 9/11 changed the nature of O'Keefe's enlistment: "9/11 ignited that desire I had always had to defend my country. I grew up in Lexington, Massachusetts, surrounded by Revolutionary War history, and fell in love with the idea of fighting against tyranny in the name of freedom."

O'Keefe thought he would head off to Afghanistan, but one of his drill instructors at boot camp explained to the recruits that they would probably end up in Iraq as part of a long war that might kill several of them. This talk framed O'Keefe's experience: "All my training was literally preparing me for when I would go to war. So when I arrived in Iraq, I saw it as equivalent to graduating from college and entering the real world, the world of combat." O'Keefe served in the Fixed-Wing Marine Fighter Attack (All-Weather) Squadron 224 as an ordnance technician, loading bombs on fighter jets: "It was the best job I've ever had, and probably the best job I'll ever have." He quickly formed powerful bonds with his fellow marines, serving several deployments with them and becoming "family." Iraq was another matter:

Iraq was a strange place; the hottest, coldest, dirtiest place I have ever been. We were on this airbase in the middle of the desert in Al Anbar province, and you could look in any direction and there was absolutely nothing as far as the eye could see. . . . It was not what I pictured a desert in the Middle East to look like; there were no sweeping sand dunes, just flat ground with hard, caked sand.

. . . During winter the temperatures at night averaged close to zero. I remember one night I was in the cockpit performing an electrical check, and the thermometers for the engine compartment's display read −8° F. I wore four or five layers to keep warm. . . . I was on the arm/dearm crew. We were the last to touch the jets before they took off because we had to arm all the ordnance, and since we flew with forward firing ordnance this arming took place at the end of the runway, with the jet pointing at absolutely nothing.

. . . The base used to get hit with mortar fire a lot. When this happened, the air raid siren would come on and everyone was supposed to take cover. However, if we were out in the arming area, we had to stay where we were to ensure the safety of the jets. . . . We had been there maybe a week when I experienced my first mortar attack. I was out in the arm/dearm area in the canvas covered Humvee with no doors. Our staff sergeant came driving up and handed us our rifles, flak jackets, and kevlars, wished us luck, and then drove back to the safety of the HAS. As time went on, I got used to them. I used to listen to my ipod while waiting for the jets, and would turn the volume up when I could hear the mortars and air raid sirens blaring. We realized there was nothing we could do. The mortars were going to land wherever they were going to land, and if we happened to be in that spot then oh well. I figured that if I got hit with a mortar that I deserved it.

There was a lot of downtime on the base, which the marines filled with a wide range of activities. They would jump into the wake of the jet engines, which, if caught just right, could launch a person thirty feet backwards: "Eventually some officer discovered this little game and we were told not to do it anymore. We still did it. It was fun. It was something to do." O'Keefe had a digital camera, which he used to record his duties and strange skits which he would post on the web: "It was a constant struggle to stay one step ahead of the monotony. . . . I did a lot of thinking during downtime, which wasn't always a good thing." Eventually he came to question what he was doing in Iraq.

When he saw a video of the results of one of his bombs, a building disintegrating into smoke and flying rubble, O'Keefe noticed a human figure cartwheeling through the air: "He was a bad guy and deserved to die. That's what I told myself." He did not question the necessity of his involvement, which meant "the difference between life and death, failure and victory," for his fellow soldiers. But he was troubled by the unquestioning celebration of violence: "Iraq would be my last deployment as an active duty Marine." On leave in the United States to attend the funeral of a friend, O'Keefe saw the sorrow and pain of his friend's family. In that moment, he recognized the humanity of the Iraqi people, both insurgents and civilians—that they, too, must have families that mourned a painful loss: "Eventually I realized that the Iraqi people were not my enemy, nor could I treat their deaths as just so much collateral damage. Their pain is no less real or important." O'Keefe did not reenlist in the Marines. Returning to college and to his religious roots, O'Keefe now devotes himself to helping other veterans who must also contend with a culture that glorifies and rewards violence in one context and then demands that all its effects be left behind on the battlefield.[85]

Individual soldiers have learned valuable lessons from their participation in America's current wars; whether the nation has done so remains in question. Addressing the cadets at West Point in 2011, Secretary of Defense Robert M. Gates stated that "any future defense secretary who advises the president to again send a big American land army into Asia or into the Middle East or Africa should 'have his head examined,' as General MacArthur so delicately put it."[86] One hopes that Gates will prove correct, but his message has been stated many times before. Most veterans now have less confidence in the wisdom of future political leaders. As one said, "We'll do our duty and feel betrayed later."[87]

At the start of America's democratic experiment, Friedrich von Steuben persuaded his troops to treat one another like brothers, to risk their lives for their comrades-in-arms. The same logic holds today, as American military personnel risk their lives for people they had not previously known who are wearing the same uniform. Thanks to significant change within the military, those fellow soldiers, sailors, and pilots include all ethnicities and both genders, regardless of sexual orientation. With time, that democratic sense of equality and shared sacrifice convinces the majority of those who serve that they are all Americans, and in it together. It is a sentiment that many veterans miss from their years in service, and hope to see extended to civilian society. Those who have served in the American military have created a viable community of the line, which may well serve as a positive example to the rest of the country.

# Notes

## Introduction

1. Geoffrey Perret, *A Country Made by War* (New York: Vintage, 1990). See also Chris Hedges, *War Is a Force That Gives Us Meaning* (New York: Anchor, 2003).

2. Paul Leicester Ford, *The True George Washington* (Philadelphia: J.B. Lippincott, 1898), 269; John F. Marszalek, *Sherman: A Soldier's Passion for Order* (Carbondale: Southern Illinois University Press, 2007), 477.

3. Stuart A. Herrington, *Silence Was a Weapon: The Vietnam War in the Villages: A Personal Perspective* (Novato, CA: Presidio, 1982), xiii.

4. But if you are, see William C. Westmoreland, *A Soldier Reports* (New York: Dell, 1980).

5. Personal conversation, 1994.

6. My lawyer acquaintance desires to remain anonymous.

7. Nancy Sherman, "A Crack in the Stoic's Armor," *New York Times*, May 30, 2010. Also see Sherman, *The Untold War: Inside the Hearts, Minds, and Souls of Our Soldiers* (New York: W.W. Norton, 2010); and Jonathan Shay, *Achilles in Vietnam: Combat Trauma and the Undoing of Character* (New York: Simon & Schuster, 1994).

8. Ray Raphael, *A People's History of the American Revolution: How Common People Shaped the Fight for Independence* (New York: The New Press, 2001); David Williams, *A People's History of the Civil War: Struggles for the Meaning of Freedom* (New York: The New Press, 2005); Jonathan Neale, *A People's History of the Vietnam War* (New York: The New Press, 2003).

9. In this context, see Studs Terkel, *"The Good War": An Oral History of World War Two* (New York: Pantheon, 1984).

10. Alfred F. Young, *The Shoemaker and the Tea Party: Memory and the American Revolution* (Boston: Beacon, 1999), vii. See also Young, *Masquerade: The Life and Times of Deborah Sampson, Continental Soldier* (New York: Knopf, 2004).

11. For two recent examples, see Michael Barbaro and David M. Halbfinger, "Colleague Says Blumenthal Claims Grew in Time," *New York Times*, May 18, 2010; Abdon M. Pallasch, "Kirk Says He 'Misremembered' Military Record," *Chicago Sun-Times*, June 4, 2010.

12. Tim O'Brien, *The Things They Carried* (Boston: Houghton Mifflin, 1990), 65–66.

13. Tyler E. Boudreau, *Packing Inferno: The Unmaking of a Marine* (Port Townsend, WA: Feral House, 2008), 8.

14. Personal conversation, 1977, and many times thereafter. On Jack Veness, see Will R. Bird, *The Two Jacks* (Toronto: Ryerson, 1954).

15. William James, "The Moral Equivalent of War," *McClure's Magazine* 35 (1910): 463.

16. Ernie Pyle, *Here Is Your War: Story of G.I. Joe* (Lincoln: University of Nebraska Press, 2004), 12, 83.

17. See Veterans History Project, Central Connecticut State University, http://www .ccsu.edu/page.cfm?p=673; Veterans History Project, Library of Congress, http://www .loc.gov/vets/; the Legacy Project, http://warletters.com/.

18. Malcolm Potts and Thomas Hayden, *Sex and War: How Biology Explains Warfare and Terrorism and Offers a Path to a Safer World* (Dallas, TX: Benbella Books, 2008), 67.

19. "Slide Show: The Ten Worst Members of Congress You've Never Heard Of," *The Nation*, April 8, 2011, http://www.thenation.com/slideshow/159804/slide-show-10 -worst-members-congress-youve-never-heard.

20. Personal interview with the author, 1994.

21. Presentation to History 395, Central Connecticut State University, November 2009.

22. Thomas Pinney, ed., *The Letters of Rudyard Kipling: 1911–19* (Iowa City: University of Iowa Press, 1999), 521–22.


## 1. The American Revolution

1. Thomas Paine, *Common Sense; Addressed to the Inhabitants of America* (London: H.D. Symonds, 1792), 12.

2. *Journal and Letters of Rev. Henry True, of Hampstead, New Hampshire* (Marion, OH: Printed for Henry True, 1900), 31–33.

3. "Simon Fobes," *Historical Collections of the Mahoning Valley* 1 (1876): 349–50.

4. "Amos Farnsworth's Diary," *Massachusetts Historical Society Proceedings*, 2nd series, 12 (1897–99): 78–84. Punctuation inserted and some spelling corrected.

5. George Washington to Lund Washington, August 20, 1775, Edward G. Lengel, ed., *This Glorious Struggle: George Washington's Revolutionary War Letters* (New York: HarperCollins, 2007), 18.

6. Washington to Richard Henry Lee, August 29, 1775, ibid., 19–20.

7. Washington to John Hancock, September 25, 1776, ibid., 71.

8. Joseph Plumb Martin, *A Narrative of Some of the Adventures, Dangers and Sufferings of a Revolutionary Soldier* (Hallowell, ME: Glazier, Masters, 1830), 25–28.

9. "A New Song, Written by a Soldier," Frank Moore, ed., *The Diary of the American Revolution* (New York: Washington Square, 1967), 481.

10. George Morison, *An Interesting Journal of Occurrences During the Expedition to Quebec* (Hagerstown, PA: James Magee, 1803), 14–15.

11. Charles Royster, *A Revolutionary People at War: The Continental Army and American Character, 1775–1783* (New York: W.W. Norton, 1979), 296.

12. Walter Clark, ed., *The State Records of North Carolina* (Goldboro, NC: Nash Bros., 1898), 15:187–88.

13. "Narrative of John Hempstead," William W. Harris, ed., *The Battle of Groton Heights: A Collection of Narratives, Official Reports, Records, &c.* (New London, CT: William Harris, 1870), 34.

14. To the Officers of the New Jersey Line, July 19, 1783, *Proceedings of the New Jersey Historical Society* (Newark, NJ: Daily Advertiser, 1853), 5:14.

15. "Memoirs of Brigadier-General John Lacey, of Pennsylvania," *Pennsylvania Magazine of History and Biography* 25 (1901): 345–46.

16. "Diary of Surgeon Albigence Waldo, of the Connecticut Line," *Pennsylvania Magazine of History and Biography* 21 (1897): 306–16, 319–20.

17. Martin, *A Narrative of Some of the Adventures*, 72–80.

18. "Journal of Ensign Daniel Gookin," in Frederick Cook, ed., *Journals of the Military Expedition of Major General John Sullivan Against the Six Nations of Indians in 1779* (Auburn, NY: Knapp, Peck & Thomson, 1887), 104.

19. William S. Powell, "A Connecticut Soldier Under Washington: Elisha Bostwick's Memoirs of the First Years of the Revolution," *William and Mary Quarterly*, 3rd series, 6 (1949): 101.

20. Josiah Atkins, *The Diary of Josiah Atkins* (New York: Arno Press, 1975), 38.

21. Robert D. Meade, *Patrick Henry: Practical Revolutionary* (Philadelphia: Lippincott, 1969), 167–68.

22. Letter of Josiah Atkins, Mattatuck Museum, Waterbury, CT.

23. Royster, *A Revolutionary People at War*, 241.

24. "Journal of Oliver Boardman of Middletown," *Collections of the Connecticut Historical Society* 7 (1899): 225–35; some punctuation added.

25. E.P. Walton, ed., *Records of the Council of Safety and Governor and Council of the State of Vermont* (Montpelier, VT: J. & J.M. Poland, 1873–80), 1:93.

26. Douglas R. Egerton, *Death or Liberty: African Americans and Revolutionary America* (New York: Oxford University Press, 2009); Woody Holton, *Black Americans in the Revolutionary Era: A Brief History with Documents* (Boston: Bedford/St. Martin's, 2009).

27. Boyrereau Brinch, *The Blind African Slave, or, Memoirs of Boyrereau Brinch* (St. Albans, VT: Harry Whitney, 1810), 147.

28. Ibid., 156–70, 200–201.

29. Cornwallis to Clinton and to Phillips, April 10, 1781, Charles Ross, ed., *Correspondence of Charles, First Marquis Cornwallis* (London: John Murray, 1859), 1:86–87.

30. "Diary of Captain James Duncan , of Colonel Moses Hazen's Regiment, in the Yorktown Campaign, 1781," *Pennsylvania Archives*, 2nd series, 15 (1893): 746–52.

31. James Thacher, *Military Journal, During the American Revolutionary War, from 1775 to 1783* (Hartford, CT: Silas Andrus & Son, 1854), 284–92.

32. Washington to General John Armstrong, January 10, 1783, Worthington Chauncey Ford, ed., *The Writings of George Washington* (New York: G.P. Putnam's Sons, 1891), 10:140–41.

33. Alexander Hamilton to Washington, February 7, 1783, Washington to Hamilton, March 4, 1783, John C. Hamilton, ed., *The Works of Alexander Hamilton* (New York: John F. Trow, 1850), 1:328, 341; Washington to Benjamin Lincoln, October 2, 1782, Jared Sparks, ed., *The Writings of George Washington* (Boston: Russell et al., 1835), 8:354.

34. Richard Severo and Lewis Milford, *The Wages of War: When America's Soldiers Came Home—From Valley Forge to Vietnam* (New York: Simon & Schuster, 1989), 32–33.

35. Sidney Kaplan, "Veteran Officers and Politics in Massachusetts, 1783–1787," *William and Mary Quarterly* 9 (1957): 36–37.

36. David P. Szatmary, *Shays' Rebellion: The Making of an Agrarian Insurrection* (Amherst: University of Massachusetts Press, 1980), 58–60, 82–87.

37. Martin, *A Narrative of Some of the Adventures*, 179–80. For additional material on the experiences of common Revolutionary soldiers, see Alexander Graydon, *Memoirs of a Life, Chiefly Passed in Pennsylvania, Within the Last Sixty Years* (Harrisburg, PA: John Wyeth, 1811); James Hawkes, *A Retrospect of the Boston Tea-Party* (Boston: S.S. Bliss, 1834); "Battle of Princeton, by a Sergeant," *Army and Navy Chronicle* 1 (1835): 394; "Journal of Simeon Lyman of Sharon," *Connecticut Historical Society Collections* 7 (1899): 111–34; Nicholas Cresswell, *The Journal of Nicholas Cresswell, 1774–1777* (New York: Dial, 1924); Margaret W. Willard, ed., *Letters on the American Revolution, 1774–1776* (Boston: Houghton Mifflin, 1925); John C. Dann, ed., *The Revolution Remembered: Eyewitness Accounts of the War for Independence* (Chicago: University of Chicago Press, 1980); Alfred F. Young, *The Shoemaker and the Tea Party: Memory and the American Revolution* (Boston: Beacon, 1999).

## 2. The War of 1812

1. Lawrence Downes, "The Star-Strangled Banner," *New York Times*, April 12, 2006.

2. Richard Severo and Lewis Milford, *The Wages of War: When America's Soldiers Came Home—From Valley Forge to Vietnam* (New York: Simon & Schuster, 1989), 83–84; poll of 140 students conducted at Central Connecticut State University, 2010.

3. Michael Bellesiles, "Experiencing the War of 1812," in Julie Flavell and Stephen Conway, eds., *Britain and America Go to War: The Impact of War and Warfare in Anglo-America, 1754–1815* (Gainesville: University Press of Florida, 2004), 205–40.

4. James D. Richardson, comp., *Messages and Papers of the Presidents, 1789–1907* (New York: Bureau of National Literature and Art, 1897–1917), 1:499–505.

5. William Ray Barlow insisted that the Far West was equally outraged over violations of maritime rights. "The Coming of the War of 1812 in Michigan Territory," *Michigan History* 53 (1969): 91–107.

6. The best work on the causes of the war remains Bradford Perkins, *Prologue to War: England and the United States, 1805–1812* (Berkeley: University of California Press, 1961). There has been surprisingly little work done on the historiography of the War of 1812. See Warren H. Goodman, "The Origins of the War of 1812: A Survey of Changing Interpretations," *Mississippi Valley Historical Review* 28 (1941): 171–86.

7. See *Annals of the Congress of the United States*, 12th Cong., 1st sess., pt. 1 (Washington, DC: Gales and Seaton, 1853).

8. Ibid., 446.

9. Ibid., 518.

10. "Justifying the War of 1812: Toward a Model of Congressional Behavior in Early War Crises," *Social Science History* 4 (1980): 453–77. See also Leland R. Johnson, "The Suspense Was Hell: The Senate Vote for War in 1812," *Indiana Magazine of History* 65 (1969): 247–67.

11. Jefferson to Hull, March 21, 1807, *Michigan Pioneer Collections* 8 (1886): 583; Hull to Dearborn, December 11, 1807, *Michigan Pioneer Collections* 40 (1929): 228.

12. See, for instance, *Michigan Pioneer Collections* 8 (1886): 602; Clarence E. Carter, ed., *Territory of Michigan, 1805–1820*, vol. 10 of *Territorial Papers of the United States* (Washington, DC: GPO, 1942): 303, 319.

13. Lawrence Delbert Cress, *Citizens in Arms: The Army and the Militia in American Society to the War of 1812* (Chapel Hill, NC: University of North Carolina Press, 1982), 150–71.

14. One of the most interesting early histories of the War of 1812 makes roughly this point, citing Washington and other Revolutionary leaders to reject a reliance on the militia and explain the utter necessity of trained troops and officers. George W. Cullum, *Campaigns of the War of 1812–15, Against Great Britain, Sketched and Criticized* (New York: James Miller, 1879), 9–35. For a modern study of the impact of the militia myth on the War of 1812, see Carl Edward Skeen, *Citizen Soldiers in the War of 1812* (Lexington, KY: University Press of Kentucky, 1999).

15. Jefferson to Hull, March 21, 1807, *Michigan Pioneer Collections* 8 (1886): 583.

16. William Henry Harrison, "Militia Discipline," *National Intelligencer* (Washington, DC), September 21 and October 1, 1810; Robert S. Lambert, ed., "The Conduct of the Militia at Tippecanoe: Elihu Stout's Controversy with Colonel John P. Boyd, January, 1812," *Indiana Magazine of History* 51 (1955): 237–50; Gale Thornborough and Dorothy Riker, eds., "Journals of the General Assembly of Indiana Territory, 1805–1815," *Indiana Historical Collections* 32 (1950): 2–17, 392–401, 409–16, 421, 426–33, 478; Michael A. Bellesiles, *Arming America: The Origins of a National Gun Culture* (New York: Knopf, 2000), 208–60.

17. John C. Parish, ed., *The Robert Lucas Journal of the War of 1812 During the Campaign Under General William Hull* (Iowa City: The State Historical Society, 1906), iii.

18. Skeen, *Citizen Soldiers*, 105; Allan S. Everest, *The War of 1812 in the Champlain Valley* (Syracuse, NY: Syracuse University Press, 1981), 91–92.

19. Parish, ed., *The Robert Lucas Journal*, 7–11, 14–15, 20–21, 27–35, 39–42, 52, 55–64. Some punctuation added.

20. See William Hull, *Defence of Brigadier General W. Hull: Delivered Before the General Court Martial* (Boston: Wells & Lilly, 1814) and *Memoirs of the Campaign of the North Western Army of the United States* (Boston: True & Greene, 1824).

21. Ernest Cruikshank, ed., *Documentary History of the Campaigns on the Niagara Frontier in 1812–14* (Welland, ON: Tribune, 1902–1908) 4: 85–88, 162–63, 174–75, 181–82.

22. Skeen, *Citizen Soldiers*, 98; Gen. Amos Hall to Governor Tompkins, July 4, 1812, Buffalo and Erie Historical Society, Buffalo, NY, reel 2; Van Rensselaer to Governor Tompkins, July 23, 1812, in Cruikshank, ed., *Documentary History* 3:142. On the Niagara frontier in 1812 there was no artillery heavier than a six-pounder and no artillerymen. At most, there was sufficient ammunition for ten rounds each for one thousand men. Florence and Mary Howard, eds., "The Letters of John Patterson, 1812–1813," *Western Pennsylvania Historical Magazine* 23 (1940): 100.

23. General Van Rensselaer to Governor Tompkins of New York, August 31, 1812, in Howard, eds., "The Letters of John Patterson," 102; Benson J. Lossing, *Pictorial Field-Book, of the War of 1812* (New York: Harper & Brothers, 1868), 384–85.

24. Theodore Crackel, "The Battle of Queenston Heights, 13 October 1812," in Charles Heller and William Stofft, eds., *America's First Battles, 1776–1965* (Lawrence, KS: University Press of Kansas, 1986), 33–56.

25. Cullum, *Campaigns of the War of 1812–15*, 69. On other militia units refusing to cross into Canada, see Parish, ed., *The Robert Lucas Journal*, 27.

26. See Robert Malcomson, *A Very Brilliant Affair: The Battle of Queenston Heights, 1812* (Toronto: Robin Brass Studio, 2003).

27. Statement of Bill Sherman, December 3, 1812, in Cruikshank, ed., *Documentary History*, 4:247. See also the newspaper accounts on these events, ibid., 4:281–85; *Niles' Weekly Register* 3 (Dec. 19, 1812), 252.

28. New York *Evening Post*, December 10 and 24, 1812, in Cruikshank, ed., *Documentary History* 4:238, 282–84.

29. *Buffalo Gazette*, December 8 and 22, 1812, ibid., 4:291–95, 335.

30. Glenn Tucker, *Tecumseh: A Vision of Glory* (New York: Cosimo, 2005), 200.

31. In 1816 Tenskwatawa told Lewis Cass that he had not ordered the attack, which had been launched without his knowledge by some Winnebagos. Alfred A. Cave, *Prophets of the Great Spirit: Native American Revitalization Movements in Eastern North America* (Lincoln: University of Nebraska Press, 2006), 121.

32. "John Tipton's Tippecanoe Journal," *Indiana Magazine of History* 2 (1906): 170–84. Some punctuation and spelling corrections added.

33. Robert M. Owens, *Mr. Jefferson's Hammer: William Henry Harrison and the Origins of American Indian Policy* (Norman: University of Oklahoma Press, 2007), 211–26.

34. Robert V. Remini, *Andrew Jackson and His Indian Wars* (New York: Penguin, 2002), 62–79.

35. Elias Darnell, *A Journal Containing an Accurate and Interesting Account of the Hardships, Sufferings, Battles, Defeat, and Captivity of Those Heroic Kentucky Volunteers and Regulars* (Philadelphia: Lippincott, Grambo, 1854), 11, 25–26.

36. Ibid., 11–20, 26–35, 38–41, 47–56.

37. See, for example, ibid., 42; Samuel White, *History of the American Troops, During the Late War* (Baltimore: B. Edes, 1830), 11–15.

38. Darnell, *Journal*, 40.

39. Tipton, "Tippecanoe Journal," 171.

40. Jacob Catlin, *The Horrors of War* (Stockbridge, MA: H. Willard, 1813). See also Kiah Bayley, *War a Calamity Greatly to Be Dreaded* (Hallowell, ME: N. Cheever, 1812); Nathan S.S. Beman, *A Sermon, Delivered at the Meeting House of the Second Parish in Portland, August 20, 1812* (Portland, ME: Hyde, Lord, 1812); John S.J. Gardiner, *A Discourse, Delivered at Trinity Church, Boston, April 9, 1812, on the Day of Publick Fast* (Boston: Munroe & Francis, 1812); James Abercrombie, *Two Sermons* (Philadelphia: Moses Thomas, 1812); Lemuel Haynes, *Dissimulation Illustrated* (Rutland, CT: Washington Benevolent Society, 1814); John Lathrop, *A Discourse on the Law of Retaliation, Delivered in the New Brick Church, February 6, 1814* (Boston: James W. Burditt, 1814).

41. James Flint, *God a Refuge and an Habitation in Times of Calamity and Danger* (Boston: C. Stebbins, 1814).

42. Brown Emerson, *The Causes and Effects of War* (Salem, MA: J. Cushing, 1812), 12, quoted in Peter Karsten, *Soldiers and Society: The Effects of Military Service and War on American Life* (Westport, CT: Greenwood, 1978), 26.

43. Howard, eds., "The Letters of John Patterson," 101.

44. It was a good thing for Jackson that he did not actually have to fire, as "the musket he had used so effectively was too ancient a weapon to be fired." Robert V. Remini, *Andrew Jackson and the Course of American Empire, 1767–1821* (New York: Harper & Row, 1977), 199.

45. John Lovett to Joseph Alexander, November 4, 1812, in Cruikshank, ed., *Documentary History* 4:181.

46. Livingston to General Smyth, November 4, 1812, in ibid., 4:180.

47. General Smyth to General Dearborn, November 9, 1812, in ibid., 4:186–87.

48. General Izard to the Secretary of War, November 2, 1814, in ibid., 2:284.

49. White, *History of the American Troops*, 5–19.

50. *National Intelligencer* (Washington, DC), December 22, 1812.

51. Cullum, *Campaigns of the War of 1812–15*, 294–96.

52. Edward D. Ingraham, *A Sketch of the Events Which Preceded the Capture of Washington* (Philadelphia: Carey and Hart, 1849), 44–45.

53. George Robert Gleig, *The Campaigns of the British Army at Washington and New Orleans, in the Years 1814–1815* (London: John Murray, 1836), 114.

54. Cullum, *Campaigns of the War of 1812–15*, 299.

55. "Col. McLane's Visit to Washington, 1814," *Bulletin of the Historical Society of Pennsylvania* 1 (1848): 18.

56. Jon Latimer, *1812: War with America* (Cambridge, MA: Harvard University Press, 2010), 305.

57. Henry Theodore Tuckerman, *The Life of John Pendleton Kennedy* (New York: G.P. Putnam & Sons, 1871), 71–80. See also John S. Williams, *History of the Invasion and Capture of Washington, and of the Events Which Preceded and Followed* (New York: Harper & Brothers, 1857).

58. Cullum, *Campaigns of the War of 1812–15*, 285–87; John R. Elting, *Amateurs, To Arms! A Military History of the War of 1812* (New York: Da Capo, 1995), 198–243.

59. Gleig, *The Campaigns of the British Army*, 156.

60. Culum, *Campaigns of the War of 1812–15*, 289.

61. Madison to Anna [her sister], August 23, 1813, "Her grand-niece," *Memoirs and Letters of Dolly Madison* (Boston: Houghton Mifflin, 1887), 110.

62. Alfred T. Mahan, *Sea Power in Its Relations to the War of 1812*, 2 vols. (Boston: Little, Brown, 1905).

63. Samuel Leech, *Thirty Years from Home: or, A Voice From the Main Deck* (Boston: Tappan & Dennet, 1843), 122–36, 179–89. See also Moses Smith, *Naval Scenes in the Last War* (Boston: Gleason's, 1846).

64. Lt. Colonel John Gurwood, ed., *Selections from the Dispatches and General Orders of Field Marshal the Duke of Wellington* (London: John Murray, 1842), 792.

65. Latimer, *1812: War with America*.

66. Arsène Lacarrière Latour, *Historical Memoir of the War in West Florida and Louisiana in 1814–15*, trans. H.P. Nugent (Philadelphia: John Conrad, 1816), 142.

67. John Spencer Bassett, ed., "Major Howell Tatum's Journal," *Smith College Studies in History* 7 (1922): 122–29. See also Samuel Stubbs, *A Compendious Account of the Most Important Battles of the Late War* (Boston: William Walter, 1817); "A Contemporary Account of the Battle of New Orleans by a Soldier in the Ranks," *Louisiana Historical Quarterly* 9 (1926): 1–15.

68. Cullum, *Campaigns of the War of 1812–15*, 144–45, 150; Skeen, *Citizen Soldiers*, 106; *Niles' Weekly Register* 4 (June 19, 1813), 261; *Military Monitor* 1 (June 28, 1813): 350; General John Stricker to General Smith, September 15, 1814, in Nathaniel Hickman, ed., *The Citizen Soldiers at North Point and Fort McHenry, September 12 & 13, 1814* (Baltimore: J. Young, 1858), 89–90; General Brown to Governor Daniel D. Tompkins, June 1, 1813, in Cruikshank, ed., *Documentary History* 5:283–87; Richard G. Carlson, ed., "George P. Peters' Version of the Battle of Tippecanoe (November 7, 1811)," *Vermont History* 45 (1977): 41.

69. Skeen, *Citizen Soldiers*, 101; Inspection Reports of Captain William King, attached to Gen. Smyth to Speaker of the House Langdon Cheves, Feb. 8, 1814, *Annals of Congress*, 13th Cong., 2d sess., appendix, docs. 11 (2487), 18 (2483–84).

70. Diary of Cushing, Lindley, ed., *Fort Meigs*, 115. William Dunlop offers a good example of the inexperience of American troops: "I once saw a solder of the 32nd take two American sentries prisoners, by placing his cap and great coat on a bush, . . . waited till both of their firelocks were discharged" at the coat, and then took them prisoner. Dunlop, *Recollections*, 69.

71. Diary of Cushing, Lindley, ed., *Fort Meigs*, 111. See also *Orderly Book of Captain Daniel Cushing's Company of Heavy Artillery* (there is no publication information on the title page of this nineteenth-century book, which can be found in the Newberry Library, Chicago), 104.

72. Darnell, *Journal*, 11, 19–20. See also Cruikshank, ed., *Documentary History* 3:283.

73. John to Levina Patterson, February 20, 1813, Howard, eds., "The Letters of John Patterson," 106.

74. Darnell, *Journal*, 29.

75. Cullum, *Campaigns of the War of 1812–15*, 207.

76. Quoted in Cullum, *Campaigns of the War of 1812–15*, 207. From the other side, William Dunlop described how at the battle of Chrysler's Farm the Americans were "driven off by the bayonet." Dunlop, *Recollections*, 19.

77. Quoted in the *National Intelligencer* (Washington, DC), February 16, 1815.

78. *Annals of Congress*, 13th Cong., 3d sess., House 1155–57, 1167, 1174, 1184–85, 1191, 1194; Senate, 233–34, 238–43, 250, 253, 258–59, 274; Appendix, 1966–67.

79. *Annals of Congress*, 13th Cong., 3d Sess., House, 538, 1200–1201.

80. Ibid., 1208, 1212, 1216, 1221, 1223, 1230–34, 1251–54; Skeen, *Citizen Soldiers*, 175–84.

81. *Annals of Congress*, 13th Cong., 3d Sess., Senate, 287, 291–92, 297–98; House, 1266–67, 1271–73. The regular army was reduced to six thousand in 1821. *Annals of Congress*, 16th Cong., 2d Sess., House, 1789–99; Skeen, "Calhoun, Crawford, and the Politics of Retrenchment," *South Carolina Historical Magazine* 73 (1972): 141–55.

82. Bellesiles, *Arming America*, 261–304.

83. George S. Pappas, *To the Point: The United States Military Academy, 1802–1902* (Westport, CT: Praeger, 1993), 99–322.

### 3. The Mexican War

1. See, for instance, Jacob Oswandel, *Notes of the Mexican War* (Philadelphia: n.p., 1885).

2. Kevin Dougherty, *Civil War Leadership and Mexican War Experience* (Jackson: University of Mississippi Press, 2007).

3. Francis Paul Prucha, *Broadax and Bayonet: The Role of the United States Army in the Development of the Northwest, 1815–1860* (Lincoln: University of Nebraska Press, 1995), 36–42.

4. David M. Pletcher, *The Diplomacy of Annexation: Texas, Oregon, and the Mexican War* (Columbia: University of Missouri Press, 1973).

5. For a fascinating contemporary presentation of the Mexican view of the war, see Albert C. Ramsey, ed. *The Other Side: or, Notes for the History of the War Between*

*Mexico and the United States* (New York: John Wiley, 1850). Joshua H. Corwin, *Mexican War Letters* (n.p., 1847), offers an on-the-ground view of the first confused encounters.

6. See the careful consideration of the border issue in Pletcher, *The Diplomacy of Annexation*.

7. Robert W. Johannsen, *To the Halls of the Montezumas: The Mexican War in the American Imagination* (New York: Oxford University Press, 1985), 21–44.

8. On these events, see T.R. Fehrenbach, *Lone Star: A History of Texas and the Texans* (New York: Da Capo, 2000), 190–246.

9. W.A. Croffut, ed., *Fifty Years in Camp and Field: Diary of Major-General Ethan Allen Hitchcock, U.S.A.* (New York: G.P. Putnam's Sons, 1909), 189, 192, 194–95, 198–203, 212, 214, 224, 228.

10. John S. D. Eisenhower, *So Far from God: The U.S. War with Mexico, 1846–1848* (Norman: University of Oklahoma Press, 2000), 29–70.

11. Justin H. Smith, *The War with Mexico* (New York: Macmillan, 1919), 1:138–346.

12. Smith, *The War with Mexico* 1:347–400, 2:1–16; Eisenhower, *So Far from God*, 113–94; Johannsen, *To the Halls of the Montezumas*, 108–43, 241–69.

13. Thomas Bailey, a musician with the Indiana Volunteers, did his duty by playing stirring martial music and headed back home at the first opportunity. "Diary of the Mexican War," *Indiana Magazine of History* 14 (1918): 134–47.

14. Letter dated July 9, 1846, George Meade, *Life and Letters of General George Gordon Meade: Major-General United States Army* (New York: Charles Scribner's Sons, 1913), 1: 109–10.

15. Benjamin Franklin Scribner, *Camp Life of a Volunteer: A Campaign in Mexico* (Philadelphia: Grigg, Elliot, 1847), 11–68. See also George C. Furber, *The Twelve Months' Volunteer* (Cincinnati: J.A. & U.P. James, 1847).

16. Smith, *The War with Mexico* 1:347–400, 2:1–16; Eisenhower, *So Far from God*, 113–94; Johannsen, *To the Halls of the Montezumas*, 108–43, 241–69.

17. Benjamin Franklin Scribner, *How Soldiers Were Made; or the War as I Saw It Under Buell, Rosecrans, Thomas, Grant and Sherman* (New Albany, 1887).

18. The 1846 class included McClellan, Thomas "Stonewall" Jackson, John Gibbon, George Pickett, and A.P. Hill. John C. Waugh, *The Class of 1846: From West Point to Appomatox: Stonewall Jackson, George McClellan and Their Brothers* (New York: Ballantine, 1999).

19. William Starr Myers, ed., *The Mexican War Diary of George B. McClellan* (Princeton: Princeton University Press, 1917), 18, 31–32, 36–39. See also Robert Anderson, *An Artillery Officer in the Mexican War, 1846–7: Letters of Robert Anderson, Captain 3rd Artillery, U.S.A.* (New York: G.P. Putnam's Sons, 1911).

20. Patterson would live down Collins's judgment at the beginning of the Civil War when he failed to move quickly to retake Harpers Ferry and was outmaneuvered by Confederate General Joe Johnston, who reinforced rebel forces in time for the Battle of Bull Run. Patterson was removed from command and his military career ended.

21. Collins resigned his commission in 1849 and became a lawyer in Ohio, where he died in 1882. Maria Clinton Collins, ed., "Journal of Francis Collins: An Artillery Officer in the Mexican War," *Quarterly Publication of the Historical and Philosophical Society of Ohio* 10 (1915): 40–57. See also George W. Hartman, *A Private's Own Journal*

(Greencastle, PA: E. Robinson, 1849), which recorded every step of the march from Veracruz to Mexico City, respecting the bravery of both sides.

22. Ibid.

23. Smith, *The War with Mexico* 2:17–59; Eisenhower, *So Far from God*, 253–83, 298.

24. Smith, *The War with Mexico* 2: 2: 60–18; Eisenhower, *So Far from God*, 292–343.

25. George Washington Patten would continue to write poetry, though it is now largely forgotten. See, for instance, Patten, *Episodes of the Mexican War: A Poem* (New York: Brentano's Literary Emporium, 1878).

26. Emma Jerome Blackwood, ed., *To Mexico with Scott: Letters of Captain E. Kirby Smith to His Wife* (Cambridge, MA: Harvard University Press, 1917), 103, 127, 131–38, 151–52, 155–56, 192–205, 216–17.

27. Smith, *The War with Mexico* 2:210–52, 294–309; Eisenhower, *So Far from God*, 345–68; Richard Griswold del Castillo, *The Treaty of Guadalupe Hidalgo: A Legacy of Conflict* (Norman: University of Oklahoma Press, 1990).

28. Edward Waldo Emerson and Waldo Emerson Forbes, eds., *Journals of Ralph Waldo Emerson* (Boston: Houghton Mifflin, 1912), 7:206.

29. Nathaniel Hawthorne, *The Works of Nathaniel Hawthorne: Tales, Sketches, and Other Papers* (Boston: Houghton Mifflin, 1883), 399.

30. Thomas Irey, "Soldiering, Suffering, and Dying," in Odie B. Faulk and Joseph Allen Stout, *The Mexican War: Changing Interpretations* (Chicago: Sage Books, 1973), 110.

31. Ulysses S. Grant, *Personal Memoirs of U.S. Grant* (New York: Charles L. Webster, 1885), 1:51–56. See also William H. Richardson, *Journal of William H. Richardson, a Private Soldier in the Campaign of New and Old Mexico* (New York: D. Fanshaw, 1849); Jacob S. Robinson, *A Journal of the Santa Fe Expedition Under Colonel Doniphan* (Torrington, WY: Narrative, 2001).

## 4. The Civil War

1. Russell F. Weigley, *The American Way of War: A History of United States Military Strategy and Policy* (Bloomington: Indiana University Press , 1977); Jay Luvaas, *The Legacy of the Civil War: The European Inheritance* (Lawrence: University Press of Kansas, 1988); Herman Hattaway and Archer Jones, *How the North Won: A Military History of the Civil War* (Champaign: University of Illinois Press, 1991); Michael A. Belleisles, *Arming America: The Origins of a National Gun Culture* (New York: Knopf, 2000), 372–429. For the contrary view, see Paddy Griffith, *Battle Tactics of the Civil War* (New Haven, CT: Yale University Press, 2001).

2. The heroic construction of war is well presented in the letters of Allan Alonzo Kingsbury, a Union soldier killed in the Peninsula Campaign in 1862; *The Hero of Medfield* (Boston: John M. Hewes, 1862).

3. Oliver Wendell Holmes Jr. Papers, Special Collections, Harvard Law School Library, Microfilm reel 15. See also Eben Stone Hannaford, "In the Ranks at Stone River," *Harpers New Monthly Magazine* 27 (Jan. 1864): 809–15.

4. Oliver Wendell Holmes Jr., *Speeches by Oliver Wendell Holmes* (Boston: Little, Brown, 1896), 2–12.

5. G. Edward White, *Justice Oliver Wendell Holmes: Law and the Inner Self* (New York: Oxford University Press, 1993), 488.

6. Leander Stillwell, *The Story of a Common Soldier* (Erie, KS: Hudson, 1920), 40–53. See also James H. Leonard in R.J. Plumb, ed., "Letters of a Fifth Wisconsin Volunteer," *Wisconsin Magazine of History* 3 (1919): 50–83.

7. On the issue of motivation, see Gerald F. Linderman, *Embattled Courage: The Experience of Combat in the American Civil War* (New York: Free Press, 1987); James M. McPherson, *For Cause and Comrades: Why Men Fought in the Civil War* (New York: Oxford University Press, 1997).

8. Abolitionist leaders Wendell Phillips and William Lloyd Garrison.

9. "Letters of a Badger Boy in Blue: The Vicksburg Campaign," *Wisconsin Magazine of History* 4 (1920): 431–56; 5 (1921): 66–68. See also Jenkin Lloyd Jones, *An Artilleryman's Diary* (n.p.: Democrat Printing, 1914); William Tecumseh Sherman, *Memoirs of Gen. W. T. Sherman* (New York: Charles L. Webster, 1892). For an outstanding analysis of Sherman's revolutionary approach to warfare, see Charles Royster, *The Destructive War: William Tecumseh Sherman, Stonewall Jackson, and the Americans* (New York: Vintage, 1993).

10. Warren Lee Goss, "Recollections of a Private," *Century Illustrated Monthly Magazine* 29 (1884–1885): 279, 767.

11. Lonnie R. Speer, *Portals to Hell: Military Prisons of the Civil War* (Mechanicsburg, PA: Stackpole Books, 1997), 16.

12. Olynthus B. Clark, ed., *Downing's Civil War Diary* (Des Moines: Historical Department of Iowa, 1916), 234. See also Oscar Osburn Winther, ed., *With Sherman to the Sea: The Civil War Letters, Diaries & Reminiscences of Theodore F. Upson* (Baton Rouge: Louisiana University Press, 1943).

13. John L. Ransom, *Andersonville Diary* (Auburn, NY, 1881), 15, 28, 41, 50–51, 77–81.

14. John Vestal Hadley, *Seven Months a Prisoner* (New York: Charles Scribner's Sons, 1898), 72–73, 93–94.

15. Abner R. Small, "Personal Observations and Experiences in Rebel Prisons, 1864–1865," *War Papers, Read Before the Commandery of the State of Maine—Military Order of the Loyal Legion of the United States* (Portland, ME: Thurston Print, 1898), 1:295.

16. Ella Lonn, *Desertion During the Civil War* (Lincoln: University of Nebraska, 1998).

17. Brough to Brig. General J.B. Fry, February 6, 1865, Fred C. Ainsworth and Joseph W. Kirkley, comp., *War of the Rebellion: A Compilation of the Official Records of the Union and Confederate Armies*, series 3, vol. 4 (Washington, DC: GPO, 1899), 1,150; Eugene C. Murdock, *One Million Men: The Civil War Draft in the North* (Madison: State Historical Society of Wisconsin, 1971), 74–78.

18. For an excellent discussion of opposition to the draft and community support for desertion, see David Williams, *A People's History of the Civil War: Struggles for the Meaning of Freedom* (New York: The New Press, 2005), 244–83.

19. W.E.B. Du Bois, *Black Reconstruction in America 1860–1880* (New York: Free Press, 1998), 55.

20. Frank Moore, *Anecdotes, Poetry, and Incidents of the War: North and South, 1860–1865* (New York: the author, 1866), 263–64; Benjamin Quarles, *The Negro in the Civil War* (Boston: Little, Brown, 1953), 78–81; H. Donald Winkler, *Stealing Secrets:*

*How a Few Daring Women Deceived Generals, Impacted Battles, and Altered the Course of the Civil War* (Naperville, IL: Cumberland House, 2010), 51–88, 143–58.

21. On aid for escaped Union soldiers, see Henry L. Easterbrooks, *Adrift in Dixie; or, A Yankee Officer Among the Rebels* (New York: Carleton, 1866); *Famous Adventures and Escapes of the Civil War* (New York: Century, 1893).

22. Quarles, *The Negro in the Civil War*, 26–27; William Seraile, "The Struggle to Raise Black Regiments in New York State, 1861–1864," *New-York Historical Society Quarterly* 58 (July 1974): 215–33.

23. Quarles, *The Negro in the Civil War*, 25–26.

24. "Reply to a Committee from the Religious Denominations of Chicago," September 13, 1862, John G. Nicolay and John Hay, eds., *Abraham Lincoln: Complete Works* (New York: Century, 1894) 2:235; Quarles, *The Negro in the Civil War*, 27–29.

25. William Douglas Hamilton, *Recollections of a Cavalryman of the Civil War After Fifty Years, 1861–1865* (Columbus, OH: F.J. Heer, 1915), 136–38; Benjamin Quarles, *The Negro in the Civil War*, 81–99.

26. P.H. Aylett to Brig. Gen. John H. Winder, March 15,1864, Fred C. Ainsworth and Joseph W. Kirkley, comp., *War of the Rebellion: A Compilation of the Official Records of the Union and Confederate Armies*, series 2, vol. 6 (Washington, DC: GPO, 1899), 1053.

27. L. Earnest Sellers, "Robert Smalls of South Carolina: Civil War Hero," *Negro Digest* 13 (April 1964), 26.

28. Cobb to Secretary of War J.A. Seddon, Jan. 8, 1865, *American Historical Review* 1 (1896): 97.

29. I have changed this quotation from its original, in which the white author attempted to give a sense of slave dialect. Hepworth has asked Tom if it is true that slaves all love their masters. "Lieutenant, I know dey says dese tings; but dey lies. Our masters may talk now all dey choose; but one ting's sartin,— dey don't dare to try us. Jess put de guns into our hans, and you'll soon see dat we not only knows how to shoot, but who to shoot. My master wouldn't be wuff much ef I was a soldier." George H. Hepworth, *The Whip, Hoe, and Sword; or, The Gulf-Department in '63* ( Boston: Walker, Wise, 1864), 187.

30. Frederic May Holland, *Frederick Douglass: The Colored Orator* (New York: Funk & Wagnalls, 1891), 301.

31. Ira Berlin, Joseph P. Reidy, and Leslie S. Rowland, eds., *Freedom's Soldiers: The Black Military Experience in the Civil War* (Cambridge: Cambridge University Press, 1998).

32. Nicolay and Hay, eds., *Abraham Lincoln: Complete Works*, 2:288.

33. Ira Berlin and Leslie S. Rowland, eds., *Families and Freedom: A Documentary History of African-American Kinship in the Civil War* (New York: The New Press, 1997), 79. The government took the view that former slaves who joined the military should be content with their freedom, not receiving the bounties offered to white enlistees. Their pay was also inferior, $10 per month rather than the $13 paid to white soldiers. This disparity ended on June 15, 1864, when Congress equalized the pay of all military personnel and offered the same bounty regardless of race: $100 for a one-year enlistment, $300 for three years. James M. McPherson, *The Negro's Civil War: How American Negroes Felt and Acted During the War for the Union* (New York: Pantheon Books, 1965); Gerald Astor, *The Right to Fight: A History of African Americans in the Military* (Cambridge, MA: Da Capo, 2001), 20–42.

34. James McPherson, *What They Fought For, 1861–1865* (New York: Anchor, 1995), 56–63, quote on 62; John David Smith, ed., *Black Soldiers in Blue: African American Troops in the Civil War Era* (Chapel Hill: University of North Carolina Press, 2002), 5–6. Susie King Taylor, an African American woman who worked with the Women's Relief Corps, offers a fascinating view of camp life and racial relations in the Union army; *Reminiscences of My Life in Camp with the 33rd U.S Colored Troops* (Boston: by the author, 1902).

35. Lincoln responded in turn that for every Union soldier enslaved, a Confederate POW would be put to hard labor. Quarles, *The Negro in the Civil War*, 180; Ira Berlin et al., eds., *Free at Last: A Documentary History of Slavery, Freedom, and the Civil War* (New York: The New Press, 1992), 447–51.

36. Henry Steele Commager and Erik Bruun, eds., *The Civil War Archive: The History of the Civil War in Documents* (New York: Workman, 2000), 544.

37. William Wells Brown, *The Negro in the American Rebellion* (Boston: Lee & Shepard, 1867), 138–41.

38. Lori J. Kenschaft, *Lydia Maria Child: The Quest for Racial Justice* (New York: Oxford University Press, 2002), 94.

39. James Henry Gooding, *On the Altar of Freedom: A Black Soldier's Civil War Letters from the Front*, ed. Virginia M. Adams (Boston: University of Massachusetts Press, 1991), 38.

40. Luis F. Emilio, *History of the Fifty-Fourth Regiment of Massachusetts Volunteer Infantry, 1863–1865* (Boston: The Boston Book, 1894), 67–104; Joseph T. Glatthaar, *Forged in Battle: The Civil War Alliance of Black Soldiers and White Officers* (Baton Rouge: Louisiana State University Press, 1990), 275–78.

41. R.J.M. Blackett, ed., *Thomas Morris Chester, Black Civil War Correspondent: His Dispatches from the Virginia Front* (Baton Rouge: Louisiana State University Press, 1989), 115.

42. Ulysses S. Grant, *Personal Memoirs of U.S. Grant* (New York: Charles L. Webster, 1886), 2:138; Albert Castel, "The Fort Pillow Massacre: An Examination of the Evidence," in Gregory J.W. Urwin, ed., *Black Flag over Dixie: Racial Atrocities and Reprisals in the Civil War* (Carbondale: Southern Illinois University Press, 2004), 89–103; Andrew Ward, *River Run Red: The Fort Pillow Massacre in the American Civil War* (New York: Penguin, 2005).

43. Glatthaar, *Forged in Battle*, 155–57; David J. Coles, "'Shooting Niggers Sir': Confederate Mistreatment of Union Black Soldiers at the Battle of Olustee," in Urwin, ed., *Black Flag over Dixie*, 65–88; Lonnie R. Speer, *War of Vengeance: Acts of Retaliation Against Civil War POWs* (Mechanicsburg, PA: Stackpole Books, 2002).

44. "Assassination of Lincoln," Report #104, *The Reports of the Committees of the House of Representatives Made During the First Session Thirty-Ninth Congress, 1865–66* (Washington, DC: GPO, 1866), 2.

45. Glatthaar, *Forged in Battle*, 155–57; Lonnie R. Speer, *Portals to Hell: Military Prisons of the Civil War* (Lincoln: University of Nebraska Press, 2005), 107–18.

46. Nicolay and Hay, eds., *Abraham Lincoln: Complete Works*, 1:576.

47. Randall C. Jimerson, *The Private Civil War: Popular Thought During the Sectional Conflict* (Baton Rouge: Louisiana State University Press, 1988), 96.

48. Berlin and Rowland, eds., *Families and Freedom*, 95–117.

49. Ibid., 102–3, 112. For a similar story from the perspective of the father serving in the Union army, see Ira Berlin et al., eds., *Free at Last*, 481–82.

50. Edward K. Spann, *Gotham at War: New York City, 1860–1865* (New York: SR Books, 2002), 74.

51. Lori D. Ginzberg, *Women and the Work of Benevolence: Morality, Politics, and Class in the 19th-Century United States* (New Haven, CT: Yale University Press, 1990), 133–73; Mary A. Livermore, *My Story of the War: A Woman's Narrative of Four Years Personal Experience* (Hartford, CT: A.D. Worthington, 1892).

52. Mary Livermore, an agent of the U.S. Sanitary Commission, wrote that they knew of four hundred women soldiers in the Union army, and estimated that many more escaped detection. Mary Livermore, *My Story of the War* (Hartford, CT: Worthington, 1888), 120–21.

53. Elizabeth Kelly Kerstens, "Disguised Patriots: Women Who Served Incognito," *Ancestry* 18 (March/April 2000): 17. For other examples of women discovered serving in the Union army, see Philip H. Sheridan, *Civil War Memoirs* (New York: Webster, 1888), 253; Annie Wittenmyer, *Under the Guns: A Woman's Reminiscences of the Civil War* (Boston: Stillings & Co., 1895), 17–20; Barbara A. Smith, ed., *The Civil War Letters of Col. Elijah H. C. Cavins, 14th Indiana* (Owensboro, KY: Cook-McDowell, 1981), 132; Elizabeth Brown Pryor, *Clara Barton: Professional Angel* (Philadelphia: University of Pennsylvania Press, 1987), 99.

54. Wakeman to her parents, June 5, 1863, Lauren Cook Burgess, ed., *An Uncommon Soldier* (New York: Oxford University Press, 1994), 31.

55. Ibid., 58, 60.

56. There was at least one other woman serving with Wakeman in this campaign, Jennie Hodgers, known as Private Albert D.J. Cashier of the 95th Illinois Infantry. Ibid., 67.

57. Ibid., 71.

58. The details of Edmonds's story have been largely confirmed by the excellent scholarly work of Sylvia Dannett, *She Rode with the Generals* (New York: Thomas Nelson & Sons, 1960).

59. S. Emma E. Edmonds, *Nurse and Spy in the Union Army* (Hartford, CT: W.S. Williams, 1865), 120–21, 262–63, 270–73. For another spy narrative, see *Famous Adventures and Escapes of the Civil War* (New York: Century, 1843), 83–101, which covers William Pittenger, who took part in the famous Chattanooga railroad raid and was tried as a spy.

60. Emmy E. Werner, *Reluctant Witnesses: Children's Voices from the Civil War* (Boulder, CO: Westview, 1998), 37.

61. Allen Thorndike Rice, *Reminiscences of Abraham Lincoln by Distinguished Men of His Time* (New York: North American, 1886), xxv. For a view from the ground of the battle, see Charles Bardeen, *A Little Fifer's Diary* (Syracuse, NY: C. W. Bardeen, 1910).

62. James I. Robertson, *Soldiers Blue and Gray* (Columbia: University of South Carolina Press, 1998), 130.

63. Bell Irvin Wiley, *The Life of Billy Yank: The Common Soldier of the Union* (Baton Rouge: Louisiana State University Press, 2008), 199.

64. Oliver Willcox Norton, *Army Letters, 1861–1865: Being Extracts from Private Letters to Relatives and Friends* (Chicago: O.L. Deming, 1903), 106–7.

65. See, for instance, John D. Billings, *Hardtack and Coffee, or, The Unwritten Story of Army Life* (Boston: George M. Smith, 1888); Charles E. Benton, *As Seen from the Ranks: A Boy in the Civil War* (New York: G.P. Putnam's Sons, 1902).

66. Harold Adams Small, ed., *The Road to Richmond: The Civil War Letters of Major Abner R. Small of the 16th Maine Volunteers* (New York: Fordham University Press, 2000), 85. See also Lydia Minturn Post, ed., *Soldiers' Letters, from Camp, Battle-Field and Prison* (New York: Bunce & Huntington, 1865).

67. Robert J. Burdette, *The Drums of the 47th* (Indianapolis: Bobbs-Merrill, 1914), 101–8.

68. James V. Murfin, *The Gleam of Bayonets: The Battle of Antietam and Robert E. Lee's Maryland Campaign, September 1862* (Baton Rouge: Louisiana State University Press, 1993), 187–88.

69. K. Jack Bauer, ed., *Soldiering: The Civil War Diary of Rice C. Bull, 123rd New York Volunteer Infantry* (Novato, CA: Presidio, 1995), 231–32.

70. *Inaugural Addresses of the Presidents of the United States* (Washington, DC: GPO, 1961), 127–28.

71. Stuart McConnell, *Glorious Contentment: The Grand Army of the Republic, 1865–1900* (Chapel Hill: University of North Carolina Press, 1992), 10.

72. *New York Herald*, May 24, 1865. None of the papers mentioned that the black 52nd Pennsylvania Regiment did not parade, but was sent on to Philadelphia, where they were demobilized.

73. Walt Whitman, *Specimen Days* (Boston: Godine, 1971), 60.

74. Walter Lowenfels, ed., *Walt Whitman's Civil War* (New York: Knopf, 1960), 292; Justin Kaplan, *Life of Walt Whitman* (New York: Bantam, 1982), 26.

75. Theodore J. Karamanski, *Rally 'Round the Flag: Chicago and the Civil War* (Lanham, MD: Rowman & Littlefield, 2006), 240–41.

76. Mary Rulkotter Dearing, *Veterans in Politics: The Story of the G.A.R.* (Westport, CT: Greenwood, 1974), 54.

77. George G. Meade, "The Soldiers' and Sailors' Home," *Army and Navy Journal*, October 28, 1865, 154; Alexander H. Bullock, "Provision for Disabled Soldiers," *Army and Navy Journal*, January 13, 1866, 331.

78. Patrick J. Kelly, *Creating a National Home: Building the Veterans' Welfare State, 1860–1900* (Cambridge, MA: Harvard University Press, 1997), 23.

79. *Documents of the U.S. Sanitary Commission* (New York: Wm. C. Bryant, 1866), vol. 2, #67:5.

80. Edward T. Devine and D. Kinley, eds., "Disabled Soldiers and Sailors," *Preliminary Economic Studies of the War* (New York: Carnegie Endowment for Peace, 1919), 47.

81. Edith Abbott, "Civil War and the Crime Wave of 1865–70," *Social Service Review* 1 (1925): 212–44, quote on 227; "American Prisons," *North American Review*, October 1866, 383–412.

82. See, for instance, Nathaniel Hawthorne, "Chiefly About War-Matters by a Peaceable Man," *Atlantic Monthly* 10 (1862): 455; T. Wemyss Reid, ed., *Life, Letters, and Friendships of Richard Monckton Milnes: First Lord Houghton* (London: Cassell, 1890), 2:242.

83. Peter Karsten, *Soldiers and Society: The Effects of Military Service and War on American Life* (Westport, CT: Greenwood Press, 1978), 245–46. See also Karamanski, *Rally 'Round the Flag*, 240–41; Dearing, *Veterans in Politics*, 54; Meade, "The Soldiers' and Sailors' Home," 154; Bullock, "Provision for Disabled Soldiers," 331; Kelly, *Creating a National Home*, 23; *Documents of the U.S. Sanitary Commission*, vol. 2, #67:5; Edward T. Devine and D. Kinley, eds., "Disabled Soldiers and Sailors," 47.

84. *The Soldier's Friend*, June 1866, quoted in Dixon Wecter, *When Johnny Comes Marching Home* (Boston: Houghton Mifflin, 1944), 184.

85. Wecter, *When Johnny Comes Marching Home*, 186.

86. "The Disease of Mendicancy," *Scribner's Monthly* 13 (1876): 416–17; Michael A. Bellesiles, *1877: America's Year of Living Violently* (New York: The New Press, 2010), 110–43.

87. David Courtwright, "Opium Addiction as a Consequence of the Civil War," *Civil War History* 24 (1978): 101–11; Joseph J. Woodward, *Medical and Surgical History of the War of the Rebellion* (Washington, DC: GPO, 1870–1888), vol. 1, part 2:750.

88. *Leslie's Illustrated Weekly*, October 7, 1865, 39.

89. *The Nation*, May 30, 1889, 438.

90. William M. Sloan, "Pensions and Socialism," *Century Magazine*, June 1891, 185, 188.

91. In the 1890s there were three hundred GAR posts in the South serving 110,000 Union veterans, most of whom were white as the GAR continued to fail African American veterans. Richard Severo and Lewis Milford, *The Wages of War: When America's Soldiers Came Home—From Valley Forge to Vietnam* (New York: Simon & Schuster, 1989), 165.

92. Charles R. Williams, *Life of Rutherford Burchard Hayes* (New York: Houghton Mifflin, 1914), 2:338; Sophonishba P. Breckenridge, *Public Welfare Administration in the United States: Select Documents* (Chicago: University of Chicago Press, 1938), 308; *Boston Advertiser*, September 8, 1865; *New York Tribune*, November 16, 1866, 4; Mary H. Stephenson, *A Memoir of Dr. Stephenson* (Springfield, IL: 1894), 49–50; Severo and Milford, *The Wages of War*, 151–59; McConnell, *Glorious Contentment*, 18–30.

93. Wallace E. Davis, "The Problem of Race Segregation in the Grand Army of the Republic," *Journal of Southern History* 13 (1947): 354–72.

94. Donald L. McMurry, "The Political Significance of the Pension Question, 1885–97," *Mississippi Valley Historical Review* 9 (1922): 23.

95. *The Nation*, May 30, 1889, 439; see also Allen R. Foote, "Degradation by Pensions," *The Forum*, December 1891, 29.

96. "An Unpleasant Contrast," *The Nation*, May 15, 1890, 386.

97. M.B. Morton, "Federal and Confederate Pensions Contrasted," *The Forum*, September 1893, 73–74; McConnell, *Glorious Contentment*, 149–62.

98. George Worthington Adams, *Doctors in Blue: The Medical History of the Union Army in the Civil War* (Baton Rouge: Louisiana State University Press, 1996), 114. On medical care during the war, see also Sophronia E. Bucklin, *In Hospital and Camp* (Philadelphia: John E. Potter, 1869); Jane Stewart Woolsey, *Hospital Days* (New York: D. Van Nostrand, 1868); Martha Derby Perry, ed., *Letters from a Surgeon of the Civil War* (Boston: Little, Brown, 1906); Walt Whitman, *The Wound Dresser: A Series of Letters Written from the Hospitals in Washington During the War of the Rebellion*, ed. Richard Maurice Bucke (Boston: Small, Maynard, 1898).

99. Adams, *Doctors in Blue*, 14.

100. Oliver Wendell Holmes, *Soundings from the Atlantic* (Boston: Ticknor and Fields), 266–68. See also Ira B. Gardner, *Recollections of a Boy Member of the Maine 14th* (Lewiston, ME: Lewiston Journal, 1902).

## 5. Indian Wars

1. President Andrew Jackson's predecessors, while still giving priority to white settlers, pursued a less hostile policy toward the Native population. Henry Knox, the first secretary of war, had established a policy of respecting Indian treaties. While state and territorial governments often violated this policy, the federal government worked to maintain stable relations with the Native peoples through the presidency of John Quincy Adams. See Bernard W. Sheehan, *Seeds of Extinction: Jeffersonian Philanthropy and the American Indian* (Chapel Hill: University of North Carolina Press, 1973); William G. McLoughlin, *Cherokee Renascence in the New Republic* (Princeton, NJ: Princeton University Press, 1986); Gregory E. Dowd, *A Spirited Resistance: The North American Indian Struggle for Unity* (Baltimore: Johns Hopkins University Press, 1992); Reginald Horsman, *Expansion and American Indian Policy, 1783–1812* (Norman: University of Oklahoma Press, 1992); Laurence M. Hauptman, *Conspiracy of Interests: Iroquois Dispossession and the Rise of New York State* (Syracuse, NY: Syracuse University Press, 1999); Tim Alan Garrison, *The Legal Ideology of Removal: The Southern Judiciary and Native American Nations* (Athens: University of Georgia Press, 2002).

2. The Five Civilized Tribes was a name applied to the Cherokee, Chickasaw, Choctaw, Creeks, and Seminoles in recognition of their advanced social organization.

3. For another account of this patrol, see George A. McCall, *Letters from the Frontiers: Written During a Period of Thirty Years' Service in the Army of the United States* (Philadelphia: J.B. Lippincott, 1868).

4. John T. Sprague, *The Origin, Progress, and Conclusion of the Florida War* (New York: D. Appleton, 1848), 43, 360–67, 374–76.

5. W.A. Croffut, ed., *Fifty Years in Camp and Field: Diary of Major-General Ethan Allen Hitchcock, U.S.A.* (New York: G.P. Putnam's Sons, 1909), 90.

6. Croffut, ed., *Fifty Years in Camp and Field*, 120–22, 125.

7. However, the code contained a telling exception in that it worked on the assumption that civilian populations would obey military authority and that opposing forces would remain clearly demarcated by uniforms. In the case of insurgency, the military was allowed to act summarily, even to the execution of suspected saboteurs and guerrillas (called partisans at the time). As it turned out, this equation of guerrillas and their supporters with "highway robbers or pirates" would prove a sizable loophole that would be used to justify a number of horrific actions. *Instructions for the Government of Armies of the United States* (New York: D. Van Nostrand, 1863), 22.

8. This war is further obscured by a wide variety of names, including the Dakota War, Dakota Uprising, Sioux Outbreak of 1862, and Little Crow's War. Even the excellent *Oxford Companion to American Military History* gives the conflict but a single clause in a sentence; John Whiteclay Chambers II, ed., *The Oxford Companion to American Military History* (New York: Oxford University Press, 1999), 476.

9. Kenneth Carley, *The Dakota War of 1862: Minnesota's Other Civil War* (St. Paul: Minnesota Historical Society, 2001).

10. "Letters of a Badger Boy in Blue: The Letters of Chauncey H. Cooke," *Wisconsin Magazine of History* 4 (1920): 81–86, 96–97, 100.

11. Maurice Fitzgerald, "The Modoc War," *Americana* 21 (1927): 520–21. See also Arthur Quinn, *Hell with the Fire Out: A History of the Modoc War* (New York: Faber & Faber, 1998).

12. Brigham D. Madsen, *The Shoshoni Frontier and the Bear River Massacre* (Salt Lake City: University of Utah Press, 1985); Stephen E. Ambrose, *Crazy Horse and Custer: The Parallel Lives of Two American Warriors* (New York: Meridian, 1975), 61–65; Albert L. Hurtado, *Indian Survival on the California Frontier* (New Haven, CT: Yale University Press, 1988); Duane P. Schultz, *Month of the Freezing Moon: The Sand Creek Massacre, November, 1864* (New York: St. Martin's, 1991).

13. Ambrose, *Crazy Horse and Custer*, 313–24.

14. Andrew J. DeKever, *Here Rests in Honored Glory* (Bennington, VT: Merriam, 2008), 113; Dee Brown, *The Fetterman Massacre: An American Saga* (London: Barrie and Jenkins, 1972).

15. John G. Bourke, *On the Border with Crook* (New York: Scribner's, 1896), 311–16. See also William Parnell, "Operations Against Hostile Indians with General George Crook, 1867–68," *United Service*, n.s. 1 (1889): 482–98, 628–35.

16. Joseph Marshall III, *The Journey of Crazy Horse: A Lakota History* (New York: Penguin, 2005), 221–38; Ambrose, *Crazy Horse and Custer*, 411–34.

17. W.A. Graham, "The Lost is Found: Custer's Last Message Comes to Light!" *Cavalry Journal* 32 (July–August, 1942), 62–66.

18. Bourke, *On the Border with Crook*, 334.

19. Michael A. Bellesiles, *1877: America's Year of Living Violently* (New York: The New Press, 2010), 68.

20. Hamlin Garland, "General Custer's Last Fights as Seen by Two Moon," *McClure's Magazine* 11 (September 1898): 444–48.

21. For the most thorough account of the war, see Jerome A. Greene, *Nez Perce Summer 1877: The U.S. Army and the Nee-Me-Poo Crisis* (Helena: Montana Historical Society Press, 2000).

22. Reuben Gold Thwaites, ed., *Original Journals of the Lewis and Clark Expedition, 1804–1806* (New York: Dodd, Mead, 1905), 5:18.

23. Greene, *Nez Perce Summer 1877*, 389n46.

24. C.E.S. Wood, "Chief Joseph, the Nez Perce," *Century Illustrated Monthly Magazine* 28 (1884): 135–42.

25. Young Joseph, "An Indian's Views of Indian Affairs," *North American Review* 128 (April 1879): 412–33.

26. Bellesiles, *1877*, 86–87.

27. These Congressional Medals of Honor remain controversial, with many Native people and historians insisting that they should be withdrawn, especially those awarded for killing women and children attempting to hide or flee.

28. Robert M. Utley, *Last Days of the Sioux Nation* (New Haven, CT: Yale University Press, 1963); Rani-Henrik Andersson, *The Lakota Ghost Dance of 1890* (Lincoln: University of Nebraska Press, 2009).

29. There remains some disagreement over the exact number killed. At least 153 Indians, including 44 women and 18 children, were killed on the spot; another 20 to 30 died of their wounds. Twenty-five soldiers were killed, several by friendly fire.

30. Turning Hawk was one of the leaders of the Oglalas (a Sioux people) at Pine Ridge, a reservation in South Dakota.

31. A prominent Oglala chief and opponent of the Ghost Dance.

32. *Fourteenth Annual Report of the Bureau of Ethnology to the Secretary of the Smithsonian Institution, 1892–93* (Washington, DC: GPO, 1896), pt. 2: 868–70, 884–86; also known as James Mooney, *The Ghost-Dance Religion and the Sioux Outbreak of 1890*.

33. Hugh McGinnis and Olive Glasgow, "I Took Part in the Wounded Knee Massacre," *Real West: True Tales of the American Frontier* 8 (January 1966), 31–34. See also Edward S. Godfrey, "Cavalry Fire Discipline," *Journal of the Military Service Institution of the United States* 19 (1896): 257–59.

6. The Wars of Empire

1. Oliver Wendell Holmes Jr., *Speeches by Oliver Wendell Holmes* (Boston: Little, Brown, 1896), 56–66.

2. Carl Schurz, "The Venezuelan Question," in Frederic Bancroft, ed., *Speeches, Correspondence and Political Papers of Carl Schurz* (New York: G.P. Putnam's Sons, 1913), 5:250.

3. Theodore Roosevelt, *The Strenuous Life: Essays and Addresses* (New York: Century, 1902), 32–33, 37.

4. John T. Flynn, *As We Go Marching* (New York: Doubleday, 1944), 218.

5. The full quote is revealing: "It has been a splendid little war; begun with the highest motives, carried on with magnificent intelligence and spirit, favored by that Fortune which loves the brave." John Hay to Theodore Roosevelt, July 27, 1898, William Roscoe Thayer, *John Hay* (Boston: Houghton Mifflin, 1915), 2:337.

6. The use of the word "possessions" was almost instantaneous with their conquest; see, for instance, Andrew Carnegie, "Distant Possessions—The Parting of the Ways," *North American Review* 157 (August 1898): 239.

7. Smedley D. Butler, *War Is a Racket: The Antiwar Classic by America's Most Decorated General* (Port Townsend, WA: Feral House, 2003).

8. Richard Hofstadter found a total of thirty-five magazine articles published on the Philippines in the United States between 1818 and 1898, while military intelligence relied on the *Encyclopædia Britannica* for information on the islands. Richard Hofstadter, *The Paranoid Style in American Politics, and Other Essays* (Cambridge, MA: Harvard University Press, 1965), 169; T. Bentley Mott, "The Organization and Functions of a Bureau of Military Intelligence," *Journal of the Military Service Institution of the United States* 32 (1903): 185–86.

9. R. Cross, *The Voyage of the Oregon from San Francisco to Santiago in 1898* (Boston: Merrymount, 1898). Some spelling has been corrected. See also the memoir by future congressman Richard P. Hobson, *The Sinking of the "Merrimac"* (New York: Century, 1899).

10. Arthur M. Schlesinger Jr., *The Imperial Presidency* (New York: Houghton Mifflin, 1973), 303.

11. "War History in Private Letters," *The Outlook* 59 (1898): 921, 1021. See also ibid., 919–23, 968–73, 1,016–21.

12. Herschel V. Cashin and others, *Under Fire with the Tenth U.S. Cavalry* (New York, 1899), 61–62, 70–72, 82–85, 89, 92–106. See also John H. Parker, *History of the Gatling Gun Detachment, Fifth Army Corps, at Santiago* (Kansas City, MO: Hudson-Kimberly, 1898).

13. Theodore Roosevelt mentions the Cuban insurgents only briefly, twice referring to them as "tatterdemalion," and dismissed them as useless in battle. Theodore Roosevelt, *The Rough Riders* (New York: Charles Scribner's Sons, 1902), 81, 119.

14. Once more, Roosevelt has little respect for non-American soldiers, finding the Spanish lackluster and their fire far from deadly. Roosevelt, *The Rough Riders*, 109.

15. Roosevelt, *The Rough Riders*, 260–61.

16. Mary T. Sarnecky, *A History of the U.S. Army Nurse Corps* (Philadelphia: University of Pennsylvania Press, 1999), 29–34.

17. The *New York Times* ran several articles on these events, August 1–6, 1898. On blaming the soldiers for getting ill, see Russell A. Alger, *The Spanish-American War* (New York: Harper and Brothers, 1901), 411–24.

18. Named for Colonel Charles Wikoff who died at the Battle of El Caney.

19. Charles Johnson Post, *The Little War of Private Post* (Boston: Little, Brown, 1960), 305–6.

20. These events appear in few modern histories of the Spanish American War. For an exception to this historical amnesia, see David F. Trask, *The War with Spain in 1898* (Lincoln, NE: Bison Books, 1996), 324–35.

21. Post, *The Little War of Private Post*, 311–17.

22. Ibid., 335.

23. A fact evident to the public from an early date; *New York Times*, August 30, 1898.

24. *New York Journal* and *New York Herald*, August 26, 1898.

25. Post, *The Little War of Private Post*, 301.

26. *East-Hampton Star*, August 26, 1898, quoted in Richard Severo and Lewis Milford, *The Wages of War: When America's Soldiers Came Home—From Valley Forge to Vietnam* (New York: Simon & Schuster, 1989), 202. This book has an excellent discussion of the disaster at Camp Wikoff, 197–210.

27. Letter from Mrs. Chadwick, *New York Times*, August 27, 1898, quoted in Severo and Milford, *The Wages of War*, 203.

28. *New York Times*, August 6, 1898.

29. *New York Times*, August 26, 1898.

30. *New York Times*, September 12, 1898.

31. Alger, *The Spanish-American War*, 446. For Alger's outrageously untruthful account of these events, see ibid., 424–54.

32. Post, *The Little War of Private Post*, 336.

33. The most notable such case was that of Edward Findley (sometimes Finley) of New Rochelle, New York, whose wife and four children were literally cast onto the street when their home was sold at auction. *New York Herald*, August 4, 1898.

34. "The Battle of Manila Bay," *Century Illustrated Monthly Magazine* 56 (1898): 611.

35. Joel Evans, "Narrative of Joel C. Evans, Gunner of the *Boston*," *Century Illustrated Monthly Magazine* 56 (1898): 624–27.

36. Richard F. Pettigrew, *The Course of Empire: An Official Record* (New York: Boni & Liveright, 1920), 259.

37. Rudyard Kipling, *The White Man's Burden: A Poem* (New York: Doubleday and McClure, 1899).

38. Julie A. Tuason, "The Ideology of Empire in National Geographic's Coverage of the Philippines, 1898–1908," *Geographical Review* 89 (1999): 34–53.

39. Susan K. Harris, *God's Arbiters: Americans and the Philippines, 1898–1902* (New York: Oxford University Press, 2011), 14.

40. Elwell S. Otis, *Annual Report of the Major-General Commanding the Army*, pt. 2 (Washington, DC: GPO, 1899), 78.

41. Mary Curtis, *The Black Soldier, or the Colored Boys of the United States Army* (Washington, DC: Murray Brothers, 1915), 41.

42. Christopher Paul Moore, *Fighting for America: Black Soldiers—The Unsung Heroes of World War II* (New York: Presidio, 2005), 43.

43. "From a Colored Soldier in Manila," *The Public* (Chicago), October 14, 1899, 12–13.

44. Brian McAllister Linn, *The Philippine War, 1899–1902* (Lawrence: University of Kansas Press, 2000), 63. This quotation is also attributed to Aguinaldo, *Affairs in the Philippine Islands: Hearings before the Committee on the Philippines of the United States Senate* as in vol. 2 (Washington, DC: GPO, 1902): 895.

45. Mark Twain, "To the Person Sitting in Darkness," *The Public* 3 (1900): 718.

46. Peter Maguire, *Law and War: An American Story* (New York: Columbia University Press, 2001), 63–64.

47. Moorfield Storey and Julian Codman, *Secretary Root's Record: "Marked Severities" in Philippine Warfare* (Boston: G.H. Ellis, 1902), 33. Waller's version of these events was validated by three other officers; B.O. Flower, "Some Dead Sea Fruit of Our War of Subjugation," *The Arena* 27 (1902): 652–53.

48. Root to President Roosevelt, July 12, 1902, War Department, *General Orders and Circulars, Adjutant General's Office, 1902* (Washington, DC: GPO, 1903), 3.

49. "Punishing Torture and Inhumanity," *The Chautauquan* 35 (1902): 536.

50. *New York Times*, July 11, 1899, p.6.

51. Storey and Codman, *Secretary Root's Record*, 13–17, 34–36, 40–41.

52. Stuart C. Miller, *"Benevolent Assimilation": The American Conquest of the Philippines, 1899–1903* (New Haven, CT: Yale University Press, 1982), 213.

53. "Three Forms of Torture Applied by Americans to Natives in the Philippines," *New York World*, April 18, 1902.

54. Flower, "Some Dead Sea Fruit," 647. The private killed was Edward C. Richter.

55. John A. Hobson, *Imperialism: A Study* (London: George Allen & Unwin, 1902). Hobson's book is still in print.

56. Democrat of Utah, 1897–1903.

57. Frederick T. Dubois, a Republican from Idaho, switched to the Democrats after the 1900 election; senator, 1891–97, 1901–1907.

58. A large palm.

59. Charles H. Dietrich, Republican from Nebraska, a proponent of empire, led efforts to draft basic legislation for the Philippines; senator, 1901–1905.

60. Albert J. Beveridge, progressive Republican senator from Indiana and leading advocate of American expansionism, another good friend of President Roosevelt; senator, 1899–1911.

61. Thomas M. Patterson, Democrat from Colorado; senator, 1901–1907.

62. Tennessee Democrat Edward W. Carmack, a bitter opponent of Ida B. Wells for exposing the reality of lynching, was shot and killed by someone he had angered in a newspaper column; senator, 1901–1907.

63. A water buffalo.

64. Senate Document #331, 57th Congress, 1st Session, *Affairs in the Philippine Islands: Hearings Before the Committee on the Philippines of the United States Senate* (Washington, DC: GPO, 1902), 1538–1541, 2548–2552. For another version of the attack on Barrio la Nog, see Flower, "Some Dead Sea Fruit," *The Arena* 27 (1902): 650.

65. John R.M. Taylor, *The Philippine Insurrection Against the United States* (Washington, DC: Bureau of Insular Affairs, 1906).

66. Report of Major Cornelius Gardner, December 16, 1901, *Affairs in the Philippine Islands: Hearings before the Committee on the Philippines of the United States Senate* (Washington, DC: GPO, 1902), 2:884–85.

67. Stuart C. Miller, "Our My Lai in 1900: Americans in the Philippine Insurrection," *Transaction* 7 (1970): 22.

68. Twain, "To the Person Sitting in Darkness," 718.

69. Stanley Karnow, *In Our Image: America's Empire in the Philippines* (New York: Ballantine Books, 1990); Philip Caputo, *A Rumor of War* (New York: Henry Holt, 1996); Stephen Kinzer, *Overthrow: America's Century of Regime Change from Hawaii to Iraq* (New York: Times Books, 2007); Alfred W. McCoy, *Policing America's Empire: The United States, the Philippines, and the Rise of the Surveillance State* (Madison: University of Wisconsin Press, 2009); Alfred W. McCoy, ed., *Colonial Crucible: Empire in the Making of the Modern American State* (Madison: University of Wisconsin Press, 2009).

## 7. World War I

1. G. John Ikenberry, *American Foreign Policy: Theoretical Essays* (London: Longman, 2002), 148; Paula Marantz Cohen, *Silent Film and the Triumph of the American Myth* (New York: Oxford University Press, 2001), 57; Kathleen Burk, *Britain, America and the Sinews of War, 1914–1918* (Boston: Allen and Unwin, 1985); Martin Horn, *Britain, France, and the Financing of the First World War* (Montreal: McGill-Queen's University Press, 2002); Brett Gary, *The Nervous Liberals: Propaganda Anxieties from World War I to the Cold War* (New York: Columbia University Press, 1999).

2. George W. Norris, *Fighting Liberal: The Autobiography of George W. Norris* (Lincoln, NE: Bison Books, 1972), 196. See also William E. Leuchtenburg, *The Perils of Prosperity, 1914–1932* (Chicago: University of Chicago Press, 1993), 26; David M. Kennedy, *Over Here: The First World War and American Society* (New York: Oxford University Press, 1980).

3. Meirion and Susie Harries, *The Last Days of Innocence: America at War, 1917– 1918* (New York: Random House, 1997), 49–50; Joseph E. Persico, *Eleventh Month, Eleventh Day, Eleventh Hour: Armistice Day, 1918: World War I and its Violent Climax* (New York: Random House, 2005), 138.

4. For an excellent summary of the war, see John Keegan, *The First World War* (New York: Knopf, 1999).

5. Malcolm Brown, *The Imperial War Museum Book of the Somme* (London: Pan Books, 2002).

6. See David F. Trask, *The AEF and Coalition Warmaking, 1917–1918* (Lawrence: University Press of Kansas, 1993); Mark Ethan Grotelueschen, *The AEF Way of War: The American Army and Combat in World War I* (New York: Cambridge University Press, 2007).

7. Keegan, *The First World War*, 321.

8. George C. Marshall to John J. Pershing, October 24, 1930, Larry I. Bland, ed., *The Papers of George Catlett Marshall* (Baltimore: Johns Hopkins University Press, 1981), 1:360–61.

9. Harries, *The Last Days of Innocence*, 251.

10. Colonel Albertus W. Catlin, a Medal of Honor recipient for action in Veracruz, Mexico, in 1914, survived his wounds. The French government awarded him a Croix de Guerre for bravery at Belleau Wood and made him an Officer of the Legion of Honor.

11. Kemper Cowing and Courtney Cooper, eds., *Dear Folks at Home* (Boston: Houghton Mifflin, 1919), 141–44. Private Wahl's lieutenant was Dan Daly, one of only two marines—the other being General Smedley Butler—to receive the Medal of Honor for two separate military engagements. Daly became famous for having shouted to his men at Belleau Wood, "Come on, you sons of bitches! Do you want to live forever?" See also John W. Thomason Jr., *Fix Bayonets!* (New York: Charles Scribner's Sons, 1926).

12. Keegan, *The First World War*, 411.

13. Cowing and Cooper, eds., *Dear Folks at Home*, 79–81. See also Leslie Buswell, *With the American Ambulance Field Service in France: Personal Letters of a Driver at the Front* (Boston: Houghton Mifflin, 1916).

14. Even the reconnaissance ability of aircraft in World War I was often exaggerated. For instance, the Russian air force was the second largest in Europe at the start of the war, yet completely failed to detect the movement of massive German armies in August 1914. Keegan, *The First World War*, 144.

15. James McConnell, *Flying for France: With the American Escadrille at Verdun* (Garden City, NY: Doubleday, Page, 1917).

16. Alfred A. Cunningham Papers (PC 459), Marine Corps Museum Collections Unit, Building 198, Washington Navy Yard; copies are available at the museum as Graham A. Cosmas, ed., *Marine Flyer in France: The Diary of Captain Alfred A. Cunningham, November 1917–January 1918* (Washington, DC: GPO, 1974).

17. Hamilton Coolidge, *Letters of an American Airman* (Boston: Plimpton, 1919), viii, 160–63.

18. Hervey Allen, *Toward the Flame* (New York: George H. Doran, 1926), vii.

19. A theme brilliantly captured in Dalton Trumbo, *Johnny Got His Gun* (New York: J.B. Lippincott, 1939).

20. Paul Fussell, *The Great War and Modern Memory* (New York: Oxford University Press, 1975); Modris Eksteins, *Rites of Spring: The Great War and the Birth of the Modern Age* (New York: Houghton Mifflin, 1989).

21. Ernest Hemingway, *A Farewell to Arms* (New York: Charles Scribner's Sons, 1929), 184–85.

22. Cowing and Cooper, eds., *Dear Folks at Home*, 56–62. See also Eldon Canright, "Some War-Time Letters," *Wisconsin Magazine of History* 5 (1922): 171–200.

23. Peyton Randolph Campbell, *The Diary-Letters of Sergeant Peyton Randolph Campbell* (Buffalo, NY: Pratt & Lambert, 1919), 29, 64–65, 87–89, 126–29, 133–35, 138–42.

24. Cowing and Cooper, eds., *Dear Folks at Home*, 88–92.

25. William March, *Company K* (New York: Harrison Smith, 1933), 55.

26. B.H. Liddell Hart, *The Real War, 1914–1918* (Boston: Little, Brown, 1930), 130.

27. "Art Notes," *New York Times*, May 21, 1913.

28. Diary in possession of author. For the military memoirs of another child of German immigrants, see Raymond Wunderlich, *From Trench and Dugout* (Stockton, CA: printed for the author, 1919).

29. Priscilla Murolo and A.B. Chitty, *From the Folks Who Brought You the Weekend: A Short, Illustrated History of Labor in the United States* (New York: The New Press, 2003), 160–73.

30. Patricia Sullivan, *Lift Every Voice: The NAACP and the Making of the Civil Rights Movement* (New York: The New Press, 2009), 61–100.

31. Doris Weatherford, *A History of the American Suffragist Movement* (New York: MTM, 2005), 193–243.

32. June A. Willenz, *Women Veterans: America's Forgotten Heroines* (New York: Continuum, 1983), 10–15.

33. Shaking paralysis, or Parkinson's disease.

34. Cowing and Cooper, eds., *Dear Folks at Home*, 16–20.

35. Captain Linda L. Hewitt, *Women Marines in World War I* (Washington, DC: History and Museums Division, U.S. Marine Corps, 1974), 73.

36. Gerald Astor, *The Right to Fight: A History of African Americans in the Military* (Cambridge, MA: Da Capo, 2001), 108.

37. Ibid., 108; Charles H. Williams, *Sidelights on Negro Soldiers* (Boston: B.J. Brimmer, 1923), 62–67, 71–77.

38. Williams, *Sidelights on Negro Soldiers*, 38–47.

39. *The Crisis* 18 (May 1919): 18.

40. Williams, *Sidelights on Negro Soldiers*, 70–71.

41. Astor, *The Right to Fight*, 109–10; Williams, *Sidelights on Negro Soldiers*, 162–88, 197–208, 211–40.

42. Williams, *Sidelights on Negro Soldiers*, 138–55.

43. Astor, *The Right to Fight*, 112–13.

44. Studs Terkel, *"The Good War": An Oral History of World War Two* (New York: Pantheon, 1984), 11.

45. Tim McNeese, *Brown Versus Board of Education: Integrating America's Schools* (New York: Chelsea House, 2007), 45.

46. War Department, General Orders No. 45 (1919).

47. French restaurants at this time had private rooms, often associated with intimate relations, known as *cabinets particuliers*.

48. *The Crisis* 18 (May 1919): 16–18. Published with the original French documents.

49. Astor, *The Right to Fight*, 125.

50. *The Crisis* 18 (May 1919): 29. See also *Complete History of the Colored Soldiers in the World War* (New York: Bennett & Churchill, 1919); Arthur M. Little, *From Harlem to the Rhine: The Story of New York's Colored Volunteers* (New York: Covici, Friede, 1936); Arthur E. Barbeau and Florette Henri, *The Unknown Soldiers: African-American Troops in World War I* (Cambridge, MA: Da Capo, 1996).

51. Astor, *The Right to Fight*, 134.

52. Running for president in 1920, Republican Warren G. Harding proclaimed, "America's present need is not heroics, but healing; not nostrums, but normalcy; . . . not experiment, but equipoise; not submergence in internationality, but sustainment in triumphant nationality." His vision of a return to an imagined past before the experimentation of the Progressive Era won the largest landslide since the uncontested 1820 victory of James Monroe. Frederick E. Schortemeier, ed., *Rededicating America: The Life and Recent Speeches of Warren G. Harding* (Indianapolis: Bobbs-Merrill, 1920), 223.

53. Lieutenant Carl H. Christine later admitted to being the author of this document. Jennifer D. Keene, *Doughboys, the Great War, and the Remaking of America* (Baltimore: Johns Hopkins University Press, 2003), 252n62. A copy of "Facts and Questions Concerning the N.R.E.F." can be found at the National Archive, College Park, MD, Record Group 120.

54. *Detroit Free Press*, April 15, 1919; Benjamin D. Rhodes, *The Anglo-American Winter War with Russia, 1918–1919: A Diplomatic and Military Tragicomedy* (Westport, CT: Greenwood, 1988), 92, 95. See also David W. McFadden, *Alternative Paths: Soviets and Americans, 1917–1920* (New York: Oxford University Press, 1993); David S. Foglesong, *America's Secret War Against Bolshevism: U.S. Intervention in the Russian Civil War, 1917–1920* (Chapel Hill: University of North Carolina Press, 1995); Robert L. Willett, *Russian Sideshow: America's Undeclared War, 1918–1920* (Dulles, VA: Brassey, 2003).

55. Robert K. Murray, *Red Scare: A Study in National Hysteria, 1919–1920* (Minneapolis: University of Minnesota, 1955), 3–17.

56. *New York Times*, April 9, 1919, quoted in Thomas A. Rumer, *The American Legion: An Official History, 1919–1989* (New York: M. Evans, 1990), 34.

57. Fred G. Holmes, "Making Criminals out of Soldiers," *The Nation*, July 22, 1925, 114–16.

58. Charles Merz, "The Betrayal of Our War Veterans," *Century* 18 (August 1924): 435–41. See also *Hearings Before the Select Committee on Investigation of Veterans' Bureau*, U.S. Senate, 67th Congress (Washington, DC: GPO, 1923). For an excellent study of the corruption of the Veterans' Bureau in the 1920s, see Richard Severo and Lewis Milford, *The Wages of War: When America's Soldiers Came Home—From Valley Forge to Vietnam* (New York: Simon & Schuster, 1989), 247–63.

59. Paul Dickson and Thomas B. Allen, *The Bonus Army: An American Epic* (New York: Walker, 2004), 26–27.

60. Dickson and Allen, *The Bonus Army*, 26; Roger Daniels, *The Bonus Army: An Episode of the Great Depression* (Westport, CT: Greenwood, 1971), 36, 39.

61. Dickson and Allen, *The Bonus Army*, 28.

62. Walter W. Waters, *B.E.F.: The Whole Story of the Bonus Army* (New York: John Day, 1935), 9.

63. Dickinson and Allen, *The Bonus Army*, 153–83.

64. William Manchester, *American Caesar: Douglas MacArthur, 1880–1964* (Boston: Little, Brown, 1978), 161–66.

65. Springs wrote this book under the name John MacGavock Grider, *War Birds: Diary of an Unknown Aviator* (New York: George H. Doran, 1926), 268. See also Alan Seeger, *Poems by Alan Seeger* (New York: Charles Scribner's Sons, 1916); Sam K. Cowan, *Sergeant York and His People* (New York: Grosset & Dunlap, 1922), 229–56. See also Laurence Stewart, *Rainbow Bright* (Philadelphia: Dorrance, 1923).

## 8. World War II

1. Paul Fussell, *Wartime: Understanding and Behavior in the Second World War* (New York: Oxford University Press, 1989), ix.

2. The designation "GI," which first appeared in 1917, is thought to have originally meant "galvanized iron," "government issue," or "general issue."

3. Ernie Pyle, *Here Is Your War: Story of G.I. Joe* (Lincoln: University of Nebraska Press, 2004), 83.

4. Bruce Henderson, *Down to the Sea: An Epic Story of Naval Disaster and Heroism in World War II* (New York: HarperCollins, 2007), 131.

5. Louise Steinman, *The Souvenir: A Daughter Discovers Her Father's War* (Berkeley, CA: North Atlantic Books, 2008), 61; E.B. Potter, *Bull Halsey* (Annapolis, MD: Naval Institute Press, 2003), 13.

6. Diane Burke Fessler, *No Time for Fear: Voices of American Military Nurses in World War II* (East Lansing: Michigan State University Press, 1996), 14.

7. Fessler, *No Time for Fear*, 16. See the memoir of Rose DelMonico, CCSU Veterans History Project.

8. Diary of Robert T. Smith, CCSU Veterans History Project.

9. See also Robert L. Scott Jr., *God Is My Co-Pilot* (New York: Scribner's, 1943); Daniel Ford, *Flying Tigers: Claire Chennault and His American Volunteers, 1941–1942* (New York: HarperCollins, 2007).

10. The pacifist Jeannette Rankin of Montana, who had also voted against U.S. entry to World War I.

11. Fussell, *Wartime*, 4.

12. Stephen E. Ambrose, *Eisenhower: Soldier, General of the Army, President-elect, 1890–1952* (New York: Simon & Schuster, 1984), 149.

13. Geoffrey Perrett, *Days of Sadness, Years of Triumph: The American People, 1939–1945* (Baltimore: Coward, McCann & Geoghegan, 1973), 67.

14. Louis Simpson, *Collected Poems* (New York: Paragon House, 1988), 275.

15. Robert Kotlowitz, *Before Their Time* (New York: Anchor Books, 1999), 50.

16. Studs Terkel, *"The Good War": An Oral History of World War Two* (New York: Pantheon, 1984), 66.

17. Terkel, *"The Good War"*, 40.

18. Pyle, *Here Is Your War*, 246.

19. Martin Rockmore retired from the Marine Corps in 1964 as a brigadier general. In 1962 he established the Marine Corps Scholarship Program to aid the children of marines. Rockmore died in 1992.

20. This account is from interviews with Don Moss and documents he provided, available at the CCSU Veterans History Project. See also the journals of William E. Carey, Lyle H. Cate, William T. Gresh, and Robert McCulloch CCSU Veterans History Project.

21. Named for General George F. Elliott, the commandant of the Marine Corps, 1903–1910.

22. On the naval war in the Pacific, see Alvin Kernan, *Crossing the Line: A Bluejacket's World War II Odyssey* (Annapolis, MD: Naval Institute Press, 1994); Theodore C. Mason, *Rendezvous with Destiny: A Sailor's War* (Annapolis, MD: Naval Institute Press, 1997); C. Snelling Robinson, *200,000 Miles Aboard the Destroyer Cotton* (Kent, OH: Kent State University Press, 2001).

23. Peleliu remains controversial. The battle lasted two months, September to November 1944, at a cost of ten thousand American casualties. The First Marine Division lost one-third of its men and could not return to service until April 1945. Halsey did try to prevent the attack but was overruled by MacArthur. See E.B. Sledge, *With the Old Breed at Peleliu and Okinawa* (Novato, CA: Presidio Press, 1981); Bill Sloan,

*Brotherhood of Heroes: The Marines at Peleliu, 1944—The Bloodiest Battle of the Pacific War* (New York: Simon & Schuster, 2005).

24. This account is from interviews with Don Moss and documents he provided, available at the CCSU Veterans History Project. See also the journals of William E. Carey, Lyle H. Cate, William T. Gresh, and Robert McCulloch, CCSU Veterans History Project.

25. Terkel, *"The Good War"*, 38–39. See also the interviews with Joseph A. Hatala, Lawrence A. Busha, and Anthony Buemi, CCSU Veterans History Project.

26. Kotlowitz, *Before Their Time*, 101. See also the journal of Morton Katz, CCSU Veterans History Project.

27. Personal conversations with the author, 1984.

28. S.L.A. Marshall, *Men Against Fire: The Problem of Battle Command* (New York: William Morrow & Co., 1947).

29. Stephen E. Ambrose, *Band of Brothers: E Company, 506th Regiment, 101st Airborne from Normandy to Hitler's Eagle's Nest* (New York: Simon & Schuster, 1992).

30. Terkel, *"The Good War"*, 39.

31. Ibid., 40, 48.

32. Diary of Timothy L. Curran, CCSU Veterans History Project.

33. Charles Whiting, *Siegfried: The Nazis' Last Stand* (New York: Stein and Day, 1982), 228.

34. Sledge, *With the Old Breed at Peleliu and Okinawa*, 22.

35. Michael Lee Lanning, *The African American Soldier* (New York: Citadel, 2004), 162–64.

36. Ibid., 182.

37. Jack D. Foner, *Blacks and the Military in American History* (New York: Praeger, 1974), 172–73, 241; Perrett, *Days of Sadness, Years of Triumph*, 10.

38. *Negro Digest* 2 (1943): 47.

39. Lanning, *The African American Soldier*, 185. See the interview with Connie Nappier Jr., a Tuskegee airman, CCSU Veterans History Project.

40. *Army Service Forces Manual M5: Leadership and the Negro Soldier* (Washington, DC: GPO, 1944), 4.

41. Arnold Rampersad, ed., *The Collected Poems of Langston Hughes* (New York: Vintage, 1994), 271–72.

42. Wallace Terry, *Bloods: An Oral History of the Vietnam War by Black Veterans* (New York: Random House, 1984), 149–52.

43. Daniel K. Gibran, *The 92nd Infantry Division and the Italian Campaign in World War II* (Jefferson, NC: McFarland, 2001), 35. See also the diary of Francis Villano and interview with Pasquale J. D'Amato, CCSU Veterans History Project.

44. Elliot V. Converse III et al., *The Exclusion of Black Soldiers from the Medal of Honor in World War II* (Jefferson, NC: McFarland, 1997); Charles M. Blow, "My Very Own Captain America," *New York Times*, July 29, 2011. See also Phillip McGuire, ed., *Taps for a Jim Crow Army: Letters from Black Soldiers in World War II* (Lexington: University of Kentucky Press, 1993).

45. Willie James Macon interview, CCSU Veterans History Project; with special thanks to Eileen Hurst.

46. Craig S. Pascoe, "The Monroe Rifle Club: Finding Justice in an 'Ungodly and Social Jungle Called Dixie,'" in Michael A. Bellesiles, ed., *Lethal Imagination:*

*Violence and Brutality in American History* (New York: New York University Press, 1999), 398.

47. Robert F. Williams, *Negroes with Guns* (New York: Marzani & Munsell, 1962), 14.

48. Greg Robinson, *By Order of the President: FDR and the Internment of Japanese Americans* (Cambridge, MA: Harvard University Press, 2001); Jeanne Wakatsuki Houston and James D. Houston, *Farewell to Manzanar: A True Story of the Japanese American Experience* (Boston: Houghton Mifflin, 1974).

49. Ted Nakashima, "Concentration Camps: U.S. Style," *New Republic* 106 (June 15, 1942): 822-23.

50. The Editors, "Issei, Nisei, Kibei," *Fortune* 29 (April 1944): 118.

51. Terkel, *"The Good War"*, 30-31.

52. Lyn Crost, *Honor by Fire: Japanese Americans at War in Europe and the Pacific* (Novato, CA: Presidio, 1997).

53. "Gold Star Honor Nisei Killed in Action," *Los Angeles Times*, November 18, 1944, 4. See also the journal of Martin Gonzales, CCSU Veterans History Project.

54. Sledge, *With the Old Breed at Peleliu and Okinawa*, 252.

55. Giulio Douhet, *The Command of the Air*, trans. by Dino Ferraro (Tuscaloosa: University of Alabama Press, 2009), 58.

56. Randall Hansen, *Fire and Fury: The Allied Bombing of Germany, 1942–1945* (New York: NAL Caliber, 2008), 102.

57. Franklin Roosevelt, "Address at Chicago," Oct. 5, 1937, in J.B.S. Hardman, ed., *Rendezvous with Destiny: Addresses and Opinions of Franklin Delano Roosevelt* (New York: Dryden, 1944), 148.

58. Tsuyoshi Hasegawa, "Were the Atomic Bombings of Hiroshima and Nagasaki Justified?" in Yuki Tanaka and Marilyn B. Young, eds., *Bombing Civilians: A Twentieth-Century History* (New York: The New Press, 2009), 118.

59. Two of the finest books written on this subject cover the two primary theaters of war: Hansen, *Fire and Fury*; John Dower, *War Without Mercy: Race and Power in the Pacific War* (New York: Pantheon, 1987).

60. United States Strategic Bombing Survey, *Over-All Report (European War)* (Washington, DC: GPO, 1945); Albert Speer, *Inside the Third Reich: Memoirs* (New York: Macmillan, 1970).

61. United States Strategic Bombing Survey, *Summary Report (Pacific War)* (Washington, DC: GPO, 1946).

62. Robert Sherrod, "The Marines at Tarawa: November 1943," in *Reporting World War II* (New York: Library of America, 1995), 1:709-11. See the interview with John E. Pease, CCSU Veterans History Project.

63. Terkel, *"The Good War"*, 44-45.

64. Ibid., 66.

65. Ambrose, *Band of Brothers*, 79.

66. Robert S. La Forte et al., *With Only the Will to Live: Accounts of Americans in Japanese Prison Camps 1941–1945* (Wilmington, DE: SR Books, 1994).

67. Stanley L. Falk, *Bataan: The March of Death* (Norwalk, CT: Easton Press, 1962); David Foy, *For You the War Is Over: American Prisoners of War in Nazi Germany* (New York: Stein and Day, 1984); Ronald Searle, *To the Kwai—and Back: War Drawings, 1939–1945* (London: Imperial War Museum, 1986); Telford Taylor, *The Anatomy of the Nuremberg Trials: A Personal Memoir* (New York: Knopf, 1992).

68. Max Hastings, *Overlord: D-Day and the Battle for Normandy* (New York: Vintage, 2006), 253. On "friendly fire," see also Samuel W. Mitcham Jr. and Friedrich Von Stauffenberg, *The Battle of Sicily: How the Allies Lost Their Chance for Total Victory* (Mechanicsburg, PA: Stackpole Books, 2007), 130–32; Anthony Tucker-Jones, *Falaise: The Flawed Victory: The Destruction of Panzergruppe West, August 1944* (Barnsley, UK: Pen and Sword, 2008).

69. Leon J. Peragallo memoir and additional materials at CCSU Veterans History Project. See also interview with Stephen J. Stupak, CCSU Veterans History Project.

70. Harry Lichtenbaum, CCSU Veterans History Project. See also James J. Fahey, *Pacific War Diary, 1942–1945* (Boston: Houghton Mifflin, 1963); Thomas Hayes, *Bilibid Diary: The Secret Notebooks of Commander Thomas Hayes* (Hamden, CT: Archon Books, 1987).

71. Richard Prendergast, in Terkel, *"The Good War"*, 49–53; Kurt Vonnegut, *Slaughterhouse-Five* (New York: Delacorte, 1969).

72. I.C.B. Dear, ed., *The Oxford Companion to World War II* (New York: Oxford University Press, 1995), 546.

73. Lieutenant Paul Boesch received numerous medals during the war, including the Silver Star and the French Croix de Guerre. After the war he became a well-known wrestling promoter.

74. Arthur C. Neriani, CCSU Veterans History Project; this narrative is based on two different accounts by Neriania.

75. William M. Blair interview, CCSU Veterans History Project.

76. Barrett Tillman, *Whirlwind: The Air War Against Japan, 1942–1945* (New York: Simon & Schuster, 2010).

77. See the interview with William T. Burrows, CCSU Veterans History Project.

78. See Leslie R. Groves, *Now It Can Be Told: The Story of the Manhattan Project* (New York: Harper & Row, 1962); Richard Rhodes, *The Making of the Atomic Bomb* (New York: Simon & Schuster, 1986).

79. See Sledge, *With the Old Breed at Peleliu and Okinawa*.

80. Richard Rasmus and Richard Prendergast, in Terkel, *"The Good War"*, 47, 57.

81. Sweeney wrote a controversial account of his mission, *War's End: An Eyewitness Account of America's Last Atomic Mission* (New York: Avon Books, 1997). See also Paul W. Tibbets, *Return of the Enola Gay* (Columbus, OH: Mid Coast Marketing, 1998).

82. William L. Laurence, "Atomic Bombing of Nagasaki Told by Flight Member," *New York Times*, September 9, 1945.

83. Robert B. August, CCSU Veterans History Project. August died in January 2010. For an eyewitness account of the bombing, see Michihiko Hachiya, *Hiroshima Diary: The Journal of a Japanese Physician, August 6–November 30, 1945*, trans. Warner Wells (Chapel Hill: University of North Carolina Press, 1955).

84. Kotlowitz, *Before Their Time*, 152.

85. On women in the military in World War II, see Paula N. Poulos, *A Woman's War Too: U.S. Women in the Military in WWII* (Washington, DC: National Archives, 1996); Michael E. Stevens and Ellen D. Goldlust, eds., *Women Remember the War, 1941–1945* (Madison, WI: State Historical Society of Wisconsin, 1993).

86. Robert Lekachman, in Terkel, *"The Good War"*, 68.

87. Russell D. Buhite and David W. Levy, eds., *FDR's Fireside Chats* (Norman: University of Oklahoma Press, 1992), 264.

88. John Morton Blum, *V Was for Victory* (New York: Harcourt, Brace, 1976), 223.

89. Robert M. Hutchins, "The Threat to American Education," *Collier's*, December 30, 1944, 20–21, quoted in David Nasaw, *Schooled to Order: A Social History of Public Schooling in the United States* (New York: Oxford University Press, 1979), 178.

90. Willard Waller, *The Veteran Comes Back* (New York: Dryden, 1944), 6, 16.

91. Bernard I. Bell, "The Church and the Veteran," *Atlantic Monthly* 174 (December 1944): 64–68.

92. J. Gordon Chamberlin, *The Church and Demobilization* (New York: Abingdon-Cokesbury, 1945), 14.

93. "Veterans' New Dealer," *Collier's*, November 24, 1945, 24, quoted in Lawrence J. Korb et al., *Serving America's Veterans: A Reference Handbook* (Santa Barbara, CA: ABC-CLIO, 2009), 30.

94. Richard Prendergast, in Terkel, *"The Good War"*, 57–58.

95. Ambrose, *D-Day*, 330.

96. June A. Willenz, *Women Veterans: America's Forgotten Heroines* (New York: Continuum, 1983), 177–79; Richard Severo and Lewis Milford, *The Wages of War: When America's Soldiers Came Home—From Valley Forge to Vietnam* (New York: Simon & Schuster, 1989), 303.

97. Richard Prendergast, in Terkel, *"The Good War"*, 58.

98. Richard Rasmus and Richard Prendergast, in Terkel, *"The Good War"*, 48.

## 9. Cold Wars: Korea and Vietnam

1. Robert Dallek, *Harry S. Truman* (New York: Henry Holt, 2008), 107; Max Hastings, *The Korean War* (New York: Simon & Schuster, 1987), 329.

2. Lisle A. Rose, *The Cold War Comes to Main Street: America in 1950* (Lawrence: University Press of Kansas, 1999), 186.

3. Dennis Wainstock, *Truman, MacArthur, and the Korean War* (Westport, CT: Greenwood, 1999), 18.

4. Harry G. Summers Jr., "The Korean War—A Fresh Perspective," *Military History* 13 (1996): 2.

5. James L. Holloway, *Aircraft Carriers at War: A Personal Retrospective of Korea, Vietnam, and the Soviet Confrontation* (Annapolis, MD: Naval Institute Press, 2007), 46.

6. David Halberstam, *The Coldest Winter: America and the Korean War* (New York: Hyperion, 2007), 147.

7. Clay Blair, *The Forgotten War: America in Korea, 1950–1953* (Annapolis, MD: Naval Institute Press, 2003), 78.

8. Lt. Col. Bob E. Edwards sent a report to Washington, DC, on these executions, complete with photographs, which can be found in the National Archive.

9. Charles J. Hanley, Sang-Hun Choe, and Martha Mendoza, *The Bridge at No Gun Ri: A Hidden Nightmare from the Korean War* (New York: Henry Holt, 2001), 74–75; Grace M. Cho, *Haunting the Korean Diaspora: Shame, Secrecy, and the Forgotten War* (Minneapolis: University of Minnesota Press, 2008), 19–22, 50–79.

10. O.H.P. King, *Tail of the Paper Tiger* (Caldwell, ID: Caxton, 1961), 245.

11. Sahr Conway-Lanz, *Collateral Damage: Americans, Noncombatant Immunity, and Atrocity after World War II* (New York: Routledge, 2006), 99–100; U.S. Department of the Army, *No Gun Ri Review* (January 2001), xii.

12. Hanley, Choe, and Mendoza, *The Bridge at No Gun Ri*, 80.

13. Ibid., 85.

14. Ibid., 75. Since the publication of this important book, some authors have questioned whether direct orders to strafe civilians were in fact given, suggesting that pilots may have been under an erroneous impression that such orders were in place. Sahr Conway-Lanz offers a careful examination of the evidence and concludes that such orders had been given. *Collateral Damage*, 92–103.

15. Hanley, Choe, and Mendoza, *The Bridge at No Gun Ri*, 90.

16. Ibid., 151–52.

17. Charles J. Hanley, "No Gun Ri: Official Narrative and Inconvenient Truths," *Critical Asian Studies* 42 (2010): 589–622.

18. Blair, *The Forgotten War*, 77.

19. Matthew B. Ridgway, *The Korean War* (Garden City NY: Doubleday, 1967), 63. Dean Acheson declared the Chinese attacks "the worst defeat of U.S. forces since Bull Run. The generalship was even more stupid. . . . MacArthur's true nature was never plainer than in defeat. He first lost his head . . . and then started to blame his government for his own assininity." Ray Geselbracht and Dean C. Acheson, eds., *Affection and Trust: The Personal Correspondence of Harry S. Truman and Dean Acheson, 1953–1971* (New York: Knopf, 2010), 115.

20. Hastings, *The Korean War*, 165.

21. Donald Dugay journal, CCSU Veterans History Project. See also Bob Drury and Tom Clavin, *The Last Stand of Fox Company* (New York: Atlantic Monthly Press, 2009).

22. Truman's removal of MacArthur has remained controversial from 1951 through the present; see Richard H. Rovere and Arthur M. Schlesinger Jr., *The General and the President* (New York: Farrar, Straus, and Giroux, 1951); Michael D. Pearlman, *Truman & MacArthur: Policy, Politics, and the Hunger for Honor and Renown* (Bloomington: Indiana University Press, 2008).

23. Halberstam, *The Coldest Winter*, 496.

24. Hastings, *The Korean War*, 271.

25. Arpad J. Ostheimer, CCSU Veterans History Project.

26. Donald G. Martin, CCSU Veterans History Project, with special thanks to Vincent Roche.

27. Hastings, *The Korean War*, 329.

28. See, for instance, Harold Martin, "How Do Our Negro Troops Measure Up?" *Saturday Evening Post* 223 (June 16, 1951): 30–31, 139, 141.

29. Gerald Astor, *The Right to Fight: A History of African Americans in the Military* (Cambridge, MA: Da Capo, 2001), 350–98.

30. Astor, *The Right to Fight*, 352.

31. Charles M. Bussey, *Firefight at Yechon: Courage and Racism in the Korean War* (Lincoln: University of Nebraska Press, 2002), 102–4.

32. Karin L. Stanford, ed., *If We Must Die: African American Voices on War and Peace* (Lanham, MD: Rowman & Littlefield, 2008), 200–205.

33. Astor, *The Right to Fight*, 385–86.

34. U.S. Army Center of Military History.

35. Astor, *The Right to Fight*, 393, 396–97.

36. Susan L. Carruthers, *Cold War Captives: Imprisonment, Escape, and Brainwashing* (Berkeley: University of California Press, 2009), 194. See also José Mares, Experiencing War: Stories from the Veterans History Project, Library of Congress.

37. *New York Times*, April 21, 1953.

38. Paul M. Edwards, *To Acknowledge a War: The Korean War in American Memory* (Westport, CT: Greenwood, 2000), 34.

39. "A Few Come Home," *Life*, May 3, 1953, 39.

40. Ibid., 36.

41. *Newsweek*, August 17, 1953, 21.

42. William Pencak, ed., *Encyclopedia of the Veteran in America* (Santa Barbara, CA: ABC-CLIO, 2009), 1:256–57.

43. *New York Times Magazine*, August 9, 1953; Pencak, ed., *Encyclopedia of the Veteran in America*, 1:255–56.

44. Richard Severo and Lewis Milford have an excellent chapter on this strange moment in America's military history, *The Wages of War: When America's Soldiers Came Home—From Valley Forge to Vietnam* (New York: Simon & Schuster, 1989), 334–44. See also Lori Lyn Bogle, *The Pentagon's Battle for the American Mind: The Early Cold War* (College Station: Texas A&M University Press, 2004).

45. "Why Did So Many G.I. Captives Give In?" *U.S. News & World Report*, February 24, 1956, 56–72, quote on 61.

46. Harding College, now Harding University, in Searcy, Arkansas.

47. John Greenway, "The Colonel's Korean 'Turncoats,'" *The Nation*, November 10, 1962, 302–5.

48. For the repetition of Mayer's assertions as fact, see Eugene Kinkead, *In Every War But One* (New York: W.W. Norton, 1959).

49. Hugh D. Scott Jr., "The Other Gap: A Flaw in Our National Character," *American Bar Association Journal* 45 (1959): 480–81.

50. T.R. Fehrenbach, *This Kind of War: A Study in Unpreparedness* (New York: Macmillan, 1963), 66, 84, 378. Incredibly, these quotes remain in the 2000 edition of the book, *This Kind of War: The Classic Korean War History* (Dulles, VA: Brassey's, 2000).

51. Betty Friedan, *The Feminine Mystique* (New York: W.W. Norton, 1963), 398.

52. Eric Alterman, *When Presidents Lie: A History of Official Deception and Its Consequences* (New York: Viking, 2004), 200.

53. For an excellent summary of these events, see Stanley Karnow, *Vietnam: A History* (New York: Penguin, 1997), 364–92.

54. Mark Clodfelter, *The Limits of Air Power: The American Bombing of North Vietnam* (New York: Free Press, 1989); Earl H. Tilford Jr., *Setup: What the Air Force Did in Vietnam and Why* (Honolulu, HA: University Press of the Pacific, 2002); Ronald B. Frankum Jr., *Like Rolling Thunder: The Air War in Vietnam, 1964–1975* (Lanham, MD: Rowman & Littlefield, 2005).

55. Marilyn B. Young, *The Vietnam Wars, 1945–1990* (New York: HarperCollins, 1991), 129–32, 191.

56. James William Gibson, *The Perfect War: The War We Couldn't Lose and How We Did* (New York: Vintage, 1988), 374–75.

57. Jonathan Neale, *A People's History of the Vietnam War* (New York: The New Press, 2004), 79.

58. John Clark Pratt, ed., *Vietnam Voices: Perspectives on the War Years, 1941–1975* (Athens: University of Georgia Press, 1999), 650–51.

59. Gibson, *The Perfect War*, 225, 319. See also Admiral Ulysses S. Grant Sharp, *Strategy for Defeat: Vietnam in Retrospect* (Novato, CA: Presidio, 1998).

60. Karnow, *Vietnam: A History*, 33–34. See also Keith Nolan, *House to House: Playing the Enemy's Game in Saigon, May 1968* (St. Paul, MN: Zenith, 2006).

61. Christian Appy, *Working Class War: American Combat Soldiers and Vietnam* (Chapel Hill: University of North Carolina Press, 1993), 17–38.

62. David Cortright, *Soldiers in Revolt: GI Resistance During the Vietnam War* (Chicago: Haymarket Books, 2005), 5, 10–15, 273. See also Michael Herr, *Dispatches* (New York: Knopf, 2009), 172–73. Even some senior officers came to feel that they could not serve in such a war and reluctantly left the service. See, for example, the books by three colonels: William R. Corson (marines), *The Betrayal* (New York: W.W. Norton, 1968); Jack Broughton (air force), *Thud Ridge* (Philadelphia: J. B. Lippincott, 1969); Anthony Herbert (army) and James T. Wooton, *Soldier* (New York: Holt, Rinehart and Winston, 1973).

63. See, for instance, Cincinnatus, *Self-Destruction: The Disintegration and Decay of the United States Army During the Vietnam Era* (New York: W.W. Norton, 1981), 70–82; Herbert and Wooton, *Soldier*, 267–68.

64. Colonel Robert D. Heinl Jr., "The Collapse of the Armed Forces," *Armed Forces Journal*, June 7, 1971, p.38. In general on this point, see Shelby L. Stanton, *The Rise and Fall of an American Army: U.S. Ground Forces in Vietnam, 1965–1973* (Novato, CA: Presidio, 1985).

65. Cortright, *Soldiers in Revolt*, 106–37.

66. Andrew Hunt, *The Turning: A History of Vietnam Veterans Against the War* (New York: New York University Press, 1999).

67. United States Senate, *Legislative Proposals Relating to the War in Southeast Asia: Hearings Before the Committee on Foreign Relations*, U.S. Senate, 92d Congress, First Session (Washington, DC: GPO, 1971), 179–85.

68. Donald Jackson, "Confessions of 'The Winter Soldiers,'" *Life*, July 9, 1971, 22–27. The casual racism of the Vietnam War can be rather surprising to the modern reader. In a memoir of his captivity published in *U.S. News & World*, Lieutenant Commander John McCain repeatedly refers to his captors as "gooks." *U.S. News & World Report*, May 14, 1973.

69. Pratt, ed., *Vietnam Voices*, 653.

70. Herbert and Wooton, *Soldier*. In 1973 the CBS television show *60 Minutes* questioned Herbert's honesty based largely on the testimony of an officer whom the army had removed from his command for throwing a Vietnamese out of a helicopter. Herbert instituted a libel suit that dragged through the courts for the next thirty years before a U.S. Court of Appeals ruled for Herbert.

71. Bernard Edelman, *Dear America: Letters Home from Vietnam* (New York: W.W. Norton, 1985), 209–10.

72. Wallace Terry, *Bloods: An Oral History of the Vietnam War by Black Veterans* (New York: Random House, 1984), 235.

73. Letter dated September 2, 1966, in Edelman, *Dear America*, 61.

74. Pratt, ed., *Vietnam Voices*, 647–50.

75. Olsen to Rosemary Dresch, Aug. 31, 1969, in Edelman, ed., *Dear America*, 118.

76. Terry, *Bloods*, 4–5.

77. Arthur Wiknik Jr., *Nam Sense: Surviving Vietnam with the 101st Airborne Division* (Havertown, PA: Casement, 2005), xi–xii, 6–7, 9, 21, 23. With thanks to the author for allowing me to quote at length from his book.

78. Edelman, ed., *Dear America*, 103.

79. Karnow, *Vietnam*, 34.

80. Lieutenant Robert C. Ransom of the Eleventh Light Infantry, April 1968, in Edelman, ed., *Dear America*, 181.

81. Eric M. Bergerud, *The Dynamics of Defeat: The Vietnam War in Hau Nghia Province* (Boulder, CO: Westview, 1991), 229.

82. Terry, *Bloods*, 12.

83. Ibid., 173.

84. Karnow, *Vietnam*, 482.

85. Michael Bilton and Kevin Sim, *Four Hours in My Lai* (New York: Viking, 1992), 130–31.

86. Bilton and Sim, *Four Hours in My Lai*, 119–23. See also John Sack, *Lieutenant Calley: His Own Story* (New York: Viking Press, 1974).

87. Hugh Thompson, personal conversation with author, 1996.

88. Ibid.; Bilton and Sim, *Four Hours in My Lai*, 135–41.

89. Richard Goldstein, "Hugh Thompson, 62, Who Saved Civilians at My Lai, Dies," *New York Times*, January 7, 2006.

90. Joseph Tuso, *Singing the Vietnam Blues: Songs of the Air Force in Southeast Asia* (College Station: Texas A&M University Press, 1990), 185; John Whiteclay Chambers, ed., *The Oxford Companion to American Military History* (New York: Oxford University Press, 1999), 459; Jonathan Schell, *The Jonathan Schell Reader: On the United States at War, the Long Crisis of the American Republic, and the Fate of the Earth* (New York: Avalon, 2004), 52–55.

91. Terry, *Bloods*, 213.

92. Ibid., *Bloods*, 218.

93. Richard R. Moser, *The New Winter Soldiers: GI and Veteran Dissent During the Vietnam Era* (Brunswick, NJ: Rutgers University Press, 1996), 67.

94. Mark Lane, *Conversations with Americans* (New York: Simon & Schuster, 1970), 242. Tim O'Brien also reports a fragging incident against a sergeant thought to be racist; *If I Die in a Combat Zone, Box Me Up and Ship Me Home* (New York: Broadway Books, 1999), 172–73.

95. James William Gibson, *The Perfect War: The War We Couldn't Lose and How We Did* (New York: Vintage, 1988), 210.

96. David H. Hackworth and Julie Sherman, *About Face: The Odyssey of an American Warrior* (New York: Simon & Schuster, 1990), 604.

97. David Cortright, *Soldiers in Revolt: GI Resistance During the Vietnam War* (Chicago: Haymarket Books, 2005), 38.

98. Wiknik, *Nam Sense*, 216.

99. Ibid., 217, 248.

100. Pratt, ed., *Vietnam Voices*, 651.

101. Wiknik, *Nam Sense*, 35.

102. Edelman, ed., *Dear America*, 48.

103. Terry, *Bloods*, 66.

104. See, for example, W. D. Ehrhart, *Vietnam-Perkasie: A Combat Marine Memoir* (Boston: University of Massachusetts Press, 1995), 111, 247; Terry, *Bloods*, 25; Edelman, ed., *Dear America*, 97, 143; Pratt, ed., *Vietnam Voices*, 314, 398, 417, 575, 649.

105. Ron Kovic, *Born on the Fourth of July* (New York: Akashic Books, 2005), 65, 116.

106. Terry, *Bloods*, 55.

107. Ibid., 134.

108. Private Reginald Edwards, in ibid., 16–17.

109. Harold Bryant, in Terry, *Bloods*, 29.

110. Terry, *Bloods*, 219.

111. Appy, *Working Class War*, 17.

112. Karnow, *Vietnam*, 34–35.

113. *Army Magazine* (the Journal of the Association of the United States Army) 4 (1953): 25.

114. One often ignored aspect of the Vietnam War is the increased number of women who served in the military—and the failure of the Veterans Administration to offer adequate care to them after the war. By the 1980s there were 1.2 million women veterans, yet the VA offered few of the services women needed, such as gynecologists. June A. Willenz, *Women Veterans: America's Forgotten Heroines* (New York: Continuum, 1983), 184. See also Lynda Van Devanter with Christopher Morgan, *Home Before Morning: The Story of an Army Nurse in Vietnam* (New York: Beaufort Books, 1983).

115. Among the many novels, see, for instance, Larry Heinemann, *Close Quarters* (New York: Farrar, Straus and Giroux, 1977) and *Paco's Story* (New York: Farrar, Straus and Giroux, 1986); James Webb, Fields of Fire (Englewood Cliffs, NJ: Prentice-Hall, 1978); John M. Del Vecchio, *The 13th Valley* (New York: St. Martin's, 1982); Robert Olen Butler, *A Good Scent from a Strange Mountain* (New York: Henry Holt, 1992). For memoirs, see Ronald J. Glasser, *365 Days* (New York: George Braziller, 1971); Kovic, *Born on the Fourth of July*; Philip Caputo, *A Rumor of War* (New York: Henry Holt, 1977); Frederick Downs, *The Killing Zone: My Life in the Vietnam War* (New York: W.W. Norton, 1978); Robert Mason, *Chickenhawk* (New York: Viking, 1983); Michael Lee Lanning, *The Only War We Had: A Platoon Leader's Journal of Vietnam* (New York: Ballantine Books, 1987)

116. Tim O'Brien, *The Things They Carried* (Boston: Houghton Mifflin, 1990), 65–66, 68.

117. Tim O'Brien, *Going After Cacciato* (New York: Delacorte, 1978), 320–21.

118. William D. Ehrhart, ed., *Carrying the Darkness: The Poetry of the Vietnam War* (Lubbock: Texas Tech University Press, 1989), 130.

119. Donald Jackson, "Confessions of 'The Winter Soldiers,'" *Life*, July 9, 1971, 27.

120. Bruce Weigl, "The Way of Tet," in *Song of Napalm: Poems* (New York: Grove Atlantic, 1988), 6.

121. Harry G. Summers Jr., *On Strategy: A Critical Analysis of the Vietnam War* (Novato, CA: Presidio, 1995), 1.

122. Karnow, *Vietnam*, 20–21. Giap's view has found wide acceptance among those who have studied the strategic nature of the war. In addition to Summers, *On Strategy*, see General Bruce Palmer Jr., *The 25-Year War: America's Military Role in Vietnam* (Lexington: University of Kentucky Press, 1984).

## 10. Iraq and Afghanistan

1. Peter B. Lane and Ronald E. Marcello, eds., *Warriors and Scholars: A Modern War Reader* (Denton: University of North Texas Press, 2005), 123. General Meyer defended his portrayal of a "hollow army" before Congress in 1983. *Department of*

*Defense Authorization for Appropriations for Fiscal Year 1984* (Washington, DC: GPO, 1983), 2:556.

2. Daniel P. Bolger, *Americans at War, 1975–1986: An Era of Violent Peace* (New York: Random House, 1991); David Locke Hall, *The Reagan Wars: A Constitutional Perspective on War Powers and the Presidency* (Boulder, CO: Westview, 1991).

3. Daniel Wirls, *Buildup: The Politics of Defense in the Reagan Era* (Ithaca, NY: Cornell University Press, 1992).

4. The Powell Doctrine is often seen as an elaboration of the Weinberger Doctrine, developed by Secretary of Defense Caspar Weinberger in 1984. Colin L. Powell, "U.S. Forces: Challenges Ahead," *Foreign Affairs* 72 (1992–93): 32–45; Caspar W. Weinberger, *Fighting for Peace: Seven Critical Years in the Pentagon* (New York: Warner Books, 1990).

5. It should be noted that the 1989 U.S. invasion of Panama followed the Powell Doctrine in many ways. President George H.W. Bush ordered Operation Just Cause in order to seize General Manuel Noriega, who had once been a loyal client of the United States Capturing Noriega cost the lives of 23 American and 205 Panamanian soldiers, as well as an estimated two to four thousand civilians. See Thomas Donnelly, Margaret Roth, and Caleb Baker, *Operation Just Cause: The Storming of Panama* (Lanham, MD: Lexington Books, 1991); The Independent Commission of Inquiry on the U.S. Invasion of Panama, *The U.S. Invasion of Panama: The Truth Behind Operational 'Just Cause'* (Boston: South End, 1999).

6. Rick Atkinson, *Crusade: The Untold Story of the Persian Gulf War* (Boston: Houghton Mifflin, 1993); Michael R. Gordon and General Bernard E. Trainor, *The Generals' War: The Inside Story of the Conflict in the Gulf* (Boston: Back Bay Books, 1995).

7. Penny Coleman, *Flashback: Posttraumatic Stress Disorder, Suicide, and the Lessons of War* (Boston: Beacon, 2006 ), 161.

8. David Bolger, *Savage Peace: Americans at War in the 1990s* (Novato, CA: Presidio, 1995); Mark Bowden, *Black Hawk Down* (New York: Signet Books, 1999); Ann R. Markusen and Sean S. Costigan, eds., *Arming the Future: A Defense Industry for the 21st Century* (New York: Council on Foreign Relations Press, 1999); Robert C. DiPrizio, *Armed Humanitarians: U.S. Interventions from Northern Iraq to Kosovo* (Baltimore: Johns Hopkins University Press, 2002); Peter Dombrowski and Eugene Gholz, *Buying Military Transformation: Technological Innovation and the Defense Industry* (New York: Columbia University Press, 2006); Harvey Sapolsky et al., eds., *US Military Innovation Since the Cold War: Creation Without Destruction* (New York: Routledge, 2009).

9. Seth G. Jones, *In the Graveyard of Empires: America's War in Afghanistan* (New York: W.W. Norton, 2009).

10. Richard A. Clarke, *Against All Enemies: Inside America's War on Terror* (New York: Free Press, 2004). Fabrication by the Pentagon became routine in these wars; see Rick Bragg, *I Am a Soldier, Too: The Jessica Lynch Story* (New York: Knopf, 2003); Jon Krakauer, *Where Men Win Glory: The Odyssey of Pat Tillman* (New York: Random House, 2009).

11. White House press release, May 29, 2003, "Interview of the President by TVP, Poland."

12. Lloyd G. Gardner, *The Long Road to Baghdad: A History of U.S. Foreign Policy from the 1970s to the Present* (New York: The New Press, 2008), 172.

13. Ibid., 200–204, 238.

14. Barton Gellman, *Angler: The Cheney Vice Presidency* (New York: Penguin Press, 2008), 132–33, 173–79, 346–50; "Former President George W. Bush Defends

Torture," *New York Daily News*, May 29, 2009; Ali H. Soufan, *The Black Banners: The Inside Story of 9/11 and the War Against Al Qaeda* (New York: W.W. Norton, 2011).

15. Seymour M. Hersh, *Chain of Command: The Road from 9/11 to Abu Ghraib* (New York: HarperCollins, 2004); Mark P. Denbeaux and Jonathan Hafetz, eds., *The Guantánamo Lawyers: Inside a Prison, Outside the Law* (New York: New York University Press, 2009); Rajiv Chandrasekaran, *Imperial Life in the Emerald City: Inside Iraq's Green Zone* (New York: Vintage, 2007). There were also individual cases of atrocities committed by U.S. troops; see, for example, "Discrediting the US Military: US Soldier Admits Killing Unarmed Afghans for Sport," *The Guardian*, March 23, 2011.

16. Martin Schram, *Vets Under Siege: How America Deceives and Dishonors Those Who Fight Our Battles* (New York: Thomas Dunne Books, 2008); Jason Leopold, "Court Demands Mental Health Care Reform for Veterans, Cites VA's 'Unchecked Incompetence,'" *Truthout*, May 13, 2011. Since the appointment of General Eric Shinseki as secretary of veterans affairs, there is some evidence that the VA is making real efforts to treat veterans with greater respect. Lawrence Downes, "The V.A. Tries to Get Beyond Its Culture of No," *New York Times*, July 16, 2011.

17. Nadia Prupis, "Veteran Suicides Outnumber US Military Deaths in Iraq and Afghanistan," *New York Times*, October 22, 2010; Bob Herbert, "The Way We Treat Our Troops," *New York Times*, October 22, 2010; Torrey Shannon, "The VA Joins Big Banks in the Foreclosure Business," *Huffington Post*, January 21, 2011; Beth Ford Roth, "Bank of America Settles Suit over Military Family Foreclosures," *Home Post*, May 26, 2011; Dan Briody, *The Halliburton Agenda: The Politics of Oil and Money* (New York: John Wiley & Sons, 2004); Jeremy Scahill, *Blackwater: The Rise of the World's Most Powerful Mercenary Army* (New York: Nation Books, 2007).

18. Jones, *In the Graveyard of Empires*, 97; Gary Bernstein and Ralph Pezzullo, *Jawbreaker: The Attack on Bin Laden and Al Qa'ida* (New York: Crown, 2005).

19. Jones, *In the Graveyard of Empires*, 113–15.

20. Tommy Franks and Malcolm McConnell, *American Soldier* (New York: Regan Books, 2004), 324.

21. The U.S. increased its Iraq commitment to 6.5 per thousand in 2005. Jones, *In the Graveyard of Empires*, 119; James T. Quinlivan, "Burden of Victory: The Painful Arithmetic of Stability Operations" (Santa Monica, CA: Rand Corporation, 2003), available at the Rand website.

22. "Afghanistan's Marshall Plan," *New York Times*, April 19, 2002.

23. Michael Buchanan, "Afghanistan Omitted from US Aid Budget," BBC News, February 13, 2003; Clarke, *Against All Enemies*; Seymour M. Hersh, "The Other War: Why Bush's Afghanistan Problem Won't Go Away," *New Yorker*, April 12, 2004.

24. Jones, *In the Graveyard of Empires*, 166–68, 174–75; Selcan Hacaoglu, "Iraq Suffers from Dirty Water, Fears About Cholera," AP, August 1, 2008; see also the blog *Ranger Against War* for August 5, 2008.

25. Ken Adelman, "Cakewalk in Iraq," *Washington Post*, February 13, 2002; Naomi Klein, *The Shock Doctrine: The Rise of Disaster Capitalism* (New York: Picador, 2008), 409–84. For the formulation of "shock and awe" for American military use, see Harlan K. Ullman and James P. Wade, *Shock and Awe: Achieving Rapid Dominance* (Washington, DC: National Defense University, 1996).

26. Jones, *In the Graveyard of Empires*; Keith L. Shimko, *The Iraq Wars and America's Military Revolution* (New York: Cambridge University Press, 2010).

27. Benjamin Tupper, *Greetings from Afghanistan, Send More Ammo: Dispatches from Taliban Country* (New York: NAL Caliber, 2010), 135. NPR broadcast several pieces from Tupper, all of which can be found on NPR.org.

28. See *My War*, http://cbftw.blogspot.com/. Wired.com has many articles on military blogging. See, for instance, the following articles by Noah Shactman, "Army Bullies Blogger, Invades YouTube," March 23, 2007; "New Army Rules Could Kill G.I. Blogs (Maybe E-mail, Too), May 2, 2007; "Air Force Backtracks on Social Network Ban," May 16, 2008; Noah, "Bosses Delete Outspoken Army Blog," July 2, 2008. See also David Axe, "Navy Hearts Blogs," April 15, 2008.

29. See, for instance, the excellent *The Destroyermen*, http://destroyermen.blogspot.com/.

30. Matt Gallagher, *Kaboom: Embracing the Suck in a Savage Little War* (Cambridge, MA: De Capo, 2010), 11. Gallagher's posts are archived at http://kaboomwarjournalarchive.blogspot.com/.

31. Gallagher, *Kaboom*, 37–38.

32. Ibid., 44.

33. Ibid., 91–95.

34. Helen Benedict, *The Lonely Soldier: The Private War of Women Serving in Iraq* (Boston: Beacon, 2009), 140.

35. Ibid., 142.

36. Tupper, *Greetings from Afghanistan*, 7.

37. Ibid., 146.

38. Private communication with author.

39. Tupper, *Greetings from Afghanistan*, 43–45.

40. Joseph O'Keefe, personal memoir, in author's possession.

41. Gallagher, *Kaboom*, 103.

42. Ibid., 15.

43. Ibid., 58.

44. Ibid., 60.

45. Ibid., 240.

46. Tyler E. Boudreau, *Packing Inferno: The Unmaking of a Marine* (Port Townsend, WA: Feral House, 2008), 41.

47. Ibid., 8.

48. Ibid., 9.

49. Ibid., 10.

50. Tupper, *Greetings from Afghanistan*, 243–44.

51. Boudreau, *Packing Inferno*, 15.

52. Benedict, *The Lonely Soldier*, 89; Thomas Ricks, *Fiasco: The American Military Adventure in Iraq* (New York: Penguin Books, 2007), 36, 68–75.

53. Martin van Creveld, *The Culture of War* (New York: Random House, 2008), 395–410.

54. *Lioness*, directed by Meg McLagan and Daria Sommers (Room 11 Productions, 2008); Benedict, *The Lonely Soldier*; Kayla Williams, *Love My Rifle More Than You: Young and Female in the U.S. Army* (New York: W.W. Norton, 2005).

55. D'Ann Campbell, "Women in Combat: The World War II Experience in the United States, Great Britain, Germany and the Soviet Union," *Journal of Military History* 57 (1993) 322.

56. Carrie Antlfinger, "Hundreds Turn out to Remember Slain Soldier," AP, April 15, 2004.

57. Benedict, *The Lonely Soldier*, 99. See also Paul Rieckhoff, *Chasing Ghosts: A Soldier's Fight for America from Baghdad to Washington* (New York: Penguin Books, 2006).

58. Benedict, *The Lonely Soldier*, 99.

59. Ibid., 138.

60. Ibid., 4.

61. Kate Harding, "The Tragic Story of LaVena Johnson," *Salon*, June 27, 2008; http://lavenajohnson.com/.

62. Laurean fled to Mexico, but was eventually extradited, found guilty, and sentenced to life in prison. "Former Marine Gets Life in Prison for Killing Pregnant Colleague," Associated Press, August 24, 2010.

63. Ann Wright, "Is There an Army Cover Up of Rape and Murder of Women Soldiers?" Common Dreams, April 28, 2008.

64. Maureen Murdoch and K.L. Nichol, "Women Veterans' Experiences with Domestic Violence and with Sexual Harassment while in the Military," *Archives of Family Medicine* 4 (1995): 411–18; Maureen Murdoch, "Prevalence of In-service and Post-service Sexual Assault among Combat and Noncombat Veterans," *Military Medicine* 169 (2004): 392–95; Anne G. Sadler et al., "Factors Associated with Women's Risk of Rape in the Military Environment," *American Journal of Industrial Medicine* 44 (2003): 262–73; Anne G. Sadler et al., "Gang and Multiple Rapes During Military Service," *Journal of American Medical Women's Association* 60 (2005): 33–41.

65. Benedict, *The Lonely Soldier*, 94.

66. Ibid., 107.

67. Mark Benjamin, "Out of Jail, Into the Army," *Salon*, February 2, 2006; Lizette Alvarez, "Army Giving More Waivers in Recruiting," *New York Times*, February 14, 2007; Alvarez, "Moral Waivers and the Military," *New York Times*, February 20, 2007; Michael Massing, "The Volunteer Army: Who Fights and Why," *New York Review of Books*, April 3, 2008.

68. Andrew Tilghman, "I Came over Here Because I Wanted to Kill People," *Washington Post*, July 30, 2006; Jim Frederick, *Black Hearts: One Platoon's Descent into Madness in Iraq's Triangle of Death* (New York: Crown, 2010).

69. Rod Nordland, "For Soldiers, Death Sees No Gender Lines, " *New York Times*, June 21, 2011.

70. Ali Kefford, "The Woman at the Helm in the US Navy," *The Guardian*, June 23, 2011.

71. Janet E. Halley, *Don't: A Reader's Guide to the Military's Anti-Gay Policy* (Durham, NC: Duke University Press, 1999), 58.

72. Allan Bérubé, *Coming Out Under Fire: The History of Gay Men and Women in World War Two* (New York: Penguin, 1990); Randy Shilts, *Conduct Unbecoming: Gays and Lesbians in the U.S. Military: Vietnam to the Persian Gulf* (New York: St. Martin's Press, 1993).

73. Allan Bérubé, *My Desire for History: Essays in Gay, Community, and Labor History* (Chapel Hill: University of North Carolina Press, 2011), 128.

74. With gratitude to Charlie and Karen Morgan for sharing their experiences in a series of emails.

75. Elisabeth Bumiller, "Out and Proud to Serve," *New York Times*, September 20, 2011; Josh Seefried, ed., *Our Time: Breaking the Silence of "Don't Ask, Don't Tell"* (New York: Penguin, 2011).

76. Ricks, *Fiasco*.

77. Ray Suarez, "Under Armored," PBS, December 9, 2004; William Kristol, "The Defense Secretary We Have," *Washington Post*, December 15, 2004; Rieckhoff, *Chasing Ghosts*, 27–28; Donald Rumsfeld, *Known and Unknown: A Memoir* (New York: Sentinel, 2011), 645–66.

78. Frank Rich, *The Greatest Story Ever Sold: The Decline and Fall of Truth from 9/11 to Katrina* (New York: Penguin, 2006), 101–2. President Bush's statement of July 2, 2003, is not without precedent, as General Westmoreland had invited similar attacks just before the Tet Offensive. When asked by a *Time* magazine interviewer if he thought the communists might stage a major attack, Westmoreland responded, "I hope they try something, because we are looking for a fight." Stanley Karnow, *Vietnam: A History* (New York: Penguin, 1997), 527.

79. Boudreau, *Packing Inferno*, 6.

80. Ibid.

81. Ibid., 10–11, 43. See also Buddhika Jayamaha et al., "The War as We Saw It," *New York Times*, August 19, 2007.

82. Dina Rasor and Robert Bauman, *Betraying Our Troops: The Destructive Results of Privatizing War* (New York: Palgrave, 2007), 6–22; Michael Massing, "Iraq: The Hidden Human Costs," *New York Review of Books*, December 20, 2007; *Iraq for Sale: The War Profiteers*, documentary directed by Robert Greenwald (Culver City, CA: Brave New Films, 2006); Department of Defense Inspector General, "Audit of Potable and Nonpotable Water in Iraq," Report # D-2008–060 (2008).

83. Gardner, *The Long Road to Baghdad*, 227–29; Rasor and Bauman, *Betraying Our Troops*, 59–70, 99–116, 231–42; Scahill, *Blackwater*; Pratap Chatterjee, *Halliburton's Army: How a Well-Connected Texas Oil Company Revolutionized the Way America Makes War* (New York: Nation Books, 2009).

84. Benedict, *The Lonely Soldier*, 102.

85. Joseph O'Keefe memoir.

86. "Warning Against Wars Like Iraq and Afghanistan," *New York Times*, February 25, 2011.

87. Joseph O'Keefe before History 395, CCSU, December 4, 2009.

# Index

Abu Ghraib prison, 298–99
Acheson, Dean, 355n19
Adams, John Quincy, 341n1
Afghanistan, war in. *See* twenty-first-century wars (Iraq and Afghanistan)
African American soldiers: American Revolution, 31–35; Buffalo Soldiers, 166–71; Civil War, 110–16, 336n33; distinguished service medals for, 114, 166, 213, 234, 235–36, 272; Korean War and integration of the military, 269–73; Lincoln and, 111, 112, 115; Marines, 235, 272; Ninety-second Infantry Division on European Front, 235; service in the Philippines, 178–79, 236; Spanish-American War, 166–71, 178–79; veterans of World War II, 236–37; veterans World War I, 215, 217; World War II, 222, 233–37; World War I service in France, 212–15
Agent Orange, 293–94
Aguinaldo y Famy, Emilio, 176–79
air combat: bombing of civilian centers, 238–40, 260; first Persian Gulf War, 297; Iraq and Afghanistan, 301; Korean War, 260, 265–66; "shock and awe," 238, 300; Vietnam War and Operation Rolling Thunder, 277–78; World War I, 193–97; World War II, 223–26, 239–40
Alejandrino, Jose, 179
Alexander, Joseph, 49
Alger, Russell A., 175
Allen, Ebenezer, 32
Almond, Edward M., 235, 262, 269
Ambrose, Stephen, 231
American Legion, 217, 255
American Revolution, 11–43; advent of war, 11–17; African American soldiers, 31–35; attack on Cornwallis's army and defeat of British, 35–40; Battle of Bunker Hill, 14–15; Battle of White Plains, 26–27; combat horrors, 26–28; hardships and lack of provisions, 18–26, 40; mental health breakdowns and battle fatigue, 27–28; reasons soldiers enlisted and fought, 17–26; soldiers' professionalism

and competence, 28, 36–38, 39; soldiers' sense of duty and commitment to fellow soldiers, 21–23, 26, 27; veterans and promised pensions, 40–43; Washington and the new Continental Army, 15–17, 23, 32; winter encampment at Valley Forge, 17, 21–26
Anderson, William T., 170
Andersonville prison, 105–8
Andreotta, Glenn, 288
Angier, Billy, 3
Antietam (1862), Battle of, 95, 118–19, 123–24
Anti-Imperialist League, 152, 181
*Apocalypse Now* (film), 293
Armistead, Walker K., 132
Armitage, Richard, 300
*Army Magazine*, 293
*Army Service Forces Manual M5: Leadership and the Negro Soldier* (1944), 234
Arnold, Benedict, 28, 29–30
Arrears Bill (1879), 128
Atkins, Josiah, 27–28
atomic bombing of Japan, 251–53
atrocities. *See* wartime atrocities
August, Robert B., 252–53
Aylett, P.H., 111
Ayres, Harold, 259

Ball's Bluff (1861), Battle of, 96–97
Bailey, Thomas, 333n13
Bainbridge, William, 63
Baker, Edward, 96
Ball, George, 239, 277
Banks, Nathaniel, 117
Barberis, Cesidio, 269
Barnett, George, 194
Barney, Joshua, 63
Barrett, Amos, 11–13
Barth, George, 259
Barton, Clara, 116
Barton, Miriam, 312, 313
Bataan Death March, 241
Bauman, Robert, 320
Beal, Thomas, 67
Bell, Bernard I., 255

# Celebrating 20 Years of
# Independent Publishing